New Interpretations
in Naval History

New Interpretations in Naval History

Selected Papers
from the
Eighth Naval History Symposium

Edited by

William B. Cogar

Naval Institute Press
Annapolis, Maryland

Copyright © 1989
by the United States Naval Institute,
Annapolis, Maryland

Library of Congress Cataloging-in-Publication Data

United States Naval Academy History Symposium (8th : 1987)
    New interpretations in naval history : selected papers from the
Eighth Naval History Symposium / edited by William B. Cogar.
        p.   cm.
    Includes bibliographies.
    ISBN 0-87021-495-0
    1. Naval art and science--History--Congresses. 2. Naval history-
-Congresses.   I. Cogar, William B., 1949-   . II. Title.
V27.U55 1987
359'.009--dc20   89-8334
                                                          CIP

Printed in the United States of America

9 8 7 6 5 4 3 2

First printing

Contents

vii

Foreword

The Eighth Naval History Symposium was held at the United States Naval Academy on 24-25 September 1987. The following papers represent twenty of the nearly sixty-five papers delivered in the Symposium's twenty-two sessions. In all, there were about 120 proposals for papers to be read at the conference. As with past symposia, this year's conference attracted scholars from as far away as Singapore, Germany, and France, not to mention many of the states and provinces of the United States and Canada, respectively. All of the participants who delivered papers were invited to submit their papers for possible publication. The following twenty were selected on their academic merit and with an eye to producing a balanced volume which would reflect the generally eclectic nature of the biennial Naval History Symposium as well as the growing interest in naval history of all periods and nations.

Begun in 1971 and sponsored by the History Department of the Naval Academy, the first few conferences were rather limited in that retired naval officers were asked to speak on specific topics. Since then the conference directors and the History Department have attempted to expand the conference along the lines of other scholarly historical conferences but to include all facets which fit within the title of "naval history." It was decided then and it has remained a policy that the conference have no specific theme. Instead conference directors have elicited papers on topics of naval history as different as archeological findings of a naval port near Gibraltar and the continuing controversy over the Tonkin Gulf Incident, just two of the papers found in this volume.

As a result of this policy the scope and tenor of the conferences have grown considerably. At the 1977 conference, the keynote speaker, Dr. David Trask, believed that naval historical scholarship had come a long way from the usual belief that naval history is simply the study of ships, battles, tactics, and guns. While not undermining these important aspects of naval history, scholars have broadened the field considerably. The Naval History Symposium has likewise grown in size and reputation, becoming the largest and one of the most prestigious conferences of its type in the United States and perhaps around the world. The following papers demonstrate the increasing quality and diversity of modern research and scholarship in naval history.

The 1987 Symposium proved not only to be a conference of high scholarly standards but an enjoyable time for participants as well as for all attendants. Such a conference cannot be put on without the unselfish efforts of many people. The executive committee included Professor William R. Roberts, as Associate Director, Lieutenant Commander Thomas J. Cutler, USN, as Assistant Director, and Mrs. Connie J. Grigor, as Secretary. Speaking as the director, no one could be more fortunate than I to work with these fine colleagues and friends on my committee. Many others deserve notice for their efforts, without which the symposium could not have happened. The Superintendent of the Naval Academy, Rear Admiral Ronald F. Marryott, USN; the Academic Dean, Dr. Karl A. Lamb; Colonel Frederick T. Fagan, USMC, Director of the Division of English and History; Professor Frederick C. Harrod, Chairman of the History Department; Lieutenant Commander Don T. Sine, USN, Executive Assistant of the History Department; Ensign Mary Kelly, USN; Second

Lieutenant Paul Aanonsen, USMC; and all the members of the History Department were extremely helpful, and much gratitude is extended to each of them.

Of course, so much of the success of the Symposium must go to all the participants who read papers as well as to those distinguished scholars who graciously and professionally acted as session moderators and commentators. They included: Dr. Dean Allard, Naval Historical Center; Dr. Samuel E. Barns, Washington, D.C.; Mr. James P. Barry, Ohioana Library Association; Professor Daniel A. Baugh, Cornell University; Captain Edward L. Beach, USN (Ret.); Mr. William Jeffrey Bolster, Baltimore, Maryland; Professor Carl Boyd, Old Dominion University; Professor William R. Braisted, University of Texas at Austin; Mr. Wesley A. Brown, Washington, D.C.; Mr. Philip M. Callaghan, Virginia Polytechnic Institute and State University; Professor Lionel Casson, New York University; Mr. James W. Cheevers, U.S. Naval Academy Museum; Ms. Cynthia Chermely, University of Cincinnati; Professor Ira Dye, University of Virginia; J. Worth Estes, M.D., Boston University Medical Center; Professor William H. Flayhart, Delaware State College; Dr. Keith Fleming, Marine Corps Historical Center; Professor Robert Foulke, Skidmore College; Professor William M. Fowler, Jr., Northeastern University; Mr. Benis M. Frank, Headquarters United States Marine Corps; Professor Klaus Friedland, International Commission for Maritime History; Professor Janice Gabbert, Wright State University; Dr. Mary A.Y. Gallagher, Queens College; Mr. Joseph A. Goldenberg, Virginia State College; Professor John W. Gordon, The Citadel; Professor Barry M. Gough, Wilfrid Laurier University; Mr. James E. Hair, New York; Dr. William S. Hanable, Alaska Historical Commission; Dr. John Hattendorf, Naval War College; Professor George C. Herring, University of Kentucky; Professor Ted C. Hinckley, San Jose State University; Professor Calvin W. Hines, Stephen F. Austin State University; Professor Alfred C. Holden, St. John's University; Lieutenant Colonel James F. Holden-Rhodes, New Mexico; Dr. Fred W. Hopkins, Jr., University of Baltimore; Dr. Sari Hornstein, U.S. Naval Academy; Mr. H.J.K. Jenkins, Peterborough, England; Professor Gerald Jordan, York University;

Professor Jacob W. Kipp, Kansas State University; Major Randy Kolton, USA, U.S. Military Academy; Mr. Emory Kristof, National Geographic Society; Professor Frederica de Laguna, Bryn Mawr College; Professor Harold Langley, Smithsonian Institution; Dr. Archibald Lewis, Peabody Museum; Professor Brian M. Linn, Old Dominion University; Dr. Philip K. Lundeberg, Smithsonian Institution; Dr. David Lyon, National Maritime Museum, Greenwich; Lieutenant Colonel James Madison, USA, U.S. Military Academy; Dr. Timothy P. Maga, University of Maryland, Asian Division; Ms. Mary Malloy, Peabody Museum; Professor John McCusker, University of Maryland, College Park; Professor Christopher McKee, Grinnell College; Commander Norman Myer, USNR (Ret.), New Mexico; Professor Malcolm Muir, Naval Historical Center; Dr. Malcolm Murfett, National University of Singapore; Professor Keith W. Olson, University of Maryland, College Park; Dr. Michael Palmer, Naval Historical Center; Dr. Forrest C. Pogue, Arlington, Virginia; Dr. Werner Rahn, Militärgeschichtliches Forschungsamt; Mr. Fred Rainbow, U.S. Naval Institute; Professor Eugene Rasor, Emory and Henry College; Captain Rosario Rausa, USNR, Naval Aviation History; Professor Marcus Rediker, Georgetown University; Dr. Clark G. Reynolds, Naval and Maritime Museum, South Carolina; Dr. Donald A. Ritchie, Senate Historical Office; Professor Timothy J. Runyan, Cleveland State University; Professor Paul R. Schratz, Arnold, Maryland; Mr. Donald G. Shomette, Nautical Archaeological Associates; Mr. Jack Shulimson, Marine Corps Historical Center; Professor Geoffrey S. Smith, Queens University; Professor Joel Sokolsky, Royal Military College of Canada; Professor Chester Starr, University of Michigan; Mr. Paul Stillwell, U.S. Naval Institute; Professor Jon Sumida, University of Maryland, College Park; Professor J.E. Talbott, University of California, Santa Barbara; Captain Joseph K. Taussig, USN (Ret.), Department of the Navy; Dr. Geoffrey Till, Royal Naval College, Greenwich; Dr. Frank Uhlig, Naval War College; Mr. Martin Wilcox, Applied Sonics Corporation; Mr. Dana M. Wegner, David W. Taylor Naval Ship Research and Development Center; Dr. Victoria Wyatt, University of Washington; Mr. Dana R. Yoerger,

Woods Hole Oceanographic Institution; Mr. Thomas-Durell Young, Washington, D.C.

At last, special thanks must be extended to Paul Wilderson and John Cronin of the U.S. Naval Institute, and especially to my good friends and colleagues Professors Craig Symonds and John Kolp, who worked with me so enthusiastically and patiently on new technical procedures for publication. Finally, but far from least, the greatest thanks and appreciation go to my wife, who once again endured far beyond the call of duty.

William B. Cogar
U.S. Naval Academy

About the Contributors

James A. Barber, Jr., is a graduate of the NROTC regular program at the University of Southern California and holds a Ph.D. in Political Science from Stanford University. Retiring from the navy after a career that included command of the USS *Hissem* (DER-400), *Schofield* (DEG-3), and *Horne* (CG-30), he is currently Executive Director and Publisher of the U.S. Naval Institute.

Jeffrey G. Barlow received his Ph.D. in International Studies from the University of South Carolina. He is a historian with the Contemporary History Branch of the Naval Historical Center, Washington, D.C., where he is writing an official history entitled *The U.S. Navy and National Security, 1945-1964.*

Merrill L. Bartlett is a retired Marine Corps lieutenant colonel. From 1977 until 1983, he taught history at the Naval Academy where he won the William B. Clements Award as the outstanding military educator for 1979-80. He has also received the Navy

Achievement Medal and the Legion of Merit. He is the editor of *Assault from the Sea: Essays on the History of Amphibious Warfare* (1983), and his essays and book reviews have appeared in *American Neptune*, the *Marine Corps Gazette*, and the *U.S. Naval Institute Proceedings*.

Paolo E. Coletta received the doctorate in history from the University of Missouri. He taught at the Naval Academy for thirty-seven years before retiring in 1983. His publications, mostly spanning the period since 1865, include biographies of political and naval leaders, a naval history text, and naval and Marine Corps bibliographies.

Patricia K. Crimmin received the M.Phil. from the University of London. She is Lecturer in History at the University of London (Royal Holloway and New Bedford College) teaching eighteenth and nineteenth century British history and a course on British naval history from 1688 to 1830. Her present research interests include a study of the treatment and administration of prisoners of war in Britain from 1793 to 1816 as well as the role of the Royal Navy in the eastern Mediterranean from the late seventeenth to mid-nineteenth centuries.

Jeffery Dorwart received the Ph.D. from the University of Massachusetts in 1971. Currently an Associate Professor of History at Rutgers University, he is the author of *The Office of Naval Intelligence* (1979) and *Conflict of Duty* (1983) and is writing "The Good Men: Eberstadt, Forrestal, and the Creation of a National Security Establishment."

Frederick C. Drake received the Ph.D. in 1970 from Cornell University and is now Professor of History at Brock University, St. Catherines, Ontario. Besides publications in numerous scholarly journals, his monograph, *The Empire of the Seas: A Biography of Rear Admiral Robert Wilson Shufeldt, USN* (1984), won the John Lyman Prize in U.S. Naval History, awarded by the North American Society for Oceanic History. He is currently working on the study of *The War of 1812: Naval Operations*, the companion volume to George Stanley's *The War of 1812: Land Operations*.

William S. Dudley received the Ph.D. from Columbia University in 1972 and now heads the Early History Branch at the Naval Historical Center in Washington, D.C. He is the editor of two multi-volume series, *Naval Documents of the American Revolution* and *The Naval War of 1812: A Documentary History*.

Donald D. Horward is Professor of History at Florida State University. He is author or editor of nine books and some thirty articles on subjects related to the Napoleonic period. His articles have appeared in journals throughout western Europe, and he has presented papers in the United States and Europe. He has received international acclaim for his work on Napoleon, Iberia, and the Peninsula War.

George H. Lobdell received the Ph.D. in 1954 from the University of Illinois. An army veteran of World War II, he retired in 1967 from the U.S. Army Reserve as a lieutenant colonel. He has written, with Arlan Helegson and Richard Brown, *The United States of America: A History for Young Citizens* (1964) and has contributed articles to the *Dictionary of American Biography* (1973), *American Secretaries of the Navy* (1980), and the *Dictionary of American Military Biography* (1984). He is now Professor Emeritus at Ohio University where he taught for thirty-three years.

Edward J. Marolda has written extensively on the Vietnam War. His most recent works include *From Military Assistance to Combat, 1959-1965*, volume II of the U.S. Navy's official series, and *Carrier Operations*, a volume in the Bantam series, *An Illustrated History of the Vietnam War*. He is head of the Naval Historical Center's Contemporary History Branch in Washington, D.C.

Edwin E. Moise studied the history of Southeast Asia and China at the University of Michigan, where he obtained the Ph.D. degree in 1977. He is now Professor of History at Clemson University. The author of *Land Reform in China and North Vietnam* and *Modern China: A History,* he is currently writing a book centering on the Tonkin Gulf Incidents of 1964.

Elizabeth M. Nuxoll is Project Director and coeditor of the Papers of Robert Morris at Queens College of the City University of New York. Her project is publishing Morris's papers as Superintendent of Finance and Agent of Marine of the United States from 1781 to 1784. Seven volumes have appeared to date. She received the Ph.D. in 1979 from the City University of New York. Her dissertation was "Congress and the Munitions Merchants: The Secret Committee of Trade during the American Revolution, 1775-1777," published in 1985.

Geraldine N. Phillips has been the Director of the Textual Projects Division of the National Archives in Washington, D.C., since October 1988. She has held a number of other administrative and supervisory positions since coming to the National Archives in 1970 and has a special interest in the National Archives' holdings relating to the U.S. Navy in the 19th and 20th centuries. She holds degrees from Skidmore College and from the University of Pennsylvania.

Ronald L. Pollitt is currently Professor of History at the University of Cincinnati, where he has also served as Associate Dean and as Dean of the McMicken College of Arts and Sciences. He has published extensively in maritime history, and has a volume in the publications of the Navy Records Society, *Arming the Nation, 1568-1585,* in press, and is also finishing a book on English preparations for the Armada.

Norman E. Saul, who received his doctorate in history from Columbia University in 1965, teaches at the University of Kansas in history and Soviet and East European Studies. His publications include *Russia and the Mediterranean, 1797-1807, Sailors in Revolt: The Russian Baltic Fleet in 1917,* and a number of articles on

Russian naval history. His current research and writing focuses on Russian-American relations from the 1760s to 1917.

David Curtis Skaggs received the Ph.D. from Georgetown University in 1966. He is Professor of History at Bowling Green State University in Bowling Green, Ohio, where he has taught since 1965. Among his writings are *Roots of Maryland Democracy, 1753-1776* (1973), *The Old Northwest in the American Revolution* (1977), and over forty articles in professional journals. A colonel in the Army Reserve, he currently holds a mobilization assignment as the command historian, U.S. European Command, Stuttgart, West Germany.

Sherill L. Spaar is an ancient historian who has studied the port sites of Roman Spain and traced the ancient shoreline of Andalucia. She also has participated on both underwater and land excavations in Greece, and has recently joined the excavation team for the Greco-Roman port at Phalasarna, Crete. During the academic year, she serves as an associate professor at East Central University in Ada, Oklahoma.

Spencer C. Tucker received the Ph.D. from the University of North Carolina, Chapel Hill. He has published articles in several journals, including the *U.S. Naval Institute Proceedings* and the *American Neptune*. His book, *Arming the Fleet: U.S. Navy Ordnance in the Muzzle-loading Era*, appeared in early 1989. Enjoying a Fulbright Fellowship to France and a term as a Visiting Research Associate at the Smithsonian, he is a Professor of History at Texas Christian University in Fort Worth where he teaches modern European and military history.

David M. Williams is a Lecturer in Economic and Social History at the University of Leicester in the United Kingdom. He is a specialist in maritime history post-1700 and has published widely on the North American trade, seamen, shipping efficiency, commercial policy, and government intervention.

Part I

Creating and Maintaining
a Navy

Carteia: An Ancient Naval Port on the Bay of Gibraltar

Sherill L. Spaar

Continued research by classicists has unearthed, sometimes quite literally, aspects of naval history inaccessible to conventional naval historians. In this essay, Professor Spaar relies upon ancient and modern sources as well as archaeological findings to show the naval and maritime significance of the Roman seaport of Carteia, now extinct, on the southeast coast of Spain.

In ancient times, the southern Spanish littoral served as the western terminus of the civilized world (see Baetica map). It was occupied by various historical peoples, among whom were the Carthaginians, Greeks, and Romans, and each added to the cultural, political, and economic history of the area, but the Romans made the greatest impact. Having conquered the area from the Carthaginians during the Second Punic War, they converted it into a distant province, initially called Hispania Ulterior, and later Baetica, a name derived from the great river which flows westward to the Atlantic from its headwaters in the Sierra Nevada mountains. This river, the *Betis fluens* of antiquity, takes its present name, the Guadalquivir, from the Arabs who inhabited much of Spain in the Middle Ages.

The Guadalquivir and the rio Guadiana to its northwest, both of which are navigable in their lower courses, allowed the Romans easy access to the interior. They used these routes to pacify the native Iberian tribal folk, and to establish strong urban centers in

1

which to attract large numbers of settlers from Italy and elsewhere in the Mediterranean sphere. These settlers, lured by the rich natural resources of southern Spain, faced a long and arduous journey by sea to what was regarded at the time as the end of the world. Although there were fragmentary land routes in the western provinces, and eventually a complex road system built by the Romans to accommodate troops and travellers, the sea remained the most practicable means of communication from Italy to Spain in the entire history of Roman occupation.

More than thirty Roman sites have been identified along the coast of Baetica, starting in the east at Carthago Nova, the finest natural harbor of this littoral, and extending to the rio Guadiana in the west, the present Spanish-Portuguese border. Of course, not all sites were major port cities or naval bases. Many were small entrepôts which served as end points for local products from the interior. Most were located at the mouths of intermittent streams, and had rudimentary port facilities, if any. Problems of loading and unloading supplies may have been overcome by beaching the smaller ships, or by larger ships laying at anchor offshore while dinghies brought stores back and forth. On the Atlantic side, tide action was sufficient to float ships into and out of estuaries, even though this practice must have been risky and unreliable. Whatever the process, it appears as if there were few places which were suitable for large scale defensive or mercantile operations.

Of those locations which proved practical for providing defense or building harbor installations, that is, Carthago Nova, Malaca, Carteia, and Gades, Carteia was perhaps the most strategically located for the control of maritime activities during the later Roman Republican period (second and first centuries B.C.). It lies on the inner curve of the Bay of Gibraltar, and commands a position at once defensible and suitable as a lookout for ships sailing through the Strait. The Strait itself, which was known to the ancients by various names--the pillars of Hercules, the strait of Hercules (*fretum Herculeum/Columnae Herculis*), the strait of Gades (*fretum Gaditanum*), or simply the jaws (*fauces*) or gateway (*ostium*),[1] is only fourteen kilometers wide at its narrowest point, and can pose difficult and even hazardous navigational problems

BAETICA: The Roman Coast
(Map produced by Ken Hite)

Anas F.

BAETICA

Corduba

Italica
F. Baelis
F. Singilis
Astigi

F. Urium
F. Luxia
Ilipla
Hispalis

Onoba

Ebura Cerealis
Turris Caepionis
Olaastrum
Gades
ad Herculem
Mercablum
Promunturium Iunonis

Asta Regia
F. Lacca
Portus Gaditanus
Menesstheus
Baesippo

Clavicum
Maenoba
Suel
Cilniana
Salduba
Carteia
Baelo
Mellaria
Celruamo
Lunae Insulam
Barbesula
Mons Calpe
Iulia Traducta
Portus Albus
GADITANUM
FRETUM
Mons Abyla
Tingis

Selambina

Sexi
Malaca
Iugum Barbetium

Adra

Turaniana
Murgi
F. Abla
Urci

SINUS Veneris Iugum.
URCITANUS

Baria
Promunturium
Charidemi

MARE
INTERNUM

OCEANUS
ATLANTICUS

Lixus

to oar- and sail-driven vessels. Beset by two opposing wind and four opposing sea currents, it has rocks and shallows on both sides, and a dearth of shelter.

Ancient authors wrote that it was not possible to sail from the European to the African side by the shortest route (Tarifa to Tangier). Instead, ships stayed well to the east or west for the north-south crossing, forced to hug a perilous shoreline once they had made it to the other side.[2] The major geographical feature of the Strait of Gibraltar, and one of the most famous landmarks in the world, is a massive rock outcropping which the Romans knew as *mons Calpe*. There is an equivalent outcropping on the African shore called Djebal Musa (*Abila*). Strabo even refers to the town of Carteia as *Calpe* (3.1.7), and indicates that the Greeks called it *Heracleia*, from the myth that Heracles parted the monolithic rocks to create the connecting seaway between the Mediterranean and the Atlantic.

The Roman site of Carteia is aligned northeast-southwest on a hill with two successively higher ridges (see Gibraltar map). It is flanked on the south by the sea, and defensive walls from more recent times, within which are gun emplacements. The Roman walls, described as "massive" or "great" by Strabo (3.1.7), fall inside and at a slight elevation to the present-day seawalls. Still extant near the seaside of the Roman walls is an Islamic watchtower (called the "torre de Cartagena") built on a Roman foundation. The entire system of Roman fortifications encompassed the sixty-five acre site, and has been surveyed and partially excavated by archaeologists. The tower measures six meters by seven meters at the base with courses about one meter in height.

The extensive Roman walls were at least partially erected on the base of earlier walls which protected a settlement of native Iberian peoples. These Iberian walls date to the third century B.C. There are some finds from the Iberian town,[3] and Strabo refers to an "Iberian naval base" there (3.1.7.). Before the Iberian town, a Punic site (the Cerro del Prado) has been located in the area, which dates to the seventh-sixth centuries B.C., and lies about three kilometers north of the Ibero-Roman city.[4] Both sites took advantage of a perennial stream now flowing some three hundred

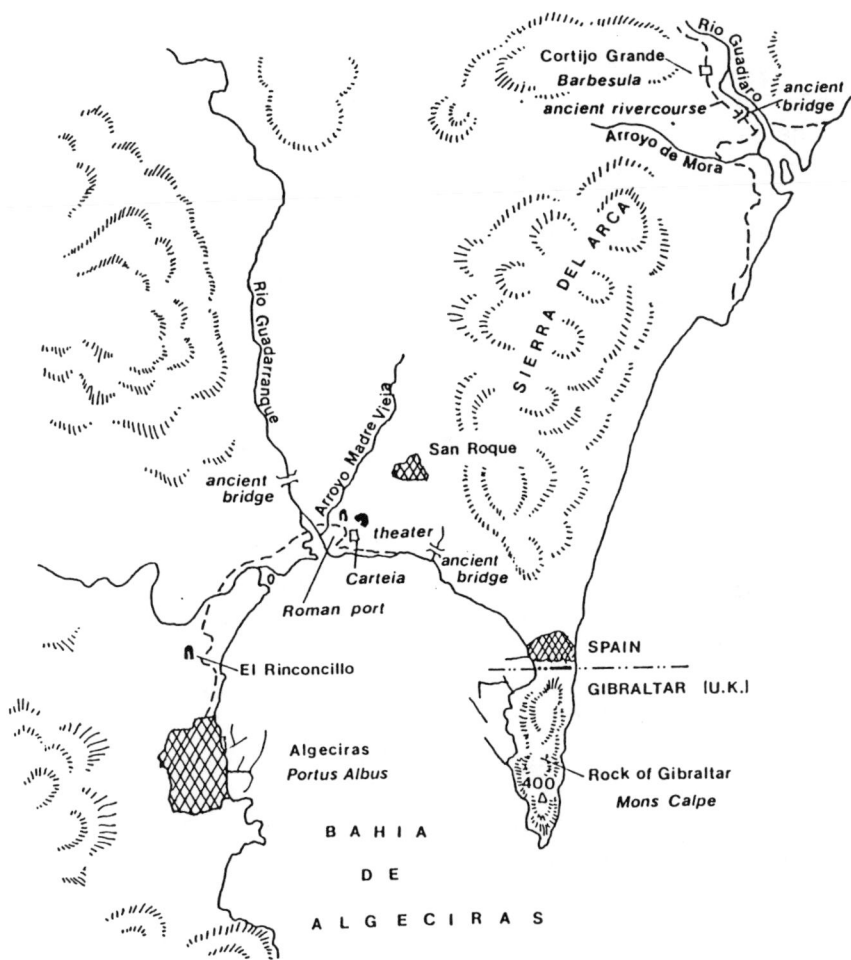

Rio Guadiaro

Cortijo Grande
Barbesula
ancient rivercourse
Arroyo de Mora

ancient
bridge

SIERRA DEL ARCA

Rio Guadarranque

Arroyo Madre Vieja

San Roque

ancient
bridge

theater

Carteia

ancient
bridge

Roman port

El Rinconcillo

SPAIN

GIBRALTAR (U.K.)

Algeciras
Portus Albus

400

Rock of Gibraltar
Mons Calpe

BAHIA

DE

ALGECIRAS

GIBRALTAR
(Map produced by Ken Hite)

meters to the west of the Roman walls. This stream, called the rio Guadarranque, is still navigable by small craft up to a kilometer inland. In antiquity, the entire area from the Punic site to the sea was unstable or marshy ground, and the Roman bridge, which continues to span the river adjacent to the modern coastal highway, is evidence that the Roman road ran well inland to avoid the saltmarsh, as does the modern highway.

The structures from the Roman period include a theatre; bath complexes; the cella of a temple; cisterns; a drainage system, which appears to flow directly into what might have been the ancient river bed or estuary; a wide, well-constructed road; garum-vats for making fish paste; and a necropolis to the east of the walled precinct.[5] A basilica has been conjectured,[6] and a mosque may have been built later by the Muslims.[7] The site has been destroyed partially by tectonic activity, the dates of which are uncertain. Nonetheless, Byzantine, Visigothic, and Islamic populations inhabited it at least to the twelfth century A.D., when an Arabic text mentions a long mole constructed of stone at the mouth of the Guadarranque.[8]

The ancient harbor, which most likely was to the northwest of the lower ridge, would have been protected by the Levante, a dry, hot wind emanating from the Sahara. This location also would have made the harbor invisible to ships sailing west past the Rock of Gibraltar into the Bay or through the Strait. It is probable, based on the location of the ancient drainage system, and also on drawings from an eighteenth century A.D. source,[9] that the river ran much closer to the hill in earlier centuries. Another probability is that the river was set in its course by a series of retaining walls, similar to those which line its banks today. In addition, a sizable stream, the Arroyo Madre Vieja, flows into the Guadarranque just to the north of the Roman site. In antiquity, the conjunction of this stream with the river itself could have created a broad backwater. The curvature of the marsh in this area is semicircular and appears to have been purposely dug out in this shape. In 1975, three large conglomerate blocks were visible in the marsh, and may have indicated ancient remains. Sadly, these blocks had disappeared by 1978, having been removed or buried beneath a modern parking lot. The marsh had been filled in and the semicircular configuration had been destroyed as well.

There are several historical sources which bear out the capacity of the harbor. Livy illustrates this point in a passage recounting a confrontation between the Roman commander Laelius and the Carthaginian commander Adherbal in 206 B.C., during the Second Punic War. The passage also reflects the difficult problem of navigating the currents in the Strait:[10]

> Laelius meantime sailed down the strait into the Ocean [west of Gibraltar] and came with his fleet to Carteia.[11] This city is situated on the coast of the Ocean where the sea begins to open out after the narrow entrance. Of Gades, as has been said above, he had hoped without a battle to gain possession by betrayal, since men actually came into the Roman camp to make such a promise. But the betrayal was prematurely revealed, and Mago arrested all the conspirators and turned them over to Adherbal, the magistrate, to be transported to Carthage. Adherbal placed the conspirators on a quinquereme and after sending it in advance, because it was slower than a trireme, himself followed with eight triremes at no great distance. The quinquereme was already entering the strait when Laelius, also on a quinquereme, sailed out from the harbour of Carteia followed by seven triremes, and steered for Adherbal and his triremes, feeling quite sure that the quinquereme, caught in the swift current of the strait, could not reverse its course in the face of the tide. The Carthaginian in the unexpected situation was troubled for the moment and uncertain whether to follow his quinquereme or to turn his prows toward the enemy. The hesitation in itself deprived him of the power to refuse a battle; for they were already within range and the enemy was pressing them from all sides. The tide also had deprived them of control of their ships. Nor was the fight like a naval battle; for there was no initiative, no skill or strategy. The nature of the strait and its tide alone

7

controlled the entire engagement, carrying men, vainly struggling to row in the opposite direction, against their own ships or those of the enemy. And one might have seen a fleeing ship swung about by a swirl and borne against the victors, and a pursuing ship, if it chanced upon an opposite current, turning away as if in flight. In actual combat now one ship, aiming to ram a ship of the enemy with its beak, turning aslant would itself receive the blow of the other's beak. Another ship, exposing its beam to the enemy, would suddenly be turned bow foremost. While between the triremes an indecisive battle controlled by chance was now in progress, the Roman quinquereme, whether because she was steadier by reason of her weight or more easily steered as her more numerous banks of oars cleft the swirling waters, sank two triremes and shooting past another swept away the oars on one side. In addition, she would have seriously damaged the rest of the ships with which she had closed, had not Adherbal with five remaining ships crossed over to Africa under sail. Laelius as victor sailed back to Carteia...[28.30.3-12 and 28.31.1].

Another passage, from Dio Cassius, reflects a skirmish during the civil war between the forces of Caesar and Pompey (49-45 B.C.), and even more specifically mentions the harbor:

Then there were those who came to him [Pompeius] from Africa, among others his brother Sextus, and Varus, and Labienus with his fleet. Elated...he proceeded fearlessly through the country....For though Caesar also had generals in Spain, namely Quintus Fabius Maximus and Quintus Pedius, yet they did not regard themselves as a match for Pompey, but remained quiet themselves and kept sending urgently to Caesar....When he [Pompeius] discovered that Caesar was coming from Rome, he got scared, retired to Baetica, and began to suffer defeat [43.30.4-5].... The sea, moreover, straightaway became hostile to him, and Varus was defeated in a naval battle near Carteia by Didius; indeed, had he not escaped to the land and sunk a row of anchors side by side at the mouth of the harbour, upon which the foremost pursuers were wrecked as upon a reef, he would have lost his whole fleet [43.31.3].

And further,

[after Munda], Pompey, who had escaped in the rout, reached the sea, intending to use the fleet that lay at anchor at Carteia, but found that the men had gone over to the victor's side. He then embarked on a vessel, expecting to escape in this manner; but being wounded in the course of the attempt, he lost heart and put back to land, and then, taking with him some men who had assembled, set out for the interior. He met Caesennius Lento and was defeated; and taking refuge in a wood, perished there. Didius, ignorant of his fate, while wandering about in hope of meeting him somewhere, met some other troops and perished [43.40.1-2].

De Bello Hispaniensi, a source often attributed to Caesar, provides an alternative version of the same historical incident, and also mentions Carteia:

...Pompeius, who was wounded, seized twenty warships, and took to flight....On the fourth day of their voyage Pompeius' party put into land, since they had been ill provided and without water when they sailed from Carteia. While they were getting water Didius [who had pursued from Gades] hastened up with his fleet, captured some of their ships, and burned the rest [37].

There is further evidence of the importance of Carteia as a military base. Roman troops, veterans of the Second Punic War, were known to have intermarried with native women in the early part of the second century B.C. Their numbers were large enough that they formally petitioned the Roman Senate for citizenship for their children (Livy 43.3.2-5). Moreover, the Senate chose to grant Latin status to the town, making Carteia the first Latin colony founded on Spanish soil, and one of the first veteran colonies

9

established under Roman authority. As such, it was enfranchised in 171 B.C. as a *Colonia civium latinorum et libertorum*, a colony of free Latin citizens, and was governed by *quattuorviri*, who also oversaw the minting of the plentiful bronze coinage.[12] The coinage is very diverse and offers even more evidence to Carteia's maritime, and specifically naval, orientation. The most frequent motives are the heads of Saturn, Hercules, Neptune/Poseidon, and Tyche, combined with the rudder, a ship's prow, dolphin, boy on a dolphin, and seated fisherman.

Judging from both the material and literary evidence, it can be surmised that Roman Carteia was a large enough harbor to accommodate several warships, at least up to twenty triremes, and doubtlessly more; that it was regarded as a regular naval base, with substantial fortifications, and possibly a shipyard or drydock facilities; and, that it was the only Roman Republican harbor between Carthago Nova and Gades which could provide these features, along with a very strategic location. This latter point becomes even more imperative by the recognition that there is no indication that the Romans felt it necessary to protect these waters or shores with a more systematic line of defense. Granted, Carteia is not necessarily the site upon which the Romans would have founded a naval facility had one been pre-planned. Nonetheless, it was sufficient to provide adequate defense for the long settlement period after the Second Punic War, and was still serving the needs of the area in the late first century B.C.

Unfortunately, the sources are silent regarding the history of Carteia under the Empire. It no longer appears to have been used as a naval port, but may have been a center of commercial activity. At least one inscription suggests the presence of foreign merchants,[13] and several kilns have been excavated around the perimeter of the Bay for the manufacture of amphoras, that is, at el Rinconcillo. Garum was the main product, but local viticulture may have assumed some importance as well.[14] Strabo (3.2.7) mentions oysters, eels, murex (shell used for purple dye), and other varieties of fish for which Carteia was noted. However, other towns of coastal Baetica eclipsed its importance. The main base of naval operations in Spain continued to be Carthago Nova on the east

10

coast; and Malaca became the commercial center of the Costa del Sol. On the Atlantic, Gades and Hispalis (*Sevilla*) served as entrepôts for the massive quantities of oil produced in and around the Betis Valley.

Perhaps the silting process continued to plague Carteia, so that it may not have been feasible or desirable to dredge or make the harbor usable as a continuing naval port. Also, the province of Baetica had been pacified. In A.D. 44, northwest Africa was divided into two Roman provinces, Mauretania Tingitana and Mauretania Caesariensis, and permanent troops had not been stationed in Baetica from the time of Augustus. As a result, Rome's idea of *mare nostrum* had become a reality and the urgency of protecting the Strait from enemies was no longer present. At some unspecified date in the early Empire a new port (Portus Albus) was built on the west side of the Bay, although it does not appear to have been extensive. As the material remains suggest, Carteia continued to have importance as a waystation and embarkation point for the shipping of various products from the surrounding area; and, solid evidence from later centuries suggests that the town did not suffer extinction until well into the Middle Ages.

Notes

[1]See R. Thouvenot, "Le Détroit de Gibraltar chez la Géographie Ptolémée," *Revue des Études Anciennes*, 53 (1951): 185-202, and A. Schulten, "Die 'Saulen des Herakles'," in Otto Jessen, *Die Strassen von Gibraltar* (Berlin, 1927), 174-206. Jessen's geological study of the Strait has become the standard reference.

[2]Michel Ponsich, "La Navigation Antique dans le Détroit de Gibraltar," *Litterature Gréco-Romaine et Geographie Historique--Mélanges offerts à Roger Dion* (Paris, 1974), 269. Domingo Manfredi Cano, *Biografía del Estrecho* (Madrid, 1956), throughout discusses wind, tide, and currents in more detail regarding present-day navigation of the Strait. Strabo (3.2.5) also mentions the difficulty of navigating this channel.

[3]See Daniel Woods, "Excavations at Carteia, Southern Spain 1965-1967," *American Journal of Archaeology*, 73 (1969): 247-9, for a synopsis of the finds and dates.

[4]See Pierre Rouillard, "Brève note sur le Cerro del Prado, site Phénicien de l'ouest, à l'embochure du Rio Guadarranque (San Roque - Cadix)," *Madrider Mitteilungen*,

19 (1978): 152-60, and Manuel Pellicer, L. Menanteau and Pierre Rouillard, "Para una metodología de localización de colonias fenicias en las costas ibéricas: El Cerro del Prado," *Habis*, 8 (1977): 217-51.

[5]General finds are described in Daniel Woods, et al., *Carteia* (Madrid, 1967) [*Excavaciones Arqueológicas en España*, no. 58]; E. Romero de Torres, "Las Ruinas de Carteia," *Boletín de la Academía de Historia*, 54 (1937): 247-54; César Péman, *Memoria sobre la situación arqueológica de la Provincia de Cádiz en 1940* (Madrid, 1942) [*Informes y Memorias* 1]: 28-9; Pelayo Quintero, "Excavaciones de Carteya," *Memorias de la Junta Superior de Excavaciones y Antigüedades*, 99 (Madrid, 1929): 10-12, discusses the necropolis and two late Roman sarcophagi. The necropolis was never thoroughly excavated, and is now on inaccessible industrial property. The garum industry is well-attested in the ancient sources. M. Ponsich and M. Tarradell, *Garum et industries antiques de salaison dans la Mediterranée Occidentale* (Paris, 1965), 83, record the remains of garum-vats "sur la plage," but there is no sign of them today. Some vats recently have been excavated on the first ridge overlooking the sea, but have not been published.

[6]Péman, *Memoria...Cádiz en 1940*, 29, and R. Thouvenot, *Essai sur la province Romaine de Bétique* (Paris, 1940), 659, both suggest this possibility.

[7]A. García Bellido, "Un importante texto arabe valioso para nuestra historia antigua," *Archivo Español de Arqueología*, 52 (1943): 307.

[8]A. García Bellido, "Las colonias romanas de Hispania," *Anuario de Historia del Derecho Español*, 29 (1959): 450f. While excavating Carteia in 1975, I glimpsed an intriguing set of rectangular-cut stones even with the ground surface about fifty meters to the east of the river and near the present seashore. When I had another chance to investigate these stones in 1978, they had been covered by a paved area for parking.

[9]As reproduced in Juan del Alamo, *Gibraltar ante la historia de España* (Madrid, 1942), figs. 28 and 45.

[10]All translated passages are from the Loeb editions.

[11]Laelius was probably based at Carthago Nova.

[12]García Bellido, "Colonias romanas," 450f., provides commentary on this event. The known city magistrates are published in Alberto Prieto, "Estructura social del 'Conventus Gaditanus'," *Hispania Antigua*, 1 (1971): 147-68, in the accompanying charts. Also helpful for commentary is Rainer Wiegels, "Zum Rechtsstatus von Carteia Während des Prinzipats," *Madrider Mitteilungen*, 15 (1974): 203-08.

[13]L. A. García Moreno, "Málaga y los comerciantes orientales en la Península Ibérica s. V-VII," *Habis*, 3 (1972): 136.

[14]The villas to the north of Carteia, such as those around ancient Oba, were wine-producing. See Concepción Blanco, "El mosaico de 'Marchenilla' (Jimena de la Frontera, Cádiz)," *Noticiario Arqueológico Hispánico*, 8-9 (1964-65): 190-2, and Julio Mas, "Relaciones comerciales entre ciudades Augusteas, a traves de la ánforas

imperiales hispánicas," *Ciudades Augusteas*, 2 (Zaragoza, 1976): 242, mentions that three kilns along the coast west from Malaga produced wine amphoras, and two of these are in the Bay of Algeciras (Gibraltar).

The Spanish Armada and the Mobilization of English Resources, 1570-85

Ronald L. Pollitt

Four hundred years after the event, the defeat of the Spanish Armada continues to attract the attention of scholars. Most have concentrated on the diplomatic background, the military preparations, and the battle itself. In the following essay, Professor Pollitt shows that England was preparing for the possibility of just such an encounter with Spain nearly two decades before 1588, and that Queen Elizabeth and her councillors were clearly beginning to understand the modern concept of "national security."

Few events in British history have received as much attention through the centuries as the defeat of the Spanish Armada. From the public proclamations and broadsheets that appeared as the Duke of Medina Sidonia struggled upon his "north about," to the spate of books, articles, and media events that accompany the quatercentenary of the Armada, this great clash between two Atlantic naval powers, one ascending and the other beginning its decline, has never wanted for analysts to recount the details of ships, guns, strategy, tactics, advantages, and disadvantages, and a myriad of other matters related to Philip II's "Enterprise of England." Most of those accounts, while interesting and often enlightening, tend to concentrate with varying degrees of subtlety on the painfully obvious David and Goliath theme, with tiny England bravely and successfully defying the might and determination of the largest and most powerful empire in the West. While there is a large kernel of truth in the nationalist, or for foreigners, Anglophile, recounting of the defeat of the Armada, there have rarely been many attempts, until recent years, to explain what, beyond providing fuel for nationalistic fires, the Armada meant as a key event in Western history, much less in the evolution of England and Spain as states.

World War II, because of the parallel between England's position compared to Spain in the sixteenth century and Hitlerian Germany in the twentieth century, sparked interest in the Armada. But the nature of that interest changed significantly from what might be called the "tight little island" school of historiography that characterized earlier writings on the topic. During the 1930s and into the war years, Michael Lewis conducted a thorough investigation of the armament used by the combatants. He inspired other scholars to question what the Armada could reveal about late sixteenth century European technology.[1] Colin Martin's fascinating work on the naval archaeology of the Armada, particularly on gun-founding, is part of the tradition established by Lewis.[2] Garret Mattingly's magisterial study, while contrasting with Lewis's work in its focus on the European context of the Armada rather than on military technology, provided a balanced and crafted account of the conflict that remains the most respected study of the Armada. Most recently, David Howarth's study, in telling the Spanish side of the story, has provided a thoughtful and artfully written account of the Armada.[3] But despite the virtues of these and many other post-war works, they all concentrate on the diplomatic maneuvering, the preparations that preceded the clash in the Channel, and the military encounter proper.

To date, no student of the Armada has asserted that the roots of England's success in 1588 stretch back much further than the middle or early 1580s. There is, however, considerable evidence to show that English preparation for the clash with Spain was neither, as Froude argued, too little, too late, constrained by Elizabeth's parsimony, and too reliant on muddling through, nor was that preparation a child of the 1580s, born of the necessities accompanying direct English military intervention in the Netherlands and undeniable intelligence that Philip II was preparing a mighty force to subdue the English. On the contrary, Elizabeth and her councillors recognized the Spanish danger as early as 1569, and, albeit modestly at first but with increasing intensity as causes for concern multiplied during the 1570s, took stock of the national resources--especially the naval ones--and not altogether metaphorically girded up the nation's loins for the challenge that finally came late in 1588. Perhaps it would be best to begin at the beginning.

The Northern Rebellion of 1569 is usually portrayed as the last futile attempt of feudal, Roman Catholic England to break the hold of the Reformation and return the nation to the "Old Religion."[4] Begun in November, an unlikely time in the north to mount a rebellion, and aimlessly led by the lackluster Earls of Northumberland and Westmorland, the rising provided what many have viewed as an appropriate epitaph for a way of life that was in its death throes. Since the rebels failed to accomplish more than the brief reintroduction of the Roman service in Durham Cathedral and the capture of Barnard Castle, the episode has not been regarded as seriously as, for example, Sir Thomas Wyatt's uprising against Queen Mary, where the rebels came close to capturing London and the Queen. Despite its almost comic opera character, although there was nothing especially amusing about the hanging of some six hundred rebels, the Northern Rebellion was taken very seriously by Elizabeth's government. More important, it had a profound effect on English attitudes relating to national security.

It was not so much the aims of the rebellion--to restore Roman Catholicism, and, by implication, remove Elizabeth from power--that disturbed the government so deeply and led them to change their thinking about defence. Rather, it was the strategy of the rebel leadership that forced the crown to face certain unpalatable facts about England's vulnerability. During the spring and summer of 1569, when the rebellion began smoldering and the likelihood of striking a blow for the "old ways" grew from vague possibility to imminent reality, the leaders decided that they would not simply go it alone, as had Wyatt and his followers in 1554 or the rebels in the Pilgrimage of Grace in 1536. Since the Counter Reformation was gaining momentum on the Continent, and the emerging politico-military leader of that movement was King Philip

16

II of Spain, the rebels sensibly decided to seek his help in returning England to her proper course of national development.

While it is unclear how the conspirators approached the Spanish for help--traditionally it has been thought that Geurau de Spes, Spain's Ambassador to England, was the intermediary--there can be no doubt that the strategy they evolved posed for Elizabeth and her councillors the worst of all possible threats, a powerful domestic uprising coordinated with a determined invasion by foreign troops.[5] Whether de Spes ever made known to the Duke of Alva his commitment of support to the rebel leadership is unclear. Never troubled by such details, de Spes habitually promised more than he could deliver to all who plotted with him to overthrow the Elizabethan regime. It should come as no surprise that he misled the leaders of the Northern Rebellion and, if unintentionally, was the architect of their ruin. In any event, the Spanish Ambassador made his promise and the earls believed him. The consequence was that the rebels expected that foreign troops would be forthcoming. Accordingly, seizure of a port suitable for the landing of the dreaded Spanish tercios was given the highest priority by the rebel leadership.

They did not, of course, know that de Spes was not only untrustworthy, but that he revealed their plans to people entirely loyal to Elizabeth's government.[6] As a result, the crown knew of the grand strategy of the northern rebels, dooming the rebellion to failure. It was pointless for the rebel leadership to assign the job of seizing Hartlepool to Christopher Neville, one of the seemingly innumerable relatives of the Earl of Westmorland, just as it was futile for Neville to succeed in capturing the port of Hartlepool, for Elizabeth's government had at the beginning of the crisis acted to interdict any landing in the north in support of the rebellion by foreign troops under the command of Alva or any of his minions.[7]

The government ordered the Navy Board to man and equip the *Aid*, a ship of the line built in the rearmament program of the early 1560s, and the *Bark of Boulogne*, and the *Phoenix*, two older smaller ships built during the reign of Henry VIII. Captain John Henshaw commanded the squadron with orders to blockade the Yorkshire-Durham coast, to anticipate intercepting a fleet from the

Netherlands carrying troops and supplies for the rebels, and to pay particular attention to Hartlepool as the likely landing point. Whether the three ships could have stopped a determined effort by Alva is debatable, for none of them were armed with "ship-killing" ordnance. However, they might have inflicted heavy casualties on an invading force with their lighter armament and thus made the reinforcement effort questionable in value. In any event, the point is moot since the Duke of Alva made no effort to aid the English rebels. Alva's failure to participate does not diminish the significance of Henshaw's assignment for this action by Elizabeth's government is instructive in three important ways. First, it shows the quality of intelligence being sent to London and the willingness of the crown to act on that information. Second, it suggests a recognition by the government of the military danger posed by the Spanish in the Low Countries, thus delineating for the Queen and her councillors an appropriate framework for considering future matters of national security. Finally, and perhaps most significantly, Henshaw's assignment underscores the government's decision to give the naval line of defense a high priority when considering what actions might be needed after the suppression of the Northern Rebellion.[8]

Events immediately following the defeat of the rebellion only served to ensure that official thinking concerning the role of the navy in matters of national security would not change. The flight of the rebel leaders from their refuges in Scotland to Alva's Court in the Netherlands understandably focused English attention on the danger posed by the powerful Spanish force across the Channel. English agents there reported relentless plotting by the exiled rebels, serving to heighten concern in London about a reprise of the domestic rebellion supported by a foreign invasion.[9] Just how seriously this threat was taken can perhaps best be judged by the reaction in London in the summer of 1570 when Anne of Austria began her trek to become Philip II's queen.

Owing to the Habsburg-Valois rivalry, the Spanish were unwilling to risk an overland journey for Anne that would place her at the mercy of the French. They opted instead for a sea passage from the Netherlands down the Channel. As a matter of courtesy,

Philip's representatives requested and received from Queen Elizabeth a safe conduct through the Channel. They were not, however, sufficiently confident of English control of it to arrange for Anne's passage without substantial protection. In fact, the Spanish were so concerned about English and French pirates--the seizure of Alva's pay-ships was still fresh in the Spanish mind then--that they determined to protect their prospective queen with a substantial force of their own.[10] When the escorting fleet set sail, it numbered at least ninety ships of all sizes. The preparation of such an armada did not escape the attention of the English agents in the Netherlands. Their reports, coming as they did in the wake of plans to reinforce a domestic rebellion with a foreign invasion, had a dramatic effect in London. To a certain extent it is easy to sympathize with the English reaction. After all, the Armada of 1588 only had forty ships more than Anne's escort. But in 1570, Elizabeth and her advisors, when faced with the prospect of disputing any action by such a large number of potential enemy ships, found themselves for all intents and purposes helpless. The Royal Navy could muster only seventeen men-of-war, three of them being galleys. It did not take a brilliant strategist to conclude that if Anne's voyage was a guise for a scheme to invade England, which was by no means an absurd proposition in the atmosphere of July and August 1570, then some emergency measures needed to be taken to defend the realm.[11] Those measures proved to be the first major step toward preparing England for the real challenge to sovereignty that was to come nearly two decades later.

Toward the end of July 1570 the Privy Council began to supplement the Royal Navy with merchant vessels and sailors from various ports of England for use in this crisis. Orders were issued to stay all mariners in the Isle of Wight and to survey the maritime population of Devonshire. Other areas, like Dorset, Portsmouth and Hampshire, Essex, Bristol, Sussex, Yorkshire, Norfolk, and Suffolk, were directed to detain available mariners and to reserve ships then in port for use by the Queen if necessary.[12] By the end of August, Elizabeth was able to direct the Lord Admiral to send to sea a fleet of ten Royal Navy men-of-war and thirty armed merchantmen. Under the command of Charles Howard and

William Winter, the fleet was purportedly to escort Anne of Austria through the Channel but in reality it was to prevent a Spanish invasion. It may have been a fleet less than half what the Spaniards had mustered, but it was the best England could manage at the time under short notice.[13]

All this surveying and mustering of naval resources could be viewed as an isolated series of events provoked by the Northern Rebellion and resultant paranoia if there had been no sequel to it. However, its significance is that there was further action in the 1570s that showed a definite change by the government toward the navy's role in defending the realm. Whether he officially articulated this new position by the crown, it probably was not coincidental that John Montgomery's *Treatise Concerning the Navy of England*, finished in 1570, was used by the Navy Board and others to advance the case in the Parliament for a strengthened naval defense.[14] Much of what Montgomery wrote was as self-evident to Elizabethans as it is today, for the basic principles of sea power were understood long before Captain Mahan summarized them so effectively. There were, however, two very timely and, in retrospect, profoundly influential points advanced in the treatise. One was that the Royal Navy was too small and poorly supported and that it needed a substantial expansion if it was to do its job. The other was that merchant shipping should be viewed as an integral part of the naval defence of the island.[15] Montgomery never specifically referred to the dangers posed by the Northern Rebellion and Anne of Austria's voyage. There would have been little reason for him to do so. No one among the Elizabethan power elite would have needed more than an inferential reminder.

John Montgomery's eloquent and persuasively argued case for increased naval defense perhaps captured the mood of English political leadership by the end of 1570 more than anything else. Thus his treatise seems to have laid a course for crown action throughout the decade. If the lessons learned from the Northern Rebellion and Anne's voyage, bolstered by Montgomery's arguments, needed any more enhancement, it came in 1571 with the Ridolfi Plot. That incredibly complicated and woefully misunderstood episode, which appeared to include a domestic uprising combined with a foreign invasion from both Iberia and the Netherlands, to say nothing of the murder of Elizabeth and most of her councillors, ensured that England's leadership would be very remiss if they did not take immediate and forceful steps to improve the nation's defenses.[16] While unsatisfactory to John Montgomery and his friends at the Navy Board, those steps nevertheless prepared England for the challenge that came in 1588.

The crown took action in two areas. The better known one concerned an expansion of the military navy. Early in the 1560s, as part of a general rearmament program, the Royal Navy was strengthened. In 1563 alone, four warships were added to the Queen's fleet.[17] But aside from the construction of the *White Bear* in 1564 and the purchase of the *Elizabeth Bonaventure* in 1567, nothing further was done to expand the fleet. In the aftermath of the Northern Rebellion, Anne of Austria's passage and the Ridolfi Plot, however, the navy was significantly strengthened in the numbers of ships and in their fighting quality. Eight new warships, among them the *Foresight*, the *Dreadnought*, and the *Revenge*, were built in the 1570s.[18] Two smaller ships, the *Tiger* and the *Bull*, were rebuilt during the same time. But equally important as the numerical strengthening of the Royal Navy was the type of ships they were. Designed as fast and maneuverable fighting vessels, probably best represented by the Hawkings-designed and Pett and Baker-built *Revenge*, these new additions to Elizabeth's navy were as much a revolution in shipbuilding conceptualization as they were valuable increments to the defense of the realm. Moreover, the crown did not simply authorize the building of several new ships and neglect to provide the administrative and supply systems necessary to maintain them. While they groused endlessly over insufficient financial support, the Navy Board received healthy increases in its allocations throughout the decade.[19] But it was not in this more familiar area of Royal Navy expansion that the most important action occurred. It was, rather, in the sphere of mobilizing privately owned shipping and mustering seafaring manpower that the Queen and her councillors introduced their most noteworthy innovations during the 1570s.

The crises of 1569-70 taught the government that it could

ill-afford to be not merely incapable of mustering a force likely to meet a determined foreign challenge successfully, but generally ignorant of what resources were at hand to muster should the need arise. The Council's orders for surveys and stays of shipping and mariners showed that this was significant. It also showed that it was not forgotten once the crisis had passed. It gave the English an advantage of system over their adversaries. Quite simply, what the Queen and her advisors learned in 1570 and continued to remember throughout the decade is that they needed to know how strong the naval forces of England were and how difficult it would be to mobilize them in a crisis. Perhaps the most graphic demonstration of crown concern in this area came shortly after the exposure of the Ridolfi Plot.

Coinciding with the discovery of Ridolfi's scheme in 1571, the Council ordered Thomas Colshill, Surveyor of the Port of London, to identify all the ships "being in all the Ports and Creeks within the realm of England," and to inform the government which private vessels were available to supplement the fleet.[20] Colshill completed an extraordinarily thorough survey. Whereas before 1569, the government had no recourse save reliance on the vice admirals of the counties if the need arose to supplement the Royal Navy, with Colshill's survey, the Queen and her councillors now had abundant information to use in their planning. Newcastle, for instance, could provide thirty-six ships ranging from one hundred tons and upwards to six tons in displacement. That knowledge could only have reassured the Queen and the Council if it became necessary to bolster the Royal fleet with armed merchantmen. Valuable as it was, however, this collection of data on shipping and personnel was only one part of the new policy by the government in the increasingly tense atmosphere of the 1570s.

Recurring threats to the realm during that decade only encouraged Elizabeth and her councillors to take radical steps to ensure that what was now seen as the first line of defense, the navy, would be as prepared as possible for whatever eventuality. To an extent, these official fears were the product of the paranoia that began in the years 1569 to 1571, but as the Armada eventually proved, the fears were well-founded and the preparations entirely appropriate. Some concern focussed directly on the invasion of England proper like, for example, John Hawkins's report to Lord Burghley in September 1571, calling attention to Spanish plans to invade England. The credence Burghley placed in these and similar reports is evident in his orders in 1572 that the coast be prepared for invasion, that likely landing places be watched, and that several ships be kept in readiness for immediate action.[21] There were also those in the government who believed that "He that would England win, with Ireland he must begin."[22] This view had its advocates both in England and among England's enemies, and the machinations of such Irish rebels as Thomas Stuckley and James Fitzmorris during the 1570s only increased the fear the Spanish would seize Ireland as a staging area for the real plan of invading England.

Precisely how the country was invaded probably did not much matter to those responsible for seeing that the enterprise failed. What is consequential is what the crown did during the decade to raise the level of national security. Besides expanding and strengthening the Royal Navy and identifying merchant shipping suitable to supplement the fleet, there were other ways that helped prepare for the clash that came in 1588. Some of these actions were obvious. Any island nation concerned about security would ensure, for example, that castles and forts of the Kentish coast were prepared, or that Portsmouth and the Isle of Wight had the necessary men, equipment, and facilities for defense.[23] But other actions revealed a new and more sophisticated approach toward national security. Census surveys of the male population of England and Wales for military purposes qualifies as an administrative innovation and consistent with the policy of collecting data as exemplified by the surveys of shipping and the maritime population.[24] The crown compiled information on the whereabouts and ownership of furnaces and iron works for casting guns and shot, and it prohibited the export of guns cast in England.[25] Measures were also taken to identify and make available for strategic purposes the name of all "ports, creeks, and landing places in England and Wales."[26] Indeed, the government's preparatory activities ranged from such mundane matters as surveying the state of the Royal Navy to collecting data on the hemp and flax available in England and the number of trees in the Royal forests suitable for use by the navy.

By the end of the decade, sufficient information and practical measures put England in a much better state of readiness than that in 1569. It was probably a good thing, too, that the period had brought about a reorientation in thinking and practice pertaining to national security, for by 1579 the government believed that an assault on the island was inevitable. Nicholas Bacon, for example, prepared for Elizabeth an analysis of the dangers facing the realm complete with suggested remedies. Secretary Wilson wrote a "Discourse touching the Kingdom's peril," and Lord Burghley made an assessment of the perils confronting the realm.[27] These alarming documents prepared by experienced senior members of Elizabeth's government were not the product of paranoid delusions about Spanish intentions. By 1580, the government amassed a substantial corpus of intelligence reports and recollections on thwarted plots and bungled attempts at invading England and Ireland, and they served to lead the Queen and her advisors to conclude that what they had done during the 1570s was a necessary course of action. Thus by 1582 when Lord Admiral Lincoln was directed to compile his remarkable survey of the shipping and maritime population of the kingdom which gave the crown an invaluable picture of available naval resources when the Armada came six years later, the government was well experienced in gathering strategic information and using it for planning purposes.[28] When Burghley prepared his plan in 1584 for frustrating the Spanish onslaught, it was not so much the result of his grasp of naval strategy as it was the product of over a decade of recognition of the threat to security and knowledge of what could be employed to counter that threat. Without the data at the disposal of Elizabeth's government, it is very doubtful if the Spanish assault could have been met either in the way it was or with the success enjoyed by the English.

Much of what Elizabeth and her officers did in the 1570s to prepare for the clash with Spain was not preparing England militarily as such. To be sure, the Royal Navy was strengthened and many measures were employed to prepare England militarily. But what really happened during that decade to be consequential both for contending with the immediate issue of the Spanish threat and, in future years, improving the means by which government met its obligations, was the recognition that in order to be able to act effectively, it was crucial to know what resources were at the crown's disposal. When the Queen and her advisors were challenged by the Northern Rebellion, they had very little idea of what could be used in their defence and ended up muddling through a crisis that collapsed under the weight of rebel ineptitude. Eighteen years later and a more serious threat, the Queen and her officials knew with considerable certainty what they could use to defend themselves. One needs only to look at the maritime surveys of 1572 and 1582 and to the English order of battle in 1588 to see how valuable that information was. Some have argued that the circumstances of an impossible mission, not English naval power, defeated the Spanish Armada in 1588. There is also much to recommend that the navy which fought the Spanish was the best that the crown could field at the time, and that it came into being because of government policies begun nearly twenty years before Medina Sidonia entered the Narrow Seas.

Notes

[1]Lewis's work on armaments is in *The Mariner's Mirror*, 28 (1942): 41-73, 104-49, 231-45, 259-90, and 29 (1943): 3-39, 100-21, 163-78, 203-31. Those findings, embellished by later research, are nicely synthesized in his *Armada Guns* (London, 1961). Some criticism of his conclusions has appeared in light of more knowledge of European gun-founding. Technical errors notwithstanding, however, Lewis's part in reorienting the direction of Armada scholarship is indisputable.

[2]Colin Martin, *Full Fathom Five* (New York, 1975). See especially, pp. 59, 157, 179, 203-24.

[3]Garret Mattingly, *The Armada* (Boston, 1959), and David Howarth, *The Voyage of the Armada* (New York, 1981).

[4]The Northern Rebellion still awaits its chronicler, although scholars have examined some aspects of it. For example, see Cuthbert Sharp, ed., *Memorials of the Rebellion of 1569* (London, 1840), M.E. James, "The Concept of Order and the Northern Rising of 1569," *Past and Present*, 60 (August 1973): 49-83, and R. Pollitt,

"An 'Old Practizer' at Bay: Thomas Bishop and the Northern Rebellion," *Northern History*, 16 (1980).

[5]See Great Britain, *Calendar of Letters and State Papers Relating to English Affairs, Preserved Principally in the Archives of Simancas* (London, 1894), II, 201 for evidence of de Spes' knowledge of the rebels' plans.

[6]De Spes hopelessly compromised the uprising by communicating its strategy to his contacts in the Low countries attached to the Duke of Alva. English agents, most notably John Marsh, Governor of the Company of Merchant Adventurers, learned of the plans through contacts at Alva's Court and promptly relayed that information to London. Elizabeth's government thus knew of the rebellion and that its strategy included an invasion from the Netherlands. For details, see R. Pollitt, "The Abduction of Dr. John Story and the Evolution of Elizabethan Intelligence Operations," *Sixteenth Century Journal*, XIV (1983).

[7]See Great Britain, Public Record Office [hereafter PRO], Audit Office Declared Accounts A01/1682/5 for details on the vessels sent to prevent any landing on the Yorkshire coast. Captain John Henshaw was sent to blockade the coast, and his action effectively made it impossible for Alva to land troops, even if he had the wherewithal and desire to do so, which apparently was not the case.

[8]Henshaw's instructions were possibly the first to employ an English fleet in such a deliberately planned interdiction. While many invasion scares occurred in earlier decades, especially after the dissolution of the Reformation Parliament, the crown's strategic thinking was always confined either to using the navy to carry the war to the enemy on the Continent or to allowing the invasion to occur, then defeating the invader with land forces while the navy cut off the line of retreat and interfered with communications and supplies.

[9]John Lee, one of Cecil's ablest agents in the Netherlands, had managed to work his way into the confidence of the exiled rebels. Among other achievements, this enabled Lee to report in accurate detail the activities of the English exiles. See PRO, State Papers [hereafter SP] 15/20-23 for examples of Lee's work in Antwerp.

[10]Great Britain, *Calendar of Letters and State Papers Relating to English Affairs, Preserved Principally in the Archives of Simancas* (London, 1894), V.II (1568-79), nos. 191, 195.

[11]For all Royal Navy vessels available for service in 1570, see M. Oppenheim, *A History of the Administration of the Royal Navy* (London, 1896), 120.

[12]PRO, SP 12/71/54,56,57,64,74,75,76; SP12/73/14,15.

[13]PRO, SP 12/73/36.

[14]British Library [hereafter BL], Arundel MSS, vol. XXII, includes both the original 1570 text, the emendation by Montgomery in 1588, and some striking illustrations. Montgomery's treatise has never been reproduced in its entirety in print. Some of it is in E. Bridges, *Censura literaria* (London, 1805), Vol. V. Amongst other material, the entire Arundel version is to be included in my forthcoming

volume in the Navy Records Society publications entitled *Arming the Nation, 1568-1585.*

[15]BL, Arundel MSS, vol XXII, ff. 9r and 9v.

[16]My study of the Ridolfi Plot for the North American Conference on British Studies series, *Studies in British History and Culture*, is nearing completion. A fascinating, if sometimes strangely reasoned, account of the Plot is F. Edwards, *The Marvellous Chance* (London, 1968). Sir William Cecil's (at the time of writing he had become Lord Burghley) terse account of the Ridolfi Plot, entitled "The Order in Time," exists only in manuscript form in PRO, SP 12/85/11.

[17]Oppenheim, *History of the Administration*, p. 120.

[18]Financial records attesting to the specifics and costs of these new constructions are scattered throughout the Pipe Office Accounts in the PRO, E351/2208-2216 series of rolls.

[19]The PRO, E351 series of Pipe Office Accounts for the Office of Navy Treasurer and Office of Surveyor of the Victuals, provides convincing evidence of an ascending curve of government support for the maintenance of the Royal Navy.

[20]This remarkable survey of all privately owned shipping in England, entitled "Merchant Ships in England, Anno 1572," is in PRO, SP15/22. It is an invaluable source of information about the maritime status of England toward the end of the third quarter of the Tudor century and will be included in its entirety in *Arming the Nation*.

[21]Hawkins' letter to Burghley is in PRO, SP12/81/7. An example of Burghley's orders to prepare for invasion and counter is found in PRO, SP12/89/15.

[22]Great Britain, *Calendar of State Papers, Foreign Series, of the Reign of Elizabeth, 1579-80* (London, 1904), Vol. XIV, no. 336.

[23]See PRO, SP12/90/1, 17.

[24]PRO, SP12/95/63 is a five folio abstract, dated June 1573, of the men both "able and unable" to serve in a military capacity in England and Wales.

[25]See Pro, SP12/95/15, 21, 22, 70, and 79 for information about iron works and gun founding during the 1570s.

[26]PRO, SP12/96/218r-227r. On 1 June 1574 the Earl of Bedford was given instructions against invasion, and a few months later he reported that the Spanish navy was ready to invade. See PRO, SP12/97/2; BL, Lansdowne MSS, Vol. 18, no. 76.

[27]For Bacon's analysis, see BL, Harleian MSS, Vol. 168, no. 23. For Wilson's study, see PRO SP12/123/17.

[28]Lincoln's survey is an invaluable resource for the analysis of military preparations in anticipation of the Armada and for the general study of the maritime history of England. Sixty-three folios in length, it is in PRO, SP12/156/45.

The American Navy, the "War of Finance," and the Quest for Specie

Elizabeth M. Nuxoll

Despite its claim as the father of the modern U.S. Navy, the Continental Navy of the American Revolution suffered tremendous obstacles and difficulties during its brief history. Not least of its problems was that of financial support. In this essay, Dr. Nuxoll examines the desperate need for ready and hard money which faced the Continental Navy, and the significant role played by the financier and overseer, Robert Morris.

The American Revolution, like most wars, was not only a conflict of arms, but a war of finance in which the ability to obtain and to mobilize the economic resources needed to carry on the war was a major aspect in the outcome.[1] The American navy was always linked to this war of finance. Navies are expensive, and the effort to create from scratch one capable of contending with the world's greatest naval power posed a threat to the limited funds of the revolutionary government. However, naval missions could also raise needed money through the sale of prizes and could simplify the transportation of supplies and money. They could protect American trade, thus lowering the cost of war to the United States, and could capture enemy shipping, thereby raising the cost of war for the British. The navy could therefore help make or break the war effort. The interaction between naval and financial affairs was best personified in the career of Robert Morris when the Continental Congress assigned him the dual positions of Superintendent of

Finance and Agent of Marine from 1781 to 1784, the period on which this paper will focus.

A similar situation had prevailed earlier in the war when Morris simultaneously served as chairman of the Secret Committee of Congress in charge of international procurement of military supplies and as one of the most active members of the Marine Committee of Congress. In these capacities he had often intermixed naval and commercial ventures and funds to make each voyage as cost-effective as possible.[2] Morris had great maritime expertise from more than twenty years service as active partner of the great Philadelphia mercantile firm of Willing and Morris. He had an adventurer's enthusiasm for naval operations and naval heroes, becoming one of the patrons of John Paul Jones, John Barry, and other great American naval captains. He has long been considered one of the founders of the American navy.[3]

Nevertheless, even at his most optimistic moments Morris had no illusions about the possibility of creating a naval power significant enough to defeat the British navy alone or even to protect American trade singlehandedly. From the earliest days of the war he had been involved in the effort to secure French and Spanish participation, in large part in order to obtain their naval help. He also hoped to force the British navy to spread itself so thin to preclude its effective blockade of the United States and its destruction of American trade. Some congressional agents with whom he was associated even sought to manufacture incidents likely to provoke open warfare between Britain and France sooner than either power wished. To a large degree this effort to speed things up failed. France did not wish to act without Spain, and Spain had no intention of making herself prey to the British navy and privateers until after her specie ships arrived from Latin America. The European powers went to war when it suited their convenience, although some shrewd diplomacy by Benjamin Franklin did help move things along. Nevertheless, the maneuvers well illustrate that foreign financial aid was not enough to ensure American independence. Active military, particularly naval, support from European powers was also needed.[4]

When he returned to national office in 1781 Morris was already quite familiar with the intricate linkage between naval operations, supply operations, diplomacy, and public finance. He viewed the navy not in terms of battles and maneuvers, but in terms of its strategic contributions to the total war effort. His policies as Superintendent of Finance and Agent of Marine continued and built upon his earlier practices, although he was somewhat more sensitive than previously to questions of conflict of interest, departmental jurisdiction, and explicitness in the definition of his powers and authority. While attempting to rebuild the American navy, he continued to rely on foreign naval support on crucial occasions. Since his resources remained precarious throughout his administration, he always had to subordinate naval to financial considerations, giving top priority to policies that would preserve his credit and that of the government and "keep the money machine going."[5]

This subordination of naval to financial and commercial concerns has sometimes offended naval historians, just as military historians often complain bitterly about his treatment of the army. William Fowler, for example, asserts that "In Morris's scheme of things the navy had a low priority, and indeed after Yorktown it is likely it had no priority at all." Particularly irking has been Morris's use of naval ships to carry supplies and dispatches and his efforts to make the navy as self-supporting, even profitable, as possible. Such commercial considerations tend to be regarded as crass and the transport missions as mundane and boring misuses of naval talent and resources.[6]

In justification of his policies it must be stressed that Morris's funds were minimal and he came to office when the navy had been largely destroyed. His elaborate financial wheeling-and-dealing gave the navy a longer lease on life than might otherwise have been expected, and he did make one last abortive effort to obtain French financial support for rebuilding the navy that has been largely overlooked.[7] He also publicized naval exploits in order to sustain public morale (and possibly to flatter his glory-seeking and often disgruntled naval captains).[8]

Moreover, Morris did not assign naval vessels to errand-running lightly. He used naval ships as packets only when communications via merchant vessels were virtually non-existent, and to ferry money or supplies only when the blockade was largely impregnable or the need for them desperate.[9] That conducting such missions instead of cruising created many problems for the navy is undeniable. Nevertheless, no one reading the accounts of these missions will consider them in practice at all boring or routine. They required great speed and maneuverability of ships, and sometimes more skill than their naval officers could muster, since some ended in capture.[10] By 1782, Morris was assigning his most trusted and swashbuckling seamen to them. Furthermore, they were all crucially important to the war of finance; their potential contributions to victory and the establishment of the new nation were far greater than any naval cruises could have accomplished. Among the most significant of the naval missions were those designed to secure the safe arrival of specie into the United States.

When Morris served in Congress from 1775 to 1777 he was able to finance many of his supply and naval operations with paper money. By the time he returned to power in 1781, however, this paper money was "not worth a Continental." New financial resources were needed. It was necessary to rely in part on hard money and to create a new paper medium of exchange in which the public would have confidence. The United States had no mines and no mint; specie had to be imported from abroad.[11] It could be obtained either through trade or through foreign aid, but in either case it had to be transported by ship and could be obstructed by a British naval blockade.

When Morris took office in 1781 the specie supply in the United States was high (although by no means sufficient for the needs of the entire American economy). Trade was good. Spain had recently agreed to permit American trade with Cuba, where large amounts of Spanish silver (public and private) were stockpiled because of the risks inherent in transporting it to Spain once that nation entered the war.[12] The Spanish need to provision their forces in the Caribbean encouraged trade with the United States and brought substantial amounts of privately owned silver into American ports. Merchants began to avoid dealing in the now hopelessly depreciated Continental currency and relied more heavily on specie transactions. Although there were restrictions and substantial duties on exporting specie from Havana, American merchants were apparently quite adept at bypassing many of these regulations. For example, one of Morris's clerks, James Rees, recalled that he and Morris secretly unloaded at night sugar barrels filled with specie from Havana.[13] Expenditures by the French and British armies in America had also brought in a large stock of specie in 1780-81.[14] Thus, when Morris began formulating his policies it was both necessary to think in terms of specie-based financial transactions because the currency had collapsed, and possible to do so because there had been a recent inflow of specie.

Morris's policies reflected this condition in various ways. First, he sought to have the states levy taxes toward Continental requisitions in specie or its equivalent rather than in commodities or depreciated paper.[15] He then made many public engagements payable in specie, particularly the military contacts he initiated, to replace unwieldy and expensive congressional procurement agencies. The financier also tried to create new non-depreciating paper instruments that would be equivalent to specie and could be used both for commercial transactions and for the payment of taxes. In this way he could expand the money supply sufficiently to enable people to pay taxes to support the war and restore public confidence in government, particularly among the commercial classes.[16] The sound money he sought to create in the form of bank notes and of Morris's notes were to be backed in part by private credit. However, they also were to be exchangeable for specie and redeemed by the levying of taxes payable with such notes. Combined with the careful regulation of the flow of money, such policies would create a medium of exchange to finance the war effort and promote American economic growth.[17] For this program to work smoothly, however, the stock of specie had to remain reasonably high and its circulation had to be maintained. Morris, therefore, first had to insure that specie continued to come into the country from abroad; for this, the navy proved essential.

Morris created the Bank of North America in 1781 with an intended capitalization of $400,000. Unable to obtain sufficient capital for the bank from private sources, he sought to obtain the requisite funds from Spain and France.[18] He sent the *Trumbull* to Havana in 1781 to convert bills of exchange drawn against an anticipated Spanish loan into specie to be invested in the bank. The *Trumbull*'s capture en route to Havana foiled that plan. As Morris later told his friend, Horatio Gates, "The Capture of the Trumbull Frigate was a great loss to the Public and a disapointment to a most promising plan I had for turning, as you desired I shou'd, our paper into Silver. However, we have learnt to bear losses and endure disapointments and what is still better we have the courage to try again...."[19]

Morris's optimism was justified by the safe arrival in August 1781 of a French frigate at Boston bearing specie as part of a French loan. Although he needed some of the cash to finance the Yorktown campaign, Morris managed to hold on to enough to invest about $250,000 of it in bank stock, a sum sufficient to allow the bank to open in January 1782.[20] Although Morris was unable to secure much private investment in bank stock he was able to win enough confidence in the bank to get merchants and French officials to deposit specie there and to use bank notes.[21] He is also reputed to have created the impression that more specie was available in the bank than there was by "dazzling the public eye by the same piece of coin, multiplied by a thousand reflectors." The bank allegedly displayed piles of silver on the counter, employed workers in conspicuously raising and lowering boxes containing silver, or supposed to contain it, to and from the cellar, and hired men to follow those who had demanded specie from the bank to urge them to accept notes instead.[22]

The British soon figured out how to counter America's newfound weapon in the war of finance. They encouraged illicit trade for British manufactured goods with British-occupied New York to drain specie from the surrounding American countryside. In the aftermath of their defeat at Yorktown they largely abandoned land warfare, but renewed naval warfare with a vengeance. They mounted a tight naval blockade along the coast, with special emphasis on the Delaware and Chesapeake Bays, largely destroying American trade in that region. New specie could not come in from abroad. The supply in the bank dwindled and that fledgling institution had to limit or suspend its discounts. Money became tight. Taxes could not be easily paid and the states became more reluctant than ever to try to comply with congressional tax requisitions. Moreover, Robert Morris could not raise money by selling bills of exchange drawn against foreign loans. Merchants did not need overseas bills when it was virtually impossible for their ships to leave port safely. All Morris's sources of revenues were being endangered.[23]

As a result, by mid-1782 Morris was involved in an all-out effort to renew American naval strength, to obtain increased French and Spanish naval help, and to protect American trade in general and specie shipments in particular. First, he cooperated with other Philadelphia merchants in obtaining a ship for the defense of the Delaware, using funds borrowed from the bank. The widely publicized victory of the *General Washington* under the command of Captain Joshua Barney over the *General Monk* on 8 April 1782, gave a great lift to the spirits of the mercantile community and increased confidence that effective naval action could protect American trade.[24] Nevertheless, the British naval depredations remained largely unabated.

Therefore, Morris continued his efforts to acquire naval power. Although he expended more than he could afford, his attempts to complete the long-delayed construction of the *America* and the *Bourbon* were hampered by shortages of supplies and funds. His quest to acquire the superb frigate *South Carolina* for use by John Paul Jones was also frustrated by the unfavorable terms offered and his lack of the requisite funds. Morris leased the *General Washington* and sent Barney to the West Indies with dispatches to French and Spanish naval officials seeking convoys for American trade, particularly the lucrative tobacco trade with the Chesapeake. The British naval victory at the Battle of the Saints in the West Indies devastated the French navy and undermined this plan. Nevertheless, part of the French fleet under Vaudreuill did sail up the coast in August and remained in the United States in late 1782 providing limited protection for American trade. Finally, Morris began to elicit the support of French minister La Luzerne for the rebuilding of the American navy--largely through loans from France. La Luzerne did pass on the proposals to his superiors, but the drive was largely abandoned because of the opening of peace negotiations. In the meanwhile La Luzerne promoted writings in newspapers advocating a rebuilding of the navy and calling for the tax revenues necessary to finance it.[25]

Parallel to these efforts to repair the trade predicament, Morris ordered Barney to sail to Cuba after delivering his dispatches and to pick up any specie merchants there wished to remit to the United States. Barney's return in July 1782 with $60,000 in privately owned specie, together with the long awaited arrival of merchant ships from Havana in the Chesapeake under convoy by Alexander Gillon of the South Carolina navy, brought in enough specie to help end a suspension of discounting. The bank continued to be able to make public and private loans.[26]

Nevertheless, Morris's financial difficulties mounted. Taxes failed to arrive on time. Public creditors became increasingly restive; their losses in trade were eroding their patience. Unable to pay the major army contractors on schedule, Morris was forced to renegotiate a new contract at substantially higher prices in exchange for three months' credit. Word of army unrest came from Washington, who insisted some army pay had to be provided. Morris reported this to Congress and to the states and obtained permission to request substantial new foreign loans.[27]

Morris then sent Barney to France with dispatches urgently requesting an additional French loan, a portion of which was to be placed on board his ship. At the same time, he launched a secret mission to send the newly acquired *Duc de Lauzun* to Havana bearing a cargo and bills of exchange drawn in an elaborately circuitous negotiation against a newly opened Dutch loan, the proceeds of which Morris would otherwise have trouble employing for the United States. Specie obtained by the sale of the public cargo and bills was to be transported to the United States aboard the *Duc de Lauzun*, aboard John Barry's frigate *Alliance* should it arrive on time in Havana, or aboard any other merchant vessels that the naval ships could safely convoy to the United States.[28] Although it does not appear in any of the official instructions, the

35

vessels were also to freight any private specie merchants in Havana wished to ship.[29] Private specie deposits in the bank were almost as important to Morris's program as public specie was. Because of the great danger of capture, the details of this voyage were kept secret from Congress; only Washington was given any inkling of its purpose. Morris promised Washington that if the plan was successful, most of the proceeds would be used for army pay.[30]

Shortly after the *Lauzun's* departure, the need to provide for army pay became more urgent. A committee from the army arrived in Philadelphia demanding back pay, settlement of their accounts, and fulfillment of promises of half-pay pensions made to officers who agreed to serve for the duration of the war.[31] Morris, after first refusing to pay the army, referring only obliquely to the uncertainty of the success of the measures he had taken to provide for it, eventually relented. Gambling on the success of Barney's loan appeal and of the *Lauzun's* mission, he agreed to issue one month's pay to the troops in cash at the rate of roughly fifty cents a week. Although the "piddling" manner in which this pay was to be advanced offended the army, Morris had great difficulty assembling even that much money. Only the military contractors who arranged to sell needed goods to the army in exchange for assignments of the promised pay saved him from disaster. Unlike the troops, the contractors could afford to wait for their money; moreover, they made substantial profits on the sale of goods to the army.[32]

Morris's difficulties in meeting this commitment to the army stemmed largely from the naval situation. Military historians have tended to assume that Morris refused to pay the army and kept the impending specie shipments secret only because he wanted to maintain the army as a pressure group for Continental taxes, particularly the impost amendment that had to be ratified by all the states.[33] They greatly underestimate the tremendous risks involved in his specie operation--both the financial risks and the naval ones.

The *Lauzun*, commanded by John Green and with former Marine Secretary John Brown as supercargo, reached Havana safely by early January 1783.[34] Barry's *Alliance* arrived shortly afterward. But Brown was unable to sell the requisite number of bills because of lack of confidence in the American financial predicament.[35] Having sold the cargo and some $67,000 worth of bills, he could not obtain permission to set sail with the specie. The French and Spanish fleets were planning to assemble at Porto Cabello for an attack on Jamaica. To prevent information of their plans from leaking out Spanish officials clamped a close embargo on the port of Havana. No ship could leave until the Spanish fleet set sail, and there was no telling when that would be. Green, Barry, and all American merchant captains in port were trapped in Havana until early March 1783. Barry and Green sailed with the first Spanish vessels to leave harbor.[36]

What followed was one of the most exciting naval voyages of the war, culminating in the last naval battle of the revolution, all vividly described in accounts by Barry, Green, and Barry's mate, John Kessler. The *Alliance* and the *Lauzun* narrowly escaped one battle off the Florida keys, then engaged in another with three ships off Cape Canaveral. Barry later accused Green of having deliberately jeopardized the *Alliance* to save his own ship.[37] The *Duc de Lauzun* was a poor sailor, overburdened with private cargo belonging to the captain and crew who were seeking one last opportunity for profit before peace officially arrived. Barry therefore insisted that all the public specie be transferred to his ship. Off the North Carolina coast the two ships were separated. Encountering British frigates in the fog at the entrance of Delaware Bay, Barry sailed instead to Rhode Island, landing safely with the cargo of public specie and some private specie. While a portion of this went to pay the army and some to pay off army contractors, much of the public specie had to be used to pay the crew and refit the damaged *Alliance*.[38] The proceeds of the voyage were by no means sufficient to make one month's pay to the army, estimated at about $250,000 per month,[39] and Morris's caution about its prospects for success was more than justified.

Meanwhile, the *Lauzun* succeeded in slipping past the British frigates in the Delaware and landed her cargo of private goods and specie at Philadelphia. While reports of the amount of specie aboard varied, it was soon deposited in the bank.[40] Supplemented by the timely arrival at Philadelphia of Joshua Barney with about $111,000 from a new French loan, this new stock of specie again saved the bank from a suspension of discounting and preserved its credit from collapse.[41] While the precise application of the funds brought by Barney has not been traceable, it apparently enabled Morris to meet his most urgent commitments and enabled the bank to continue granting some credit to the government.[42]

All the shipments put together did not, however, bring in enough to fully cover the one month's army pay, much less the three months' considered minimal to avoid upheaval as the army prepared for disbandment. Morris, who had presented a conditional resignation to Congress in January unless funds were provided to pay the interest on the public debt, was nevertheless prevailed upon to stay in office to issue three months' pay to the army in notes. He had to remain in office until they were paid along with his other major commitments. Had none of the specie arrived, and had Barney not brought news of a small new French loan, Morris would have had to resign.[43] What the consequences would have been for the army are unknown, but the troops no doubt would have obtained even less compensation than what they received for their Morris notes.

Although Morris was one of those who strongly favored a peacetime navy to protect American trade, the even greater financial precariousness of the rest of his administration led him to preside over the dismantlement of the American navy.[44] While it remained, however, the navy continued to play an important role in American finance. At Morris's suggestion Congress presented the unfinished ship *America* to France, in part to cut expenses, but largely to soften the French up for another loan request and to interest them in American ship construction for the French navy.[45] Barney was quickly sent back to France with another urgent appeal for foreign loans. The *Duc de Lauzun*, intended for sale, was sent to France transporting French officers, another effort to smooth relations with a rather exasperated French government.[46] Barry's *Alliance* was fitted out to carry a cargo of tobacco to Europe to pay the interest on the Dutch loan, and thereby sustain what little was left of American credit in Europe. When the ship sprang a leak and had to put back, it damaged American credibility and led to suspicion that Morris was not seriously trying to repay his country's foreign debt.[47] The remaining ships and naval stores were sold and the funds used to pay some of the government's domestic debts and expenses.[48]

It was Morris's hope that this dismantlement of the navy would play a role in his quest for strengthening the government. Only after they felt the consequences of doing without would the American public be willing to vote the taxes needed to sustain the American navy. Morris pithily expressed his dilemma:

> until Revenues for the Purpose can be obtained it is but vain to talk of Navy or Army or any thing else. We receive sounding Assurances from all Quarters and we receive scarce any thing else. Every good American must wish to see the United States possessed of a powerful fleet but perhaps the best way to obtain one is to make no Effort for the Purpose till the People are taught by their Feelings to call for and require it. They will now give money for Nothing.[49]

Stephen T. Powers has argued that in adopting this strategy Morris played into the hands of anti-naval forces and precipitated the extinction of the American navy.[50] This is true only from the short range perspective. There was no way in which Morris could have obtained funds for the continuance of a viable navy in the immediate post-war years. The retention of the *Alliance* or even one or two more ships would not have substantially overcome American vulnerability abroad or, with all due respect to John Barry, have deterred the Algerian pirates. The perception of total weakness that soon followed did play a role in the adoption of the United States Constitution in 1787 and in the obtaining for the government the tax power necessary eventually to recreate an American navy in 1794.[51] Thus did the navy play a major role in the final victory of the war of finance.

Notes

[1]For the revolution as a "war of finance," see Robert Morris (hereafter RM) to Alexander Hamilton, 2 July 1782, in E. James Ferguson et al., eds., *The Papers of Robert Morris, 1781-1784* (Pittsburgh, 1973-), V: 514. Hereafter *MP*.

[2]Elizabeth Miles Nuxoll, *Congress and the Munitions Merchants: The Secret Committee of Trade, 1775-1777* (New York, 1985), 80-82, 84-86, 87-89, 442-44.

[3]Samuel E. Morison, *John Paul Jones: A Sailor's Biography* (Boston, 1959), 59, 66, 67, 87, 91, 180, 181, 297, 318; Charles Oscar Paullin, *The Navy of the American Revolution: Its Administration, Its Policy, and Its Achievements* (1906; reprint New York, 1971), 90, 173-76, 182-83.

[4]Nuxoll, *Congress and the Munitions Merchants*, 289-94, 309n-310n, 409-14, 444-45.

[5]*MP*, I: 27, 63-64, 94-95, 96-97, 120-21, IV: 256, V: 121, 191-92, 203, VI: 37, 61-62. See E. Wayne Carp, *To Starve the Army at Pleasure: Continental Army Administration and American Political Culture, 1775-1783* (Chapel Hill, 1984), 208-17.

[6]William M. Fowler, Jr., *Rebels Under Sail: The American Navy during the Revolution* (New York, 1976), 85, 89-91. Stephen T. Powers gives the most complete discussion of Morris's handling of the navy. Somewhat critical of the navy's subordination to finance, he correctly links it to the failure of the "Nationalist" movement to obtain an independent revenue. "Decline and Extinction of American Naval Power" (Ph.D. diss., University of Notre Dame, 1965), 194-97. On subordination of the army's needs to finance, see William Johnson, *Sketches of the Life and Correspondence of Nathaniel Greene, Major General of the Armies of the United States*, 2 vols. (Charleston, SC, 1822), II: 253-56, and Carp, *To Starve the Army*, 214-16.

[7]*MP*, VI: 94-95, 101-103; David Freeman Hawke, *Benjamin Rush: Revolutionary Gadfly* (Indianapolis, 1971) 255-259; Lewis Leary, *That Rascal Freneau: A Study in Literary Failure* (New Brunswick, NJ, 1941), 96. Morris also included the navy as one of the long-range purposes for which future loans would be obtained once American public credit was established through his funding plan. See RM to President of Congress, 29 July 1782, and notes, *MP*, VI: 55, 65.

[8]John Barry to RM, 18 October 1782, *MP*, VI: 625. Writings by poet-polemicist-sea captain Philip Freneau also glorified American naval successes in 1782. See Leary, *Freneau*, 96, 428; Morison, *Jones*, 317-18.

[9]"State of American Commerce and a Plan for Protecting It," 10 May 1782, *MP*, V: 145-46, 148-53, 154-57.

[10]*MP*, I: 313-16; III: 523, 524-25, V: 265.

[11]Ibid., IV: 26-29, 32, 34-40.

[12]James A. Lewis, "Las Damas De La Havana, El Precursor, and Francisco De Saavedra: A Note on Spanish Participation in the Battle of Yorktown," *The Americas*, 37 (July 1980), 90-91, 94-97; Francisco de Miranda, *The New Democracy*

in America: Travels of Francisco de Miranda in the United States, 1783-1784, Judson P. Wood, trans., and John S. Ezell, ed. (Norman, OK, 1963), 3.

[13]See Edward F. Delancey's notes to "Original Documents/Sir Henry Clinton's Original Secret Record of Private Daily Intelligence," *Magazine of American History, with Notes and Queries* 11 (January-June 1884), 442n. This information appears in a footnote to the "Copy of a Letter from a Gentleman in Philadelphia to Capt. Beckwith (recd 1st. July, 1781)" which asserts "Our assembly as well as those of New Jersey, and the Delaware States, are now sitting upon the subject of the Paper money. They have it in contemplation to repeal all tender laws and levy their taxes in hard money. To take off all restrictions on trade, except to what they call the *common enemy*, and to give every possible encouragement to the trade of the French and Spanish Islands. The late very great success which the traders of this place have met with, has led to this measure. A number of arrivals from Havanna very lately (I believe since my last to you) have brought not less than 200,000 Dollars, besides a very large quantity of sugars. West India goods are generally as cheap here as in the time of peace. I should then, expect that your business as *Politicians*, would be to counteract this plan as much as possible, as well by encouraging the sending of the produce to you, as by cruizing against all such as was intended to be sent for the immediate supply of your enemies" (ibid., 442-43). See also James A. Lewis, "Anglo-American entrepreneurs in Havana: The background and significance of the expulsion of 1784-1785," in Jacques A. Barbier and Allan J. Kuethe, eds., *The North American Role in the Spanish Imperial Economy, 1760-1819* (Manchester, 1984), 120. On the relationship between the specie supply, the bank, and the British blockade, see *MP*, V: 376-77.

[14]Clarence L. Ver Steeg, *Robert Morris, Revolutionary Financier, With An Analysis of His Earlier Career* (Philadelphia, 1954; reprint New York, 1976) 53, 54-56.

[15]Delancy, *Magazine of American History*, 442 and n.; *MP*, V: 376-77, VI: xxxii.

[16]*MP*, I: xx, III: 414-15.

[17]Ibid., III: 267-68, 407-08, IV: 353-59, 609-10, 611-14, 616-20, 622, VI: xxxiii, 277-79, 499-500, VII: appendix; Ver Steeg, *Morris*, 68-70, 87-88, 102-103, 115-120, 135.

[18]*MP*, I: 224-25, 229-31, 288-89; Ver Steeg, *Morris*, 68-69; and Mary-Jo Kline, "Gouverneur Morris and the New Nation, 1775-1788" (Ph.D. diss., Columbia University, 1970, 221-35.

[19] *MP*, I: 144, 311, 314-16, 369, II: 280. Had the *Trumbull* arrived safely, the loan attempt would probably have failed since the one convoy to leave Havana with specie since Spain entered the war had just departed. However, with Spanish support, de Grasse managed to borrow money for his fleet in Havana which was used to finance his participation in the Yorktown campaign and enabled the French to lend funds for one month's army pay to the United States during that campaign. See Lewis, "Las Damas De La Havana," 95-97.

[20]*MP*, I: 66-72, 83-86, 142-43, 356, 357-62, II: 141, 180-81, 111, 497, 507-508.

[21]Ibid., V: 83; Chevalier de La Luzerne to Comte de Vergennes, 21 May, 23 June, and 1 July, Vergennes to Marquis de Segur, 22 July, Segur to Vergennes, 27 July, Vergennes to La Luzerne, 12 August, 1782, and La Luzerne to Vergennes, 10 January 1783, "Correspondance politique, Etats-Unis," XXI: 205-11, 329-30, 369-70, 433, 479-80, XXII: 55, XXIII: 49-50, Archives du Ministère des Affaires Etrangères (AMAE), Paris.

[22]The comments on "dazzling the eye" appeared first in Johnson, *Life of Greene*, II: 255. The other tales apparently originated in an anti-bank tract of the Jacksonian era. See William M. Gouge, *A Short History of Paper-Money and Banking in the United States* (New York, 1833), 35.

[23]*MP*, V: 149-50, 435, 436; La Luzerne to Vergennes, 21 May and 1 July 1782, Correspondance politique, Etats-Unis, XXI: 205-206, 369-70, AMAE; Ver Steeg, *Morris*, 138-39.

[24]Mathew Carey, ed., *Debates and Proceedings of the General Assembly of Pennsylvania, on the Memorials Praying a Repeal or Suspension of the Law Annulling the Charter of the Bank* (Philadelphia, 1786), 106; James Wilson, *Considerations on the Bank of North America* in Robert Green McCloskey, ed., *The Works of James Wilson* (Cambridge MA, 1967), II: 847.

[25]*MP*, V: 147, 148, 156-57, VI: 95, 102-103.

[26]Ibid., V: 194, 217, 218; Hulbert Footner, *Sailor of Fortune: The Life and Adventures of Commodore Barney, U.S.N.* (New York, 1940), 116-24; Ver Steeg, *Morris*, 140-41. A related mission for John Barry was abandoned (*MP*, V: 249, 250).

[27]*MP*, VI: 36-37, 39-40, 91, 95-96, 343, 357, 477, 478.

[28]Ibid., 424, 425; Footner, *Sailor of Fortune*, 125-40.

[29]See John Brown to RM, 4 March 1783 (second letter) and notes, *MP*, VII: 498-99.

[30]Ibid., VI: 601.

[31]Diary, 31 December 1782, and notes, *MP*, VII: 247-50.

[32]RM to Paymaster General, 20 January 1783, and notes, *MP*, VII: 327-42; and Notes on Debates, 7, 13 January 1783, William T. Hutchinson, et al., eds., *The Papers of James Madison* (Chicago, 1962-), VI: 18-19, 31-33.

[33]Richard H. Kohn, *Eagle and Sword: The Federalists and the Creation of the Military Establishment in America, 1783-1802* (New York, 1975), 21-22; Kline, "Gouverneur Morris," 260-62.

[34]See Barry's log or journal in the Barry Papers, Hepburn Collection, Philadelphia Maritime Museum (PMM).

[35]John Brown to RM, 4 March (first letter), and notes, and Governor of Cuba to RM, 1 March 1783, *MP*, VII: 483-84.

[36]Clark, *Gallant John Barry*, 293-95; Martin I. J. Griffin, *Commodore John Barry* (Philadelphia, 1903), 213-15.

[37]For contemporary accounts, see John Barry's Account of Proceedings on the *Alliance* and the *Duc de Lauzun*, [from ca. 11-20 March 1783], Barry Papers, Hepburn Collection, PMM; Barry to RM, 20 March, and Barry to Brown, 19 April 1783, Barry Papers and Letterbook, Library of Congress, Washington, D.C. [hereafter LC]; Griffin, *Barry*, 222-24; Brown to RM, 25 March, *MP*, VII: 605-15, 637; and Green to [Barry], 3 April 1783, Green Letterbook, PMM. For secondary accounts, see Clark, *Gallant John Barry*, 295-303; and Powers, "Decline and Extinction," 149-56.

[38]RM to George Olney, 29 March 1783, and notes, *MP*, VII: 645-46.

[39]Morris Diary, 14, 21, 29 January 1783, LC.

[40]Diary, 21 March 1783, *MP*, VII: 309, 345, 380, 618; Green to Barry, 3 April 1783, Green Letterbook, PMM.

[41]Brown to RM, 4 March 1783 (second letter), *MP*, VII: 499; Green's account, in Ledgers, I (1782-83), 323, Bank of North America Papers, Philadelphia, Pennsylvania Historical Society [hereafter PHS]; William Armstrong to Sir Guy Carleton, 1 April, in Historical Manuscripts Commission, *Report on American Manuscripts in the Royal Institution of Great Britain* (London, 1904-1909), IV: 6-7; Nathaniel Falconer to Benjamin Franklin, 23 June 1783, Minis I. Hays, comp., *Calendar of the Papers of Benjamin Franklin in the Library of the American Philosophical Society* (Philadelphia, 1908), III: 77.

[42]Morris Diary, 6 February, 7 May, 20, 30 October, 3, 10 December 1783, and RM to Franklin, 13 February 1784, Morris Letterbooks, LC; Thomas Fitzsimons, "State of Facts Respecting the National Bank," PHS.

[43]RM to President of Congress, 24 January, 26 February, 1, 3 May 1783, *MP*, VII: 361-71, 462-74, 767-81, 789-90.

[44]For Morris's continued belief in the importance of the navy, see RM to ?, 10 April, and to President of Congress, 3 May 1783, *MP*, VII (forthcoming); RM to President of Congress, 10 July 1783, Agent of Marine Letterbook, U.S. Naval Academy Library, Annapolis, Maryland [hereafter USNA]; RM to John Jay, 27 November 1783, Jay Papers, Columbia University Library. On the dismantlement of the American navy, see Powers, "Decline and Extinction," 162-187, and Fowler, *Rebels Under Sail*, 84-86. On the parallel dissolution of most of the American army, see Kohn, *Eagle and Sword*, 40-72.

[45]*MP*, IV: appendix; VI: 302, 494; Paul W. Bamford, "France and the American Market in Naval Timber and Masts, 1776-1786," *Journal of Economic History*, XII (1952): 21-34; Kline, "Gouverneur Morris," 218n., 234-35.

[46]RM to La Luzerne, 6 May, to Ferdinand Grand, 9 May, to a committee of Congress, 15 May, and to Benjamin Franklin, 26 May 1783 (two letters), Morris Letterbooks, LC; Footner, *Sailor of Fortune*, 143-44. La Luzerne to RM, 20 April, and RM to La Luzerne, 2 May, and Diary, 1 May 1783, *MP*, VII: 726-27, 766, 788.

[47]RM to Willinks and Co., 29 April, 8 May, 25 July, 18 September, 9 October 1783,

and 30 September 1784, Morris Letterbooks, LC; Vergennes to La Luzerne, 30 June, and Marbois to Rayneval, 24 August 1784, in George Bancroft, *History of the Formation of the Constitution of the United States of America*, 2 vols. (New York, 1893), I: 375, 378-80; Pieter J. van Winter, *American Finance and Dutch Investment, 1780-1805, With an Epilogue to 1840* (New York, 1977), 108-109, 128, n.108.

[48]Powers, "Decline and Extinction," 176-87.

[49]RM to President of Congress, 10 July 1783, Agent of Marine Letterbook, USNA.

[50]Powers, "Decline and Extinction," 168-74, 177-78, 261-62.

[51]See Frederick W. Marks, III, *Independence on Trial: Foreign Affairs and the Making of the Constitution* (Baton Rouge, 1973), 36-51; Powers, "Decline and Extinction," 235-57.

The Impact of the Napoleonic Wars upon Russian Priorities on Naval Development

Norman E. Saul

Historians have traditionally characterized the Russian navy of the first half of the 19th century as one in a state of steady decline, far behind other European navies in modernization and technological innovation. Professor Saul demonstrates that while the Napoleonic Wars caused the decline of the Russian navy after 1815, it was not as impotent a force as normally believed, and that the decline was not at all a steady one.

An anonymous European correspondent of the New York *Herald*, writing in 1853 on the eve of the Crimean War, analyzed the Russian navy as follows:

> Very little is known of the Russian navy in all other countries of Europe, and whatever notions may exist on the subject they are vague and all but delusive.... For a war fleet to be good for anything besides firing salutes and rotting in harbors the first thing requisite is the possession of a line of coast in the open sea, with convenient ports; next in importance come good ships, able crews, and efficient officers.

The reporter emphasized that there were serious problems in all respects, that ships deteriorated as fast as they are built and that forests had been wasted. In regard to personnel, he added,

> The fact is that Russian naval officers care very little for the profession, not that they are ignorant... The Russians

are not fond of salt water. The majority of the sailors come from the interior; they are inveterate landrats and never saw the sea until they were enlisted in the navy.[1]

He stressed that there was no tradition or naval history of which to speak.

How accurate was this assessment of the Russian navy in the first half of the nineteenth century? Was it a typically parochial English perspective on the navies of other countries? What impact did the Napoleonic Wars, the last major conflict in which the Russian navy was engaged, have on Russian naval policy in the first half of the nineteenth century and on the perception, if not the reality, of Russian naval potential?

These questions are not as easy to answer as one might expect mainly because of the paucity of reliable information about the subject. Our historical knowledge is little improved from the contemporary ignorance confronting the reporter in 1853, only perhaps more frustrating. Books available in English on the Russian navy are mainly of the survey type that concentrate on the Soviet period with a peripheral glance or two at "insignificant" periods--such as the eighteenth and nineteenth centuries.[2] Finding material in Russian can be even more exasperating, as American libraries have collected little.[3] Even *Morskoi Sbornik*, the leading Russian naval journal that has been uninterruptedly published since 1848, is a rare item.[4] For the Napoleonic Wars there is more material thanks to the Russian tendency to celebrate great victories. But even here the overwhelming attention paid to the army is striking, considering that the Russian navy was quite active in the early phases. Only in the post World War II era have Soviet historians, led by Evgenyi Tarle, focused on the naval history of the period, usually with the goal of celebrating victories and worshipping *Russian* heroes by extolling Russian military achievements.[5]

The Russian naval record was a very impressive one in the early Napoleonic Wars, chiefly in the Mediterranean campaigns. Building on a solid foundation of major naval accomplishments under Catherine the Great in the last half of the eighteenth century, the

Russian navy was as prepared as any for the sophisticated and difficult tasks it faced. True, much of this should be credited to foreign assistance, mainly British, in supervising ship and port construction, in serving directly in command positions, and for training Russian officers to carry out Catherine's ambitious foreign policy goals at sea.[6] The rewards of this foreign aid came early with the decisive Russian victory in the eastern Mediterranean over the Turks at Chesme in 1770. As a result, naval power made important contributions to successes in the Second Russo-Turkish War (1787-92), which featured America's own John Paul Jones in command of the Black Sea sailing fleet, and also in the Baltic against the Swedes. In fact, the balance of Russian military power in the late eighteenth century seemed to be shifting from the land armies to the navy.

Responding to the French move into the eastern Mediterranean after the Treaty of Campoformio in 1797 and the destruction of the Venetian Republic, Russia joined the Second Coalition against France and actively supported the maintenance and restoration of legitimacy in the area. Ironically, considering the predominant direction of Russian military deployment at the time, this new predicament generated an alliance with the Ottoman Empire and the first opportunity in Russian history to send a fleet through the Dardanelles into the Mediterranean. The joint Russo-Turkish liberation of the Ionian Islands from the French under direction of Admiral Fedor Ushakov was important in slowing the French penetration of the Balkans and cutting one supply route to Egypt and the Near East. Russia thus entered the long Napoleonic conflict by sea--in sharp contrast to the way it would leave it.[7] The navy then supported the coalition's Italian fronts, spearheaded by Suvorov's expeditionary army, while another squadron carried several battalions for a joint Anglo-Russian landing in Holland, an exercise often ignored in general accounts of the Napoleonic Wars. All this far-flung Russian military activity was partially inspired by, then jeopardized by, the Emperor Paul's infatuation with being the Grand Master of the Order of Malta and his consequently erratic (at least to many of his contemporaries) foreign policy that finally precipitated a sudden reversal of alliances in 1800.[8]

With Paul's assassination a few months later, at least partly provoked by his non-traditional, "unRussian" goals, and the ascendancy of his son, Alexander I, Russia charted a course of greater stability and peace that, however, maintained a solid commitment to the eastern Mediterranean and support for a naval force based at Corfu. Resumption of military activity in 1804 resulted in a series of reinforcements from the Baltic fleet that enabled the combined arms in the Mediterranean under Admiral Dmitri Seniavin to expand the sphere of Russian occupation to include mainland enclaves along the Adriatic coast and the siege of Ragusa (Dubrovnik).[9] This major port was on the point of falling to the Russian-Montenegrin encirclement when French victories on land and the Treaty of Tilsit sharply reversed Russia's military alliances and the Ionian Islands were abruptly, and apparently thoughtlessly, ceded back to France.[10]

The resulting Franco-Russian pax-Europa was disastrous for the Russian navy. The ships and supporting units in the Mediterranean were left helpless in the face of overwhelming British superiority and, without secure bases, ended up in the hands of the British, French, or Austrians. This was a self-imposed calamity comparable to the sinking of much of the Black Sea fleet at the entrance to Sevastopol almost fifty years later.[11] The remainders of the Baltic and Black Sea fleets meanwhile engaged the Swedes in the north and the Turks in the south following the pattern of the eighteenth century. In neither did the navy particularly distinguish itself, using the excuse of British naval support to Sweden in the Baltic. The resulting victory there by 1809 was credited chiefly to the Russian army's occupation of Finland and to French diplomatic and military support. Still, the navy's role in preventing Swedish reinforcement was important in the peace settlement by which Russia annexed the rest of Finland.[12] In the south, the Turks--in another separate war--generally avoided the Russians at sea, as the Russians stayed clear of the British in the north. A strategy seemed to be emerging after Trafalgar that fleets should avoid confrontation in open sea against an enemy considered to be superior or equal. The risk of a crushing, irreparable naval defeat was too great and irretractable.

This was also a period of continuation and expansion of Russian exploration voyages in eastern waters, following those of Bering, Chirikov, Billings, Sarychev, and others in the eighteenth century. The establishment of Russian settlements in northwest America in the 1790s and the chartering of the Russian-America Company in 1799 provided additional incentive and justification for Pacific voyages.[13] Under the command of British-trained German-Estonian Ivan Kruzenstern and Iurii Lisianskii two small ships managed the first Russian circumnavigation of the earth in 1804-06.[14] A highlight of the expedition was a Russian embassy to Japan headed by Nikolai Rezanov. Although more points in the Pacific were added to the Russian inventory, the effort to open Japan failed. The expedition is thus best remembered for its 1812 penetration into California to establish a base for hunting sea otter and for the supply of Alaska.

Even Hawaii was nearly added to the Russian Pacific "possessions" in 1815 through the independent action of George Sheffer, an employee of the Russian-America Company.[15] There were even plans to establish a naval base in Haiti in the Caribbean, while direct diplomatic relations were expanded to include Brazil and the United States. Supporting these maritime extensions in high government circles were Minister of Commerce and then Foreign Minister and Vice-Chancellor Nikolai Rumiantsev and many of the early advisors of Alexander I--Adam Czartoryski, Viktor Kochubei, Pavel Stroganov, Aleksandr Novosiltsev, and Aleksandr and Semen Vorontsov. Russia appeared in 1807 to be on the threshold of a major global expansion of economic interests and military power that especially involved naval forces.

Tilsit, the continental system, and, finally, the famous Great Fatherland War that began with the French invasion of Russia in June 1812 turned Russian attention inward, however, and forced a military concentration on land unequalled since the Livonian War of the sixteenth century. The navy thus became a low priority during this last climactic struggle against Napoleon, although a Russian squadron under Vice Admiral Egor Tet (George Tate) did play a minor role in bolstering British control of the North Sea in those years.

At first glance the Napoleonic Wars would appear to have

dramatized to Russians the importance of naval power. After all, the British navy had done as much as the Russian army to defeat France through victories at the Nile, at Trafalgar, and elsewhere and by effectively controlling European waters and breaking the continental system. Moreover, Russians could point to their own achievements at sea and their first genuinely Russian naval heroes--Admirals Ushakov and Seniavin--and progressive naval administrators such as Admirals Nikolai Mordvinov, Aleksandr Shishkov, and Pavel Chichagov. Several young Russian officers had received valuable battle experience, not only in their own fleet actions but also in those of the British, including some attached to the British fleet under Nelson at Trafalgar.[16] Even after the necessary concentration on the land fronts after 1812, in terms of expertise, Russia enjoyed in 1815 as solid a foundation for naval power as ever in its history.

Alexander I also stood at the Congress of Vienna as the guardian and guarantor of peace under the Holy Alliance, the jurisdiction of which was mainly the European continent but would naturally include the waters around it and European extensions abroad, such as in Latin America. Long-perceived obstacles to Russian naval power--a very limited merchant marine and little open coastline in need of defense--were at least partially mitigated by the annexation of Finland in 1809, which had an active maritime commerce with several shipping companies that sponsored trans-Atlantic voyages.[17] The opening of the Black Sea to international trade, symbolized by the arrival of the first American vessel in Odessa in 1810 and the annexation of Bessarabia in 1813, is additional proof of Russia's expanding commercial base. The growing markets for Russian naval stores--hemp, sailcloth, and iron--only served to enhance Russia's own maritime potential.[18]

These factors in support of Russian naval power were more elusive than real. Trafalgar could just as easily show the futility of challenging British sea power, and who else was left to challenge at sea after 1812? Moreover, the other war of that year might appear to prove that British sea power had definite limitations against a continental enemy that had a very small navy, and that an improvised, mainly privateering fleet could be quite effective in neutralizing formidable naval power. The idea of a "gunboat" navy might, therefore, apply to Russia as to Jefferson and Madison's America--not that Russians thought much about any long-term naval strategy, for their minds were on borders and the land beyond. The fact that the wars had practically destroyed Swedish naval power and seriously weakened the Turkish gave Russia a dominant position in the Baltic and Black Seas, but also removed at least some of the incentive to compete.

At Tilsit, Alexander I withdrew from the Mediterranean, an often ignored success of Napoleonic diplomacy, and relinquished naval power. By this treaty and his invasion of Russia, Napoleon forced Russia to concentrate on continental conflicts and incidentally to leave the seas to the British.[19] Directly and indirectly, Napoleon was responsible for the years of Russian naval neglect that were to follow.

The first sign came with the shift of resources and personnel to the army. The best example is the command by Admiral Chichagov of a field army from 1812 to 1814. Another illustration is the American naval officer, George Sontag of Philadelphia, who had joined the Russian navy and commanded a frigate against the Turks in 1810. In 1814, Sontag led a regiment all the way to Paris.[20] Rising to general rank, he remained in the army during his long career in Russian service. Many of the leading naval commanders of the Napoleonic era--Ushakov, Seniavin, Chichagov, Kruzenstern, Lisianskii--were retired from service, while others, such as Mordvinov and Shishkov, shifted to important posts in civil administration. The experience and potential in naval leadership created by the wars was thus wasted.

A new voyage of Pacific exploration was launched in 1815, promoted by Kruzenstern and commanded by Otto Kotzebue, but it was financed privately by Rumiantsev.[21] Though apparently successful in terms of scientific goals, Kotzebue--like Vasilyi Golovnin who followed him--was critical of the operations of the Russian-American Company, hastened the end of Sheffer's Hawaiian adventure for Russia, and even supported the Spanish governor's view that the Russian base in California was illegal.[22] Though other minor expeditions of exploration followed, in most respects the Russian-American Company was left to its own devices and its own limited resources of money and talent, which meant increasing reliance on, and invitation to, American ships for help.[23]

Above all, the invasion of 1812 and its aftermath had created an almost hysterical concern in Russia for strengthening land defenses. A foreign army penetrating so deep into Russian territory and occupying and destroying Moscow, the largest city and ancient capital, was a shock from which Russians would perhaps never recover. The very large army that Russia amassed in the closing stages of the war remained at full strength after 1815, absorbing an inordinate share of Russia's potential military talent. This also created a large continuing fiscal burden on top of an already enormous war debt.

The navy's share of the military budget, which had already declined dramatically during the last phase of the war, thus remained at a much lower level in the years of peace that followed than in the late eighteenth century. While the navy's expenditures were one-third of the army's in the years 1800 to 1805, before Tilsit, they had fallen to one-tenth by 1810, rising only slightly by 1825.[24] The result was a considerable decline in the relative position of the navy in military expenditures and probably an actual budget reduction for the navy, though the amount is difficult to calculate accurately because of the rapid depreciation of the ruble during this period.

More important, perhaps, were the psychological effects of the diminished attention to the navy. Already in 1814, a British naval surgeon, serving with the Russian North Sea squadron that was ferrying guards' regiments back to Russia observed:

> The difference of the *esprit du corps* between the army and navy is obvious. The former know and feel the value, not only of their usual weight in the country; the latter appear to labour under a feeling of inferiority, as if aware they were only a lower link in the chain of national power. Several of the lieutenants regretted they had no means of acquiring distinctions, compared with the army; and two

even thought of relinquishing the service of Neptune for that of Mars.[25]

He stressed that the "guards" lorded it over the seamen, and that the ship's officers had to give up their cabins to army officers and serve the meat in the officers' mess. The spirit of Peter the Great, "the same spirit [which] continued to influence his successors till lately," he said, was "from all appearances...rapidly declining."[26]

In the years that followed the Napoleonic Wars, the Russian navy literally rotted away. One of the few capable and experienced officers still active, Vasilyi Golovnin, who assumed charge of shipbuilding in 1823, frankly admitted: "If the rotten, badly and poorly equipped vessels, the elderly, ailing, ignorant, and lost-at-sea admirals of the fleets, the inexperienced captains and officers, and the peasants who passed for sailors and enrolled for ship's crews can produce a navy, then we have one."[27] Overseeing this mess, and symptomatic of it, was an aging French emigré, Jean-François, Marquis de Traversay. Though serving as Russian Minister of Navy for almost twenty years (1809-28), his name fails to appear in any major Russian encyclopedias or biographical works--and deservedly so. Another, but more capable, "foreigner," Admiral Otto Moller, succeeded him. For Traversay's appointment and the general *malaise* in naval affairs, one must ultimately blame Alexander I, something that Russian/Soviet historians have been disinclined to do.[28]

These non-Russian officeholders point to another "disadvantage" under which the navy labored in the post-Napoleonic years. This was being labelled "foreign," or, perhaps even worse, "Western." This was an era of the rapid development of a conservative Russian national consciousness and the birth of the Slavophile movement, which emphasized *Russian* culture and institutions. The navy would be identified with Peter the Great and the West (though later historians would justify naval pursuits by digging up every little boat that could be found in one thousand years of Kievan and Muscovite history).[29] This was an especially sensitive issue with the development of as radical circles that advocated basic governmental changes that stemmed from Western examples, culminating in the Decembrist Revolt of 1825. Though some sources claim that naval officers had a larger proportional role in revolutionary circles of the nineteenth century than other segments of the population, for example, army officers, the available evidence does not support this conclusion. This may have been simply a case of guilt by association: "the navy was Western, therefore...." The contemporary result, however, was that the navy had another obstacle to overcome. Naval officers were likely to be more familiar with the West and modern science and technology than other Russians. Loyalty to the tsar and the country was another matter.

Russia's naval doldrums ended soon after Nicholas I ascended the throne at the end of 1825 when he appointed a Committee on the Reformation of the Navy. There were several reasons for this. First, Russia's naval glories were never entirely forgotten but kept alive by the publication of new histories and memoir accounts, especially by Pavel Svin'in and Vladimir Bronevskii on their experiences in the Mediterranean campaigns.[30] The same is true of the effects of the publicity and narrative accounts about the exploring voyages of Kotzebue, Golovnin, and Ferdinand von Wrangell.

Also, that "generation" of largely British-trained officers survived, endured, and gradually rose in rank and influence. The Seniavinites and Trafalgarites in the Russian navy could not be completely buried and ignored. A leading example is Mikhail Lazarev, who distinguished himself at the Battle of Navarino and rose to command and rebuild the Black Sea fleet in the 1830s and 1840s. Included in his accomplishments were the rebuilding and expansion of the fortresses and naval facilities at Sevastopol, which, fortuitously, would become a symbol of nineteenth century military defeat for Russia and the navy.[31]

Nicholas I, a Napoleonic officer himself, should receive some of the credit for revitalizing the navy. The new emperor is best known for his strict autocratic regime and military bearing, as "the gendarme of Europe," but he is seldom regarded as a sailor. Though not inclined to wear a naval uniform as was his great grandson and namesake, Nicholas I, he showed an interest in, and knowledge of, naval affairs.[32] He assigned a wealthy, dilettantish but influential favorite, Prince/General Aleksandr Menshikov, to head the Naval General Staff under Moller and then to succeed him, essentially to be in charge of the navy for twenty-eight years, until the eve of the Crimean War. He encouraged his second son, Constantine, to immerse himself in naval lore from an early age, even outfitting his room in the Winter Palace as the interior of a fighting ship. Upon Admiral Seniavin's death in 1831, Nicholas I assumed personal command of the honor guard of sailors at the funeral.[33] Spending many summer days aboard the imperial yachts, he delighted in naval reviews and calls on visiting foreign warships, like the USS *Independence* in 1837.[34]

The famous Battle of Navarino in the summer of 1827 did much to rekindle interest in naval power. In a joint operation, British, French, and Russian Mediterranean squadrons destroyed an Egyptian-Turkish fleet and "saved" Greece for independence. This refocus on the eastern Mediterranean, reminiscent of the Second Coalition of 1798, revived the importance of warships and in turn stirred up the Eastern Question. The revitalization of the Black Sea fleet, reconstruction of Sevastopol, establishment of a new shipbuilding center at Nikolaevsk, and plans for a major ship construction program followed.

In 1830, after another Russo-Turkish War drew to a close, Nicholas sent Admiral Aleksandr Avinov, a veteran of Trafalgar, on a mission to Britain and the United States in an effort to catch up on the new naval technology. After surveying shipyards, Avinov purchased in New York for the Russian navy its first "modern" warship, the steam corvette *Kensington*, renamed the *Prince of Warsaw*, to serve as the flagship of the Baltic fleet.[35] In fact, the neglect of naval affairs for so many years forced Russia to take shortcuts to modernization through expensive purchases of warships abroad, a practice that would continue into the Soviet period. Another important example was the contracting and building of the 4,000-ton steam frigate *Kamchatka* in New York in 1840.[36]

Although many of the new capital ships were traditional sailing ships of the line with seventy-four and even over one hundred guns virtually unchanged in design from the Napoleonic epoch, a few new steam vessels were also built in Russia, especially under the supervision of Russia's leading naval construction engineer, Mikhail Grinval'd at the New Admiralty shipyards in St. Petersburg. After spending two years touring facilities in Holland and Britain, Grinval'd returned to Russia in 1835 to lay down Russia's first steam frigate, the *Bogatyr*, and the ironclad *Inkkerman*, promoted by Lazarev, was launched at Nikolaevsk in 1838.[37]

The revitalization of the Russian navy in the 1830s under Nicholas I was expensive and the naval budget increased rapidly. Even though the army was not neglected in that period, the navy's share of military expenditures doubled to about 20-25 per cent of the total and comparable to that of other naval powers.[38] Though fortunately the Napoleonic Wars helped provide Russia with experienced and progressive leadership needed for a major regeneration, central administration, heavily dominated by the army, and state resources were not adequate to the task. In the 1840s the naval budget failed to grow, while that of the army increased rapidly. Though regaining much of its earlier ship and manpower strength by 1850, the Russian navy had fallen again to its pre-1825 budget share. It had sadly failed to sustain the buildup of the 1830s and suffered the costly neglect of the technological advances of the 1840s; by 1852, facing another threat of war in the South, another "catch up" was attempted by sending another high level naval mission to the United States. Erratic and inconsistent naval policy was becoming a Russian tradition.

The destruction of the Turkish fleet at Sinope in 1853 demonstrated that some constructive naval advances had been made under Nicholas I. Why then did the Russian navy play such a defensive and inconsequential role in the Crimean War that followed? Perhaps one only needs to mention another enduring legacy of the Napoleonic Wars--the mystique of Trafalgar, the ghost of Horatio Nelson. Each day as the sun set the shadow of Nelson's column in London fell across the Admiralty in St. Petersburg. More realistically, the Russian navy was severely hampered by the period of neglect and disruption from 1807 to 1826 and by the failure to sustain a major modernization effort in

56

the 1840s. In conclusion, the *Herald* reporter was correct in his assessment of the Russian navy on the eve of the Crimean War, but the reasons for its poor condition had more to do with historical circumstances and the nature of imperial leadership than with limited coastlines and backward peasants. But the question still remains: was the Russian navy really unimportant in the Crimean War, or did its strength play a part at least in limiting the war? For that answer, another paper, another time.

Notes

[1]New York *Herald*, 18 Sep 1853.

[2]The best general history of the Russian navy is Donald W. Mitchell's, *A History of Russian and Soviet Sea Power* (New York, 1974), though it has some definite drawbacks. An older one by Mairin Mitchell, *The Maritime History of Russia* (London, 1948) is worth consulting as is a more popular work by David Woodward, *The Russians at Sea: History of the Russian Navy* (New York, 1966).

[3]From several bibliographic sources, but chiefly from *Sistematicheskii katalog biblioteki morskogo ministerstva: otdely voenno-morskoi i voennyi* (Petrograd, 1916), eighteen references in Russian were identified pertaining particularly to the Russian navy in the first half of the nineteenth century. Of these only eight could be found in the readily available reference catalogs such as the *National Union Catalog*, the British Library *Catalog*, and the catalog of the Slavonic Division of the New York Public Library; only three have thus far been obtainable through inter-library loan. What is probably a key work by N. Korguev, *Russkii flot v tsarstvovanie Imperatora Nikolaia I* (St. Petersburg, 1896), appears not to exist in the West.

[4]The most complete holdings of *Morskoi Sbornik* are in the Library of Congress, the New York Public Library Slavonic Division, and Columbia University's Butler Library.

[5]Even the more recent Soviet publications tend to ignore the nineteenth century, except for biographical studies of naval heroes. An exception is L. G. Beskrovnyi, *Russkaia armiia i flot v XIX veke: voenno-ekonomicheskii potentsial Rossii* (Moscow, 1973), but even the bulk of this is devoted to the army and the last half of the century.

[6]For British officers in Russian service, see R. C. Anderson, "British and American Officers in the Russian Navy," *Mariners Mirror*, 33 (1947): 17-27; M. S. Anderson, "Great Britain and the Growth of the Russian Navy in the Eighteenth Century," *Mariners Mirror*, 42 (1956): 132-78; and A. G. Cross, "Samuel Greig, Catherine the Great's Scottish Admiral," *Mariners Mirror*, 60 (1976): 251-66.

[7]For the background on this period, see the author's *Russia and the Mediterranean, 1797-1807* (Chicago, 1970), A. M. Stanislavskaia, *Russko-angliiskie otnosheniia i problemy sredizemnomor'ia, 1798-1807* (Moscow, 1962); and E. V. Tarle, *Tri ekspeditsii russkogo flota* (Moscow, 1956).

[8]For the best examination of Paul's shift in alliances, see Hugh Ragsdale, *Detente in the Napoleonic Era: Bonaparte and the Russians* (Lawrence, KS, 1980).

[9]Seniavin's activities are examined by the author, Stanislavskaia, and Tarle, in works cited above, and by A. L. Shapiro, *Admiral D.N. Seniavin* (Moscow, 1958).

[10]Saul, *Russia and the Mediterranean*, 220-21.

[11]For parts of the tragedy of the Russian fleet, see Dmitri Fedotoff White, "The Russian Navy in Trieste during the Wars of the Revolution and the Empire," *American Slavic and East European Review*, XI, nos. 18-19 (1947): 25-52; and Donald D. Horward, "Portugal and the Anglo-Russian Naval Crisis (1808)," *Naval War College Review*, 34 (1981): 43-73.

[12]The meaning and impact of the annexation of Finland is reviewed by Juhani Paasivirta, *Finland and Europe: International Crises in the Period of Autonomy, 1808-1914*, edited by David G. Kirby (London, 1981), 6-25; and Paivio Tommila, *La Finlande dans la politique Européenne en 1809-1815* (Helsinki, 1962).

[13]The best accounts of Russia's early Pacific attempts are by Glynn Barratt, *Russia in Pacific Waters, 1715-1825* (Vancouver, 1981), and James R. Gibson, *Feeding the Russian Fur Trade: Provisionment of the Okhotsk Seaboard and the Kamchatka Peninsula, 1639-1856* (Madison, WI, 1969). The papers of a Soviet-American conference on the history of Russian America sponsored by the Kennan Institute are also useful: Frederick Starr, ed., *Russia's American Colony* (Durham, 1987).

[14]V. Nevskii, *Vokrug sveta pod russkim flagom: pervoe krugosvetnoe puteshestvie russkikh na korabliakh "Nadezhda" i "Neva"* (Moscow-Leningrad, 1953); and V. M. Rasetskii, *Ivan Fedorovich Kruzenshtern* (Moscow, 1974).

[15]See Richard A. Pierce, *Russia's Hawaiian Adventure, 1815-1817* (Berkeley, 1965), 1-13. ·

[16]Russians attached to the British fleet at Trafalgar and who were later to rise to prominence in the Russian navy included Avinov and Lazarev.

[17]Paasivirta, *Finland and Europe*, 44.

[18]For Russia's rising commercial position in the Napoleonic era, see Alfred W. Crosby, Jr., *America, Russia, Hemp, and Napoleon: American Trade with Russia and the Baltic, 1783-1812* (Columbus, 1956).

[19]The best work on Russia's manipulation of the continental system is M. F. Zlotnikov, *Kontinental'naia blokada i Rossiia* (Moscow-Leningrad, 1966).

[20]Sketchy details of Sontag's career in Russia come from Americans who visited him in the 1830s: John Lloyd Stephens, *Incidents of Travel in Greece, Turkey, Russia and Poland* (New York, 1838), I: 264; Henry Wikoff, *Reminiscences of an Idler* (New York, 1880), 235-36; and Edwin Forrest manuscript diary, Pusey Theatre Library,

Harvard University.

[21]The explorer himself described the voyage: Otto von Kotzebue, *A Voyage of Discovery...*, 3 vols. (London, 1823). Another excellent account of the Kotzebue voyage is by Adelbert von Chamisso, *A Voyage around the World with the Romanzov [sic.] Exploring Expedition in the Years 1815-1818 in the Brig "Riurik"*, Captain Otto von Kotzebue (Honolulu, 1986). Chamisso was a French nobleman who joined the expedition as a naturist.

[22]Chamisso, *Voyage Around the World*, 115-16; Pierce, *Russia's Hawaiian Adventure*, 17-20.

[23]For the Russian-American Company's reliance on American shipping, see Mary E. Wheeler, "Empires in Conflict and Cooperation: the 'Bostonians' and the Russian-American Company," *Pacific Historical Review*, 40 (1971): 419-41; James R. Gibson, "Bostonians and Muscovites on the Northwest Coast, 1788-1841," in *The Western Shore: Oregon Country Essays Honoring the American Revolution*, ed. Thomas Vaughan (Portland, 1975), 81-119; and Barratt, *Russia in Pacific Waters*, 143-62.

[24]Beskrovnyi, *Russkaia armiia i flot*, 482-83, 599; S. F. Ogorodnikov, *Istoricheskii obzor razvitiia i deiatelnosti Morskago Ministerstva za sto let ego sushchestvovaniia, 1802-1902* (St. Petersburg, 1902), 130.

[25]*A Voyage to St. Petersburg in 1814, with Remarks on the Imperial Navy, by a Surgeon in the British Navy* (London, 1822), 8.

[26]Ibid., 9, 15.

[27]As quoted in N. A. Bestuzhev, *Opyt istorii rossiskogo flota* (Leningrad, 1961), 9.

[28]A good biography of Alexander I, especially covering the last ten years of his reign, does not exist. Most sources agree, however, that he fell more and more under the influence of conservative and religious officials such as Minister of War A. A. Arakcheev and Minister of Education A. N. Golovin. For an able recent appraisal of his successor, see W. Bruce Lincoln, *Nicholas I: Emperor and Autocrat of all the Russias* (Bloomington, 1978).

[29]Ogorodnikov, *Istoricheskii*, 83. For political theory and ideology during this period, see Nicholas Riasanovsky, *Nicholas I and Official Nationality in Russia, 1825-1855* (Berkeley, 1961).

[30]Pavel Svin'in, *Vospominaniia na flot Pavla Svin'ina* (St. Petersburg, 1819); and Vladimir Bronevskii, *Pis'ma morskago afitsera*, 4 vols. (Moscow, 1825).

[31]V.F. Golovachov, *Istoriia Sevastopolia, kak russkago porta* (St. Petersburg, 1872), 238-56.

[32]Most Western scholarly sources on Nicholas' reign fail to even mention the navy, for example: Lincoln, *Nicholas I*; John Shelton Curtiss, *The Russian Army under Nicholas I, 1825-1855* (Durham, 1965); and Walter McKenzie Pintner, *Russian Economic Policy under Nicholas I* (Ithaca, 1967).

[33]Mitchell, *Russian and Soviet Sea Power*, 134. For a detailed examination of the

naval upbringing of Grand Duke Constantine, see Jacob W. and Maia A. Kipp, "The Grand Duke Konstantin Nikolaevic: The Making of a Tsarist Reformer, 1827-1855," *Jahrbuch fur Geschichte Osteuropas* 34 (1986): 3-18. A description of the young grand duke's room in the Winter Palace is in Mary Anne Pellew Smith, *Six Years Travels in Russia, by an English Lady* (London, 1859), I: 111-12.

[34]George Mifflin Dallas, *Diary of George Mifflin Dallas*, ed. Susan Dallas (Philadelphia, 1892), 8; *National Intelligencer*, 23 Sept 1837.

[35]"Vospominanie o zhizni i sluzhbe Admirala Aleksandra Pavlovicha Avinova," *Morskoi Sbornik*, May 1855: 71-72, 78-79. For the interesting story about the dismasting of the *Kensington* in a storm and its repair and dispatch by a generous American, see Silas E. Burrows, *America and Russia: Correspondence, 1818 to 1848* (N.p., n.d.), copy in the Library of Congress.

[36]*New York Herald*, 25 Nov 1840, and 10 July 1841.

[37]David R. Jones, "Main Admiralty," *Encyclopedia of Russian and Soviet Military History*, 3 (1981): 117.

[38]Ibid.; Beskrovnyi, *Russkaia armiia i flot*, 483-84, 492-97, 600-601; Ogorodnikov, *Istoricheskii*, 130.

"A Community of Interest and Danger": British Naval Power in the Eastern Mediterranean and the Levant, 1783-1815

Patricia K. Crimmin

In this essay, Ms. Crimmin examines the shift of diplomatic alignments among Britain, France, Russia, and the Ottoman Empire, the role of British sea power in those diplomatic maneuvers, and the impact the maneuvering had on Britain's naval and commercial presence in the eastern Mediterranean.

The quotation in the above title comes from a letter of 29 July 1798 by Spencer Smith, British chargé d'affaires at Constantinople, to Rear Admiral Horatio Nelson. It conveyed the fears of the Ottoman Empire at the recent French invasion of Egypt and of Smith's own "wearisome endeavours" to wean the Turks away from their pro-French attitude into an alliance with Britain. Recent events had confirmed Ottoman suspicions of French ambition in the Near East, and only formalities remained to convert "the community of interest and danger which must serve as the basis of such an union" into a strict alliance between Britain and the Porte. The Sultan would depend on "the succour of His Majesty's fleet" against French attack and Smith had already circulated orders to the principal parts of the empire "for the more hospitable reception of the British flag." Enclosed in his letter was an imperial edict commanding all pashas in the area to consider the British fleet as though it were Ottoman and to supply it with all necessaries at current prices. To the latest news of French progress in Egypt, Smith added a plea for some encouraging information for the

Porte, suffering from painful suspense and looking "with an anxious eye towards the British fleet."[1]

When news of Nelson's victory at the Nile on 1 August 1798 arrived at Constantinople at the end of the month, its reception was dramatic. The Grand Vizier and other pro-French members of the government were arrested and exiled on 30 August. On 2 September Pierre Ruffin, French chargé d'affaires, and about two thousand Frenchmen in the capital were imprisoned. A week later the Porte formally declared war on France. On 3 January 1799 Russia and Turkey signed an alliance against France. Britain joined on 5 January, guaranteeing the integrity of the Ottoman Empire for the next eight years.[2] This was a dramatic reversal of former alliances.

Britain was not a natural Mediterranean power. Her interest there was primarily commercial and her naval presence was to protect that trade. The Levant Company exported English woolen cloth in return for raw silk and cotton, mohair, and a range of other goods. By the last quarter of the eighteenth century this trade had declined in volume and value, outstripped by that of the East and West Indies. British exports to Turkey were badly affected by the war with France. They reached their lowest level in 1797, when they fell to a real value of £23,532, partly as a result of the evacuation of the British fleet from the Mediterranean the year before. Imports also suffered, the lowest point being in 1798-99, when the full effect of that withdrawal was felt and real values fell from £104,838 in 1797, to £42,285 in 1798, and to £33,091 in 1799.[3] The naval force usually available for the trade's protection before 1798 was two frigates and a sloop of war. Britain was unwilling to commit more forces to protect a shrinking commerce in seas dominated by a neutral nation, traditionally allied to France, when there was no threat to strategic British interests. The constant fear of riots and violence against foreigners and of official Ottoman reprisals against the factories and officials of the Levant Company led British consuls to ask often for naval protection as the one thing the Turks feared and respected.[4] After 1798 fear of officially sponsored attacks diminished, though in 1806-07 the British ambassador was sufficiently alarmed at the supposed threat to his life and those of the British merchant community in the capital to take refuge on board the HMS *Endymion* and sail to the protection of the squadron at Tenedos. The factory at Smyrna, similarly alarmed, also went on board the HMS *Glatton*.

British trading interests were not a primary concern to the Ottoman Empire. France was more favored by the Porte and engrossed more of the Empire's total European trade; in 1798 an estimated three-fifths as compared with Britain's one-fifth. The traditional friendship of the two states was not, at first, disturbed by the French Revolution. When Selim III (1787-1807) wished to reform the Ottoman armed forces, he turned to France for the necessary experts.[5] But despite traditional ties, when war broke out the Porte hoped to remain uninvolved. The main preoccupation of the Ottoman Empire was with its territorial integrity which, before 1798, seemed more threatened by Russia and Austria than by France. There were powerful reasons, too, why the Turks should adopt an attitude of cool neutrality to Britain before 1798. The Porte's traditional enemy, Russia, was seen by Britain for most of the eighteenth century, as a natural ally against France. As the dominant Baltic power after 1720, Russia controlled the supply of vital naval stores Britain needed to maintain her maritime and naval strength. Russian hostility during Britain's war with her American colonies and the Franco-Russian commercial agreement of 1787 shook this belief, but with the outbreak of the revolution Russia again seemed a bulwark against France.[6]

With the outbreak of war the Royal Navy's role was extended from trade protection to the destruction of French commerce, the defeat of French naval power, and the support of allies in this region. The practical difficulties were formidable. The nearest dockyard was at Gibraltar, the other end of the Mediterranean, though the capture of Minorca in 1798 and of Malta in 1800 eased the problem of repairs and supplies. Limited facilities were periodically available at Leghorn, Naples, Palermo, Lissa (modern Vis) from 1810, and at Ottoman ports, though subject to the fluctuations of war and diplomacy. The whole area, with its innumerable bays, islands, and headlands, swarmed with privateers and pirates; it was too extensive to control completely; its waters were largely uncharted and unknown to British warships.[7]

Of French commerce in the first years of the war, it was not the actions of British squadrons in the Levant, but bitter conflicts in France and between Frenchmen in the Ottoman Empire which disrupted it.[8] As the war continued, British naval power in the Mediterranean, virtually unchallenged after 1809, meant that the French Levant trade suffered severely. Although French squadrons escaped into the Mediterranean, they were unable to extend the consistent protection to their merchantmen that Britain could provide.

In search of allies against France in these waters, British naval officers often found themselves cooperating with a motley crowd of curious characters: semi-bandits, like Ali Pasha of Janina, or Pasvan Oglu of Widdin; unlikely clerics, like Fra Diavolo, head of a partisan band in Calabria, shot by the French there in 1806, or the "ferocious Baroness Laura Fava," also operating in Calabria, who escaped to Sicily in 1806. This was the world of John Buchan, almost of James Bond. In 1813 Captain William Hoste collaborated with the Montenegrins, "a lawless banditti not to be depended upon," to drive the French out of the town and fortress of Cattaro (modern Kotor), and as early as 1799 Captain Samuel Hood, commanding the blockading squadron off Alexandria, supplied arms and ammunition to Calabrian partisans in return for fresh beef for his little force.[9]

In 1794 British naval officers, attempting to destroy French commerce and influence in the Levant by capturing French ships in Ottoman ports, found themselves embroiled in violations of Ottoman neutral waters which so irritated the Turks to promote the French cause at Constantinople.[10] Ottoman sensibilities remained acute even when the Empire became Britain's ally. The official French view, Panglossian in its optimism that their occupation of Egypt would benefit everyone, including the Ottoman Empire, did not convince the Porte which did not wish to see Egypt used as a stepping stone for "Frankish" ambitions in the Levant or farther east. The Porte desired neither the ruin of British commerce nor the destruction of British possessions in

India, as the French hoped, nor the extirpation of French ideas, government, and commerce, as the British expected. Its motto was "a plague on both your houses." Though prepared to support British naval attempts to oust the French from Egypt and Syria, the Porte did not desire a British military presence there either, and it resented the British expeditions to Egypt in 1801 and 1807. Britain failed to see this, because she was convinced of the purity of her motives in desiring the French defeat, and obsessed with the danger to British India from Napoleon's eastern ambitions.

The actions of Captain Sir Sydney Smith, brother of Spencer Smith, in Egypt and Syria in 1799, though hostile to the French, also alarmed the Ottoman Empire. At the siege of Acre, Smith showed the Turks what British sea power could achieve. The port did not fall to the French because it was supplied by sea and supported by his tiny squadron of two ships of the line which captured the French siege train sent from Egypt. Smith was in touch with the local Arab chiefs in Egypt and Syria, with the Druze in the Lebanese mountains and with the mameluke beys, still holding out against the French in Egypt, all whom he tried to stir up against the French and exploit in British interests, though not necessarily in Ottoman interests. But British support for the mamelukes displeased the Sultan, who hoped to restore his direct rule in Egypt once the French were removed. Furthermore, Smith's encouragement of Arab chiefs alarmed the Turks, who feared incipient Arab nationalism. Lord Elgin, newly appointed British ambassador at Constantinople in 1799, complained that Smith's tactless behavior, while on a visit to Jerusalem, had "given rise to an unfortunate parallel between Bonaparte's conduct and his, and had been the subject of much unpleasant discussion with the Seraglio."[11] There was a good deal of jealousy between Elgin and the Smiths, who, until Elgin's appointment, had been joint ministers plenipotentiary to the Porte. Also, Sydney Smith enjoyed a separate command in the eastern Mediterranean with the rank of commodore, which offended his naval colleagues. But it would have been better if Smith had heeded Elgin's advice that "it would be a galling sensation for a Government to see any foreign power assume the total management of transactions with the Enemy," for the Convention of El Arish, which Smith negotiated in January 1800, under which the French would evacuate Egypt on favorable terms, offended the Ottomans as much as it enraged Smith's naval superiors, who repudiated it.[12]

Following 1798 there were many examples of what British sea power could not do, as well as instances of its success. Though it helped to repulse Napoleon at Acre and probably forced him to evacuate Syria, it could neither prevent the Turkish army's defeats in 1799 and 1800 nor remove the French army from Egypt. Sea power alone could not reconquer the Kingdom of Naples, though a British squadron consistently prevented the French invasion of Sicily. It could not prevent the collapse of an alliance, formed in 1805, between Russia, Britain, and the Ottoman Empire and quickly ruined by mutual distrust. Russian hostility and Turkish fears led them to war in September 1806, into which Britain was reluctantly drawn. She made unsuccessful attempts to pressure the Turks into peace with Russia and the rejection of renewed French influence. But Vice Admiral Sir John Duckworth's imperfect demonstration of sea power could not restore the waning British prestige at Constantinople. He failed to bombard Constantinople and capture the Turkish fleet. The Turks resented British violation of the Straits and used the time, gained in negotiations, to fortify the Dardanelles, with French help, and force Duckworth to withdraw his ships from an increasingly untenable position. Yet when, in 1808, Ottoman fears were again roused by French advances in the Balkans, the Turks turned to Admiral Lord Collingwood, commander in chief in the Mediterranean, as the local embodiment of British power. These tentative overtures were translated into peace by the Treaty of the Dardanelles on 5 January 1809 at which Ottoman concessions to British commerce were balanced by British guarantees of Ottoman defense and territorial integrity.[13]

A community of British interest and Ottoman danger had again been achieved, though it was no more wholehearted an alliance than that of 1799. The Ottomans, apprehensive of French power until at least 1812, thereafter hoped that the pre-occupations of the European powers with the collapse of Napoleon's empire would leave them in peace. The British, increasingly committed to the western Mediterranean and the Peninsular War, saw little need to commit considerable forces to a passive ally and a theatre of declining importance. The region henceforth played a secondary role in British strategy.

But it was not an unimportant one. Though Napoleon had failed at Trafalgar, he did not consider himself finally defeated at sea. He planned to outbuild the Royal Navy and smash British naval power permanently. His declared aim in 1811 was a fleet of 150 sail of the line and his naval program for 1813-14 saw no reduction in this figure despite Russian defeats.[14] French yards and those in subject states at Genoa, Naples, and Venice, continued work at high pressure. Anything Britain could do, therefore, to interrupt this work or the supply of materials to it, would be useful, perhaps decisive. So the activities of British frigates, like the *Amphion* or the *Unité* in the Adriatic, from 1807, were not merely irritating. They stood between Napoleon and his naval ambitions and constituted a threat to his system of economic blockade, which intended to strangle British trade and force Britain to surrender.

Napoleon had long seen Italy as a supplier of raw materials for French industry. After the introduction of the "Continental System," he saw it as a route whereby goods from the eastern Mediterranean and the Levant could pass to France, avoiding the long sea journey which was always threatened by the British navy. Cargoes from the Adriatic would go by barge up the river Po to Piedmont and thence by wagon into France. Cargoes from Trieste would travel, either by coastal waters too shallow for warships or by the new coastal road. This was the reason behind the programs of road, river, and canal improvements launched by Eugéne as Viceroy of Italy.[15] But until these improvements were made, all trade went by sea, carried mainly in small ships, particularly that maid of all work in the Adriatic, the trabaccolo, of between fifty and seventy tons. It was among the islands and broken coastline of Dalmatia, with danger from reefs, sudden violent storms, fierce gales or sea mists, rather than from enemy warships, that British frigates thwarted and defied Napoleon's attempts to create a French-dominated trading area in which Britain would find no place. But it was not glamorous work. There was nothing particularly exciting about capturing a convoy of these small ships; there was rarely the possibility of a stimulating fight with the enemy. Between June 1808 and Christmas 1809, Captain Hoste of the *Amphion*, stationed in the Adriatic, took or destroyed 218 enemy vessels. "Can there be any greater proof of the pusillanimity of our enemies in this part of the world," he wrote to his father, "than to allow one frigate and one sloop to annoy the trade in this manner we do?" He compared his force with that of the French; six frigates, five brigs, three schooners, and many gun boats. There were also four Russian ships which, however, were as passive to the French as allies as they had formerly been to Britain.[16]

The daily grind of this work is well described in the journal written between 1805 and 1809 by Robert Wilson, a pressed man who rose to be a midshipman on the *Unité*. On 13 April 1807 near Fiume, the ship discovered 162 pieces of fine oak timber ashore, cut down and in process of seasoning "for the use of the French to build ships of war at Venice," which were subsequently loaded for themselves. On 22 August 1807 the *Unité* took three prizes, laden with deals and spars, soap, dyeing bark, acorns, and leather. On 5 February 1808 she captured a brig loaded with oil and a trabaccolo with tobacco and snuff, while on 21 February she captured one with a cargo of linen, beeswax, and nails. Two days later they discharged the cargoes of seven more trabaccolos comprising oil, almonds, hides, tallow candles, hams, cheeses, wines, and salt.

Such work dislocated the local food supply and increased costs. The cost to British ships came in endless vigilance and in individual, barely remarked deaths, like that of William Skill, a seaman who fell overboard and drowned in boisterous weather on 15 January 1807, or like the frigate *Nautilus*, "lost on the island of Cerigotto in the Archipelago...most of her crew [had] perished in famine," or the death of Captain Seccombe of the *Glatton*, killed "on some service he was on, on the coast of Calabria." But Wilson's journal also chronicles the effect of this patient, unremitting work. In March 1807 he wrote: "we so closely annoy the trade in the Adriatic that scarcely a single vessel could pass us without our examining them, especially those bound for Trieste, which makes our favour courted and our sway dreaded." In June 1807 one of a prize crew who had deserted, was recaptured, then escaped back to the *Unité*, related that "our ships and her maneuvers were the topic of conversation in many places of Dalmatia and Germany through which he passed and, in several public houses where he had been, he saw the picture of the *Unité* represented in different nautical tactics...."[17]

In these circumstances it is not surprising that a flourishing smuggling trade developed through the entire Mediterranean which engaged all the region's small ports. One firm in Dalmatia is known to have employed over five hundred horses to carry goods, coffee, sugar, and raw cotton, from the coast over the mountains to Belgrade and thence to the rest of Europe. As a result of this illicit trade, Malta became a thriving entrepôt, and the population of the island of Lissa trebled from 1803 to 1811 in response to its success.[18] French efforts to expel the British from Lissa and the Adriatic led to their resounding defeat there by Captain William Hoste on 13 March 1811, who with four frigates outmaneuvered a French force of almost double that number.[19] This was a trade which the French, lacking effective sea power, were powerless to destroy, but which sapped the success of the "Continental System" and ultimately Napoleon's plans for the region.

Collingwood and his successors in the Mediterranean were denied the long-sought fleet action against the French. Instead, there was the boredom of blockade, interspersed with small, deadly actions with enemy ships or small squadrons; work a man could get killed at, but at which it was difficult to win glory or prize money. "It is not fighting, my dear William," wrote Captain Edward Codrington to his brother after Trafalgar,

> which is the severest part of *our* life, it is the having to contend with the sudden changes of season, the war of elements, the dangers of a less shore, and so forth, which produce *no food for honour or glory* beyond the internal satisfaction of doing a duty *we* know to be the most important, although passed by others unknown and unnoticed.[20]

By its very success at this work the Royal Navy was, to some extent, the victim of its own efficiency. In 1808, when Collingwood was chasing Vice Admiral Ganteaume's squadron, he found "not the least intelligence to be obtained at sea for there is nothing on it but ourselves." Yet by sweeping clear the eastern Mediterranean of enemy shipping the navy enabled Britain's trade in the region to recover from the interruptions of the war with Turkey (1807-09) and to expand. Industrial changes in Britain, particularly in cotton spinning, led to increased demands for raw cotton and a rise in the export of manufactured cotton goods, which outstripped woolens in the Levant Company's exports by 1812. Exports to the Ottoman Empire reached their highest point in 1812 at £311,029 while imports in that year stood at £243,894. A period of renewed prosperity began for the company as British strategic interests in the area waned.

At the beginning of this period the Royal Navy was unwilling to commit itself to an area where British trade was in decline. From 1812 British trade in the Levant was reviving. Yet the Admiralty did not choose to commit additional forces to a region when its strategic interests were in the western Mediterranean and when, thanks to alliances with the Ottoman Empire, however passive, naval activity would be limited. Yet the Royal Navy frequently played a supporting role in the region. Assigned a secondary importance, its achievements there were sufficiently solid. Napoleon's remark that "wherever there is water to float a ship, we are sure to find you in the way" applies to this theater as much as to any other. Perhaps the title of this paper should be simply, "Being There," since that was the true position of the navy in this region after 1798. Never totally defeated, never completely withdrawn, and often insufficiently strong to accomplish all the tasks allotted to it, it nevertheless was there, to uphold Britain's idea of "a community of interest and danger."

Notes

[1]"Letters from Robert Liston and others to Hood, 1794-9," Greenwich, National Maritime Museum [hereafter NMM], MKH/101.

[2]British commercial interests were advanced by the Ottoman promise to open the Black Sea to British merchantmen. Spencer Smith spent much in bribes before achieving this considerable concession in 1802. By a treaty of 25 June of the same year, however, the Turks granted similar rights to the French.

[3]Alfred C. Wood, *A History of the Levant Company* (London, 1935), 140-41, 179n, 180.

[4]Lindegren to Stephens, 30 December 1791, and Bosanquet to Consul Hayes, 14 February 1794, "Levant Company Out-Letter Book, 1781-95," Public Record Office [hereafter PRO], State Papers [hereafter SP] 105/121/469, 345; Hayes to Ainslie, 2 January 1794, and Ainslie to Grenville, 25 January 1794, "General Correspondence, Turkey," PRO, Foreign Office [hereafter FO] 78/15/13-14, 15-17; Bosanquet to Nepean, 11 May, 16 June 1796, 22 October 1800, and 19 June 1805, "Levant Company Out-Letter Book, 1795-1805," PRO, SP 105/122/30, 44-45, 202, 508.

[5]Elena Frangakis, "The Balance of Trade and the Balance of Payments between Izmire and France, 1700-1789," *Communications Grecques Presentées au Ve Congrès International des Études du Sud Est-European: Belgrade 11-17 September, 1984* (Athens, 1985), 127-38; Frangakis, "The Ottoman Port of Izmire in the Eighteenth and Early Nineteenth Centuries, c. 1695-1820," *Revue de l'Occident Musulman et de la Méditerranée, no. 39* (Aix en Provence, 1985), 149-61; B. Lewis, "The Impact of the French Revolution on Turkey," *Journal of World History*, 1 (1953-54): 106-25.

[6]For the amount and value of Russian trade, see Herbert H. Kaplan, "Observations on the Value of Russia's Overseas Commerce with Great Britain during the Second Half of the Eighteenth Century," *Slavic Review*, 45 (Spring 1986): 85-94. From 1781 the French merchant Anthoine de Saint Joseph built a trade in naval stores between the Russian Black Sea naval base and Kherson and Marseilles in ships flying the Russian rather than the French flag. Britain could not view this trade with equanimity. Saint Joseph, *Essai Historique sur le Commerce et la Navigation de la Mer Noire*, 2 vols (1805). Reissued in 1820, this became a standard text on the subject of French trade in the Black Sea.

[7]Since no strategic interest was involved in the Levant seas, the Admiralty had never developed supplies of naval stores from this area, though such supplies existed. See John S. Bromley, ed., *The New Cambridge Modern History, VI: The Rise of Great Britain and Russia, 1688-1725* (Cambridge, 1970), 562. On getting cables for British warships at Constantinople or Smyrna, see Samuel Hood to S.H. Linzee, 14, 16 January 1795, and Hood to Henry Hotham, 16 January 1795, in NMM, MKH/246, "Out-Letter Book of HMS *L'Aigle*, 1794-5." Francis Beaufort was only beginning in

1812 his valuable survey of the southern Turkish coast. Dilettanti Society to Barrow, 17 September 1812, "Petitions 1811-12," PRO, Admiralty [hereafter ADM] 1/5128.

[8]Ainslie to Grenville, 17 January, 1 February, 26 March, 10 April 1794, PRO, FO 78/15/19-20, 27-28, 54-58, 69-72.

[9]Owen Connelly, *Napoleon's Satellite Kingdoms* (New York, 1965), 68; Sir Sydney Smith to Captain Hoste, 18 July 1806, Laing MSS, II: 699-700, Historical Manuscripts Commission (London: 1925); Tom Pocock, *Remember Nelson: The Life of Captain Sir William Hoste* (London, 1977), 201; William Darley to Captain Hood, 9 May 1799, NMM, MKH/101.

[10]Captain Paget of the *Romney* (50) captured the French frigate *La Sybille* (40) and three merchantmen at Mykonos in 1794. Hood, appointed to the Levant station in 1795, was caught up in the later controversy in which the Turks took the French part and demanded compensation from Britain. See Robert Liston, ambassador at Constantinople, on these events, 29 December 1794 to 13 October 1795, NMM, MKH/101.

[11]Norman Daniel, *Islam, Europe and Empire* (Edinburgh, 1966), 109; Sir Robert T. Wilson, *History of the British Expedition to Egypt* (London, 1803), II: 90, n. 1, Appendix, 22 July 1799, Napoleon to the Cairo Divan.

[12]Christopher C. Lloyd, ed., *The Keith Papers* (Navy Records Society, 1950), II: 199-203; Lord Elgin to Smith, 22 December 1799, PRO, FO 78/24.

[13]By the treaty Britain undertook to send a squadron to the Levant and supply arms to the Turks in case of French attack. She agreed to the closure of the Straits to all non-Turkish warships in peacetime. In return British exports to the Ottoman empire were to pay reduced duties of 3 percent. If an Anglo-Russian treaty was signed (Britain had been in dispute with Russia since 1807), Britain was to secure a similar treaty between Russia and the Porte which would guarantee Ottoman territorial integrity. In fact, Russian fears of French aggression led to a rapprochement with the Ottoman Empire in 1812 at the Treaty of Bucharest. The Ottoman navy had been much improved by Selim III's reforms. Between 1791 and 1799, forty-six new warships were built, four of the latest design, and by 1807 the total had risen to sixty-one ships of all sizes. Selim's naval reforms were generally more successful and less controversial than his army reforms, and by the end of his reign he had transformed the Ottoman fleet. See T. Naff, "Ottoman Diplomacy and the Great European Powers, 1797-1802" (Ph.D. thesis, University of London, 1960), 27, 36-41.

[14]Bonaparte's exposé, 29 June 1811, in Richard G. Glover, *Britain at Bay, Defence against Bonaparte, 1803-14* (London, 1973), p. 188. Bonaparte thought that by 1814, with two ships already at Venice and "with three belonging to the Kingdom of Italy, I shall have a fleet of eight ships there." Napoleon to Decres, 23 January 1813, ibid., 190.

[15]Connelly, *Satellite Kingdoms*, 43-48. The new coast road to Genoa and Nice was completed in 1812.

[16]Pocock, *Remember Nelson*, 151.

[17]Rear Admiral H.G. Thursfield, ed., *Five Naval Journals, 1789-1817* (Navy Records Society, 1951), 171, 194, 216-17, 229, 159, 164, 217, 181.

[18]Connelly, *Satellite Kingdoms*, 47.

[19]Pocock, *Remember Nelson*, 164-79; Commander W. M. Phipps Hornby, "Letters Describing the Battle of Lissa 1811," *Mariners Mirror*, 52 (May 1966): 193-98.

[20]Jane Barbara Codrington, Lady Bourchier, *The Life of Sir Edward Codrington* (London, 1873), I: 73.

Navy Pension Files in the National Archives as Manuscript Resources

Geraldine N. Phillips

Naval historians, like historians in other fields, have long cherished the valuable collections housed in the National Archives in Washington, D.C. But so voluminous is this collection, that some important elements can be overlooked. Citing a small but notable sample, Ms. Phillips demonstrates in this essay that pension files by Civil War veterans and their dependents offer much new and interesting information for the historian and are thus a new and rich source of manuscript evidence.

Pension applications filed by navy and marine corps veterans and their dependents from 1861 to 1910 have been in the custody of the National Archives for over forty years. They are part of the 1.5 million files generally described as "Civil War and later pension application files," for which the National Archives receives about thirty thousand reference inquiries annually. Those pursuing genealogical research discovered the value of these pension files for their studies long ago. Although the contents of these files are primarily documents by the Bureau of Pensions in order to grant benefits under the laws passed from 1861 until well into the twentieth century, genealogists have found in them valuable information about their families' past. Dates and places of birth, death, marriage, and sometimes divorce; names and occupations of family members; data on families' economic status found in affidavits and court documents filed to obtain benefits; and original baptismal, marriage, and discharge certificates, and, occasionally, photographs are just some of the items located in these files.

The demands placed on these pension files by those doing family research have limited their accessibility and hence their visibility for other types of inquiry. As a result, many have viewed these records as having value only for genealogical research. In 1982, the National Archives took steps to increase access to these files by initiating a pilot project to reproduce on microfiche the roughly sixty thousand files composing the four series of navy pension files from 1861 to 1910. The smallest of these series, about seven thousand files of disapproved pension applications of widows and other dependents of navy veterans, usually called "Navy Widows' Originals," has been completely reproduced on slightly over eight thousand microfiche. This series is now available for viewing in the National Archives Microfilm Reading Room and for purchase.

A second series, some twenty thousand approved pension application files of widows and other dependents of navy veterans, usually called "Navy Widows' Certificates," is now on microfiche for duplication and verification, and will be available for viewing and purchase by 1990. Microfiche publication of the last two series, about ten thousand disapproved and some twenty-four thousand approved pension application files, will follow.

The files discussed below are mainly from the series of approved and disapproved pension application files of widows and other dependents of navy veterans (i.e., veterans' children under the age of sixteen, dependent mothers and fathers, and dependent unmarried sisters under the age of sixteen). Many of the application files of these dependents also contain original applications of the navy veterans.

These applications, whether approved or disapproved, include virtually the same types of documentation requested by the Pension Bureau to support the claim. The value of these files for many other types of research lies in these supporting documents-- affidavits, depositions, transcripts of interviews, personal and official correspondence--wherein is found not only a complete record of the veteran's service but also, in most instances, some description of what he did while in the navy. Sometimes documents in these files tell what battles or operations he took part in, what foreign ports he visited, what his experiences were in the midst of battle, what his life was like aboard ship, what he did before entering the navy, how and when he entered the service, what he did following service, and, almost always, what injuries or illnesses he suffered while in the navy and their impact upon his health and later livelihood.

Many of these pension applications came from those who manned the blockade vessels protecting the over thirty-five hundred miles of southern coastline. There are applications made by men, or their survivors, who served in some of the most important operations of that war--the capture of Hatteras Inlet in August 1861, the first combined army-navy operation of the war; the attacks on Confederate Forts Walker and Beauregard, and the occupation of Port Royal, South Carolina, in November 1861; and the capture of Forts Henry and Donelson in Tennessee by Commodore Andrew H. Foote and General Ulysses S Grant in February 1862. The applicants served under Farragut at New Orleans, Vicksburg, and Mobile Bay; with Porter at Fort Fisher; with DuPont and Dahlgren at Charleston; and on the sounds and rivers of North Carolina. To date, no one has examined these files in depth for what they tell about these men's experiences during the Civil War and during other periods of the American naval past. A quite random and most unscientific sampling of some two hundred of these files reveals the following.

The pension application filed by Thomas McCabe's widow contains his original application of 16 March 1892 for a pension based on deafness and debility caused by a wound received while in the naval service. In response to the Bureau of Pension's request for additional information, McCabe submitted an affidavit telling of his part in the capture of Forts Morgan and Gaines at the entrance to Mobile Bay in August 1864 while assigned to the USS *Oneida*. McCabe recalled that the ship's doctor, a Surgeon Taylor, ordered him to the ward room pantry to light a lamp. While doing so a Confederate shell struck the *Oneida*'s starboard quarter, entered and completely demolished the captain's cabin, and killed a "Colored Steward" stationed there. The landing of the shell caused "bursting and Splintering" of the partition that separated the captain's cabin from the ward room, and a splinter struck

McCabe's right leg below the knee, causing a slight flesh wound which the doctor bandaged.

McCabe continued helping the surgeon when shortly afterward another shell landed, striking the boiler and causing steam to rush out. The surgeon's other steward ran out of the engine room into the warrant officers' quarters to escape to the deck and was severely scalded while doing so. As soon as the steam cleared, McCabe followed the steward to the deck and arrived just as the 11-inch gun began firing. McCabe said he experienced a "violent" ringing in his right ear "as if something had broke in it." Returning to the ward room he noticed that his hearing in the right ear was impaired. He told the ship's surgeon about the condition, but he lost his hearing completely in his right ear, nonetheless. McCabe also said that the wound to his right leg, although slight at first, became a sore. Because of the debilitated state of his health from repeated attacks of chills and fever, it took about six or seven weeks for the wound to heal, leaving a large scar on his right leg.[1]

C. W. Adams also took part in the naval operation to seize Mobile Bay. As was commonly done, the Bureau of Pensions asked him to provide testimony regarding the service of a shipmate, William J. Dell, who was applying for pension benefits. In a deposition filed at Chicago in February 1897, Adams stated that he commanded the Confederate ironclad *Tennessee* from her capture until her dismantling. Describing the men who served under him he said that they all "suffered severely." Yellow fever broke out on the vessel which thus spent a long time in quarantine below New Orleans. After the quarantine was lifted, the ironclad went to the mouth of the Red River where practically the entire crew experienced an epidemic of "black fever." In Adams's words, "The boat was a floating hospital. Bowel trouble was prevalent most of the time."[2]

According to his declaration for pension made in November 1875 before the U.S. Consul at Port Adelaide, South Australia, Frederick O.G. Fincke was sixteen years old when he was struck by a Confederate shell while serving on the gunboat *Cayuga*, part of the first division that crossed the chain barrier between Forts Jackson and St. Philip on 24 April 1862. As a result of this injury, and possibly because of the later medical treatment, Fincke lost his left leg. The treatment for his injury, described in documents enclosed with his application, required his transfer from the *Cayuga* to a hospital at the naval storage depot at Pilot Town, Louisiana, described as "a few ramshackle houses standing on poles in the swamp." It may be safe to assume that the hospital was equally "temporary" in nature. The young Fincke remained there for a month before being sent by steamship to the naval hospital at New York. He was apparently a patient there for almost two years before being honorably discharged. At the time he filed for pension, Fincke was twenty-seven years old and a jeweler's assistant in Australia.[3]

When Dr. Nelson C. Reed of Columbus, Ohio, applied for pension benefits, he amply described the treatment he received as a seventeen year old following enlistment in March 1864, at Cincinnati. While on the receiving ship *Grampus*, Reed contracted a severe case of diarrhea which he claimed remained with him for five months. Transferred from the *Grampus* to the gunboat *Elfin*, he remained on duty with the ship's surgeon. Transferred again in April to the *Nymph*, he was by then "so reduced, weak and emaciated, that it required great effort for me to walk upon the deck. Was mere skeleton already, of my former robust, plethoric self." The *Nymph*'s surgeon gave Reed a physical examination immediately after he came on board the vessel and as a result ordered him to sick bay where he remained until July.

Reed stated that during the latter part of his illness he became unable to digest the ship's coarse fare, described as

> truly unfit for human food. Bread often moldy, and often wormy (the latter condition being the less objectionable), and particularly the alleged 'corn beef,' at which a hungry wolf would have hesitated before acception. In the use of such diet, and stagnant Red River water, a large percent of which in May and June, is mud, slimy with vegetation, and alleged to hold in solution, or suspension, no small amount of excrement of Caymans, there could be little or no relief to a delicate and disordered stomach, which always rebelled

against, and often rejected, after a necessarily enforced ingestion of such.[4]

Edwin A. Galinda, a manufacturer in Brooklyn and Newark, and partly disabled, applied for an invalid pension on 21 July 1890. Along with other veterans and dependents of navy veterans, he filed following the passage on 21 June 1890 of the liberal Disability Pension Act (26 Stat. 182). This act allowed a Civil War veteran to apply for benefits upon submission of proof of ninety or more days of service and an honorable discharge, together with a statement of disability. This same act allowed widows and other dependents of veterans to apply for benefits regardless of the cause of the veteran's death, provided he served ninety days and received an honorable discharge.

Galinda claimed that while an acting master's mate in April 1862 on the ironclad gunboat *Galena*, flagship of the James River Squadron, he contracted swamp fever or malarial poisoning. Ordered to the *Eutaw* in 1863 and serving near Dry Tortugas, he then contracted "breakbone fever," a malady described as so painful that suicide is sometimes contemplated by its victims as a means of relief. Galinda stated that as a result of the illnesses from his naval service, he suffered from an enlarged spleen, stomach disorder, rheumatism, and blood poisoning. Galinda's widow later stated that he weighed 160 pounds before he entered the navy, but weighed only about a hundred pounds when discharged because of his bout with breakbone fever.[5]

Judging from the sample, a strikingly large number of navy and marine corps veterans filed for disability pension because of rheumatism. Veterans, aged forty and up, listed as preconditions for chronic rheumatism exposure to dampness and water while below decks, to fog and cold while standing watch in open boats at night, and to other unhealthful conditions.

Post-traumatic stress disorders are well known today, but were not well recognized in the nineteenth century. Few applications in the sample of files examined fell in this category, but the successful application of George W. Perrigo suggests some understanding of the effects of trauma on this former acting master's mate. Perrigo's post-naval career as an attorney and newspaper editor was prematurely shortened by what he described as a nervous condition which left him at the age of forty-three unable to use his legs, and only partially able to use his arms and thus feed himself.

Perrigo traced his condition to his experience on board the monitor *Milwaukee* attached to the West Gulf Blockading Squadron. On 17 March 1865, the *Milwaukee* was about to withdraw from the Blakeley River in Alabama where it had been shelling Confederate positions, when it struck a torpedo. As signal officer, Perrigo was on deck at the time of the explosion with several other officers. The vessel quickly began sinking, and there was, according to Perrigo, a frantic attempt to remove the battle hatches and iron grates to free those trapped below. Perrigo and several others were finally rescued by an ensign in a dinghy who had been searching for torpedoes and was returning to his parent ship, the *Elk*, under the cover of darkness. The *Elk* had, however, changed positions, extinguished its lights, and banked its fires for protection against the Confederate torpedoes. As a result, the dinghy with its survivors from the *Milwaukee* remained in open water for about five hours. Perrigo claimed that the trauma and exposure of this incident resulted in frequent and debilitating nervous attacks following his discharge.[6]

Many of these files tell of the wounds and illnesses of navy veterans, but some also tell much about the relationships between officers and men. Frederick Hitner, a fireman aboard the *Banshee*, testified for Walter A. Garfield, a deck officer and sailing master who claimed rheumatism originating from naval service. When asked by the pension examiner about his relationship with Garfield, he replied: "I did not have much acquaintance with him as he was an officer and I was a private. I would never speak to him except when I was called before the mast or when I had something particular to say to him."[7]

Also evident in these files are the adverse effects on navy enlistments of payment of bounties to army enlistees following passage of the Civil War Federal draft laws. Secretary of the Navy Gideon Welles made known his apprehensions regarding these laws which resulted in the navy losing experienced seamen, lured to the army by bounties. Francis Bridgewater appears to have been a case in point. Bridgewater served in the navy from 1858 until 1863. He then enlisted in June 1864 under an alias, James Williams, in Company G, 2nd Massachusetts Infantry, a unit with which he stayed until the close of the war.[8]

Aliases were common among veterans who made these pension applications. Often, the process of examining the veteran's claim for pension disclosed the reason for taking an alias. Ellen J. Gormley was nearly denied a pension based on the service of her husband, Frank T. Gormley, because he assumed the alias of a man carried on the Navy Department's rolls as a deserter. It seems that Gormley shipped aboard the USS *Massachusetts* from New York City in May 1864, transferred to the *North Carolina*, and from there to the *Union* en route to the West Gulf Blockading Squadron. While on the *Union*, he met Patrick Carrick, who in the words of the special pension examiner, proved to be "a coward and deserter." Gormley was anxious to be part of the action in the South, and he and Carrick agreed to exchange names at first call for a detail to be made. When the detail was made to the USS *Metacomet*, a vessel headed for Farragut's fleet with provisions before the attack on Mobile Bay, Gormley assumed Carrick's place and his name which he retained for the remainder of his naval service. The true Patrick Carrick, going under the name of Frank T. Gormley, later deserted.[9]

While the pension applications sampled found evidence of illiteracy, there were also files containing letters written by the men both during and after naval service. One such example are the letters found in the file of Frederick Dobbs, a third assistant engineer, who died in April 1862, of consumption or tuberculosis contracted in naval service. Dobbs's mother submitted to the Bureau of Pensions many letters written to her by her son while he was on the USS *Hartford* in the East India Squadron from 1856 until about 1861. These letters contain, amongst other matters, descriptions of the dress, language, customs, and geography of the places visited. Writing from Hong Kong in January 1860, Dobbs commented on the voyage from the Mauritius Islands and implied that the speed of the voyage to the Far East was considerably increased because the captain, Cornelius K. Stribling, on his way to become flag officer of the East India Squadron, "was in a great hurry to get to Hong Kong, as his pay was increased $500 as soon as he got on the station, or gave an order to a ship."[10] In an earlier letter to his mother written from Whampoa in 1856, Dobbs, in his version of the storming of the Chinese forts, leaves little doubt in his account that he held the English "with their usual obstinacy" fully to blame for starting the incident which resulted in their loss of over five hundred officers and men.[11]

Nearly a quarter of all Union navy enlistees during the Civil War were black. The foreign born--Irish, Italians, Germans--also made up a sizable part of the nearly eighty-five thousand men of the Civil War navy and marine corps. The files of the blacks, many of them former slaves, and of the foreign born enlistees provide considerable information about their lives before service. There are fascinating accounts throughout the files of how many blacks escaped from slavery to freedom and went on to join the navy.

K. Jack Bauer, at a 1974 National Archives Conference, questioned why younger historians trained in quantitative and other methods of the social sciences had not conducted more research into the enlisted men of the U.S. Navy.[12] A similar note was struck by Frederick S. Harrod. "Enlisted personnel," he said, "are the forgotten men of naval history. Historians write of tactics and technology but ignore the people who compose the service."[13] These pension application files provide much material for the study of enlisted men and of the navy during the years 1861-1910. Those interested in the social, economic, labor, and family structures and migration patterns during these years will find them to be important primary documentation. There is a wealth of material for tracing the exodus of Southern blacks from slavery to freedom in the 1860s and their lives into the early years of this century. Used with other resources at the National Archives and in other repositories, these files offer considerable potential for broadening our understanding of the American past.

Notes

[1]McCabe to Commissioner, Bureau of Pensions, 28 June 1892, Case Files of Approved Pension Applications of Widows, and Other Dependents of Civil War and Later Navy Veterans (hereafter Navy Widows' Certificates), 1861-1910, no. 0009746 (M1279, Microfiche NWC 0008893, Thomas McCabe), Records of the Veterans Administration, Record Group 15 (hereafter RG 15), National Archives (hereafter NA), Washington, DC.

[2]Deposition of C.W. Adams, 25 February 1897, Case Files of Disapproved Pension Applications of Widows and Other Dependents of Navy Veterans (hereafter Navy Widows' Originals), 1861-1910, Application 0011414 (M1274, Microfiche NWC 0003055, William J. Dell), RG 15, NA.

[3]Declaration for pension of Frederick O. G. Fincke, 29 November 1875, Navy Widows' Certificates, no. 0011200 (M1279, Microfiche NWC 0010297, Frederick O.G. Fincke), RG 15, NA.

[4]Sworn statement of Dr. Nelson C. Reed, 17 October 1882, Navy Widows' Certificates, 1861-1910, no. 0009881 (M1279, Microfiche NWC 0009020, Nelson C. Reed), RG 15, NA.

[5]Declaration for pension of Edwin A. Galinda, 21 July 1890, Navy Widows' Certificates, 1861-1910, no. 00011164 (M1279, Microfiche NWC 0010263, Edwin A. Galinda), RG 15, NA.

[6]Declaration for pension and affidavit of George W. Perrigo, 23 April 1887, Navy Widows' Certificates, 1861-1910, no. 0009865 (M1279, Microfiche NWC 0009005, George W. Perrigo), RG 15, NA. It is interesting to note that the official accounts of the sinking of the *Milwaukee* is very similar to that given by Perrigo, but no mention is made of Perrigo's rescue by the dinghy, or of the rescue of the remainder of the crew except to say that there were no casualties. *Official Records of the Union and Confederate Navies in the War of the Rebellion*, Series I, Volume 22 (Washington, 1908), 67, 70, 71, 73, 74, 92, 129.

[7]Deposition of Frederick Hitner for pension claim of Walter H. Garfield, 4 February 1895, Navy Widows' Certificates, 1861-1910, no. 0011170 (M1279, Microfiche NWC 0010268, Walter H. Garfield), RG 15, NA.

[8]Statement of service of Francis Bridgewater, Navy Widows' Certificates, 1861-1910, no. 0009667 (M1279, Microfiche NWC 0008858, Francis Bridgewater), RG 15, NA.

[9]Report of Special Examination 6867, April 1892, Navy Widows' Certificates, 1861-1910, no. 0009667 (M1279, Microfiche NWC 0008817, Frank T. Gormley), RG 15, NA.

[10]Letter of Frederick Dobbs to Mary Ann Dobbs, 6 January 1860, Navy Widows' Certificates, 1861-1910, no. 0002816 (M1279, Microfiche NWC 0002127, Frederick Dobbs), RG 15, NA.

[11]Letter of Frederick Dobbs to Mary Ann Dobbs (1856), ibid.

[12]K. Jack Bauer, "The Navy in an Age of Manifest Destiny: Some Suggestions for Sources and Research," *Versatile Guardian-Research in Naval History*, ed. Richard A. Von Doenhoff (Washington, DC, 1979), 165.

[13]Frederick S. Harrod, *Manning the New Navy: The Development of a Modern Naval Enlisted Force, 1899-1940* (Westport, CT, 1978), ix.

The British Government and Merchant Seamen: Efficiency and Welfare 1870-1914

David M. Williams

During the half century preceding the outbreak of World War I, British merchant sailors saw many important and permanent changes in their profession. Not least among these were the increasingly numerous and far-reaching influences which resulted in the British government assuming a more active role toward its merchant seamen population. In this essay, Mr. Williams identifies the influences at work from 1870 to 1914, examines the issues and measures taken, and evaluates the response of government.

The eminent British social investigator, Henry Mayhew, wrote in 1850 that "the reckless and improvident character of sailors, and the peculiar nature of their service, coupled with a consideration of their vast importance to our national welfare, have long induced both the legislature and Courts of Justice to treat them differently from other labourers."[1] For such reasons government intervention in the merchant service had a history stretching back over centuries as government recognized the seaman's unique conditions and location of service, his importance to the commercial marine, and his potential as a reserve for the navy.[2] The Victorian era witnessed a growth in the level of official action associated with merchant seamen, unprecedented both in terms of earlier periods and in labor generally. No other sector of the work force gained so much and so regular attention. As the nineteenth century progressed the forces generating intervention increased. In the forty years before 1914 government had to address old and new issues in response to pressures stemming from circumstance and interested parties. The outcome was much investigation and action.

The factors influencing government between 1870 and 1914 in its consideration of merchant seamen were many and varied. Some stemmed from past government policy; others emanated from general developments within British economy and society; still others arose from pressure groups associated with British shipping. Action on seamen after 1870, though extended and far-reaching, was nevertheless a continuation of policies developed in the mid-century and in some instances inaugurated much earlier. To confine discussion merely to Victoria's reign before 1870, a series of official enquiries, notably in 1836, 1843, 1849, 1858, and 1869-70, concerned themselves directly or indirectly with seamen. Involvement was not confined to investigation. The Mercantile Marine Act of 1850, which established the important Marine Department of the Board of Trade, and additional acts in 1854 and 1867, included a range of clauses touching on employment, accommodation, and terms of service.[3] Acceptance by government of such responsibilities made further action almost inevitable, and there are parallels in this field with the MacDonagh thesis of government growth.[4]

Irrespective of any pattern of administrative evolution, other aspects ensured the extension of policy. The changing role of government generally after 1870 was one such feature and in the wider context considerable stress must rest on the British seafaring tradition. To a nation indoctrinated with Hearts of Oak and which annually celebrated the glorious 21 October, government had an obligation to concern itself fully with things naval. Moreover, the popularization of the maritime England sentiment through art and culture at all levels ensured that any administration which failed to do its duty would answer to an electorate drawn from an increasing swathe of the population. Furthermore, the Empire was one bound together and dependent on the freedom of shipping lanes. The dominance of the seas by British vessels, and therefore the well-being of their crews, was an economic, strategic, and political necessity. Finally, amongst general influences there was that of technological change. Iron and steam transformed the merchant fleet and its manpower. Steam dramatically changed the lot of the individual seamen; more so, it fundamentally altered the makeup of the labor force. Under sail, the vast majority of those working at sea were seamen; with steam, there emerged a whole new class of workers below decks, engine room, or cabin staff, with none of the seaman's traditional duties or skills. Added to this non-seaman element, through the growth of passenger traffic, was a proliferation of stewards, kitchen hands, and others. Government now had to consider not one type of seafarer but a variety of workers with different job specifications.

Alongside these general influences the legislature faced often conflicting claims for attention and action from a range of interested parties. Many of these organized themselves into associations, societies, and unions which enhanced their ability to pressure and lobby government. Foremost amongst pressure groups were the shipowners and their various organizations, such as the Liverpool Steamship Owners, the Clydeside counterpart, and most notably, the Chamber of Shipping of the United Kingdom, established in 1878. Shipowners were not natural lovers of state intervention, being suspicious of anything that might curb their operating freedom and being firm opponents of any measures that would raise costs. They resisted strongly proposals they regarded as counter to their interests and protested depression, real or imaginary, as grounds for the special consideration of their position. In common with most British employers in the nineteenth century, shipowners regularly featured the labor aspect as a causal element of their problems. From the 1850s they drew attention to what they regarded as a deterioration in the quality, and a deficiency in the supply, of British seamen, which caused the increasing employment of foreigners. This, and the general problem of manning, was one which disturbed naval and nationalistic interests as the merchant seaman was traditionally viewed as a wartime strategic reserve.[5] Training sufficient young seamen became an issue far beyond the mere commercial, and the polemics of admirals, retired or active, were later reinforced by the Navy League with its formidable propaganda campaigns.[6] Drawing both on commercial and nationalistic feeling, there was concern too over the size of crews of merchant vessels vis à vis those of other nations in terms of the competitive ability of the British mercantile marine.

If shipowners and naval pressure groups were motivated by commercial and patriotic interests, there were also parties concerned more directly with seamen themselves. Politicians such as Plimsoll, Chamberlain, and Brassey made national issues of the seaworthiness of vessels and the well-being of seamen. Safety at sea was a theme assured of popular support, for man against the might of the sea was a Victorian obsession. Likewise, the welfare of seamen afloat and the need to protect them from evil and temptation ashore were widely approved. All proposals in such areas received the support in spirit, if not politically, by maritime charitable and religious bodies such as the British and Foreign Sailors Society, the Missions to Seamen, and the temperance hostel movement inspired by Dame Agnes Weston, the indefatigable "sailor's friend."[7] Seamen themselves came to develop a voice. The nature and size of steamship crews caused the first effective unions, notably the Sailors and Firemen's Union, whose leader, Havelock Wilson, gained political success and a high public profile.[8] Labor's representation on official enquiries from around 1900 was an important element to improved conditions. Finally, amongst the forces influencing action there was the Board of Trade itself. The attitude of personnel at the Board and its Marine Department were highly significant in determining the form and pace of intervention.

The concerns of the many interested parties, though quite varied, can effectively be grouped under the heads of efficiency and welfare. On the efficiency side, there were the two aspects of manning--that of the manning of individual vessels, and that of manning the mercantile fleet in terms of the number and quality of seamen. On the welfare side, the issue was one of improving the seaman's position: in particular, safeguarding his life; improving his condition afloat--contract, wages, diet, and accommodation; and ashore--tackling the problems of crimping. Of course, these two features of efficiency and welfare were in no way exclusive; indeed they were mutually reinforcing. For example, creating better and safer working conditions would help recruitment; again, seamen who felt secure and satisfied would work more effectively, yet in the main contemporaries treated them separately, though recognized the relationship. An examination of the several elements of efficiency and welfare and a consideration of the official response must precede any attempt at assessment of government action.

II

Of all matters about seamen, the one which evoked the most attention during the period 1870-1914 was the so-called "manning question." The question had various aspects. Its key theme was the quality and supply of British merchant seamen. Following this came the issues of the increasing employment of lascars and foreigners and the ability of the merchant navy to supply an adequate reserve for the Royal Navy. A separate but related consideration was the manning efficiency in terms of crew size and man/ton ratios.

The central question of manning has a long pedigree stretching back to before the eighteenth century. In the Victorian era the establishment of a Registry Office for seamen, together with special commissions in 1852 and 1859, all testify to the subject's high regard. But from around 1870 the issue took on fresh aspects and momentum. Indicative of this new phase were two reports produced by the Liverpool Committee of Shipowners. The first, in 1870, arising out of discussions with the Board of Trade, was based on a detailed questionnaire answered by over one hundred masters and shipowners in sail and steam. High percentages of respondents agreed that seamen had deteriorated as seamen, in physical condition and in subordination. A second report in 1874 focussed on the quantitative aspect and estimated total annual wastage of seamen in the British mercantile marine at sixteen thousand, logically noting that any shortfall in new British entrants would require the further employment of foreigners. These two reports were but elements of an extensive debate in the 1870s.[9] "Unseaworthy seamen," publicized more than a shade suspiciously by shipping interests, became almost as much a burning issue as "unseaworthy ships."

On the validity of assessments of declining quality and numbers, appraisal is difficult. On deterioration there was the contemporary dilemma of defining the "skill" of the seaman in a changing technological age and, as suggested, circumstances may have colored judgement. Brassey, in his 1877 seminal work, affirmed that "the alleged deterioration of British seamen is not conclusively established," but he presented a more favorable view of seamen in steam compared with sail.[10] On the quantitative side there was less controversy; a problem of labor supply with considerable annual wastage and the growing employment of foreigners was generally acknowledged. Indeed, contemporaries were more confident than present day observers since problems exist in interpreting the figures of the Registrar General of Seamen.[11]

Fortunately, in this context, there is no need for detailed statistics. It is sufficient to recognize that there was a prevailing view of a serious manning problem and to enquire what was done about it. Much debate and limited action is the short answer. But given the stress laid on the issue, accounting for the lack of progress is important, even more so because there was full agreement that the solution was in attracting more boys through either training ships or some form of apprenticeship scheme. While all parties supported such laudable aims, there was disagreement over who should bear the cost. Training thousands of boys each year could not be cheap. Official policy was made clear as early as 1872, rejecting any suggestion that "it was the duty of the state to educate sailors for the mercantile marine." Government defended this stance in debates and committees, notably in 1903 and 1907, claiming to see no economic or strategic grounds for action. In its view the attainment of an adequate supply of British seamen was to "be looked for in the improvement of their conditions rather than in the increase of facilities for training boys."[12] However, the sensitive aspects of the employment of non-whites and foreigners, and the need for a naval reserve, forbade any total dismissal of the matter. No administration could ignore patriotic appeals and the strength of tradition. On the two solutions of training ships or apprentices, government preferred the latter but was neither willing to introduce a compulsory system nor to make grants to shipowners.

For their part, shipowners favored training ships or schools where costs would be borne by others. They argued that boys in steam represented pure cost and that the conditions held to be desirable for boy sailors, supervision and separate accommodation, augmented charges. The refusal of both sides to face the financial costs saw scant progress. At times and under pressure, government did make some response, as with the unsatisfactory Ritchie Act between 1898 and 1905.[13] Again, in 1912, faced with a determined campaign by the Navy League and under the impact of the *Titanic* disaster, government conceded a modest grant for boys in sea training institutions. However, as these numbered under two thousand in 1914 this hardly promised a full solution.[14] Thus on the eve of war there was no resolution to the manning question. Seamen certainly lacked the skills of fifty years earlier, and while there was no actual labor supply problem, British-born sailors had fallen since 1891 from 68 to 60 per cent, while foreigners and lascars rose from 26 to 34 per cent.[15]

If procrastination characterized the major issue of the supply and quality of British seamen, one aspect of manning where progress occurred was desertion, a growing problem in the nineteenth century. Recent research suggests that over time perhaps 20 to 25 per cent of seamen became deserters,[16] and official returns reveal a near tripling of annual desertions between 1850 and the 1890s when the work force rose by only a third.[17] Increasing desertions were a serious cause of inconvenience and expense, and it was one area where shipowners sought official action. Government was not unsympathetic, because as the sanctity of labor contracts was highly regarded, it viewed desertion as a matter of legal and moral concern. Traditionally government relied on shipowners themselves taking action through the courts. Similarly, there were prosecutions for the encouragement of desertion and measures against crimping. However, there was limited action because much desertion occurred overseas. Desertions continued to increase despite instructions to British consuls on attitude and procedure.[18] Ultimately government saw the problem as best tackled by concentrating on the causes and ease of desertion. Improving the seaman's conditions, thereby making him less inclined to desert, was a long term solution. But the deterrent approach, making desertion more difficult, had more immediate potential. Following an enquiry in 1899, government introduced the practice of issuing seamen with Continuous Discharge Certificates. These had an immediate effect. Between 1900 and 1908 desertions in Britain fell by 70 per cent and abroad by 20 per cent.[19] The potential loss of "papers" needed for signing on proved a real deterrent. For once bureaucracy and paper work provided a more effective solution than the rigors of the law.

The remaining aspect of the contemporary manning issue, that of crew size, was one where government itself could take no direct action. Masters and owners determined the size and makeup of their crews, but though crew size was an operating decision, the subject had long been regarded as one of official concern. The matter first arose in the 1830s when fears about the competitiveness of British shipping, in particular its poor showing against United States vessels, saw the pioneering use by Board of Trade officials of man/ton ratios as a measure of efficiency.[20] After 1849 statistics were irregularly produced, but in 1870, prompted by the debate over seamen, government commenced compilation on a regular and more scientific basis. Early figures had been crude, but the new statistics showed more ingenuity and sophistication. The resulting series of tables, running from the mid-nineteenth to the early twentieth century, represents a rich storehouse of material on crewing not yet fully explored.[21] What contemporary use was made of them is conjectural, but they were a source of reference and reassurance as they showed regular and substantial improvements in man/ton ratios. In this context, however, their importance is an indication that government attached great significance to manning efficiency and appreciated the need for constructive statistical data.

III

As the opening quotation suggested, the unique position of the seaman and his economic and strategic significance meant that his welfare and conditions of employment were a matter of public interest. As early as 1729 an Act for the Better Regulation and Government of Seamen in the Merchant Service introduced a written contract stressing the seaman's terms of service and penalties for breaches of discipline, though it did give the seaman some wage protection. Down to the mid-nineteenth century the emphasis of government concern was discipline and control,[22] but in time safety and a more genuine interest in welfare came to influence action. Seamen gained some benefits from investigations into shipwrecks in 1836 and 1843, and there were slight advances too in consequence of measures concerned with emigrants. The resulting anomalous position of the seaman led to the belated introduction of minimal standards in accommodation in 1867, and in 1868 the Board of Trade issued a non-mandatory recommended diet scale.[23] Thus, down to 1870 official action on sailors' welfare was limited. There was some campaigning for reform, but shipowner opposition and antagonistic attitudes at the Board of Trade prevented progress. Thomas Farrar, the Board's permanent secretary, and Thomas Gray of the Marine Department, respectively described as "an unrepentant free trader" and "personifying the philosophy of administrative laissez faire," were to hinder reform in the mid-century and beyond.[24] Yet after 1870 various factors--Plimsoll's campaign, seamen's unions, rising general living standards, and new liberal ideas on social reform--caused government to concern itself more directly with welfare. Matters affecting welfare can be examined under three basic heads: safety, protection of the seaman ashore, and the material conditions under which he served afloat.

The Plimsoll agitation over safety at sea and Chamberlain's later efforts are familiar enough to require no detailed survey. Plimsoll announced his campaign for a compulsory load line in 1870. Though his proposals were ignored, the 1871 Merchant Shipping Act made it an offence to send an unseaworthy ship to sea. Real progress came only after the publication of Plimsoll's evocatively titled *Our Seamen*. The Somerset Commission of 1873 was generally supportive and Disraeli's government brought in a bill in 1875. Shipowner opposition and the volume of amendments saw a proposal to drop the bill which occasioned Plimsoll's famous "villains" outburst. Public opinion forced government a year later to introduce a measure whereby powers of inspection were given to the Board of Trade, but the fixing of a load line was left to owners.[25] Chamberlain's attempts to deal with the problem of over insurance and to make owners responsible to their crews for seaworthiness foundered, and it was only after more reports in 1885 and 1887 that, in 1890, effective load line legislation was introduced. Alongside these general provisions were specific regulations covering hazardous cargoes.[26] All such legislation had the final effect of creating safer conditions for seamen and thus represented a gain in welfare terms. However, required are some important provisos, notably the twenty years taken to introduce effective controls. Again, while in theory from 1871 seamen had the right to refuse to sail and to demand surveys, the attitudes of both shipowners and the courts showed that in the conflict between disciplinary and safety interests the former was given priority. Not until 1894 were there back-up arrangements for crew complaints.[27]

While measures towards safety could never fully remove the risk of loss or wreck, some problems permitted a fuller solution. One area was that of crimping.[28] Crimping, the business of serving as an intermediary in crew procurement, flourished in all the world's major ports. Crimping tended to be corrupt and exploitive though some recent writers have been less critical. In Britain crimps were mostly boarding house keepers whose chief aim was to strip seamen of their accumulated back pay and advance note future income. To obtain clients, crimps employed runners to board incoming vessels. Mid-century attempts to curb crimping made little impact, not least because Board of Trade officials refused to intervene in what they saw as the free labor market.[29] However, following initiatives by the Metropolitan Police, concerned by the criminality associated with crimping, the Board from 1878 evolved the Transmission of Wages Scheme which provided facilities for seamen to have their pay forwarded home. Two years later an act forbade runners from boarding ships. These measures separating seamen from crimps and safeguarding earnings effectively precluded the most profitable form of crimping. Giving evidence to an official enquiry in 1903, Havelock Wilson reported "that crimping had almost died out."[30]

In the third area of welfare provision, that of conditions afloat, significant action came late. Previous inadequacies are clearly intimated by the Royal Commission of 1903 which required an enquiry into "the sufficiency or otherwise of the law and practice for securing proper food, accommodation, medical attention and reasonable conditions of comfort and well-being for seamen." In practice, the key aspects were accommodation and diet. Theoretically the general Public Health Act of 1875 covered the former, but procedure under the Act was fraught with difficulty. Though periodically the matter attracted attention, and the *Lancet* published critical papers in the 1890s, real advance came only in 1906 when the Merchant Shipping Act fixed accommodation space per seaman at 120 cubic feet.[31] Around this time also many leading shipping companies were voluntarily beginning to improve conditions. To the seaman food was probably a more important creature comfort than his fo'castle surroundings. Traditionally seamen's fare was limited in variety, of poor quality, and vitamin deficient.[32] Though the problems were long appreciated, the state, lime juice apart, made no statutory provision for the diet of merchant seamen until 1906. In the nineteenth century, despite precedents, government chose not to legislate. Such was the power of shipowner opposition that, even in the 1890s, government rejected union pleas and commission recommendations. It contented itself with advocating voluntary scales and though that of 1868 was widely ignored, it adhered to this approach as late as 1903. Only, following blatant disregard, did it, two years later, accede to compulsion. However, when it did finally legislate, measures were comprehensive. The statutory diet scale halved the salt meat element and stipulated twenty food items instead of the customary mere four.[33] In addition, it instigated the inspection of food and water and the certification of cooks. "Pound and pint" had given way to relative plenty.

IV

Surveying the period 1870 to 1914, government increasingly

involved itself with seamen, as expected given the host of compelling influences. The scale of concern in terms of official enquiries and parliamentary debate was enormous. All these deliberations would appear to have borne fruit, for on the eve of war many of the issues associated with the efficiency and welfare of merchant seamen had been in some part resolved. Death and casualty through loss and wreck had been considerably reduced, and the seaman's conditions of accommodation and diet were now subject to statutory standards. Crimping had been virtually eliminated and desertion remarkably lessened. Even in the area of least progress, the manning question, 1912 had seen the beginnings of a state funded program.

In light of this it would be easy to view the period as one of great achievement through extended intervention. That progress occurred cannot be denied, but any final verdict requires some qualification. Irrespective of any reservations about the extent of advance, the chief comment must relate to the matter of timing. In almost every instance action might have been taken much sooner. An examination of the timing of measures is revealing. Despite the agitation in the early 1870s, effective load line legislation did not occur until the 1890s. Solving the age-old evil of crimping began in the 1880s, and the problem of desertion deteriorated until curbed from 1900. In the key welfare areas real progress had to wait until 1906, and on the training and supply of seamen token action came only after forty years of fierce debate.

The explanation of this pattern of delay lies primarily in the attitude of government which, until the turn of the century, was reluctant to take a firm line. In part this was because it was fully aware of the shipping interest's economic and political influence. However, though the strength of opposition represented a potential, and sometimes actual, stumbling block for legislative proposals, government's lack of committed action stemmed principally from its own disposition which was shaped by a range of laissez-faire principles. There was a belief in the efficacy of the market, an unwillingness to intervene in freely entered labor contracts, a desire to avoid expenditure, and a reluctance to compel. Instead the preferred course was one of encouraging voluntary self-regulation. These tenets, so widely subscribed to in the mid-Victorian era and which crumbled only slowly later in the century, were retarding influences in other sectors--housing, education, and factory controls--but compounding these general influences for seamen was the additional element that such attitudes were deeply entrenched in the Board of Trade and its Marine Department down to the 1890s.[34] When civil servants themselves advised against legislation and endorsed the view that "the less inspection the better," the likelihood of decisive legislation was severely checked.[35] By the turn of the century the retirement of such dogma-bound personnel had given way to more open and less prejudiced minds. This, together with evidence of the inadequacy of previous approaches, and from 1906 a government with a commitment to social reform and a greater political will, and majority, caused the more positive policies of the decade and a half before 1914. Yet the new attitude represented only a partial break with the past. The new approach of "enlightened paternalism" was a philosophy with two aims: welfare and social control--where labor was governed for its own good and kept in its place; and economic efficiency--ensuring the preservation of the free market, the security of capital, and cost competitiveness. Hence, while there was an increase in intervention after 1900 it was circumscribed by what Davidson terms an "underlying identity between the objectives of government and the self interest of employers."[36] To those in authority before 1914 the fruits of this common identity appeared as an expanding merchant fleet, regular improvements in manning ratios, and the overwhelming dominance of world shipping by the British mercantile marine. Such an impressive past record of achievement assured the continuance of a policy where the seaman, however much a meritorious cause for concern, was not the final priority.

Thus in the period 1870-1914, in consequence of all the influences working on government, there was a considerable extension of intervention. Government came to accept more responsibility in the fields of efficiency and welfare, and in both state action represented real benefit. Yet action was reluctant and tardy until laissez-faire attitudes weakened in the 1890s, and even thereafter the underlying ethos retained traditional values and objectives apparently justified by the success of British shipping. While the British merchant marine prospered, government saw definite limits to its function.

Notes

The author gratefully acknowledges the constructive comments on this paper of Professor Eugene L. Rasor of Emory and Henry College, Emory, Virginia, and Professor Gerald Jordan of York University, Ontario, Canada.

[1]*Morning Chronicle* (London), 7 March 1850. The quotation appears in Letter 40 of Mayhew's series of letters on labor in London, portions of which are in Ann Humphreys, ed., *Voices of the Poor* (London, 1971); Edward P. Thompson and Eileen Yeo, *The Unknown Mayhew* (London, 1971).

[2]For surveys of long-term government intervention in the merchant service, see Alfred G. Course, *The Merchant Navy* (London, 1963), 214-306; Conrad Dixon, "Legislation and the Sailors' Lot, 1660-1914," in *Seamen in Society*, ed. Paul Adam (Proceedings of the International Commission for Maritime History, Bucharest, Yugoslavia, 11-12 August 1980), 3: 96-106.

[3]13 & 14 Vict. C.9. On the early role of the Marine Department, see Peter G. Parkhurst, *Ships of Peace* (New Malden, 1962); Roger Prouty, *The Transformation of the Board of Trade, 1830-1855* (London, 1957). 17 & 18 Vict. C.104; 19 & 20 Vict. C.41; 30 & 31 Vict. C.124. A useful summary of mid-century legislation is in Great Britain, *Parliamentary Papers* [hereafter *Parl. Papers*], "Report of the President of the Board of Trade on Recent Legislation concerning Merchant Ships and Seamen," C.1398, 1876, 66: 333.

[4]Oliver MacDonagh, *A Pattern of Government Growth, 1800-60* (London, 1961).

[5]On the general issue of manning, see Eugene L. Rasor, *Reform in the Royal Navy* (Hamden, CT, 1976), and Stephen Jones, "Blood Red Roses: The Supply of Merchant Seamen in the Nineteenth Century," *Mariners Mirror* 58 (1972): 429-44.

[6]*The Navy League* (London, 1896). This publicity booklet and collection of papers embodies the League's aims and tactics.

[7]Doris Gulliver, *Dame Agnes Weston* (London, 1971).

[8]Joseph Havelock Wilson, *My Stormy Voyage Through Life* (London, 1925).

[9]The two reports were summarized and discussed in Thomas Brassey, *British Seamen* (London, 1877), 1-4, 35-39. Examples of contributions to the debate include: *Parl. Papers*, "Replies by certain of Her Majesty's Consuls to a Circular Letter of the Board of Trade," C.630, 1872, 53: 201; "Report of the Assistant Secretary, Marine

Department...with Reference to the Supply of Merchant Seamen," C.752, 1873, 59: 225; Thomas Brassey, *Our Reserves of Seamen* (London, 1872); James Malley, *Our Merchant Ships and Sailors* (London, 1876); William S. Lindsay, *Manning the Royal Navy and Mercantile Marine* (London, 1877); and Admiral Sir Frederick W. Grey, *Suggestions for Improving the Character of our Merchant Seamen and for Providing an Efficient Naval Reserve* (London, 1873).

[10]Brassey, *British Seamen*, 30-34.

[11]N. Cox, "The Records of the Registrar General of Shipping and Seamen," *Maritime History* 2 (1972): 168-88; V.C. Burton, "Counting Seafarers: the Published Records of the Registry of Merchant Seamen," *Mariners Mirror* 71 (1985): 305-20.

[12]Great Britain, *Hansard's Parliamentary Debates*, 3rd ser., 213 (1872): 132; *Parl. Papers*, "Report of the Committee appointed by the Board of Trade to Inquire into certain Questions Affecting the Mercantile Marine," Cds. 1607-9, 1903, 62: 15 et seq., 162: 39; "Report of the Committee appointed by the Board of Trade to Inquire into the Supply and Training of Boy Seamen for the Mercantile Marine." Cds. 3722-3, 1907, 75: 167 et seq.

[13]*Parl. Papers*, "Report of the Departmental Committee appointed to Enquire into the Manning of British Merchant Ships." C.8217, 1896, 60: 1 et seq. On the Ritchie Act see Coghlan McL. McLardy, *British Seamen, Boy Seamen and Light Dues* (London, 1899).

[14]Contemporary accounts of the pre-war manning campaign are in Clement Jones, *British Merchant Shipping* (London, 1922), 128-39; *The Times, Shipping Number*, 13 December 1912, reprinted as a book (London, 1913), 141-45.

[15]Burton, "Counting Seafarers," 318.

[16]On the problem of desertion see L. R. Fischer, "A Dereliction of Duty: The Problem of Desertion on Nineteenth Century Sailing Vessels," in *Working Men Who Got Wet*, eds., Rosemary Ommer and G. Panting (St. John's, Newfoundland, 1980), 51-70; Sarah B. Palmer, "Seamen Ashore in Late Nineteenth Century London: Protection from the Crimps," in *Seamen in Society*, ed. Paul Adam, 55-76.

[17]*Parl. Papers*, "Annual Statements of Trade and Navigation; 'Report of the Select Committee on Merchant Shipping'" (no. 530), 1860, 13: 1 et seq.; "Return showing the Number of Desertions and Failures to join in various Parts of the World," Cd. 371, 1901, 68: 73.

[18]*Parl. Papers*, "Reports from certain Foreign and Colonial Ports Respecting the Desertion of Seamen from British Ships," C.9265, 1899, 87: 119.

[19]Conrad Dixon, "The Rise and Fall of the Crimp, 1840-1914," in *British Shipping and Seamen, 1630-1960: Some Studies*, ed. Stephen Fisher (Exeter, 1984), 62-64; *Parl. Papers*, "Return showing the Number of Desertions and Failures to join in various Parts of the world," Cd. 4803, 1909, 78: 1-5.

[20]See *Parl. Papers*, "Report from the Select Committee of the House of Lords appointed to Inquire into the Operation and Policy of the Navigation Laws" (no.

431), 1847-48, 20, pt.2: 856-59. Figures by the Board of Trade were often referred to in the struggle over the navigation laws. For example, John L. Ricardo, *The Anatomy of the Navigation Laws* (London, 1847), 204-205; 'A. Barrister,' *Mr Ricardo's Anatomy of the Navigation Laws, Dissected* (London, 1848), 78-80; Jeremiah Dibs, *The Navigation Laws, Three Letters to Lord John Russell, M.P.* (London, 1848), 8-13.

[21]The form of the tables was that of creating samples of vessels, sail and steam separately, and providing full details of crew size and composition. The tables examined not merely man/ton ratios at a particular date, but also how the ratios of particular samples of vessels changed over time. They also tried to chart the changing functions of crew members and recognized the need to distinguish between those who worked and those who served the ship. The first surveys were undertaken retrospectively in 1870, thereafter at roughly five-yearly intervals, the resultant series running from the mid-nineteenth to the early twentieth centuries. The tables are in the annual *Tables showing the Progress of British Shipping*, commencing *Parl. Papers*, C.34, 1870, 60: 223.

[22]2 Geo. 2, C.36; Dixon, "Legislation and the Sailors' Lot," 98-100.

[23]*Parl. Papers*, "Report from the Select Committee Appointed to Inquire into the Causes of the Increased Number of Shipwrecks" (no. 567), 1836, 17: 373; "Report from the Select Committee Appointed to Inquire into the Shipwreck of British Vessels" (no. 549), 1843, 9:1; 30 & 31 Vict. C.124.

[24]Geoffrey Alderman, "Samuel Plimsoll and the Shipping Interest," *Maritime History* 1 (1971): 78-79.

[25]Ibid; David Masters, *The Plimsoll Mark* (London, 1955); Neville Upham, *The Load Line--A Hallmark of Safety*, Maritime Monographs and Reports, no. 33 (London, 1978); 34 & 35 Vict. C.110; Samuel Plimsoll, *Our Seamen. An Appeal* (London, 1873); 39 & 40 Vict. C.80.

[26]Geoffrey Alderman, "Joseph Chamberlain's Attempted Reform of the British Mercantile Marine," *Journal of Transport History*, n.s. 1 (1972): 169-84; 53 & 54 Vict. C.9. By the 1890 Act the load line was to be marked according to tables recommended by the Board of Trade's Load Line Committee of 1884-85; D. M. Williams, "State Regulation of Merchant Shipping, 1839-1914: the Bulk Carrying Trades," in *Charted and Uncharted Waters*, eds. Sarah Palmer and Glyndwr Williams (London, 1981), 55-80.

[27]In 1871 and 1872 an average of over five hundred seamen who had alleged unseaworthiness were imprisoned and as late as 1884 the figure was still over 100. See *Parl. Papers*, "Return of the Crews of Merchant Ships Committee to Prison in 1870, 1871 and 1872," C.83, 1873, 59: 245. Similar return for 1880-84, C.106 - Sess. 1, 1886, 59: 241; 57 & 58 Vict. C.60. This Act included schedules establishing procedure for detention, survey and appeal.

[28]On crimping, see Palmer, "Seamen Ashore"; Stephen Jones, "Blood Red Roses,"

pp. 432-38; Judith Fingard, "'Those Crimps of Hell and Goblins Damned'...the Image and Reality of Quebec's Sailortown Bosses," in *Working Men Who Got Wet*, eds. Ommer & Panting, 321-34; Dixon, "The Rise and Fall," 49-67.

[29]Acts in 1835 and 1854 (5 & 6 Will. 4 C.19; 17 & 18 Vict. C.104) imposed but modest fines for harboring deserters and for runners boarding vessels without permission. Thomas Farrar, Permanent Secretary of the Board of Trade, testified to his reluctance to interfere with a contract between master and man. See *Parl. Papers*, "Report of the Select Committee on Merchant Shipping" (no. 530), 1860, 13: Qs. 5805-23.

[30]Dixon, "The Rise and Fall," 59-61; *Parl. Papers*, "Report of the Committee... affecting the Mercantile Marine," Cds. 1607-9, 1903, 62: Qs. 5175 et seq.

[31]Ibid., iii. Port authorities were empowered to deal with complaints of insanitary conditions under the Act of 1875. However, the procedures were cumbersome and the implications of delaying a vessel's departure were a further deterrent. 6 Edw. 7, C.48.

[32]Conrad Dixon, "Pound and Pint: Diet in the Merchant Service, 1750-1980," in *Charted and Unchartered Waters*, 164-80.

[33]*Parl. Papers*, "Report of the Royal Commission on Labor," C.7421, 1894, 35: vii. The Board of Trade voluntary scale of provisions is in *Parl. Papers*, "Correspondence on the Subject of Dietary Scales in use in Merchant Ships" (no. 407), 1867-68, 63: 161-9; 6 Edw. 7 C.48. Schedules 25 & 64.

[34]For examples of the negative and obstructive attitude of senior officials of the Board of Trade, see Williams, "State Regulation"; Alderman, "Samuel Plimsoll"; Alderman, "Joseph Chamberlain"; Dixon, "Legislation and the Sailors' Lot."

[35]From a minute written by Thomas Farrar, quoted in Dixon, "Legislation and the Sailors' Lot," 102.

[36]R. Davidson, "The Board of Trade and Industrial Relations, 1896-1914," *Historical Journal*, 21 (1978): 571-91.

Part II

Successful
Combined Operations

Admiral Berkeley and the Duke of Wellington: The Winning Combination in the Peninsula

Donald D. Horward

The cooperation of land and sea forces in a joint operation can be particularly difficult, especially when there is no unified commander. In such cases, open and unselfish cooperation is essential. In this essay, Professor Horward evaluates the role of Admiral George Berkeley and his relationship with the Duke of Wellington in the British defense of Iberia during the Napoleonic Wars.

———————

During the past 175 years the military reputation of the Duke of Wellington has been enhanced as each new book has appeared about the Peninsular War and the Waterloo Campaign. However, many of those who played a crucial supporting role in his success have been relegated to his shadow and lost to the pages of history. One such figure whose abilities, commitment, and loyalty assured the success of Wellington's strategy in Iberia was Admiral George Cranfield Berkeley, who is known to scholars only through the Duke of Wellington's correspondence with him.[1] Yet without Berkeley's dedication, resourcefulness, and even his willingness to defy the Lords of the Admiralty, Wellington's unique strategy for the defense of Portugal in 1809-11 would have failed and Iberia would have been lost.

Berkeley's early career in the Royal Navy was anything but extraordinary. He advanced slowly through the ranks, often only after the recommendation of a relative. Indeed, his nominations for promotion were rejected more than once. However, he gained experience as a junior officer in a series of naval engagements between 1778 and 1805, and he served aboard several British vessels ranging from fireships to the *Victory*. By 1805, at the age of fifty-two, he had become a vice-admiral commanding the Halifax station; his direct orders led to the *Leopard-Chesapeake* controversy with the United States two years later. In 1808 he commanded the Red Squadron stationed off the coast of Portugal, and it was in that capacity that he provided a unique and valuable service for England and the Duke of Wellington, a service that has been unrecognized for almost two centuries.

In December 1808, while Sir Arthur Wellesley was in London awaiting the verdict of the Court of Inquiry about the humiliating Convention of Cintra, George Berkeley was receiving his instructions from William W. Pole, Secretary for the Lords of the Admiralty, and Wellesley's brother. Berkeley was ordered to protect British trade and retain his squadron in the Tagus River with five months' stores "in constant readiness to put to sea at a moments warning."[2] Because Napoleon had entered Spain in November 1808 with one hundred thousand reinforcements to complete the subjugation of the Peninsula, Berkeley received additional instructions before he left London. He was to complete arrangements to evacuate the British army or "afford them every assistance in his power." He was also to send supplies up the Tagus and employ gunboats to support army operations.[3]

Sailing aboard the *Conqueror*, Berkeley soon reached the Tagus where he shifted his flag to the *Ganges*. There he found arrangements almost completed for the evacuation of Lisbon and the destruction of the remaining supplies. It seemed none too soon. Sir John Moore's army had marched from Lisbon to support Spanish forces, and it was now in headlong retreat across northwestern Spain, pursued by the French. Although Moore's army was forced to evacuate La Coruna, the immediate threat to Lisbon had subsided. Accordingly, Berkeley turned to the more mundane duties of securing provisions for his squadron which had become dependent on army depots.[4]

Despite the unpromising situation, the British cabinet resolved to carry on the struggle in the Peninsula. Soon convoys from

England laden with reinforcements and supplies sailed for the Tagus. The British army began to increase in size and resources, and a formidable Portuguese army was again in existence. Flatboats were built for operations on the Portuguese rivers while cavalry transports began to reach the Tagus.[5]

On 5 April 1809, Berkeley received a letter from the Admiralty announcing the appointment of Wellesley to command the British army in Lisbon. He was expected to "comply with any requisitions from...Wellesley to convey transports with troops" to and from the Tagus.[6] His orders were clear, but Berkeley had no means to comply with the order except by "employing such vessels which [might] arrive here under orders for no particular service."[7] Captains putting in at Lisbon thus found their transports or warships commandeered by Berkeley to carry reinforcements and provisions or to escort convoys. Indeed, Berkeley admitted that without such "infringements" he could not carry out his duties. His need for vessels was further complicated by need to supply vessels for the transport of fresh fruit, by the American embargo which resulted in the trans-shipment of American cargoes from Lisbon, and by the needs of the army for its forthcoming offensive.[8] Hence, it was only by disobeying Admiralty orders that he was able to fulfill his mission. He subsequently appealed for additional vessels from England or for the authority to requisition ships that called in the Tagus.

On 25 April, Berkeley received his first letter from the recently arrived and newly appointed commander in chief of the army, Sir Arthur Wellesley, and thus began a relationship of mutual trust and dependence that continued through times of triumph and adversity. Wellesley's first request was for transports to convey eleven hundred horses to Lisbon. A week later there was another appeal to transport more horses and mules, followed by requests for troop and ordnance vessels.[9]

At the end of April, when Wellesley was satisfied with his own army of 18,500 men and the reactivated Portuguese army of almost eleven thousand troops, he began to concentrate his forces at Coimbra, 120 miles away. His goal was to attack Marshal Nicolas Soult's army occupying Oporto. Berkeley's ships conveyed some of the British infantry, cavalry, and artillery to Figueira da Foz, near Coimbra. Reinforcements en route from England were intercepted and directed to Figueira; warships were also dispatched northward to Oporto to cooperate with Wellesley.[10]

After a surprise crossing of the Douro River on 12 May, the British seized the French hospitals and baggage, and drove Soult's army out of Portugal, inflicting five thousand casualties. At the same time, intelligence reached Lisbon that another French army under Marshal Claude Victor was advancing from Alcantara into southern Portugal with almost twenty-three thousand men. Wellesley had left General Alexander Mackenzie with five thousand British and seven thousand Portuguese troops in the area, but this force could hardly oppose the French advance. Berkeley acted at once to reinforce MacKenzie. He reported to the Admiralty on 19 May, "I have made every arrangement in my power with General Mackenzie to defend the passes on the Tagus, and.... I have landed the greatest part of the marines of the squadron to occupy the citadel and take the necessary guards."[11] The admiral also dispatched a flotilla of armed transports up the Tagus to Vila Nova; ten flatboats manned by sailors moved up the river over the shoals, while heavy cannon were transported up the Tagus for use on the right bank, opposite the fords.[12] The French threat soon subsided as he began to ferry elements of Wellesley's victorious army back to Lisbon.[13] Berkeley's good judgment and decisive actions in these operations reflected the attributes of a first rate commander that did not go unnoticed by Wellesley or the Admiralty.

Because Wellesley had decided to attack Victor's army and advance on Madrid, the summer months were busy for Berkeley. He made arrangements to transport army provisions up the Tagus as far as Abrantes, eighty miles from Lisbon. At the same time, he struggled to meet Wellesley's demand for ships to transport men, horses, and provisions to half a dozen destinations.[14] From his pivotal position in the Tagus, he had an opportunity to influence or regulate much of the sea traffic. In most instances, when ships put in at Lisbon, he altered their orders to benefit Wellesley's operations. Warships were delayed until convoys could be organized, and the sailing of empty transports was postponed until the sick, prisoners, or forces in transit could be boarded.

In July 1809, Wellesley began his march up the Tagus with an army of almost twenty-three thousand men. After joining a Spanish force of some thirty thousand troops under General Gregorio de la Cuesta, they marched on Madrid to confront the armies of King Joseph. Berkeley hastened the advance by ferrying part of the army and its supplies up the Tagus in flatboats.[15] The allied army marched eastward to Talavera where it fought a bloody battle with the French. Realizing that he would see little enemy action while posted in the Tagus, Berkeley seemed to derive special satisfaction from the army's success. He described the battle to the Admiralty as a "most decisive victory,... as wonderful as it [was] glorious."[16]

The autumn was equally as demanding for Berkeley and the Red Squadron. At times criticized by the Admiralty for delays in convoy sailings, he illustrated his predicament by sending a list of the transports in the harbor, explaining that there were forty-five sail in the harbor loading or unloading and forty more awaiting naval escort.[17] This was not an isolated occurrence. Early in October he postponed the sailing of fifty transports for want of an escort. His own squadron was so widely dispersed on urgent missions, escorting convoys, resupplying Spanish forces, carrying urgent official dispatches or general officers to England, pursuing French privateers, or sailing to confront the illusionary Toulon squadron, that only his flagship remained in the Tagus. On occasion, even the flagship had to be dispatched, forcing Berkeley to transfer his flag to a transport in the Tagus and live in a house near the harbor.[18]

On 26 October 1809, Wellesley, now Viscount Wellington, wrote a confidential letter to Berkeley regarding his future strategy for the defense of Portugal. It was a daring proposal--the construction of the Lines of Torres Vedras. He wrote, "In case the enemy should make a serious attack upon Portugal, his [the French] objective, as well as that of the allies, would be the possession of Lisbon."[19] If the city fell, the only alternative would be evacuation, so Berkeley's commitment to Wellington's plan was essential. Wellington sought Berkeley's advice about defenses and a possible embarkation site if the major French army advanced along the north bank of the Tagus. Similarly, he requested a list of ships in the Tagus, their moorings and tonnage, and periodic updates, in the event the British army had to evacuate.[20]

By November Wellington had begun construction on a series of lines across the peninsula north of Lisbon. Extrapolating on the plans of Portuguese Major Jose Neves Costa, these fortifications were built on the prominent terrain controlling the approaches to Lisbon. The work was undertaken by tens of thousands of Portuguese soldiers and peasants. When the French reached the Lines in October 1810, they found 247 guns in 126 redoubts defended by forty thousand militia and regulars and Wellington's entire field army of over sixty thousand men.[21]

The year 1810 began with uncertainty for Berkeley and his squadron. To eliminate "alarm and confusion" among the populace of Lisbon, Wellington ordered that the regimental baggage be loaded aboard the transports in the Tagus to coincide with the embarkation of reinforcements.[22] Berkeley's situation was further complicated when the French overran Spanish forces and drove them to the walls of Cadiz, thereby severing land contact with Lisbon and threatening the south bank of the Tagus with invasion. The Admiralty quickly sent a convoy to Cadiz where it remained until French intentions were clearer. These arrangements, however, reduced the number of transports, and placed Wellington's army in a vulnerable position.[23]

Before the end of January, Wellington, noting the progress on the defense of Portugal, became convinced that the French could not force his evacuation. He wrote, "If I can bring thirty thousand effective British troops into the field, I will fight a good battle for ... Portugal. If the Portuguese do their duty, I shall have enough [troops] to maintain it, if they do not, nothing Great Britain can afford can save the country."[24] His opinion was received with some skepticism in London, and Lord Liverpool, Secretary for War and the Colonies, expressed reservations; by remaining too long in Portugal the safety of the army would be jeopardized. To reassure the government, Wellington asked for warships and enough transports to evacuate both the British and Portuguese armies if necessary.[25] This did not ease Liverpool's fears, and he cautioned,

"I should apprise you, however, that a very considerable degree of alarm exists in this country respecting the safety of the British army in Portugal." Liverpool suggested that Wellington withdraw "a little too soon," rather than expose his army to defeat or capture.[26] Wellington ignored the suggestion and continued to request additional transports in both his private and public correspondence.[27] He turned to Berkeley for support. "I hope the government will send us more ships," he wrote, "I think they are mistaken in sending large ships to Cadiz."[28] Three weeks later, Berkeley was still receiving requests for transports to embark army stores. "I am very anxious to have everything in such a state that we may either go or stay," dependent upon the invading force.[29]

On 6 and 7 March 1810, Liverpool announced to Wellington that forty-nine thousand tons of transports designated for the evacuation of the Allied army were either in Lisbon harbor or en route to the Tagus. Liverpool admitted that in the event of an actual evacuation the vessels might be crowded, but "without endangering the safety of the vessels, or the health of the men."[30] Despite these arrangements and Wellington's assurances, Liverpool's anxieties continued. To Berkeley, Wellington explained his predicament. "The government are terrible afraid that I shall get them, and myself, in a scrape. But what can be expected from men who are beaten in the House of Commons three times a week? A great deal might be done now, if there existed in England less party, and more public sentiment."[31]

The nagging controversy continued until the end of April when George III learned of Wellington's strategy for the Peninsula; he was so impressed with Wellington's understanding of the situation, he insisted that the Duke's strategy be carried out, "unfettered by any instructions which might embarrass him in the execution of his general plan of operations."[32] Nevertheless, Liverpool remained apprehensive. He asked Berkeley to forward complete returns of transports and other ships in the Tagus for use in a general evacuation. Wellington also wrote to Berkeley, "I am perfectly satisfied with all the arrangements for the embarkation of the army. Everything is prepared for us either to go or to stay." This letter was possibly prompted by knowledge that command at

Plymouth had been offered to Berkeley. The admiral's decision, however, was never in doubt. He rejected the position, convinced that his command in the Tagus was the most important assignment of his career.[33]

By the end of May, Berkeley began to cooperate directly with Wellington's army. He stationed vessels at Figueira da Foz to transport the sick to Lisbon. Small boats crossed the bar at Figueira and conveyed men and provisions up the Mondego to the army, posted near the Portuguese frontier.[34] Simultaneously, he took a personal role in the defenses around Lisbon. On several occasions he met with Wellington's chief engineer to discuss the location and form of the telegraph stations on the Lines of Torres Vedras. They initially agreed that naval personnel from the squadron would operate the stations. However, when Wellington was unable to provide supplemental rations and funding for them without authorization from London, they were withdrawn and replaced by army engineers. A frustrated Wellington complained to Berkeley, "It is certainly a great disadvantage to us to be deprived of this assistance which it is now, and will be, I hope, more, in your power to give us in various ways."[35] Fortunately, when the French army reached the Lines of Torres Vedras, naval personnel returned to the telegraph stations.[36]

During the summer, with the French army before the city of Ciudad Rodrigo, and Portugal facing imminent invasion, Berkeley retained the transports in the Tagus, ready for a possible evacuation. Even when he received requests to transport grain from Ireland, he refused, suggesting instead the use of empty victualers and storeships.[37] As conditions deteriorated along the Portuguese frontier in August, Wellington complained that he had hoped to transfer troops and transports from Cadiz to Lisbon, "knowing how important it will be to have a very strong fleet in the Tagus when we shall embark."[38] This was a curious comment from a man who expected to remain in Portugal, but it incited Berkeley to an even more rigorous timetable for the arrival of transports.

When the French army, under the command of Marshal André Masséna, began the actual invasion of Portugal in mid-September,

Berkeley was an anxious observer as Wellington withdrew 120 miles to the Serra de Bussaco. On 27 September, Wellington won an important tactical and psychological victory at Bussaco, but the French army outflanked his position, forcing a retreat to Lisbon and the Lines of Torres Vedras.[39] Berkeley wanted to send ships immediately to Oporto with reinforcements and supplies for a diversionary effort,[40] but Wellington reassured him, "I have very little doubt of being able to hold this country against the force which has attacked it."[41] Berkeley's anxieties remained as he wrote to the Admiralty on 4 October, "The whole French force is to the southward and against Lord Wellington." Perplexed by Masséna's "movements and conduct" which he regarded as "extraordinary," he retained every troop ship in harbor since "the crisis is so near at hand."[42] By the second week of October, Wellington's army had reached its last refuge, the Lines of Torres Vedras, and Berkeley received a terse letter from Wellington: "None of the transports ought to be sent home under the present circumstances."[43]

As Masséna's army swept toward Lisbon, the imposing Lines of Torres Vedras resolutely resisted it on 12 October. After several probes of the Lines, Masséna, convinced that the positions were impregnable, requested reinforcements and a siege train from Paris.[44] Berkeley, meanwhile, moved his gunboats up the Tagus to Alhandra to cover Wellington's right flank and the nearby island. He also occupied the large island of Lyceria, with its stockyard and corn depot.[45]

As the French army dug in before the Lines of Torres Vedras, both Wellington and Berkeley were concerned about a possible enemy attack from south of the Tagus. In such a case, Wellington believed "the defense of the country ought not to be attempted." He felt the attack was improbable but he cautioned Berkeley, "My wish therefore is to have embarked in the ships every body who cannot walk down to the beach." Berkeley took precautionary measures and sent the supply vessels out of the Tagus, leaving only the troop transports in the harbor.[46]

To retain control of the Tagus, Berkeley's gunboat squadron was reinforced near Salvaterra, and the flotilla off Alhandra was concentrated to cover Wellington's flank. After six days of inactivity caused by heavy rains and gales, the French began the construction of a bridge. Wellington, aware of the French activity, asked Berkeley to collect boats and to build several bridges across the lower Tagus in order to move troops to the south bank to observe the enemy and prevent their crossing.[47] Within three days Berkeley's seamen were moving General Henry Fane's cavalry and a brigade of Portuguese infantry across the Tagus. Since it was impossible to transport a heavy 24-pounder beyond Salvaterra, Berkeley also sent a naval crew to Fane with Congreve rockets to fire on French bridge construction sites and depots at Barquinha and Santarém.[48]

The French retained their positions until the night of 14 November when they began a withdrawal. Early the next morning, Wellington and Berkeley learned by telegraph that the French had withdrawn all along the line and were in full retreat toward Santarém. General Rowland Hill, on the right flank, advanced from Alhandra and a flotilla of gunboats proceeded up the Tagus to cover his flank. Admiral Thomas Williams collected boats and pontoons on the Tagus to transfer the army to the south bank if necessary. When the bridges were completed across the river, Hill's entire division crossed to the south bank at Valada to join Fane's troops.[49] Wellington soon realized that the French intended to halt at Santarém so he deployed his troops around the town and both armies remained in these positions for almost four months.[50]

November was a month of controversy for Berkeley. Serving both Wellington and the Admiralty, he was forced to support one and defy the other. In each case he supported Wellington. When refugees flooded into Lisbon and food supplies were reduced to a "few days [rations] for the consumption of the army and the inhabitants,"[51] he ordered twelve transports and an escort to sail for Algiers to pick up grain, ignoring the administrative struggle raging in England over the use and payment for the vessels.[52] There was also disagreement about the disposition of French prisoners. On Wellington's instructions, Berkeley had been sending them to England since April 1809. The Admiralty requested that the practice be halted. When the Portuguese government was unable to accommodate the massive numbers that accumulated in

Lisbon, Berkeley resumed sending healthy prisoners to England, despite the Admiralty's admonitions, until more than fifty thousand were in Great Britain.[53]

In military terms, the most contentious issue was Wellington's request for the kind of aid which he felt would "most materially contribute to the success of His Majesty's arms, and to the salvation of the country."[54] He requested a brigade of seamen and a battalion of marines from the squadron to serve at Fort St. Julian for training to replace the regular infantry on the Lines of Torres Vedras. Berkeley already had four hundred seamen and several hundred marines on the south side of the Tagus with Fane, while two hundred marines were on the flatboats, armed with howitzers, carronades, and two 12-pounders. The remainder of the gunboats and launches, also manned by men from the squadron, were near Alhandra. Beyond the Lines, detachments of seamen and marines manned batteries at Calhandriz and on the island of Lyceria. Despite these commitments, Berkeley did not hesitate to send the five hundred seamen and the five hundred marines requested by Wellington.[55]

Learning of his decision, the Admiralty instructed him to recall the squadron personnel but promised to send out a reserve marine battalion to replace it. In an extreme emergency, however, he could employ them "whenever you may judge it necessary." A month later, when Wellington learned of the arrival of French reinforcements, he requested one marine battalion to replace the 88th Foot in Lisbon and the reserve marine battalion to occupy Loures; he also wanted a unit of marines from the squadron to garrison St. Julian and other forts on the Tagus.[56] Berkeley reacted within the week. Rather than recall the squadron personnel as the Admiralty had ordered, he landed more marines. He defended himself, declaring,

> The necessity of adding every strength to the army under Lord Wellington has been so apparent that I have concentrated the battalion of ships marines in the citadel and the town of Lisbon...and I have garrisoned the Fort of St. Julian at the entrance of the harbor, and the fortified

positions of the army near it with 250 marines...and the marine artillery company.[57]

In January and February 1811 there was little contact between the opposing armies as they continued to entrench their positions. During the lull, Berkeley sent out ships from his squadron to cruise off Cape St. Vincent. Nevertheless, transports continued to plow the waters between the Tagus and Britain, bringing reinforcements, horses, ordnance, and provisions.[58]

As the cold and wet months of winter passed, the British army continued to grow in strength and confidence, largely because of the Royal Navy, while the abandoned yet defiant French army starved at Santarém. Finally, on 5 March, after 108 days of suffering and deprivation, the French withdrawal began. An elated Berkeley wrote to the Admiralty, "I have great pleasure in informing their Lordships of the evacuation of the strong post which the enemy possessed at Santarém and that our army are now advancing in pursuit."[59] Berkeley ordered the flatboats up the Tagus as far as Abrantes while transports sailed up the Portuguese coast to support Wellington's advancing army. Incoming vessels from England were routed directly to Figueira to land their cargoes.[60] In a letter dated 19 March he boasted to the Admiralty, "His Lordship is still in pursuit of the enemy [with]...the very men whom they boasted of driving into the sea."[61]

With the advance of the army, Wellington's demands for reinforcements, cavalry, and supplies intensified. Yet on 20 March as he neared the Spanish frontier, Wellington sent his historic and long awaited dispatch to Berkeley which announced victory. All the transports, except those for three thousand infantry and three hundred horses, were to be sent back to England.[62] Success had finally come and it was nowhere more heartily celebrated than by Berkeley, his squadron, and the nameless souls who had navigated the hazardous seas from London to the Tagus. Berkeley began making arrangements at once to send home all but his original squadron and the transports that Wellington had requested. A week later he carried out a two-stage withdrawal; the first convoys included 146 transports and supply ships, while the remaining 108 vessels sailed soon thereafter.[63]

On 30 March 1811, Berkeley sent what might be considered his victory dispatch when he wrote to the Admiralty, "I have great satisfaction in informing their Lordships that...by the time this reaches England, there will not be Frenchmen in Portugal except as prisoners." The import of this victory had far-reaching implications. Not only were the French expelled from Portugal, but the Tagus was open, Lisbon was safe, the independence of Portugal preserved, and Wellington's army had repulsed its most serious threat.[64]

The war did not end for Berkeley with the expulsion of Masséna's army. He continued to collaborate with Wellington for another sixteen months. Only at sunset on 7 July 1812 did he resign command of his squadron; he sailed down the Tagus and set a course for home. His flag was struck on 22 July at Spithead and he was rowed ashore for the last time. He was named admiral and then retired from active duty, having served his country in the finest tradition of the Royal Navy.[65]

Although eclipsed by more famous and familiar commanders, as Nelson, Jervis, Collingwood, and Cochrane, Berkeley's efforts were crucial for the final success of British arms. His clear judgment and courageous support of Wellington may not have been remembered or recorded, but it proved to be the winning combination in the Peninsula and assured the safety of England's only army. It was also a classic example of how success can be derived from the combined use of sea and land power. With a less decisive and resourceful naval commander in the Tagus, Wellington's army might have been crushed. With such a scenario, the history of Napoleon and perhaps Europe might have been drastically altered.

Notes

The author would like to acknowledge the International Department of the Calouste Gulbenkian Foundation of Lisbon for the support received to complete research in Portugal and England.

[1]John W. Fortescue, *A History of the British Army*, 13 vols. (London: Macmillan, 1899-1930), vol. VII; Charles Oman, *A History of the Peninsular War*, 7 vols. (Oxford: Clarendon Press, 1902-30), vols. III, IV. In the two most comprehensive multi-volume studies of the Peninsular War, Fortescue mentions Berkeley three times in passing; Oman ignores him completely.

[2]Great Britain, Public Record Office, Admiralty (hereafter PRO, Adm.) 2/1367, Pole to Berkeley, 16 December 1808.

[3]PRO, Adm. 2/1367, Pole to Berkeley, 24 December 1808.

[4]Ibid., 1/341, No. 11, Berkeley to Pole, 16 January 1809.

[5]Ibid., 1/341, No. 184, Berkeley to Pole, 14 February 1809; Adm. 2/1367, Pole to Berkeley, 24 December 1808.

[6]Pro, Adm. 2/1368, Pole to Berkeley, 5 April 1809.

[7]Ibid., 1/341, No. 89, Berkeley to Pole, 25 April 1809.

[8]Ibid., 1/341, No. 101, Berkeley to Pole, 26 April 1809.

[9]Arthur Wellesley, Duke of Wellington, *The Dispatches of Field Marshal the Duke of Wellington During his Various Campaigns in India, Denmark, Portugal, Spain, the Low Countries, and France, from 1799 to 1818*, 13 vols. (London: J. Murray, 1834-39) (hereafter *Wellington's Dispatches*), Wellington to Berkeley, 25 April, 2 May 1809, IV: 271, 292-93.

[10]*Wellington's Dispatches*, Wellington to Berkeley, 7 May 1809, IV: 306-307.

[11]PRO, Adm. 1/341, No. 113, Berkeley to Pole, 19 May 1809.

[12]Ibid., Adm. 1/341, no number, Berkeley to Pole, 23 May 1809.

[13]Ibid., Adm. 1/341, No. 114, Berkeley to Pole, 17, 23 May 1809.

[14]*Wellington's Dispatches*, Wellington to Berkeley, 7, 15, 21, 30 June, 5 July 1809, IV: 392, 426, 441, 476, 495.

[15]PRO, Adm. 1/341, No. 156, Berkeley to Pole, 7 July 1809.

[16]Ibid., Adm. 1/341, No. 174, Berkeley to Pole, 29 July 1809.

[17]Ibid., Adm. 1/341, No. 194, Berkeley to Pole, 11 September 1809.

[18]Ibid., Adm. 1/341, Nos. 214, 120, 145, 242, 248, Berkeley to Pole, 9 October, 1, 25 June 1809; Berkeley to Croker, 14, 25 November 1809.

[19]*Wellington's Dispatches*, Wellington to Berkeley, 26 October 1809, V: 244-45.

[20]Ibid., Wellington to Berkeley, 26 October, 26 November 1809, V, 244-46, 307-8.

[21]Donald D. Horward, "British Seapower and Its Influence Upon the Peninsular War (1808-1814)," *Naval War College Review* 31 (Fall 1978): 59-60.

[22]*Wellington's Dispatches*, Wellington to Berkeley, 24 January, 5 February 1810, V: 442-43, 515-16.

[23]PRO, Adm. 1/342, Nos. 287, 288, Berkeley to Croker, 6, 10 February 1810.

[24]*Wellington's Dispatches*, Wellington to Villers, 14 January 1810, V: 424-26.

[25]Ibid., Wellington to Liverpool, 1 March 1810, V: 538-42. See also PRO, War Office, W.O. 6/50, Liverpool to Wellington, 3 January 1810.

[26]Arthur Wellesley, Duke of Wellington, *Supplementary Despatches and Memoranda of Field Marshal Arthur Wellesley, Duke of Wellington*, 15 vols. (London: J. Murray, 1858-72) (hereafter *Supplementary Despatches*), Liverpool to Wellington, 13 March 1810, VI: 493-94.

[27]*Wellington's Dispatches*, Wellington to Berkeley, 2 March 1810, V: 542-43.

[28]Ibid., Wellington to Berkeley, 6, 8 March 1810, V: 547-48, 554-55.

[29]Ibid., Wellington to Berkeley, 21 March 1810, V: 583-84.

[30]PRO, W.O., 6/50, Liverpool to Wellington, 2 April 1810.

[31]*Wellington's Dispatches*, Wellington to Berkeley, 7 April 1810, VI: 21-22.

[32]*Supplementary Despatches*, Taylor to Liverpool, 21 April, VI: 515; Liverpool to Wellington, 25 April 1810, VI: 515.

[33]Berkeley reported that 109 vessels were available in the Tagus. PRO, Adm. 1/342, No. 355, Berkeley to Croker, 11 May 1810; Liverpool to Wellington, 5 May 1810; *Wellington's Dispatches*, Wellington to Berkeley, 8 May 1910, VI: 98; PRO, Adm. 1/342, No. 355, Berkeley to Croker, 11 May 1810.

[34]*Wellington's Dispatches*, Wellington to Berkeley, 23 May 1810, VI: 144.

[35]Ibid., Wellington to Berkeley, 9 September 1810, VI: 421.

[36]Ibid., Wellington to Berkeley, 24 June, 1810, VI: 196-97; Wellington to Liverpool, 19 October 1810, VI: 526-27.

[37]PRO, Adm. 1/342, Stuart to Berkeley, 1 July 1810; Berkeley to Stuart, 4 July 1810.

[38]*Wellington's Dispatches*, Wellington to Berkeley, 9 August 1810, VI: 336.

[39]Jean Jacques Pelet, *The French Campaign in Portugal, 1810-1811: An Account by Jean Jacques Pelet*, ed., annot., trans. by Donald D. Horward (Minneapolis: University of Minnesota Press, 1973), 157-221.

[40]PRO, Adm. 1/342, No. 467, Berkeley to Croker, 4 October 1810.

[41]*Wellington's Dispatches*, Wellington to Berkeley, 3 October 1810, VI: 482.

[42]PRO, Adm. 1/342, No. 467, Berkeley to Croker, 4 October 1810.

[43]*Wellington's Dispatches*, Wellington to Berkeley, 8 October 1810, VI: 497.

[44]Pelet, *French Campaign in Portugal*, 222-24.

[45]*Wellington's Dispatches*, Wellington to Berkeley, 16, 26 October 1810, VI: 512-14, 541.

[46]Ibid., Wellington to Berkeley, 17, 19 October 1810, VI: 518-20, 522-23.

[47]PRO, Adm. 1/342, No. 473, Berkeley to Croker, 14 October 1810; *Wellington's Dispatches*, Wellington to Berkeley, 29 October, 1 November 1810, VI: 561-63, 570.

[48]*Wellington's Despatches*, Wellington to Berkeley, 1, 3, 16 November 1810, VI: 570, 577, 591-92. Wellington had little confidence in the success of the rockets, but the government ordered him to employ them.

[49]PRO, Adm. 1/342, Nos. 509, 510, Berkeley to Croker, 20, 22 November 1809.

[50]Pelet, *French Campaign in Portugal*, 279-326.

[51]PRO, Adm. 1/342, Stuart to Berkeley, 23 November 1810.

[52]*Wellington's Dispatches*, Wellington to Berkeley, 4 November 1810, VI: 584-85; PRO, Adm. 1/342, Stuart to Berkeley, 5, 22, 23 November 1810; Transportation Board to Berkeley, 18 September 1810; Sampayo to Berkeley, 2, 21 November 1810; Berkeley to Stuart, 22 November 1810; No. 513, Berkeley to Croker, 26 November 1810; Poulden to Sampayo, 20 November 1810. See also Wellington Papers, MSS, University of Southampton (hereafter Wellington Papers), 1/319, Sampayo to Stuart, 2, 21 November 1810.

[53]Wellington Papers, 1/320, Admiralty to Croker, 6 December 1810; PRO, Adm. 1/342-3, Nos. 505, 537, 71, Berkeley to Croker, 16 November, 20 December 1810, 8 March 1811; *Wellington's Dispatches*, Wellington to Berkeley, 4 November 1810, VI: 585.

[54]*Wellington's Despatches*, Wellington to Berkeley, 10 November 1810, VI: 601-602.

[55]PRO, Adm. 1/342, Nos. 498, 504, Berkeley to Croker, 10, 16 November 1810.

[56]PRO, Adm. 2/1371, Croker to Berkeley, 24 November 1810; PRO, Adm. 1/342, Nos. 536, 545, Berkeley to Croker, 20, 27 December 1810; *Wellington's Dispatches*, 25 December 1810, VII: 70-71. The Reserve marine battalion included many foreign troops and were often regarded as less reliable.

[57]*Wellington's Dispatches*, Wellington to Berkeley, 25 December 1810, VII: 70-71.

[58]PRO, Adm. 2/1371, Croker to Berkeley, 26 December 1810, 17 January 1811; PRO, Adm. 1/343, Nos. 20, 59, Berkeley to Croker, 8 January, 2 March 1811.

[59]PRO, Adm. 1/343, No. 70, Berkeley to Croker, 8 March 1811.

[60]Ibid., Adm. 1/343, Nos. 76, 79, Berkeley to Croker, 15, 16 March 1811.

[61]Ibid., Adm. 1/343, No. 81, Berkeley to Croker, 19 March 1811.

[62]*Wellington's Dispatches*, Wellington to Berkeley, 20 March 1811, VII: 379; PRO, Adm. 1/343, No. 91, Berkeley to Croker, 23 March 1811.

[63]PRO, Adm. 1/343, No. 99, Berkeley to Croker, 28 March 1811.

[64]Ibid., Adm. 1/343, No. 101, Berkeley to Croker, 30 March 1811.

[65]Ibid., Adm. 1/344, No. 169, Berkeley to Croker, 22 July 1812; Martin to Croker, 9 July 1812.

Joint Operations During the Detroit-Lake Erie Campaign, 1813

David Curtis Skaggs

Successful combined and joint operations are a rarity in early American military annals. Between the battle at Yorktown in 1781 and the landing at Vera Cruz in 1847 the most successful such operation occurred in the Detroit-Lake Erie campaign of 1813. By examining the support by Major General William Henry Harrison of Commodore Oliver Hazard Perry's manning problems before the famous naval engagement off Put-in-Bay as well as Perry's support of Harrison's land operations in the final weeks of the campaign, Professor Skaggs demonstrates that close harmony between the two men resulted in a most successful joint operation leading to strategic victory in the Old Northwest.

Americans entered the War of 1812 with considerable optimism for an easy victory and the conquest of Canada. This optimism dissipated very quickly as the realities of British-Canadian-Indian resistance became apparent and the necessity for naval control of the Great Lakes became obvious. Even before General William Hull's ignominious surrender of Detroit, Governor William Henry Harrison of the Indiana Territory conveyed his apprehensions about that outpost's survivability in case of a combined British-Indian attack. "Commanding as they do the Navigation of the lake," wrote Harrison, "the British can with the utmost facility transfer their force from one side to the other, meet our Detachments and overpower them if they are small." But Governor Harrison's perceptive analysis of Hull's predicament did not result in a recommendation to gain control of the lakes. Rather, he urged that "a Considerable covering Army" be sent via "a laborious and circuitous march through a Swampy Country" either to aid Hull or to reclaim his post should it be lost.[1]

Shortly after the surrender of Detroit, Harrison become a major general and charged with the command of the western frontier operations. He began by moving a "Considerable covering Army" towards Detroit in a campaign reminiscent of his mentor, Anthony Wayne. An advance detachment of Kentucky and Indiana troops commanded by Brigadier General James Winchester advanced to Fort Wayne and down the Maumee River to the rapids of that stream located west of modern Toledo. There Harrison expected them to stop. Instead, Winchester's forces marched northward to modern Monroe, Michigan, where they were badly beaten in what is known as the River Raisin Massacre on 22 January 1813. Subsequently, Harrison's main party arrived at the Maumee rapids and began building Fort Meigs, an outpost he expected to become a major supply and assembly point for the sixty mile advance to Detroit. Harrison faced severe logistical problems. His major source of troops and most useful line of advance was from central Kentucky up the Wabash valley to Fort Wayne. His best source of food and forage came from "the highly cultivated part of Ohio between the Miami and Scioto Rivers." From this area, supplies could be forwarded up "Hull's trace" from Cincinnati to Fort Meigs through the infamous Black Swamp south of the Maumee. Additional troops and supplies might come from Pittsburgh through the villages of Erie and Cleveland, but this was a lightly populated region and subject to naval raiding parties sent from the Canadian shore.[2]

Thus American supply lines were either highly vulnerable to British offensive action or located along the laborious overland route from the Ohio valley. Harrison's situation could be considerably improved by the establishment of logistical lines free from such attacks over more convenient water routes. Logistics was the key to both Canadian and American success in this war and the key to logistics was control of the lakes.[3] In the winter of 1812-13, these strategic considerations finally accorded the lakes some of their due in the military calculus. As Acting Secretary of War James Monroe concluded: "It is obvious that the Command of Lake Erie would dissipate many difficulties which now weigh heavy on us."[4]

Monroe sought to alter the balance of naval power on Lake Erie via a *coup de main* against British ships icebound in the Amherstburg, Ontario, harbor at the mouth of the Detroit River. Harrison agreed to the proposal, but warned that its success depended upon the freezing of the Detroit River to allow his troops and artillery to cross to the Canadian shore. Actually, Harrison's over-the-ice campaign was more elaborate than the raid to burn the vessels proposed by Monroe. Harrison planned to seize Amherstburg and adjoining Fort Malden as part of his Detroit campaign. Two factors precluded the operation's success, however. First was Winchester's defeat at the River Raisin which cost Harrison the most likely force to make such a move. Second was the failure of the river to freeze solid enough for the troops to cross.[5] It was becoming increasingly obvious that Harrison's Northwest Army could not be rendered operationally and logistically secure without a coordination of army and navy assets unprecedented in the annals of American history.

In actuality, a spirit of interservice cooperation was the intention of Secretary of the Navy Paul Hamilton early in the war. For instance, on 20 June 1812, Hamilton notified his various port commanders (including O. H. Perry at Newport, Rhode Island) that in order "to provide against a deficiency in the munitions of war" commissary officers of the army and naval commanders should cover the deficiencies of the other service as far as possible. Hamilton added that "a mutual interchange of civilities of every kind, will become, in the event of exigencies arising, an obvious duty of patriotism."[6] Master Commandant Perry took this cooperation order to heart. On 6 February 1813 he reported to Secretary Jones that a 32-pound cannon from a wrecked gunboat had been given to the commanding officer of Fort Wolcott.[7]

In 1813 the infusion of new leadership into the two service departments--John Armstrong as secretary of war, and William Jones as secretary of the navy--reinvigorated the American efforts to coordinate the actions of both services. Armstrong had long advocated "naval ascendancy" as the key to American strategy. He and Jones drafted a memorandum of understanding containing, as Jones wrote, "joint regulations of the War and Navy Departments, for the government of their respective commanders, when acting in concert." Jones notified Perry that he would cooperate with Harrison "in support of general movements on the Lakes. In those opportunities you should avail yourself of the advantages derived from communicating such information as may be useful, and of inviting from him their reciprocation." Communicated to Perry in July, these regulations guided both Harrison and Perry in their conduct of the campaign. In fact, it can be argued that Perry and Harrison were the only two commanders in the United States military establishment that fully complied with the intent of this memorandum.[8]

Thus, when Perry was ordered to assume command of the Lake Erie squadron being constructed at Presque Isle (Erie), Pennsylvania, he took with him not only officers and sailors from his Newport detachment, but also an attitude of army-navy cooperation that would hold him in good stead in the following months. In many respects, the degree of cooperation Perry received from the army was greater than he received from his own superior, Captain Isaac Chauncey, who commanded all naval forces on the Great Lakes from his headquarters at Sacket's Harbor, New York, on Lake Ontario.

Captain Abraham R. Wooley, the army's ordnance officer at Fort Fayette, Pennsylvania, furnished Perry with several supply items unavailable for purchase in Pittsburgh. Perry was particularly impressed with Wooley's "ardent desire to promote the service either of the Army or of the Navy." General Henry Dearborn placed two hundred of his soldiers under Perry's temporary command to help in the movement of vessels from near Buffalo to Erie. In addition, Dearborn sent Captain Henry B. Brevoort, Second U.S. Infantry, who was well acquainted with Lake Erie and environs, on special assignment to Perry's squadron as a temporary marine officer. Unfortunately, the secretary of war's authorization that the two hundred soldiers remain with the Lake Erie fleet arrived after they returned to Dearborn's command. Perry also secured temporary manpower from militiamen stationed in Erie, Pennsylvania.[9]

Interservice cooperation was not a one-way street. When the

army was evacuating Fort Erie, Perry complied with General Dearborn's request that his boats transport baggage across the Niagara river.[10]

But by far the most important testimony of Perry's support of joint operations before his famous encounter near Put-in-Bay came when he left Erie to join Captain Chauncey and General Dearborn in the attack on Fort George at the mouth of the Niagara River on 27 May 1813. Chauncey and Dearborn rejected Perry's suggestion for the difficult amphibious attack, but he was able to convince Colonels Alexander Macomb and Winfield Scott, both future commanding generals of the army, to negotiate a compromise. A combined army-navy assault involving several hundred boats containing troops, horses, and artillery landed on the Canadian shore. Supported by Perry's schooners, whose gunfire kept the British from attacking the landing force, Colonel Scott's troops successfully secured a beachhead. Perry's shelling routed the fort's defenders, set fire to its log buildings, and allowed Scott's troops to take the post with few losses. One of the more interesting aspects of this operation was General Dearborn's order placing those army forces participating in the landing under the direction of the navy, thereby anticipating by about a century and a quarter amphibious command doctrine that evolved before World War II. Perry supervised the disembarkation of the army troops. Few amphibious operations of modern warfare exhibit more professionalism and cooperation in the pursuit of joint operational objectives than this hastily organized enterprise.[11]

This experience contributed to Perry's idea of joint operations when he returned to Lake Erie. There he found intraservice disputes more adversely affecting cooperation than interservice feuding. The rivalries and conflicting pressures confronting Perry and Harrison, on the one hand, and Chauncey and Secretary of War Armstrong, on the other, contributed significantly to the delay in Lake Erie operations for 1813.

When he learned of plans to gain control of the lake before waging offensive operations upon the Detroit frontier, Harrison agreed to wait. However, he refused to depend wholly upon Perry's victory for determining his operations. He expanded his Fort Meigs post throughout the spring and summer and prepared boats and pirogues at the headwaters of the Maumee to transport supplies to the rapids and to provided logistical support to a ground movement northward along the lake coast. Such a march could be accomplished without the requirement for a naval victory and the small boats might give Harrison a chance to attack Fort Malden on the Canadian side of the Detroit River even without a victory by Perry's fleet.[12]

Harrison's proposal for a land operation received a cool reception elsewhere. In Frankfort, Kentucky, Governor Isaac Shelby, a distinguished veteran of the Revolution, cautioned: "...without the command of Lake Erie it is evident to every reflecting mind, that no descent upon Upper Canada by way of Malden, can promise a favourable issue, and it will be madness in the extreme to put to hazard the best blood and interest of our country to attempt it until that event is effected."[13]

Perry's great problem was not Harrison, but rather Commodore Chauncey who, from Perry's point of view, refused to provide him enough officers and sailors to man his flotilla. In a famous exchange, Perry called the few men that came to him in July "a motley set, blacks, Soldiers and boys." To which Chauncey replied: "I have yet to learn that the colour of the skin or cut and trimmings of the coat, can effect a man's qualifications or usefulness."[14]

From 19 June until 1 August, Perry's fleet lay within the bar at Presque Isle. Though at the time the American flotilla was far superior in numbers of vessels and weight of metal to that commanded by Captain R. H. Barclay, it would be nearly equalled if the British completed a vessel then under construction at Fort Malden. Perry claimed that insufficient crews were the only thing keeping him from action. When British General Henry Procter began a campaign against army outposts at Fort Stephenson (modern Fremont, Ohio) and Fort Meigs, General Harrison pleaded for Perry to help him by relieving his garrisons and cutting off the enemy's line of retreat. It is obvious that the general was well aware of the tactical and strategic importance of naval operations upon the eventual success of his campaign. Harrison assumed that "no exertion will be omitted" on Perry's "part to give the crisis an issue of Profit & Glory to the arms of our Country."[15]

This Perry could not accomplish. The commodore's shortage of officers and men, a problem which he communicated to Harrison, became common knowledge in Washington, much to the embarrassment of Secretary Jones. Perry found his lack of manpower mortifying; Jones found his candor with Harrison notorious, tending "to embolden the enemy," to "depress the confidence of the officers and men" already in the commodore's squadron, and to constitute a justification on Perry's part for "declining to meet the Enemy."[16]

Such insults from both his immediate commander and his service secretary offended Perry's sense of honor, and raised the level of bitterness in this intraservice encounter to the point where Perry tendered his resignation. Fortunately, Chauncey ignored this request and on 30 July, Perry received sixty officers and men including Master Commandant Jesse D. Elliott, who took command of the second brig in Perry's squadron. Although his fleet was still only half manned and officered, within a few days Perry was over the bar and into the lake, seeking combat with Barclay.

At Harrison's suggestion, the young commodore anchored his flotilla at Put-in-Bay in the Bass Islands, north of Sandusky Bay, and within sight of Harrison's forces which were congregating near the mouth of the Portage River (modern Port Clinton, Ohio). From this point onward the degree of cooperation between the army and navy commanders was extraordinary. Perry called Harrison "the only *officer* we have of enterprise."[17]

Harrison immediately set out to provision the fleet and to find sailors, or at least potential sailors, within his troops. Eventually the Northwest Army provided 130 officers and men for the naval squadron. Traditionally we have assumed most of these men were Kentuckians who had been boatmen on the western rivers and who knew something about sailing. An investigation by Park Ranger Gerard Altoff of the Perry's Victory and International Peace Memorial at Put-in-Bay argues for the addition of the Pennsylvania militia, 9th, 17th, 19th, 24th, 27th, and 28th U.S. Infantry, 1st U.S. Light Dragoons, and 2nd U.S. Artillery to the list of units from which soldiers came. It seems reasonable to credit the army with roughly 40 percent of Perry's sailors and marines during the battle. Included were several officers, as well as one doctor, W.T. Taliaffero.[18]

Since it appeared for five weeks in August and early September that Barclay would not fight the Americans, the general and the commodore planned an amphibious advance on Fort Malden. Therefore, Perry and senior army officers held a joint meeting to coordinate the transport of troops to the Canadian shore.[19]

Before this effort could be launched, Barclay led his squadron into the lake and, on 10 September 1813, Perry achieved immortality with one of the most significant naval victories in United States history. Barclay's fleet was captured, Lake Erie came into American possession, and an invasion of Canada became practicable. "We have met the enemy," Perry wrote the general after the battle, "and they are ours." One of the Kentuckians aboard the *Caledonia* later recalled that Perry reputedly said "that had it not been for the [army] volunteers the battle would have been lost."[20]

While the cooperation in the victory off Put-in-Bay was significant, it is Perry's continued support of Harrison in the following weeks that truly distinguishes him in the annals of joint operations. The commodore refused to rest on his laurels. He desired to carry out the double meeting of the last word in his famous after action report. "[T]hey are ours" meant more than merely his fleet had achieved its objective. Perry seemed determined for "ours" to mean that Procter's land forces and Indian allies were now at the joint mercy of the combined forces of the two commanders.

Perry directed these efforts in five different areas: (1) providing logistical support to the army, especially in carrying supplies from Erie and Cleveland to the Detroit area; (2) transporting most of Harrison's army from the mouth of the Portage in preparation for an attack on Fort Malden that never took place because of Procter's withdrawal; (3) chasing a few light British vessels out of Lake St. Clair and using his ships to provide additional logistical support to Harrison's advance along the southern shore of that lake toward the mouth of the Thames River; (4) sailing his lightest gunboats up that river as far as they could go to provide firepower and logistical support to Harrison's movement; and (5) transporting elements of Harrison's army from the Detroit frontier to the Niagara frontier to augment the campaign in that theater.[21]

General Harrison's invasion of Canada was a two-pronged advance. Colonel Richard M. Johnson's Kentucky mounted riflemen rode north from Fort Meigs to Detroit while Harrison's main forces (both regulars and Kentucky militia) sailed across the lake to attack Fort Malden. Although Harrison had no legal command authority over Perry, the two cooperated in a unity of effort that made such authority unnecessary. Each of the service commanders brought the expertise of his service to the decision making process. Harrison, for instance, desired to cross the lake in one movement with his troops packed into the ships of Perry's fleet. Perry objected to this arrangement both on the grounds of its effect upon his ability to navigate his vessels, and also because of the potentially disastrous results in bad weather or in the event of an opposed landing. In effect, Perry became Harrison's advisor on naval problems and a member of his general staff (a term which in those days referred to flag officers).

At Perry's suggestion, the Northwest Army moved in stages with the bulk of troops transported in bateaux that had been specially made for this purpose. Built in Cleveland under the direction of Major Thomas Jessup, the landing craft were strongly built, undecked boats "high sided & very competent to the navigation of the Lake, particularly between the chains of islands & the West Shore." For example, Brigadier General Duncan McArthur moved his brigade from Fort Meigs to "the General Rendezvous" at the mouth of the Portage, via his own small boats that had transported troops and supplies down the Maumee earlier and via Perry's vessels and the bateaux sent to support these efforts.[22]

On 20-22 September, Perry transferred Harrison's forces to Put-in-Bay from the Portage mouth. When the weather cleared on 25-26 September, he moved them all to Middle Sister Island, about fifteen miles from the landing point below Malden. Middle Sister is little more than an islet of five or six acres on which some 3,500 soldiers were now assembled. On the 26th Perry took Harrison, his generals, and his ubiquitous chief engineer, Major Eleazer D. Wood, on a reconnaissance toward Fort Malden. For the invasion of a hostile enemy shore, Wood drafted and Harrison signed one of the most detailed set of orders heretofore written for an American military operation. His force consisted of at least 3,500 soldiers, Perry's sixteen vessels, and eighty to ninety landing craft. The Americans brought virtually no experience in such an expedition, except that which Perry had learned at Fort George a few months earlier. As Captain Robert McAfee of the Kentucky militia wrote, Harrison's army was "composed emphatically of raw troops,... whose officers in general were but little superior in the knowledge of tactics to the men they commanded." The minute orders tried to cover all expected exigencies, and Harrison's initial landing parties were led by some of his most experienced officers.[23]

The detail expressed in Harrison's general orders was amplified in those issued by his subordinates. For instance, Brigadier General McArthur ordered "each man... [to] take with him fire arms[,] one blankit[,] and provisions only[.] [T]he baggage[,] knapsacks[,] and camp equipage[,] and sick of each regt[.] will be left in tents pitched for that purpose." For the attack, General McArthur combined several companies across regiments and then ordered his regiments to form their companies into "platoones of equal size and strength." He required each man to be "supplied with two spare flints an[d] his box filed with Cartridges."[24] To achieve the desired objective of unit equality, Colonel John Miller of the 19th U.S. Infantry made a number of detachments and attachments from and to several of his companies. Miller divided the resulting new companies into two platoons each with one platoon commanded by the second ranking officer of the company.[25] These arrangements allowed each bateau to receive an equal number of troops.

Harrison's instructions to Perry were much less specific. Learning from the Fort George experience, Harrison directed that the "arrangement for landing the troops will be made entirely under the direction of an officer of the navy whom Commodore Perry has been so obliging as to offer for that purpose. The debarkation of the troops will be covered by the cannon of the vessels." Given that latitude, Perry assigned each warship to tow several of the bateaux during the movement from Put-in-Bay to Malden. Perry commanded the fire support from his warships while his second-in-command, Captain Jesse D. Elliott of the *Niagara*, managed "the debarkation of the troops."[26]

On 27 September, Perry's armada arrived off the Canadian coast and the warships moored about a quarter of a mile from the shore with springs on their cables in order to provide fire support. The first to disembark were the dismounted dragoons of Lieutenant Colonel James V. Ball and the riflemen commanded by Colonel James Simrall. Their instructions were to move "with the utmost celerity consistent with the preservation of good order, and... seize the most favorable position for annoying the enemy, and covering the debarkation of the troops of the line." The chief engineer, Major Wood, who seemed to enjoy changing branch insignia as often as possible, commanded a battalion of artillery which went in with the lead regiments with six pieces "mounted in bateaux--one gun in each--loaded and matches lighted--so," said the young West Point graduate, "that I could have fought as well by sea as by land." Captain Elliot's direction of the landings received "cordial assistance... from every officer of the Army, and [this combined with] his own exertion and judgement, [was sufficient to insure that] that service was most admirably performed."[27] A few shots from Perry's guns scared off the few Indians observing the landings, and Malden and Detroit fell without any British-Indian opposition.

Perry's Order Book is filled with directives to his subordinates to support later ground operations. For example, he ordered the commanders of two of his smaller vessels to "proceed to Portage River ... & take on board as many of Col. [Thomas] Smith's Regt. of Riflemen, as [your vessels] will carry & land them at Malden. If you are not able to bring them all, you will return to the River for the remainder." To Lieutenant Thomas Holdup, he wrote "You will keep as near the Army with the Caledonia as possible, that you may be enabled to deliver them provisions as called for." As he told Secretary Jones, "every possible exertion will be made by the officers & men under my command to assist the advance of the

Army, and it affords me great pleasure... to say, that the utmost harmony prevails between the Army & Navy." General Harrison confirmed this in a letter to Secretary Armstrong which noted that "Commodore Perry gives me every assistance in his power."[28]

Moreover, General Harrison appears to have consulted Perry on joint operational matters and to have heeded the commodore's technical advice not to follow a contemplated plan of advance. The pursuit of Procter could have gone either along the Thames or via water to a point on the north shore of Lake Erie where a short march would have placed the Americans in a blocking position capable of capturing the whole of Procter's force. Taking Perry's advice to use the land option rather than risk the fall storms on the lake, Harrison marched his combined columns east from Sandwich (now Windsor, Ontario) with Perry's vessels supporting him.[29]

On top of all this, Perry attached himself to Harrison's staff and fought at the Battle of the Thames, 5 October 1813, where American militiamen and a few regulars soundly beat the British-Canadian-Indian forces in a battle that for all intents and purposes eliminated any British threat to the Lake Erie basin. In this battle, Perry again showed his determination to make sure the enemy were truly "ours." Harrison lauded "my gallant friend Commodore Perry" in an after action despatch that noted how the appearance on the battlefield "of the brave Commodore cheered and animated every breast."

But it was not merely Perry's conduct on the battlefield that Harrison admired. He paid particular attention to how the commodore brought the army's baggage from Detroit protected by three gunboats, and how those gunboats covered the army's passage over the Thames and its tributaries.[30] Seldom have commanders from different services cooperated with each other in a closer and more efficient manner. One only has to compare the strategic impact of their campaign with those of Chauncey and Dearborn and note the difference in operational success given the same directions from Washington for interservice cooperation.

All this conformed to Secretary Jones' strategic plan announced in a letter of early July:

The consequences of cutting off,... [the enemy's] Naval force on Erie, would be incalculably great, and probably would be immediately followed by his abandonment of Malden, and the upper country; which would immediately induce the desertion of the Savages, and release a great part of General Harrison's army, which might immediately have been transported, by our fleet, to Niagara and produce a decisive blow in that quarter also.[31]

That no "decisive blow" was delivered on the Niagara peninsula is not really the point.

There is one more ingredient in the success of these joint operations that needs to be addressed--the personal cooperation between the senior service commanders. General Jacob L. Devers, well known for his command of the Sixth Army Group in Europe during World War II, had considerable experience in joint and combined operations. He labeled this aspect the "first concern" of such commanders. "A complete understanding of this problem is the very essence of successful leadership," Devers told the U.S. Army Command and General Staff College in 1947. The commander must know the "peculiarities of his principal subordinates" and he "must thoroughly understand the methods of approach which will secure from them their unstinted loyalty and cooperation in every endeavor."[32]

Harrison's relationship with Perry in this regard is a model worthy of considerable admiration. Harrison and Perry achieved that unity of effort that is critical to the attainment of the national objective. They overcame interservice ambitions and operational considerations to focus on a common goal. Undoubtedly some of this was because of Perry's deference to Harrison's rank, age, experience, and professionalism. Harrison exhibited a degree of respect toward his junior colleague in his laudatory reports regarding the commodore's actions. Possibly the best example of this mutual admiration came when Harrison allowed Perry to co-sign a proclamation establishing government in the recently conquered area of Upper Canada. Such an honor was indeed

133

singular, especially since none of the general officers under Harrison's command signed the document.[33]

It is probably to the great relief of Canada that neither President James Madison, Secretary of War John Armstrong, nor Secretary of the Navy William Jones were so impressed by this dynamic duo that they kept it together on the Lake Ontario front in 1814. What would have happened in that year had Harrison replaced James Wilkinson and Perry been elevated to Chauncey's post with the latter given the saltwater command awarded Perry? But that brings us into the "what-ifs" that historians are wont to discourage.

Notes

[1]W.H. Harrison to secretary of war, 12 August 1812, in Clarence Edwin Carter, ed., *The Territorial Papers of the United States, Volume VIII, The Territory of Indiana, 1810-1816* (Washington, 1939), 191.

[2]Ibid., 192.

[3]See Harrison to secretary of war, 13 October, 15 November, and 12 December 1812, and James Monroe to Harrison, 26 December 1812, in Logan Esarey, ed., *Messages and Letters of William Henry Harrison* 2 vols., (Indianapolis, 1922), II: 177-78, 212-16, 240-44, 265-69. An excellent appraisal of the strategic and logistical interconnections to relative naval control of the lakes is in John Sloane to General Thomas Worthington, 3 February 1813, in Richard C. Knopf, ed., *Document Transcriptions of the War of 1813 in the Northwest*, 10 vols. (Columbus, 1962), III: 166-68. For extended discussions of the logistics, see Brereton Greenhous, "A Note on Western Logistics in the War of 1812," *Military Affairs*, 34 (1970): 41-44; C.P. Stacey, "Another Look at the Battle of Lake Erie," *Canadian Historical Review*, 39 (1958): 41-51; Stacey, "Naval Power on the Lakes, 1812-1814," in Philip P. Mason, ed., *After Tippecanoe: Some Aspects of the War of 1812* (East Lansing, 1963), 49-59; Jeffrey Kimball, "The Fog and Friction of Frontier War: The Role of Logistics in American Offensive Failure During the War of 1812," *Old Northwest*, 5 (Winter 1979-80): 323-44. On the importance of the Lakes, see General John Armstrong to secretary of war, 2 January 1813, in Armstrong's *Notices of the War of 1812* (New York, 1836), 235.

[4]Monroe to Harrison, 17 January 1813, in Esarey, ed., *Messages and Letters*, II: 313.

[5]Monroe to Harrison, 26 December 1812, Harrison to Monroe, 4 and 6 January, 11 February 1813, in ibid., 267-68, 295-98, 301-306, 357.

[6]Circular, Hamilton to Selected Officers, 20 June 1812, in William S. Dudley, ed., *The Naval War of 1812: A Documentary History, Vol I, 1812* (Washington, DC, 1985), 140.

[7]Perry to Jones, 6 February 1813, Library of Congress Photocopies, Institute for Great Lakes Research, Bowling Green State University, Perrysburg, Ohio. (Hereafter IGLR.)

[8]Armstrong to secretary of war, 2 January 1812, in John Armstrong, *Notices of the War of 1812*, I: 235; John Jones to Perry, 10 July 1813, IGLR. A copy of the memorandum enclosed with this letter has yet to be discovered by this researcher, but when found it should show the degree of interservice cooperation expected by Armstrong and Jones. The biographies of Jones and Armstrong fail to discuss in detail the joint operational attitudes of the two secretaries. See C. Edward Skeen, *John Armstrong, Jr., 1758-1843: A Biography* (Syracuse, 1981) and Edward K. Eckert, "William Jones and the Role of the Secretary of the Navy in the War of 1812" (Ph.D. diss., University of Florida, 1969), 102-09. Clearly, Secretary Jones did not suggest interservice cooperation to mean naval subordination to the ground commanders. See Jones to Madison, February 1813, Madison Papers, Library of Congress, Washington, D.C. (Hereafter LC).

[9]Perry to Jones, 21 April, 25 June, 10 August, 1813, Jones to Perry, 3 July 1813, IGLR; Dearborn to Perry, 6 July 1813, Perry Papers, Box 1, William L. Clements Library, University of Michigan, Ann Arbor, Michigan (hereafter WLCL).

[10]Dearborn to Perry, 8 June 1813, Perry Papers, Box 1, WLCL.

[11]Alexander Slidell Mackenzie, *The Life of Commodore Oliver Hazard Perry*, 2 vols. (New York, 1843), I: 136-48; Richard Dillon, *We Have Met the Enemy--Oliver Hazard Perry: Wilderness Commodore* (New York, 1978), 86-93.

[12]Monroe to Harrison, 17 January 1813, Harrison to John Armstrong, 17, 27, and 28 March 1813, in Esarey, ed., *Messages and Letters*, II: 312-14, 387-93, 404, 406.

[13]Shelby to Harrison, 20 March 1813, in ibid., 393.

[14]Perry to Jones, 17 July 1813, Perry to Chauncey, 27 July 1813, Chauncey to Perry, 30 July 1813, IGLR.

[15]Adjutant Levi Hukill to Perry, 23 June 1813, Adjutant A.H. Holmes to Perry, 23 July 1813, Perry Papers, WLCL. See also Mackenzie, *Perry*, 164-66.

[16]Perry to Jones, 15, 19, and 28 July 1813, Jones to Perry, 10 July, 18 August 1813, IGLR; Harrison to Armstrong, 6 July 1813, in Esarey, ed. *Messages and Letters*, II: 484.

[17]Harrison to Perry, 5 July 1813, Perry to Christopher R. Perry (his father), 9 August 1813, Perry Papers, Box 1, WLCL; Perry to Jones, 4 August 1813, IGLR. Harrison first suggested the importance of Put-in-Bay in a letter to Armstrong, 25 April 1813, in Esarey, ed. *Messages and Letters*, II: 427.

[18]Harrison to Perry, 5 July, 25 August, 4 September 1813, Perry Papers, Box 1, WLCL; W. W. Dobbins, *History of the Battle of Lake Erie*, 2nd ed. (Erie, PA, 1913),

61; Gerard T. Altoff, "Deep Water Sailors–Shallow Water Soldiers" (Unpublished paper at Perry's Victory and International Peace Memorial, Put-in-Bay, Ohio, c. 1986). A copy of this paper has been graciously supplied by Park Ranger Altoff.

[19]Harrison to Perry, 4 September 1813, Perry Papers, Box 2, WLCL; Harrison to Duncan McArthur, 28 August 1983, Duncan McArthur Papers, LC microfilm in Ohio Historical Society (hereafter OHS), Columbus, reel 1. That the army intended to move on Detroit regardless of the outcome of the naval battle is found in McArthur to his wife Nancy, 12 September 1813 (McArthur did not yet know the results of the naval battle), ibid. "Whatever may be the result of the action betwixt the fleets; I expect to leave this [place–Fort Meigs] with the most of the troops." See also Harrison to McArthur, 1 September 1813, Perry to McArthur, 31 August 1813, ibid. By early August there was considerable impatience over the lack of movement by the Northwest Army. One correspondent wrote that Harrison was "lying on his Oars" and Colonel John Miller felt it was "high time we had commensed to act on the offensive, in this quarter if anything is to be done this season." William Barbee to General Thomas Worthington, 21 July 1813, Miller to Worthington, 14 August 1813, in Knopf, ed., *Document Transcriptions*, III: 216, 217.

[20]John Norris to A.T. Goodman, 7 April 1869, in Knopf, ed., *Document Transcriptions*, X: 158. On the condition of many of the soldiers serving as marines, see George Stockton to Perry, 5 September 1813, Perry Papers, Box 2, WLCL. Even after Perry's victory, soldiers continued to man the fleet. See for instance, Perry to his commanding officers, 21 September 1813, Order Book, Lake Erie, 1813, Perry Papers, Box 1, WLCL; Harrison to Armstrong, 22 September 1813, Esarey, ed. *Messages and Letters*, II: 545.

[21]For the most part, the standard secondary sources relating to this campaign pay little attention to the degree of cooperation between Harrison and Perry in the operations after Put-in-Bay. See for instance, Dillon, *We Have Met the Enemy*, 164-77; Mason, ed., *After Tippecanoe*; Theodore Roosevelt, *The Naval War of 1812* (New York, 1903), 254-81; A.T. Mahan, *Sea Power in its Relations to the War of 1812*, 2 vols.˙(Boston, 1905), II: 99-104; Beverley W. Bond, Jr., "William Henry Harrison and the War of 1812," *Mississippi Valley Historical Review*, 13 (March 1927): 499-516; Freeman Cleaves, *Old Tippecanoe: William Henry Harrison and His Time* (New York, 1939), 188-205; Alec R. Gilpin, *The War of 1812 in the Old Northwest* (East Lansing, 1958); Reginald Horsman, *The War of 1812* (New York, 1969), 107-15; John K. Mahon, *The War of 1812* (Gainesville, 1972), 177-87; John Sugden, *Tecumseh's Last Stand* (Norman, 1985); John K. Mahon, "Oliver Hazard Perry: Savior of the Northwest," in James C. Bradford, ed., *Command under Sail: Makers of the American Naval Tradition, 1775-1850* (Annapolis, 1985), 126-46; J.C.A. Stagg, *Mr. Madison's War: Politics, Diplomacy, and Warfare in the Early American Republic, 1783-1830* (Princeton, 1983), 322-31; George F.G. Stanley, *The War of*

1812: Land Operations, Canadian War Museum Historical Publication No. 18 ([Ottawa], 1983), 208-14.

[22]Harrison to McArthur, 15, 17, and 20 September 1813, Duncan McArthur Papers, LC on microfilm in OHS; Perry to Jones, 20 September 1813, IGLR; Thomas J. Jessup to John Armstrong, 1 July, 1 August 1813, in Knopf, ed., *Document Transcriptions*, VII: 2, 51; Jesup N. Couch to Worthington, 5 July 1813, ibid., III: 212.

[23]Harrison's order is in Esarey, ed., *Messages and Letters*, II: 546-50; John Armstrong to Harrison, 8 May 1813, in Knopf, ed., *Document Transcriptions*, VIII: 148; Eleazer D. Wood, *Journal of the Northwestern Campaign of 1812-1813*, ed. Robert B. Boehm and Randall L. Buchman (Defiance, OH, 1975), 31; Dillon, *We Have Met the Enemy*, 165-67; Gilpin, *War of 1812 in the Old Northwest*, 218-19. That Major Wood probably drafted the landing order is seen by the fact that a first draft in his handwriting exists. See George W. Cullum, *Campaigns of the War of 1812-15, against Great Britain* (New York, 1879), 118n.

[24]Brigade orders, Middle Sister Island, 24 and 25 September 1813, Duncan McArthur Papers, LC, microfilm OHS, reel 2.

[25]Regimental Orders, Middle Sister Island, 25 September 1813, ibid.

[26]Harrison's General Orders, 27 September 1813, in Esarey, ed., *Messages and Letters*, II: 547; Perry to Officers in charge of Prime Vessels, 22 September 1813, Order Book, Lake Erie, 1813, Perry Papers, Box 1, WLCL; Perry to Jones, [c. 27] September 1813, IGLR; Dobbins, *Battle of Lake Erie*, 136-37.

[27]Harrison's General Orders, 27 September 1813, in Esarey, ed., *Messages and Letters*, II: 546-50; Wood, *Journal*, 31. Wood participated as a cavalryman in the pursuit of General Procter and died on 17 September 1814 commanding a regiment of infantry.

[28]Order Book, Lake Erie, 1813, passim for September and October, quotes from Perry to J.E. McDonald, and to Thomas Holdup, 2 October 1813, Perry Papers, Box 1, WLCL; Perry to Jones, 20 September, 7 October, 1813, IGLR; Harrison to Armstrong, 22 September and 9 October 1813, in Esarey, ed., *Messages and Letters*, II: 545, 559, 570; Perry to Jones, [c. 27] September 1813, [c. 1 October], 23 October 1813, IGLR.

[29]Perry to Harrison, 18 August 1817, in Esarey, ed., *Messages and Letters*, II: 559; Robert B. McAfee, *History of the Late War in the Western Country* (Bowling Green, OH, 1919; originally published 1816), 411-12.

[30]Harrison to Armstrong, 9 October 1813, in Esarey, ed. *Messages and Letters*, II: 559, 561, 564.

[31]Jones to Perry, 3 July 1813, IGLR. This directive was confirmed in Armstrong to Harrison, 22 September 1813, in Esarey, ed. *Messages and Letters*, II: 544-45.

[32]Jacob K. Devers, "Major Problems Confronting a Theater Commander in Combined Operations," *Military Review*, 27 (October 1947): 14. For current doctrine

on joint operations see *FM 100-5, Operations* (Washington, 1986), 175-76; *AFSC Pub 1, Joint Staff Officers Guide* (Fort McNair, D.C., 1983).

[33]A Proclamation, 17 October 1813, in Esarey, ed. *Messages and Letters*, II: 581.

Commodore Isaac Chauncey and U.S. Joint Operations on Lake Ontario, 1813-14

William S. Dudley

Naval and military historians increasingly are turning their attention to the history of the interaction between the armed forces to reveal the dynamics of inter-service or "joint" operations. In order to discover the origins of modern American joint operations, Dr. Dudley here examines the nature of the collaboration of Commodore Isaac Chauncey's naval forces with the troops under Generals Henry Dearborn and James Wilkinson in 1813, and with Winfield Scott and Jacob Brown in 1814.

The War of 1812 on the northern lakes is a good example of the proposition that sea power is not an end in itself. It is a means to an end, that is, the victory of the combined forces of government acting in concert. The Madison administration chose to seize key points in Canada as bargaining chips in its struggle with Great Britain.[1] What little planning went into the 1812 campaign neglected the navy as an element of military operations, and there was no joint planning at all. Early army operations failed in part because, without an American squadron, British naval forces controlled the lakes. As the initial strategy of northern expansion collapsed, it became clear that Canada's conquest was not, as Thomas Jefferson put it, "a mere matter of marching."[2] President Madison soon admitted "... we were mislead by a reliance authorized by [General William Hull] on [the expedition] securing to us the command of the lakes."[3]

At the time of the declaration of war, the U.S. Navy had only the brig *Oneida* on Lake Ontario whose mission was the enforcement of the embargo laws. News of the declaration of war forced her commander, Lieutenant Melancthon Woolsey, to focus his concern on the vulnerability of American merchant schooners in the St. Lawrence River. Taking advantage of the truce between Governor General Prevost and Major General Dearborn, Woolsey moved those vessels to the relative safety of Sacket's Harbor where they became an important part of the navy's force on Lake Ontario.

When President Madison realized that General Hull's invasion of Canada at Detroit had collapsed, he ordered the construction of a dominant naval force on the lakes. To supervise that construction Secretary of the Navy Paul Hamilton selected Captain Isaac Chauncey. A skilled mariner and strict disciplinarian, Chauncey had supervised the building of the frigate *President*, serving in her under Captain Thomas Truxton during the Quasi-War with France. Commodore Edward Preble had appointed him flag captain of the *Constitution* in the Mediterranean during the attacks on Tripoli. Since Chauncey had been commandant of the New York Navy Yard from 1808 to 1812, he was knowledgeable of its resources and personnel. When Hamilton appointed Chauncey to command the lakes, he chose the officer best able to exploit the talents of the New York ship-building community.

During September and October 1812 Chauncey moved hundreds of men and immense quantities of supplies from New York City to Sacket's Harbor, and contracted with shipbuilder Henry Eckford to build warships with local timber. The schooners brought to Sacket's Harbor were modified, armed, and renamed. On 5 November 1812 Chauncey reported the following schooners ready for war service: the *Governor Tomkins*, *Hamilton*, *Fair American*, *Ontario*, *Conquest*, *Growler*, *Pert*, *Scourge*, and *Julia*. At the same time, Eckford and his men were building the corvette *Madison*, 24 guns, that was launched on 26 November after forty-five days of feverish work. Meanwhile, on 8 November Chauncey raided the Kingston naval base of the Provincial Marine with the *Oneida* and six schooners and succeeded in damaging the *Royal George*. From that day until the end of May 1813 the U.S. squadron had control of Lake Ontario. During the winter of 1812-1813, Eckford completed the fitting out of the *Madison*, commenced work on a 28-gun ship, and completed a small despatch schooner that was launched on 6 April as the *Lady of the Lake*.[4]

In early 1813 Madison's cabinet revised its war plans. Secretary of War John Armstrong and Secretary of State James Monroe argued for the capture of Kingston and the destruction of its naval base.[5] After cutting communications with Quebec and Montreal, the Americans would then attack York and Fort George. If successful, all Upper Canada would fall, virtually ending the war. The strategy was sound, but during consultations in March 1813 General Dearborn altered the basic plan and substituted Kingston for the secondary objectives of York and Fort George. Surprisingly, Armstrong did not object. This was a fatal error, and the Lake Ontario campaign never recovered.[6]

Naval cooperation was crucial to successful military ventures around the lake, and the new secretary of the navy, William Jones, framed Chauncey's orders within that context. He was to cooperate with the military when called upon, but the timing, nature, and extent of cooperation were Chauncey's decisions. Jones allowed Chauncey broad discretion in executing his instructions. When operating with the army, he was to facilitate its movements, to protect its communications, and to give battle when the British squadron threatened. When not directly engaged in supporting the army, Chauncey was to use his force to bring the enemy to battle or to blockade the opposing squadron in port so that it could neither hamper U.S. Army operations nor support those of the British army.[7]

Joint operations dominated Lake Ontario during 1813. For the most part Chauncey accepted this role with good will and energetic execution. His squadron's readiness at Sacket's Harbor in April 1813 gave him the initiative, but his main difficulty lay in bringing to action his opponent, Captain Sir James Yeo. The British commodore had arrived but recently with a Royal Navy contingent. With time, his squadron became roughly equal to Chauncey's, but Yeo, like his Yankee counterpart, was cautious and preferred to husband his strength until the perfect moment. There was also an element of restraint in Yeo's orders. The Admiralty specified a defensive role for the Royal Navy contingent under his command.

141

He was not to undertake any operations "without the full concurrence and approbation of [Prevost] or of the commanders of the forces employed under him."[8]

American preparations for amphibious operations began well in advance. Lieutenant Van de Vinter, the army's deputy quartermaster general in the north, reported to Secretary Armstrong in early April that he had purchased at Sacket's Harbor and Oswego a large number of vessels which he estimated could transport some 8,050 men, plus supplies. When added to the troop-carrying capacity of Chauncey's squadron estimated at two thousand, the total number of troops could reach ten thousand.[9]

Commodore Chauncey wrote often to his military colleagues to apprise them of his preparations and assure them of his eagerness to cooperate. On 10 April he informed General Dearborn that he was pleased to have General Pike in the expedition and that all would be ready by the time the ice thawed. To General Morgan Lewis at Niagara he stated on the same day that he hoped soon to be able "to act together against the common enemy." He advised him "to be prepared with all the force he can collect and with all the boats at Buffalo, Black Rock and Niagara." He also wanted him to spread some misinformation about an intended attack against Kingston "keeping the enemy ignorant of our real object." As the time for embarkation approached, Chauncey ordered the commanding officers of his thirteen vessels to be ready to receive the troops on board, adding: "Sirs, the success of this enterprize will very much depend upon a good understanding between the Naval and Military officers. You will use your best exertions to cultivate harmony and frown upon the first symptoms of a contrary disposition." He issued detailed squadron sailing and signal instructions on 23 April.[10]

The squadron made a false start in threatening weather at Dearborn's insistence and against Chauncey's better judgement. By the time they were out of harbor, a southeasterly gale churned the lake. Had they not turned back, they would have suffered more damage than they did and perhaps loss of life. As it was, the crew and some six hundred soldiers crowded on board the *Madison* were cold and wet. Anxious to get on with the operation lest the men become ill, Chauncey's general order of 26 April shows he had worked out an orderly disembarkation plan with his army counterparts.[11]

The landing at York began at 8:00 A.M. on 27 April. The wind disrupted the precise landing plans of the leading boats whose troops landed one half mile to leeward of their assigned positions and thus beyond protection of their naval covering batteries. However, the ships adjusted their positions and soon they had the British shore batteries under fire allowing the troops to begin their advance. Although the army lost Zebulon Pike in this battle, it captured and destroyed naval and military supplies, and burned a ship on the stocks. The sailors took possession of the *Duke of Gloucester* and sailed her back to Sacket's Harbor. There were minor naval casualties in the battle. Eight were wounded and four were killed, while six ships were affected by loss of personnel. The army suffered more severely.[12]

Though the re-embarkation of the troops went smoothly, the vessels were unable to leave immediately because of adverse winds. This caused Chauncey some concern because of fatigue and illness among the men. On 30 April Chauncey ordered Lieutenant Joseph Smith in the *Asp* to take the wounded and stores and, with the schooner transport *Gold-Hunter*, deliver these to Sacket's Harbor. The *Gold-Hunter* carried the body of General Pike, killed in the explosion of the enemy's magazine.[13]

Between the battles of York and Fort George, Chauncey sailed to Fort Niagara to land troops. He returned to Sacket's Harbor to obtain provisions and reinforcements and to check the safety of his naval base. Before departing Niagara, Chauncey ordered the schooners *Governor Tomkins* and *Conquest* "to watch the movements of the Enemy and to give every assistance to the Army in any operations against the Enemy where they may require your assistance." He informed them of an enemy sloop at Forty Mile Creek, near Burlington, and of a quantity of stores in that vicinity. Later, the vessels embarked about one hundred soldiers under Captain Willoughby Morgan, Twelfth Regiment, and raided the site at the head of the lake, capturing provisions and burning a building, which the British called "Government House."[14]

Once at Sacket's Harbor, Chauncey sent four schooners to Oswego to collect stores from New York City. He expected Colonel Winfield Scott to move his forces by boat from Oswego along the south shore of the lake. He embarked Colonel John Chandler and about a thousand men and sent three schooners ahead to Niagara. He waited until the return of the schooners *Fair American* and *Pert* before he departed, so as not to leave the base without naval protection. During this time, a detachment of sailors arrived from Boston, freeing an additional fifty seamen for Perry on Lake Erie.[15]

The commodore departed Sacket's Harbor on 22 May with 350 of General Macomb's regiment on board, but did not arrive at Niagara until the twenty-fifth because of light winds. Commodore Perry hastened from Erie to help in the Niagara attack. On the evening of 26 May Perry and Chauncey reconnoitered the shoreline and placed buoys as stations for the landing vessels. About forty-five hundred troops embarked at 3:00 A.M. the next day. Generals Dearborn and Lewis joined Chauncey on board his flagship. With no wind, the flotilla got underway using their sweeps. Chauncey stationed his schooners in position to shell the British batteries near the Lighthouse and Two Mile Creek. The *Hamilton, Asp*, and *Scourge* anchored opposite the landing beach "to scour the woods and plain" of enemy defenders. The troops landed in barges by brigades, with Colonel Scott leading the way. Once out of their barges, they had to climb a ten-foot cliff before gaining a footing on level ground. It was here that the covering fire of the schooners had good effect. Chauncey gave Perry high marks for his energetic direction of the support vessels' gunfire and for arranging and superintending the landing of the troops. The enemy batteries were quickly silenced, and the fort was in American hands by noon. The rising wind and surf threatened the safety of the squadron near the beach, so Chauncey ordered the vessels to move into the mouth of the Niagara River. The British withdrawal had begun and would not halt until they had drawn their troops back to the head of the lake.[16]

Chauncey's military counterparts praised his work. After the York landing, General Pike's aide, Lieutenant Fraser, wrote:

It is proper to state in this place the masterly cooperation of Commodore Chauncey and the naval squadron under his command. He sent his schooners mounting heavy metal to cover the landing, and kept up so well directed and incessant a fire of grape on the woods as to effectually cover our right flank and afforded us great facility in forming our platoons besides producing utmost consternation among the Indians.

From General Dearborn came the accolade, "Commodore Chauncey had made the most judicious arrangements for silencing the enemy's batteries near the point of landing. The army is under the greatest obligations to the naval commander for his cooperation in all its important movements, and especially in its operations this day."[17]

At Fort George, American naval and military cooperation had enjoyed a second successful landing. The basic plan put into effect at York was used again but with more troops. Even from the British point of view, it was an impressive show. As General Vincent put it,

the morning being exceedingly hazy neither [the enemy's] means nor his intention could be ascertained until the mist, clearing away at intervals, the enemy's fleet, consisting of 14 or 15 vessels was discovered underway standing towards the lighthouse in an extended line of more than two miles, covering from 90 to 100 large boats and scows, each containing an average of 50 or 60 men.... Being on the spot and seeing that the force under my command was opposed with tenfold numbers, who were rapidly advancing under cover of their shipping and batteries, from which our positions were immediately seen and exposed to a tremendous fire of shot and shells. I decided on retiring my little force to a position I hoped would be less assailable.[18]

Yeo's joint thrust at Sacket's Harbor on 29 May announced that the Royal Navy had arrived. Chauncey, justifiably, had long worried about the safety of the base, as would any commander, and this attack made him very hesitant to venture out.[19] He dashed back from Fort George where he had been supporting Dearborn's troops and remained in port until 21 July. The commodore's future flagship, the *General Pike*, had been partially burned by the defenders when they feared the British assault would succeed. An additional six weeks were required to repair the damage during which Chauncey's squadron withdrew from the lake and Yeo's vessels came out to harass American troops ashore at the head of the lake.

During August and September Chauncey hoped to sweep the British squadron from the western end of the lake.[20] The opposing armies were locked in an unproductive contest, with the Americans seeking desperately to hold Fort George after reverses at Stoney Creek and Beaver Dam. From the joint perspective, if Chauncey could defeat Yeo, British armies would be weakened for lack of reinforcements and provisions. Secretary Armstrong wanted to direct American military efforts against Kingston and needed to transport several thousand men from Niagara to Sacket's Harbor. Without clear naval superiority, these tasks would be difficult to accomplish.[21]

Over many weeks of maneuvering for position and wind advantage, Chauncey failed to bring his opponent to a decisive action. In early August he lost four schooners, a loss only partially offset by the completion of the heavy 10-gun schooner *Sylph* in mid-August. When he returned briefly to Sacket's Harbor on 17 September Chauncey met with Secretary Armstrong who urged him to challenge Yeo so that the army's operations at the eastern end of the lake could proceed.[22]

The long-awaited battle occurred on 28 September when Chauncey discovered the enemy at York. Yeo attempted to evade but finally the squadrons engaged. The *General Pike* severely damaged Yeo's flagship, the *Wolfe*, and might have finished her had not the *Royal George*, Captain William Mulcaster, fought a superb rear-guard action, allowing the *Wolfe* to escape. In an easterly gale, had Chauncey cast free the cumbersome schooners he was towing, he might have caught and defeated Yeo. With the enemy seeking shelter in Burlington Bay, at the extreme western end of the lake, Chauncey faced a decision: either risk the squadron by chasing the enemy into shoal water on a lee shore, or draw off and hope to catch him later. Characteristically, Chauncey followed the safer course. Having punished his enemy, he withdrew his squadron intact.[23]

Yeo's evasive tactics cost the United States valuable time. Although Chauncey's victory over Yeo allowed Wilkinson's convoy to sail from Fort George, a foretaste of winter weather disrupted the concentration and deployment of the army. By mid-October the operation had been delayed at least one month, and Secretary Armstrong changed his mind about the wisdom of attacking Kingston. Fearing that the place had been strongly reinforced, he ordered Wilkinson and Chauncey to change the objective to Montreal.[24] In a letter to Secretary Jones on 20 October, Chauncey wrote that he was "much disappointed and mortified" to learn that General Wilkinson had decided to attack Montreal instead of Kingston. After four weeks of planning, he now learned that he would be unable to participate in the attack and objected to the subordinate role he had played "as a mear attendant upon the army." He accurately forecast the disaster awaiting the American troops as they descended the St. Lawrence.[25]

The naval squadron protected the army's move by flatboat from Sacket's Harbor to a rendezvous on Grenadier Island at the head of the St. Lawrence. Chauncey also had to establish a blockade below Kingston to prevent the British flotilla from harassing the army's barge convoy. In retrospect, the expedition should never have left. Harsh weather in mid-October delayed movement and cast some boats on unpopulated islands. Finally there was a stretch of fine weather in early November and the descent began. Chauncey stationed his units at the foot of Wolfe Island, ready to go into action if Yeo decided to run down one of the two channels to intercept the flotilla. But positioning was not enough. Yeo had built small gunboats and placed a division of them under Mulcaster who then slipped downriver undetected. Chauncey refused

Wilkinson's request for an armed schooner to help in the passage of Prescott. He wanted to keep his squadron intact if Yeo came to meet him or made another attack on Sacket's Harbor. Further, he feared that headwinds and ice would trap his vessels in the river. The squadron remained in the St. Lawrence until the weather turned foul on 10 November, then departed for Sacket's Harbor.[26]

On the next day, Wilkinson's forces landed on the Canadian side of the St. Lawrence to battle what he thought were weak forces following him. British units and Canadian militia stood their ground well, and the American army withdrew to their boats. This defeat in the Battle of Chrysler's Farm, combined with General Wade Hampton's failure to join Wilkinson for an attack on Montreal, signalled a pitiful end to a misbegotten expedition. If poor conception and orchestration can be blamed on army leadership, its poor timing can be blamed partly on the navy. The later the start, the worse the weather; the worse the weather, the greater the confusion and demoralization.

The Navy Department commenced preparations for the 1814 campaign even before hearing the results of 1813. Secretary Jones expected the British to redouble their efforts to gain control of the lake.[27] On the other hand, American preparations were generally slower in 1814 than they had been in 1813 for many reasons. The navy had difficulty finding seamen willing to sign for duty on the lakes. The recruiting problem continued, even after Congress passed a special law providing for increased compensation (up to 25 per cent more) for hardship areas. The northern lakes met this criterion. Desperate for experienced hands, the Navy Department transferred to the lakes the crews of the frigates *Congress* and *Macedonian* and the sloops *Erie* and *Ontario*.[28] Chauncey spurred Henry Eckford to prepare for the 1814 season. The frigate *Superior*, 50 guns, and two 22-gun brigs, the *Jefferson* and the *Jones*, were laid down in February and launched by 2 May. Work immediately commenced on the 42-gun frigate *Mohawk* which was launched in June but not ready for sea until July.

On the northern side of Lake Ontario, Commodore Yeo had built two new frigates and renamed and rearmed his older vessels. By the end of April his squadron included two frigates, two corvettes, and two brigs, employing 1,620 men and throwing an accumulated broadside of 2,874 pounds with its 211 guns. Impressive figures, but when the U.S. naval squadron finally sailed, it exceeded the British in all categories. The advanced state of British preparations, however, gave Yeo three months of uncontested superiority on the lake.[29] Chauncey did not even attempt to confront him until the end of July. From the perspective of joint operations, British naval dominance sped their strengthening of army units at Niagara and allowed Yeo to retard the fitting out of Chauncey's squadron.[30]

As in 1813, Armstrong's plans for the army depended on American naval superiority on the lake. Although preferring an early attack on Kingston, he meekly permitted Major General Jacob Brown to march from Sacket's Harbor for a renewed attempt at Niagara. At the 7 June cabinet meeting President Madison approved plans calling for an attack on the British depot at Burlington, a naval expedition from Lake Erie to Lake Huron, and a thrust at Kingston through York.

Chauncey informed Secretary Jones that his squadron would probably be ready to sail during the first week in July providing that sufficient seamen were on hand.[31] President Madison, Secretary Jones, and General Brown assumed that once at sea, Chauncey would sail west to aid Brown's movement across the Niagara peninsula toward Burlington. In reply to Brown's letter of 21 June, however, Chauncey wrote on the twenty-fifth that he did not intend to sail until 10 July and that even then he would not sail toward Niagara unless Yeo did.[32] For two critical weeks in mid-July Chauncey's headquarters remained silent. His later explanations were: first, that the frigate *Mohawk* lacked a commanding officer since Captain John Smith on the *Congress* had fallen ill and remained in New York; second, the *Mohawk* required some blocks and ironwork before being completely ready for sea; and the final reason, not revealed until the secretary had written in harsh terms, was that Chauncey had been severely ill and incapable of taking the squadron to sea. When asked why he had not conferred his command on his immediate second, Captain Jacob Jones (formerly commander of the *Wasp*), Chauncey's excuse was that this would have required transfers of commanders in all vessels and the officers did not want to be removed from the men they had trained.[33]

President Madison, meanwhile, was overcome with anxiety by the absence of news and urged the exasperated William Jones to replace Chauncey with Captain Stephen Decatur whose ship, the *United States*, was still blockaded at New London. Jones complied but made Decatur's appointment conditional: If Chauncey had gone to sea by the time Decatur arrived, or if news of his sailing reached Decatur while traveling north, the orders were to be considered null. Chauncey did embark before Decatur's arrival and thereby escaped supersession, though not embarrassment.[34]

Criticism issued sharply from many sources, especially from General Brown. Seeking Chauncey's cooperation, Brown had sent an urgent message:

> I have looked for your fleet with the greatest anxiety since the 10th. I do not doubt my ability to meet the enemy in the field and to march in any direction over his country--your fleet carrying the necessary supplies. We can threaten Forts George and Niagara, carry Burlington Heights and York, and proceed direct to Kingston and carry that place. For God's sake, let me see you....[35]

To this plea, Chauncey responded that he had never promised Brown he would meet him on a particular day and that the fleet could not have helped his incursion into Canada; adding,

> that you might find the fleet somewhat of a convenience in the transportation of provisions and stores I am ready to believe, but Sir, the Secretary of the Navy has honored us with a higher destiny--we are intended to seek and fight the enemy's fleet. This is the great purpose of government in creating this fleet and I shall not be diverted in my efforts to effectuate it by any sinister attempt to render us subordinate to or an appendage of the army.[36]

Chauncey thus excused his own failure to act by blaming it on interservice rivalry. Military historians have condemned his views as shortsighted and parochial. Mahan rejected the argument that the squadron would have been of no service, and blamed Chauncey for the inability of the army to achieve a victory at Lundy's Lane.[37] On Chauncey's side, three arguments should be considered. First, his efforts in the 1813 campaign could not have been surpassed by any other American naval commander. He had done everything required except to force Yeo into a major defeat. This was virtually impossible because, with the example of Barclay before him, Yeo did not intend to risk all in a set battle with Chauncey's squadron. Nor was he being urged to do so. Second, Chauncey was evidently disillusioned with the army's version of cooperation. His first signs of bitterness had surfaced when the army high command changed its objective from Kingston to Montreal in October 1813. It had happened again the following May. Finally, the Royal Navy's establishment at Kingston in 1814 was much stronger than it was a year earlier and posed a genuine threat to Chauncey's naval base at Sacket's Harbor.

There is no doubt that a desperate military and naval battle would have been fought in an attempt to destroy the enemy's Kingston naval base. To defend it, Yeo would have been forced into the very battle he had successfully avoided. Instead, Chauncey was, for the third time, expected to leave his base unprotected to support the army's indirect strategy. Chauncey's reasoning was self-serving, but it was tactically sound in the absence of stronger military defenses at Sacket's Harbor.

The major strategic accomplishment of the navy under Chauncey's direction was that of holding the line on Lake Ontario. Had the enemy broken the center of the northern front, the way would have been open for attacks through New York State. Even though Chauncey did not achieve his goal--an unwavering superiority on Lake Ontario--his actions were sufficiently menacing to worry British commanders and to force them to adjust their plans according to his strengths and weaknesses.

Finally, lest Perry get all the credit for his victory on Lake Erie, Chauncey's activity on Lake Ontario weakened the enemy's Lake Erie squadron. The attacks on York and Fort George in 1813 caused fatal shortages and delays for the naval forces under the command of Commodore Robert Barclay. Perry felt that Chauncey had hampered his efforts, yet with what Chauncey provided, Perry was able to improvise and carry out his orders, allowing General William Henry Harrison to roll back the British army from Detroit to Niagara.

The dynamics of joint operations in the War of 1812 depended a great deal on the quality of leadership. General officer leadership in the army remained at a low level until 1814. Yet, even this was not fatal if the incompetent generals had able subordinates such as Zebulon Pike, Winfield Scott, and Jacob Brown. The naval officers were a much younger group. Most had been born during or after the American Revolution and had not seen action until the Quasi-War with France. The second dynamic was manpower resources. With a weak militia and a small regular army, American generals were all too ready to believe exaggerated accounts of the enemy's strength. The navy also had its manpower weaknesses. Several ships on the seacoast were deactivated so that their crews and armament could be used on Lake Ontario. Lake commodores occasionally called for soldiers to man their vessels, much to the dismay of army commanders. Yet, for the most part the army cooperated with these calls. A third important dynamic was the strength and mobility of enemy forces. The greater the pressure Chauncey felt because of Yeo's threat to his base or his own lack of equipment caused by enemy blockade, the less likely he was to cooperate enthusiastically with his army counterparts. This aspect was especially operative during July 1814. To remove himself and the greater part of his squadron to Niagara while Yeo threatened Sacket's Harbor was almost unthinkable for Chauncey. As long as he felt his squadron in control of the lake, however, Chauncey threw himself enthusiastically into joint operations.

The war on the northern lakes is the least appreciated aspect of the maritime war of 1812-15. Strategically, it was the most important theater of the war. The naval operations there were inextricably involved in the general military situation, and the most worthwhile operations were joint operations. Considering the restricted nature of the conflict, even the blockade of Kingston, a purely naval tactic, had joint aspects. Service parochialism existed without a doubt, but Chauncey gave his subordinates clear instructions to "harmonize with" their brother service. His amphibious landings at York and Fort George were planned and executed with a precision remarkable for their time.[38] There were no comparable precedents for such operations in U.S. military history at that time. The amphibious operations conducted on Lake Ontario against York and Fort George in 1813 provide the earliest examples of excellent advance planning and smooth interservice operations of the U.S. armed forces in modern times.

Notes

[1]J.C.A. Stagg, *Mr. Madison's War: Politics, Diplomacy, and Warfare in the Early American Republic, 1783-1830* (Princeton, 1983), 46-47.

[2]Thomas Jefferson to William Duane, 4 August 1812, quoted in Dumas Malone, *Jefferson and His Time*, vol. 6, *The Sage of Monticello* (Boston, 1981), 109.

[3]James Madison to John Nicholas, 2 April 1813, James Madison Papers, Library of Congress, Washington, D.C. Nicholas (1756-1819), a Virginian and former Republican member of the House of Representatives, had moved to Geneva, New York. He served in the New York state senate from 1806 to 1809 and was judge of the court of common pleas of Ontario County from 1806 to 1819.

[4]Chauncey to Hamilton, 5 November 1812, Captains' Letters Received by the Secretary of the Navy (hereafter CL), 1812, vol. 3, no. 161, Record Group (hereafter RG) 45, National Archives (hereafter NA), Washington, D.C.; Chauncey to Hamilton, 5, 13, 26 November 1812, ibid., nos. 162, 176, 192.

[5]Secretary of War John Armstrong to Major General Henry Dearborn, 10 February 1813, *American State Papers, Military Affairs*, 7 vols. (Washington, 1832-) (hereafter *ASPMA*), I: 439-40; Armstrong to Dearborn, 15 February 1813, War Department, Letters Sent, RG 107, pp. 293-94, NA; Dearborn to Armstrong, 18 February 1813, *ASPMA*, I: 440.

[6]Alfred T. Mahan, *Sea Power in its Relations to the War of 1812*, 2 vols. (1905; reprint, New York, 1969), II: 33-36.

[7]Jones to Chauncey, 27 January 1813, Secretary of the Navy Letters Sent to Officers, Ships of War, 1813, RG 45, NA [hereafter SNL].

[8]Lords Commissioners of Admiralty to Sir James Lucas Yeo, 19 March 1813, ADM 1/1376/252-264, Public Record Office, London.

[9]C. Van de Vinter to John Armstrong, 1 April 1813, Records of the Office of the Secretary of War, Unregistered Letters Received, RG 107, NA.

[10]Isaac Chauncey Letterbook Vol. 2 (April 1813-August 1813, William L. Clements Library, University of Michigan, Ann Arbor, MI (hereafter WLCL).

[11]Ibid.

[12]Chauncey to Jones, 28 April 1813, CL, vol. 3, no. 63, RG 45, NA; Ernest Cruikshank, ed., *The Documentary History of the Campaign upon the Niagara Frontier*, 4 parts (Welland, Ontario, 1896-1908) (hereafter *HCNF*), 1813, I: 183.

[13]Chauncey to Lieutenant Joseph Smith, 30 April 1813, Chauncey Letterbook, vol. 2, WLCL.

[14]Chauncey to Lieutenant Thomas Brown, 9 May 1813, ibid.; Chauncey to Jones, 11 May 1813, CL, 1813, vol. 3, no. 136, RG 45, NA. See also, Brigadier General Vincent to Governor General Prevost, 19 May 1813, *HCNF*, 1813, I: 235-36.

[15]Chauncey to Jones, 16 May 1813, Chauncey Letterbook, vol. 2, WLCL.

[16]Chauncey to Jones, 28 May 1813, CL, 1813 vol. 3, no. 190, RG 45, NA; Charles W. Elliott, *Winfield Scott: The Soldier and the Man* (New York, 1937), 89-101.

[17]Lieutenant Fraser to unknown correspondent, May 1813, published in the Philadelphia *Aurora*; *HCNF*, 1813, I: 179-82; Dearborn to Armstrong, 27 May 1813, ibid., 246-47.

[18]Brigadier General Vincent to Governor General Sir George Prevost, 28 May 1813, *HCNF*, 1813, I: 250-53.

[19]Chauncey to Jones, 2 June 1813, CL, 1813, vol. 4, no. 8, RG 45, NA; C. Edward Skeen, *John Armstrong, Jr., 1758-1843: A Biography* (Syracuse, 1981), 155.

[20]Chauncey to Dearborn, 12 June 1813, Chauncey Letterbook, vol. 2, WLCL.

[21]Armstrong to James Madison, 25 July 1813, James Madison Papers, Library of Congress, Washington, D.C.; John Armstrong, Jr., *Notices of the War of 1812*, 2 vols. (New York, 1836), II: 187-188, App. I; *HCNF*, 1813, I: 266-67.

[22]Chauncey to Jones, 25 September 1813, CL, 1813, vol. 6, no. 92.

[23]Theodore Roosevelt, *The Naval War of 1812* (New York, 1882), 250; Mahan, *Sea Power to War of 1812*, 107-108. Chauncey to Jones, 1 October 1813, CL, 1813, vol. 6, no. 115.

[24]"From the Journal of the Secretary of War," 4-5 October 1813, *HCNF*, 1813, III: 197-98; Wilkinson to Chauncey, 9 October 1813, and Chauncey to Wilkinson, 9 October 1813, *ASPMA*, I: 473; Armstrong to Wilkinson, 19 October 1813, in Armstrong, *Notices of the War of 1812*, II: 207-09.

[25]Chauncey to Jones, 30 October 1813, CL, vol. 7, no. 63.

[26]Chauncey to Jones, 4 November 1813, ibid., 76; Chauncey to Wilkinson, 4 November 1813, *ASPMA*, I: 482; Mulcaster to Yeo, 2 November 1813, *HCNF*, 1813, IV: 123-24; Chauncey to Jones, 11 November 1813, CL, vol. 7, no. 93.

[27]Jones to Chauncey, 1 December 1813, SNL; Jones to Chauncey, 15 January 1813 [1814], ibid.

[28]Jones to Chauncey, 25 February 1814, SNL; Jones to Bainbridge, 25 February 1814 (regarding the opening of a Boston rendezvous for Lake Ontario service), ibid.;

Jones to Chauncey, 18 March 1814, ibid.; Jones to Chauncey, 6 April 1814, ibid.; Jones to Chauncey, 31 May 1814, ibid.

[29]Roosevelt, *Naval War of 1812*, 354-57; E.A. Cruikshank, "The Contest for the Command of Lake Ontario in 1814," *Ontario Historical Society Papers and Records*, XXI (1924): 99-159.

[30]Chauncey to Jones, 7 May 1814, CL, 1814, vol. 3, no. 28.

[31]Twice in June Chauncey informed Jones that the *Mohawk* was making good progress and that he would be ready to sail on or before 1 July. See Chauncey to Jones, 9 and 11 June 1814, CL, vol. 4, nos. 39, 54. On 24 June Chauncey slipped his estimated departure date to "the first week in July." See Chauncey to Jones, 24 June 1814, ibid., no. 98.

[32]Chauncey to Brown, 25 June and 8 July 1814, Jacob Brown Papers, Massachusetts Historical Society, Boston.

[33]Chauncey to Jones, 10 August and 19 August 1814, CL, 1814, vol. 5, nos. 84, 113.

[34]Jones to Chauncey, 20 July, 24 July, 3 August, and 5 August, SNL; Jones to Decatur, 28 July and 5 August 1814, ibid.

[35]Brown to Chauncey, 13 July 1814, *HCNF*, 1814, pt. I, 2: 64; Brown to Armstrong, 25 July 1814, ibid., 87.

[36]Chauncey to Brown, 10 August 1814, enclosed with Chauncey to Jones, 11 August 1814, CL, 1814, vol. 5, no. 87. In another letter, Chauncey accused Brown of being "anxious to provide against a disaster and to prepare the public mind to shift responsibility from himself to me." Chauncey had given Brown adequate notice of his intentions. His concerns for the safety of his base were justified. Unfortunately, he had not taken the trouble to make his situation clear in advance to the Navy Department. Hence, there was great concern in Washington over his lack of communication and non-appearance off Niagara. See Chauncey to Jones, 19 August 1814, CL, 1814, vol. 5, no. 140.

[37]Mahan, *Sea Power to War of 1812*, II: 304-14.

[38]Roosevelt, *Naval War of 1812*, 228-33.

Commodore Sir James Lucas Yeo and Governor General George Prevost: A Study in Command Relations, 1813-14

Frederick C. Drake

It is one of the curiosities of the naval war of 1812 that while major engagements were fought on Lake Erie and Lake Champlain, there were no such battles on Lake Ontario. Historians have frequently labeled the British and American naval commanders (Sir James Yeo and Isaac Chauncey) as men who tried to avoid a fight. Professor Drake examines the role of the British naval commander and his relationship with his superior to show that the relative inaction on the lake was to the British advantage.

On 29 September 1814, Sir James Lucas Yeo, commanding the naval forces in the Canadas, complained to the Admiralty that responsibility for the defeat of the Lake Champlain squadron under Captain George Downie rested most likely with the Governor General of the Canadian Provinces, Sir George Prevost. "It appears very evident," Yeo wrote, "that Capt. Downie was urged, and even goaded on to his fate, by...[Prevost] who appears to have assumed the direction of the Naval Force." Yeo based his criticism on the letters and reports of naval officers including Captain Daniel Pring who claimed that "had [Prevost] adhered to his previous arrangement [a coordinated land attack], the Enemy's Squadron must have quitted their Anchorage, particularly their Gun Boats that lay close under their Shore, and whose heavy Metal and cool fire did more execution to our Vessels than their Ship or Brig." Yeo's complaints helped lead to Prevost's recall, a naval court-martial that exonerated Downie by placing most of the blame for the defeat on Prevost, and the latter's call for a court-martial to examine his own conduct. Prevost's death shortly before the court-martial convened sparked a controversy over Yeo's claims that prompted the governor general's family to try to clear his name.[1]

The controversy over the Lake Champlain result and the bitterness over Yeo's denunciations should not, however, mask the fact that throughout most of the war it was the cooperation between Yeo and Prevost that enabled the British to retain Upper Canada. In the long run, the eighteen months of cooperation during the war meant more than the year of recrimination after it had ended.

Cooperation between the two began early. On 23 November 1812 Prevost recommended to Whitehall that the Royal Navy promptly take command of the Great Lakes. In addition, he applied to Sir John Warren, commanding the North American Station, for additional officers.[2] While Warren eventually forwarded a small detachment from the blockading squadrons, the Admiralty began making preparations for a larger lakes force. Commanding the force as commodore was Sir James Lucas Yeo. Under him were three commanders, William Howe Mulcaster, Richard (later Sir Richard) J.L. O'Connor, and Frederick B. Spilsbury, and eight lieutenants who commanded the smaller vessels belonging to the Canadian Provincial Marine. Most of the 448 officers and men of that detachment remained with Yeo on Lake Ontario throughout the war.[3]

On 19 March 1813 Yeo received his instructions. To defend "His Majesty's Provinces of North America," his first object, clearly stating that he had to act within strategic limits, was

> to co-operate with [Prevost]...not undertaking any operations without the full concurrence and approbation of him...and on all occasions conforming yourself and employing the forces under your command according to the requisitions you may from time to time receive to this effect from the said Governor or Commander of the Forces.[4]

When Yeo arrived at Quebec, he found additional orders to place himself "under the command of...Sir John B. Warren...and follow such orders as you may receive from him...."[5] By emphasizing the connection with Warren, the Admiralty made certain that Yeo, already ordered to report to and work in close harmony with Prevost, was also seen to serve directly under Admiralty control. The result, however, meant serving Prevost, Warren, and the Admiralty, three masters who required close consultation. Such instructions placed Yeo in a position where command decisions had to be vetted by superior officers in two services, one of whom was also the supreme civilian authority. In terms of creative action or battle plans, Yeo was operating in a more limited context than his opposite number on Lake Ontario, Commodore Isaac Chauncey. Whereas some military historians have cited the virtues of a single command structure as one reason for British military success on land,[6] it also placed decision making for the naval forces within the framework of a defensive strategy determined by Sir George Prevost.

Yeo, who enjoyed a reputation for daring exploits,[7] shook down his assorted group of officers and ratings on the trip across the Atlantic. Midshipman David Wingfield declared: "The vague idea we had of the Service, and force being commanded by so gallant an officer as Sir James Yeo, made us look upon it as fraught with danger; but headed by an officer of our Commodore's known bravery made us the more anxious to come in contact with the Enemy, and the period of our sailing was most ardently desired." Midshipman John Johnston, however, detected a difference in attitude. "To begin with," he complained in letters home, "Sir Jas. who talked so smoothly in London quite altered his tone in Blue Water, particularly with the Mids, who he looks upon as a poor set of wretches sent out to be butchered for their Commissions and not worthy of the name of Officers...."[8]

On arrival at Kingston Yeo superseded Robert Barclay who was eventually given the command of the Lake Erie station. Midshipman Wingfield wrote: "The arrival of Sir James Yeo at Kingston, with this force, raised the drooping spirits of the inhabitants of that place, and generally, of the country at large, who were well aware that the fall of Kingston must necessarily involve the whole country upwards in ruin."[9]

The rival commanding officers had different strategic objectives that affected all decisions. Chauncey had three tasks. The first, for which his command of the New York Navy Yard equipped him well, was to create a naval force. This included establishing a navy yard; building, buying, or hiring vessels; appointing officers; enlisting and forwarding seamen; and purchasing naval stores. Chauncey's second task was to cooperate with the army for combined operations to reduce British fortified camps. Finally, Chauncey had to gain naval superiority on the lakes either by capturing or destroying the enemy's fleet, or by neutralizing it with a blockade.[10]

Yeo, on the other hand, found an establishment already in being. Shipbuilding yards existed at Kingston and York on Lake Ontario, and at Amherstburg on Lake Erie,[11] and he brought seamen with him to replace those of the Canadian Provincial Marine.[12] Yeo had to defend the Canadas by cooperating with the army in the upper peninsula, by providing logistical support by raiding lake bases and disrupting his opponent's supply bases on the southern shore, and by keeping lines of communication open rather than by risking all on a vainglorious search for battle. Given these dissimilar perspectives of what was expected of them by their respective governments, Yeo's and Chauncey's objectives were different. Yeo was to avoid engagement unless absolutely necessary, either from extreme disadvantage or fortunate advantage. Chauncey's goal was to *press* for a battle, threaten his enemy's lake bases, and engage in combined operations whenever possible.

The contest between Yeo and Chauncey throughout 1813 and 1814 was fought in several different ways. First, they began a shipbuilding race, which lasted periodically until the end of the war, in order to win control of the lakes. The race began with schooners and escalated to line-of-battle ships. The strategy eventually worked to Yeo's advantage on Lake Ontario, although the demand for seamen denied Barclay on Lake Erie sufficient seamen and support, thus helping to undermine the latter's attempts to retain command of Lake Erie in the summer of 1813. Second, the two commodores raided each other's lake bases. Chauncey did so at Kingston in November 1812 and at York in April 1813, both taking place before Yeo and his forces had arrived on the lakes, and again in July 1813. Yeo attacked Sacket's Harbor in late May 1813, Sodus Bay in June 1813 and, in a successful combined operation, at Oswego in May 1814. Third, Yeo and Chauncey skirmished with each other in August and twice in September 1813. In this, Yeo avoided defeat and thus maintained his squadron as a barrier to Chauncey's goal of a decisive action.

Next, the commodores cooperated with their compatriot army commanders in combined operations. Chauncey was successful on the Niagara frontier in May and June 1813 with Generals Dearborn, Winder, and Chandler. Yeo was successful with General Vincent and Colonel Harvey at Stoney Creek in June 1813, which threw the American army's invasion in reverse, and with General Drummond at the same location in the summer of 1814. Chauncey's failure in July 1814 to cooperate with General Jacob Brown in the Lundy's Lane campaign became one of the most widely known squabbles between army and navy officers during the war. Yeo was far more successful in cooperating with Prevost and his commanders than Chauncey was with his army field commanders. Both men, however, generally provided adequate logistical support for their armies. Lastly, the commodores blockaded each other's squadrons; Chauncey at Kingston in August 1814; Yeo at Sacket's Harbor in May and June 1814. Both enjoyed limited success but ultimately failed to deny the lake to the other for very long at critical times.

Each one of these activities required both tactical decision-making and strategic goals. But each interpreted the importance of naval operations differently. For example, Yeo and Prevost decided to try to take command of the lake by attacking Sacket's Harbor in late May while Chauncey was attacking Fort George at the western end of the lake. Intending to burn Chauncey's frigate, the *General Pike*, then under construction, and all the public stores, there can be little doubt that the boldness of the plan came from Yeo and not from Sir George, who later termed it a diversion to relieve pressure on Fort George. Prevost and Yeo took with them about nine hundred men from the garrison at Kingston.[13]

The attack failed because it was not pushed hard enough and because the fleet could not near the fort owing to "light and adverse winds." Unable to use the heavy guns of the fleet in support of the troops, Prevost ordered a general withdrawal. Ironically, the Americans decided to fire the yard while the battle was at its height. Both the *Gloucester*, captured at York the month before, and the *General Pike* were set afire, but the flames were doused as the British troops withdrew. The action lasted about four hours with the British suceeding in burning only the stores.[14]

Unable to tip the naval balance in his favor, Prevost ordered his forces back to Kingston, fearing that he might be trapped if Chauncey returned. Had he left that concern to Yeo and concentrated on pushing the action for another hour, especially with his artillery, he might have been able to deny Chauncey the use of the *General Pike* entirely. Although this was the main combined operation by Yeo and Prevost on Lake Ontario in 1813, and although it had ended in failure, the results went beyond its immediate aim. One suspects that Chauncey was never quite the same after the attack. Anxiety for the security of his base and the belief that the loss of the *General Pike* would have given command of the lake to the English led him to keep large numbers of troops to guard it in his absence.

Chauncey's squadron in 1813 consisted of fifteen vessels, displacing a total of 2,528 tons, and having 114 guns. Yeo's force was much smaller; six vessels of 1,421 tons and 91 guns. His squadron, however, was built for war, all completely equipped and ready for sea. His flagship, the *Wolfe*, was the largest vessel in his squadron, but smaller than the *Madison*, Chauncey's second vessel, and only half the size of Chauncey's *General Pike*.[15]

Yeo spent much of the summer of 1813 building vessels for Prevost's strategic defensive on the Niagara Peninsula. On 3 June he sailed from Kingston to Burlington Heights where he delivered badly needed supplies and reinforcements to General Vincent's forces about to counter the Americans at Stoney Creek. He next carried out a series of raids to cut off supplies to the American forces now at Fort George. Yeo's activities raised concern among some American officers. Major David Campbell, commanding the Twelfth Regiment, wrote that "Chauncey is certainly permitting the enemies fleet to remain too long without molestation if he could avoid it. They give great confidence to their troops and they may have it in their power to carry them off."[16] Captain Willoughby Morgan, also of the Twelfth Regiment, informed his commanding officer after Stoney Creek and the retreat to Fort George:

> What now are our prospects? I believe that we are waiting until Chauncey gets command of the lake or we get reinforcements--But is this certain? I am informed from the same source that Sir James Lucas Yeo went to the Harbor himself in the disguise as a farmer to sell potatoes and viewed undiscovered every thing. He landed about six hundred men a day or two afterwards covered his boats with leaves and concealed them with a view of burning our vessels at that place. His plan was fortunately discovered by a deserter and our troops marched against him and arrived just as his boats had put off. What vigilant officers are at the harbour.[17]

All spectators of the Yeo-Chauncey duel in 1813 expected to see one great battle settle the naval issue. Colonel James Miller, second in command at Fort George wrote that "we remain hobeled as usual with orders to avoid a battle with the enemy if possible until the Fleet decides their battle which we expect to take place daily."[18] Colonel Thomas Parker at Albany informed David Campbell at Fort George that "both parties are using Every Exertion to Get the Superiority on the lakes; without it we ought never to Trust An Army in that Country."[19] Captain Morgan in Fort George, on hearing that "the British are making great exertions to get a superiority upon the lake," conjectured that "unless we are quick upon them they may effect their object."[20] In Kingston, Midshipman John Johnston wrote home doubting his return by Christmas. "You must not expect me back so soon as we expected for we have now a Regular Fleet on the Lake.... We are not so numerous but have more heavy Ships.... We expect to sail in 4 or 5 days to meet the Yankees, as long as the American War lasts we shall keep a Naval Force, as the Fate of Cannada depends upon us."[21]

Yeo confided to Colonel John Harvey, leader of the successful attack at Stoney Creek, that he hoped to meet Chauncey soon but was "fully impressed with the necessity of having a *commanding Breeze* before he makes his Attack--In light ones or Calm the Enemy's Flotilla of small Vessels would have incalculable advantages." In Yeo's words the pattern of events were forecast for the summer. Neither commander would engage unless the weather conditions presented him with an overwhelming advantage.

To this point, the naval contest had remained a miniature race to turn out the heaviest vessel. Yeo led for a period with the *Wolfe* though his advantage ended when his forces failed to burn the much larger *General Pike*. Returning to Kingston he proposed to counter the Americans' ship by building an even larger one.[22]

The events of May and early June at Sacket's Harbor, and at 40 Mile Creek, set the pattern of strategy on Lake Ontario in 1813. The threat to Sacket's Harbor pulled Chauncey back to his base. As he returned, Yeo exploited the opportunity to sail up the lake to cooperate with the army defending the peninsula. The primary function of Yeo's squadron was in keeping the troops supplied, harrassing the American forces retreating down the Peninsula, attacking American bases on the southern shore, and keeping Chauncey guessing. By doing so, he could maximize tactical opportunities without endangering the strategic defensive posture adopted by the nature of his Admiralty orders and the need to serve both Warren's and Prevost's orders.

Two other aspects affected Yeo's tactical options. The composition of the squadrons and the respective attitudes of the commanders made it unlikely that either commander would risk his vessels in the conditions regarded as most favorable for his opponent.[23] Hence a general engagement, though often threatening, never happened in six weeks of uninterrupted attempts to provide one. While Yeo's squadron delivered more shot than Chauncey's force in total weight, Chauncey's squadron had almost five hundred men more and was roughly one thousand tons larger in size. Yeo had absolutely no reason to engage an enemy under these circumstances, as his orders made clear, unless he had every conceivable advantage of weather gauge, of an opponent on a lee shore or stranded, or of divided squadrons that could not easily be reunited.

Two conditions ensured that the squadrons would never engage in a general action, despite the weeks of manoeuvering. The first was the nature of the guns in each squadron. Yeo's broadside was mainly a heavy carronade. He had only nineteen long guns in his squadron throwing a total shot of 330 pounds. Yeo's seventy-two carronades, however, fired 2,312 pounds of metal, and in any single broadside thirty-six could fire 1,156 pounds of shot. Chauncey's balance was much better. In the summer of 1813, although his broadside guns changed at times, he normally had sixty-eight long guns in his squadron, firing a total of 1,219 pounds of shot. In addition, his forty-six carronades fired 1,216 pounds. Chauncey thus enjoyed at least a three to one advantage in long gun broadside metal, while Yeo had a two to one advantage with carronade fire. Yeo could only engage with a prospect of success at close range, when his heavy carronades would equalize his broadside disadvantage.

If broadside metal had been the only aspect to consider, Chauncey could well have been more successful than he proved to be. His flagship, the *General Pike*, equipped entirely with long guns, could have gained the superiority on the lake on its own by its very size and ability to absorb punishment. Simply by keeping away, Chauncey could have pounded and crippled Yeo's ships, leaving the British commander unable to reply.

However, the respective designs of each squadron counted for much, and in 1813 the British had an advantage to offset their smaller numbers, size, and weight of metal. The six vessels were designed as war vessels, and they generally combined well, though the *Earl of Moira* was reputed to be a poor sailor. Mahan considered them a good manoeuvering squadron, which might be stretching the point in an absolute sense. Compared with Chauncey's, however, they were.[24]

The American squadron was a mixture of solidly constructed war vessels and thin-skinned converted merchant schooners, the latter being very vulnerable to canister shot and having poor defensive qualities. Moreover, before 8 August 1813, these merchantmen contained over half of Chauncey's long guns. In fine weather, they served as reasonably steady gun platforms, but when it blew hard as it tended to do in June and September, the schooners were hard put to stay steady. In these circumstances, Chauncey had either to put into port, or watch over them with caution.

He resorted to towing in blowy conditions, but this merely slowed down his war vessels without giving a corresponding advantage, other than to prevent the schooners from foundering. In maneuverability, Chauncey's squadron was simply worse than Yeo's. The American commodore could have taken on the entire British squadron with his largest three ships, but that would have required a commitment to action and daring that was seemingly not in Chauncey's psyche.

Thus, though Chauncey's three war vessels were within four pounds weight of broadside metal of Yeo's first three, their much greater size and range made them more than a match for Yeo's first four. The *General Pike* could, under suitable weather conditions, have engaged all six British vessels with a good chance of success. But with the poor manoeuvering and support structure of much of Chauncey's squadron compared with the much better unit work of the British, and the various facts relating to broadside to be considered, the tactics for Lake Ontario were obvious to each commander. Chauncey would only engage in calm weather, at long range, and near sheltered anchorages to gain the maximum benefit from his schooners and long guns. Yeo could only engage in rough weather, on the open lake where his greater coordination and superiority of sailing allowed him to come to offset the broadside disparity. In order to do that, he would have had to expose his lighter vessels to Chauncey's long guns before he could bring his carronades to bear.

The result was that the two squadrons jointly occupied the lake for nearly ten weeks in 1813 and only made serious contact three times, none of which proved decisive. During 1814 the contest

165

returned to being principally a shipbuilding race. In terms of the war effort, however, the results were critical. Strategically, Chauncey should have come to grips with Yeo as often as possible but tactically it suited his purpose to remain at long distance. While Yeo avoided defeat, thereby carrying out the Admiralty's orders and its strategic purposes, he found that to bring his big guns into play he would have had to put his squadron in tactical jeopardy by risking a close encounter with Chauncey. Tactical requirements contradicted strategic necessity. However, while Yeo's purposes were served by such contradictions, Chauncey's were not.

Yeo's words to Lieutenant Colonel Harvey at Stoney Creek about the necessity of a commanding breeze showed that he was not prepared to engage indiscriminately, especially if advantage of wind and location rested with his opponent. Those words reveal that he had perceived the dilemma and accepted its consequences: avoid a damaging action, avoid defeat; prevent the enemy from gaining his purpose, and thereby win a war. Yeo's success denied the invading American forces from ever gaining the naval dominance which they defined as necessary to win. As long as Yeo's squadron remained a fleet in being which supplied the troops and threatened Chauncey's base at Sacket's Harbor and his flexibility, the British forces would be able to maintain their defensive arrangements. It also meant fulfilling Prevost's defensive strategy of holding Upper and Lower Canada.

Chauncey, on the other hand, had to win the initiative, not only tactically on the lake, but strategically by removing the impediment of his opponent's squadron. His primary concern should have been to force a showdown with Yeo. By removing Yeo's squadron, or even by crippling its maneuverability, his conjunction with land forces should have been sufficient to win the Upper Province. Chauncey could even have stood a crippling of his own squadron if he could have also crippled Yeo's in a general action, for the faster building potential of the American forces should then have ruled the day. Thus Chauncey's strategic goal should have been to press action against the British squadron first, the British bases second, and against British troops in a combined operation third. Yet his initiative in April and May 1813 scrambled that order:

York and Fort George came first and combined operations came second. He was rarely given the chance in the war to pursue the first objective, and, when the opportunity arose, with one exception, Yeo never allowed him to capitalize on it. Only once (which should have been sufficient), on 29-30 September 1813, did it appear that the first objective might be achieved when Chauncey caught the *Wolfe* and dismasted her in a wild chase towards Burlington Bay. Chauncey missed the chance. As Yeo's squadron remained a fleet-in-being, so Chauncey's hopes for victory on Lake Ontario faded. That was the extent to which the war on the lake in 1813 and 1814 became a war of nerves, played and won by Yeo.

Command relations are sometimes hammered out in battles or during combined operations. Sometimes, however, they are predetermined by superiors' orders and strategic goals. On Lake Ontario during 1813 and 1814, Yeo's relationship with Prevost was conditioned by those aspects. Had the Lake Ontario lessons been applied by the British on Lake Champlain in September 1814 where an offensive gamble by Prevost finally replaced a defensive strategy for the war, it might also have led Prevost and Downie to escape the disaster and the consequent recriminations that followed between Prevost and Yeo over the responsibility for that defeat. It would also have placed in better light the true magnitude of their efforts in Upper Canada over the previous eighteen months.

Notes

[1] Yeo to Admiralty, 29 September 1814, Admiralty Captains Letters, Public Record Office, London, Admiralty Records (hereafter ADM) 1/2737/206-207. For correspondence on the Lake Champlain defeat, see ADM 1/2737/173-207. For court martial details, see ADM 1/5450. See also William C. H. Wood, ed., *Select British Documents of the Canadian War of 1812*, 4 vols. (Toronto, 1920) I: 377, III: 336-86, 400-98.

[2] Prevost to Gray, 19 December 1812, Gray to Prevost, 12 March 1813, and Warren to Melville, 18 November, 31 December 1812, in Warren Letterbook, Correspondence with Lord Melville--American War of 1812-14, Manuscripts Division, National Maritime Museum, Greenwich; Admiralty to Yeo, 22 March 1813, Secretary's Out-Letters, ADM 2/1376/263.

[3]Establishment of officers and men for the lakes station, 8 March 1813, ADM 2/1376/183-85, 202. See John C. Spurr, "The Royal Navy's Presence in Kingston, Part I: 1813-1836," *Historic Kingston*, 25 (March 1977): 63-64, and Ernest A. Cruikshank, "The Contest for the Command of Lake Ontario in 1812 and 1813," *Transactions of the Royal Society of Canada*, 3d ser., 10 (September 1916): 161-222.

[4]Admiralty to Goulburn, 6 March 1813, and Admiralty to Yeo, 16, 19 March 1813, ADM 2/1376/131-33, 205-206, 249-52.

[5]Admiralty to Yeo, 19 and 22 March 1813, ADM 2/1376/249-63, 823.

[6]See J. M. Hitsman, *The Incredible War of 1812: A Military History* (Toronto, 1965) 45, 54-56, 67, 102-104, 243-51.

[7]On Yeo's background career, see *Dictionary of National Biography* , s.v., "Yeo, Sir James Lucas"; Spurr, "Royal Navy's Presence," 63-64, *Dictionary of Canadian Biography*, s.v., "Yeo, Sir James Lucas"; and William James, *Naval History of Great Britain from 1793-1820*, 6 vols. (London, 1837), V: 73-77.

[8]The Diary of David Wingfield, National Archives of Canada, p. 2; John Frederick Johnston to his mother, 15, 16, 17, 18, 23, 29 March, and 28 April 1813, Account of the career and death of John Frederick Johnston, RN, ca. 1816, Halsey Collection, nos. 16421, 16285, 16287, 16288, 16290, 16291 (a) and (b), 16292, Hertfordshire (England) County Records Office (hereafter HCRO).

[9]Barclay's Naval Arrangements, 5 May 1813, Barclay to Freer, 9 May 1813, Barclay to Sheaffe, 5 May 1813, and Barclay to Freer, in Wood, *Select Documents*, II: 113-18; "Narrative of the Proceedings during the Command of Captain Barclay...on Lake Erie," given in court-martial of Barclay, 9 September 1814, ADM 1/5445/29; Wingfield Diary, p. 5.

[10]Chauncey to secretary of navy, 26 September 1812, Chauncey Papers, William L. Clements Library, University of Michigan, Ann Arbor; also quoted in Alfred T. Mahan, *Sea Power in its Relation to the War of 1812*, 2 vols. (Boston, 1905) I: 361-62; C. P. Stacey, "Another Look at the Battle of Lake Erie," *Canadian Historical Review*, 39 (1958): 45-46.

[11]See Barclay to Freer, 9 May 1813, in Wood, *Select Documents*, II: 116, 129; C. P. Stacey, "The Ships of the British Squadron on Lake Ontario, 1812-1814," *Canadian Historical Review*, 34 (1953): 317-21; Spurr, "Royal Navy's Presence," 64.

[12]An adjunct of the army used mainly as a transport service before the war, it was regarded by some historians with disdain. W. A. B. Douglas, "The Anatomy of Naval Incompetence: The Provincial Marine in Defence of Upper Canada Before 1813," *Ontario Historical Society*, 81 (March 1979): 3-24.

[13]Johnston to mother, 17 June 1813, Halsey Collection, no. 16293, HCRO; Wood, *Select Documents*, II: 130-31.

[14]Prevost to Lord Bathurst, 1 June 1813, in ibid., 130-32. For the attack upon Sacket's Harbor, see Colonel Baynes to Prevost, 30 May 1813, in ibid., 123-27. British casualties (48 killed, 195 wounded, and 16 missing) are in ibid., 133-34.

Brenton to Freer, 30 May, McDouall to Freer, 29 May, Yeo to Croker, 31 May 1813, Johnston to mother, 23 June 1813, in Halsey Collection, nos. 16294, 16421, HCRO. American dispatches from Brigadier General Brown to Governor Tompkins and to secretary of war, Sacket's Harbor, 29 May and 1 June 1813, in *Niles Weekly Reader*, IV: 260-61, which also gives the American casualty figures (21 killed, 84 wounded, and 26 missing, mostly regulars). Militia casualties were not known, though probably no more than twenty-five.

[15]Chauncey's squadron in 1813 was:

Name	Tonnage	Crew	Broadside Lbs.	Armament Guns		Total
General Pike	875	326	312	26	long 24s	624
Madison	593	274	344	20	carronades 32s	688
				4	long 12s	
Oneida	243	146	201	16	carronades 24s	402
				2	long 9s	
Hamilton	76	54	84	8	carronades 18s	156
				1	long 12	
Governor Tompkins	96	64	65/57	1	long 32	122
				1	long 24	
				2	carronades 24s	
				2	long 9s	
Fair American	82	63	32/24	1	long 32	56
				1	long 24	
Conquest	82	46	30	2	long 24s	54
				1	long 6	
Growler	53	31	40	1	long 32	48
				4	long 4s	
Julia	53	36	32/12	1	long 32	44
				1	long 12	
Ontario	81	29	32/12	1	long 32	44
				1	long 12	
Pert	53	35	38	1	long 32	44
				2	long 6s	
Scourge	45	33	20	4	long 6s	40
				4	long 4s	
Asp	57	27	24/12	1	long 24	36
				1	long 12	

Name	Tonnage	Crew	Broadside Lbs.	Armament Guns	Total
Raven	50	16	18	1 long 18	18
Lady of the Lake	89	29	9	1 long 9	9
Gloucester			32/18	1 long 32 1 long 18	50
16	2,528	1,209	1313/1231	114 (68 long guns 46 carronades)	2435

Yeo's squadron in 1813 was:

Name	Tonnage	Crew	Broadside Lbs.	Armament Guns	Total
Wolfe	426	200	360	1 long 24 (pivot) 8 long 18s 4 carronades 68s 8 carronade 32s	696
Royal George	330	158	366	1 long 24 (pivot) 2 long 18s 2 carronades 68s 16 carronades 32s	708
Melville	186	95	210	2 long 18s 12 carronades 32s	420
Earl of Moira	169	90	153	2 long 9s 12 carronades 24s	306
Sir Sidney Smith	c.160	75	172	2 long 12s 10 carronades 32s	344
General Beresford	150	70	96	1 long 24 (pivot) 8 carronades 18s	168
6	1,421	688	1,357	91 (19 long guns; 72 carronades)	2642

For Chauncey's squadron, see "The Return of vessels, arms and men," Record Group 45, National Archives, Washington, DC. This was kindly supplied by the

Project Director, Hamilton Scourge Project. For Yeo's squadron, see "Statement of the Number and Force of His Majesty's Squadron upon Lake Ontario," Yeo to Warren, 29 September 1813, ADM 1/504/324.

[16]David Campbell to Edward Campbell, 19 June 1813, Campbell Family Papers, Perkins Library, Duke University, Durham, North Carolina [hereafter DUL].

[17]Willoughby Morgan to [David Campbell], 18 July 1813, ibid.

[18]See Colonel James Miller to Catherine Miller, 17 July 1813, in James Miller MSS, U.S. Military Academy, West Point, New York.

[19]Thomas Parker to David Campbell, 24 June 1813, in Campbell Papers, DUL.

[20]Willoughby Morgan to David Campbell, 20 July 1813, ibid.

[21]Johnston went on to say that "we are now as regularly fixed and as compleat a Navy form'd as if we were on the Atlantic Ocean." Johnston to mother, 25 July 1813, Halsey Collection, No. 16295 a & b, HCRO.

[22]Harvey to Baynes, 11 June 1813, in Wood, *Select Documents*, II: 153; Yeo to Prevost, 31 May and ? 1813, ibid., 129-130; Cruikshank, "Contest for Ontario," 188.

[23]"The Return of vessels, arms and men" for Chauncey's squadron, Record Group 45, National Archives. Theodore Roosevelt, *The Naval War of 1812* (Boston, 1886), 185-86 incorrectly assessed the broadside of the *Madison* and *Oneida*. "Statement of the Number and Force of His Majesty's Squadron upon Lake Ontario," Yeo to Warren, 29 September 1813, ADM 1/504/324. Yeo added the number of guns wrongly at ninety-three and he estimated the weight of metal in tons (!), not pounds. But the important revelations were the number and calibre of the guns and the size of the crew.

[24]Mahan, *Sea Power*, II: 54.

Part III

Peacetime Controversy and Crisis

The "Peacemaker" Explosion

Spencer C. Tucker

On 23 February 1844 a large gun named the "Peacemaker" exploded aboard the USS *Princeton* killing and wounding several onlookers, including the secretary of the navy. It was one of the worst accidents in American naval history and the most infamous one involving ordnance. In this essay, Professor Tucker traces the evolution of the *Princeton*'s heavy ordnance and the mechanics of wrought iron gun manufacturing in order to show the causes for this disaster as well as to show how this vessel and her armament served as an important experimental platform for technological changes in the U.S. Navy.

The War of 1812 had proved to the navy the superiority of ships armed with heavy, long-range guns. In the war's aftermath, many American naval officers believed that the logical step was to arm much larger ships with a few heavy guns and to omit the many but largely ineffective smaller ones. A fast vessel armed with only a few of the biggest guns able to fire accurately to the longest range would make all other warships obsolete. Americans were not alone in this thinking. Such a plan was under consideration by most of the world's major navies.

Besides this change in armament were extensive experiments with new types of guns and with shell. One such project was a revived interest in wrought iron guns developed by Professor Daniel Treadwell of Harvard. Wrought iron was the strongest metal then known, having about twice the tenacity of cast iron. Large forgings of shafts, common by the 1830s, were made of several wrought iron bars laid side by side, heated white hot, and welded together by repeated blows from a heavy, machine-operated hammer. Wrought iron guns were thus made in the form of a shaft, then bored out. Strong longitudinally but weak in the transverse, the chief drawbacks were the uncertainty of the welds and the cost.

Despite the failure of the Treadwell gun in this country, work on wrought iron guns continued, particularly in Britain, where the successful Armstrong breech-loading gun was built on the Treadwell principle. From Britain also came a large wrought iron gun named the "Orator," designed by the brilliant young engineer and one-time captain in the Swedish army, John Ericsson. He had been unable to convince the British authorities of the utility of his inventions.[1]

There was resistance in the U.S. Navy as there was in the Royal Navy during the 1840s to steam propulsion, ironclad vessels, and the new shell guns. Matthew C. Perry, Robert F. Stockton, and others, however, argued for change, and Stockton's considerable wealth allowed him to take leaves of absence from the navy to pursue other interests, such as the building of the Delaware and Raritan Canal in his native New Jersey. The financial panic of 1837 led him to Britain for financial assistance to complete the canal project. While there, Francis Ogden, the American consul in Liverpool and designer of steam engines, introduced Stockton to his business associate, John Ericsson. The Swede's work impressed Stockton and convinced him that Ericsson's inventions would be much better received in the United States. Before leaving England, Stockton commissioned Ericsson to build a small iron-hulled screw steamer.[2]

In December 1838 the navy ordered Stockton to join the Mediterranean Squadron. On the way he witnessed the trial of the small steamer. He and Ericsson agreed on the feasibility of a 12-inch bore wrought iron gun, and Stockton contracted with the Mersey Iron Works near Liverpool for its manufacture. The gun was subsequently shipped to the U. S. in 1841, where it was bored, and had its trunnions installed.[3] Later, both Stockton and Ericsson claimed credit as the originators of the gun, but Ericsson apparently designed it.[4]

When Ericsson arrived in the United States at the end of 1839, there was only one steam vessel in the U.S. Navy, the small 750-

176

ton side-wheeler frigate *Fulton II*, built in 1837-38. Congress authorized three additional steam warships in 1839, including the big 1700-ton side-wheel frigates *Mississippi* and *Missouri*. Both were handsome vessels, carrying two 10-inch and eight 8-inch guns, but their machinery was located above the waterline. The third was the *Union*, a vessel of 956 tons with submerged horizontal paddle wheels and four 8-inch guns.[5] Stockton sought command of the *Missouri* but failed to receive it.[6]

His disappointment was short-lived. Campaigning for William Harrison and John Tyler in the election of 1840, Stockton was offered the office of secretary of the navy by Tyler who succeeded Harrison after the latter's brief term as president. Stockton declined but prevailed on Tyler to authorize the construction of a new vessel that he would command. The disappointing result was a corvette with one gun deck, but at least Stockton was allowed to build her as he and Ericsson saw fit.[7] The new vessel was the 672-ton steam sloop *Princeton*, named for Stockton's home town and completed in 1844.[8] Conceived as an experimental vessel, Stockton and Ericsson made her the most technically advanced warship of the time.[9]

The *Princeton* was of wood, but her sides were thicker than a vessel of that size. She was the first screw-propeller steam warship ever built in any country and the first to be built with her machinery below the waterline. This made her virtually impervious to damage from enemy shot and shell; the lower location of the weight also produced greater stability. The *Princeton* was the first to burn anthracite coal, eliminating the tell-tale black smoke of commercial soft coal. She was also the first warship equipped with fan blowers to produce better combustion and hotter furnace temperatures, speeding the heating of the plant and eliminating the need for a tall smoke stack to create draft. Ericsson even designed a stack that could be lowered to conceal the fact she was a steamer.[10] She also had seawater-cooled surface condensers to recondense steam, thus eliminating the need for a resupply of fresh water. Ericsson's power plant also proved more efficient than expected. Although rated at 220 horsepower, the engine produced upwards of 260. According to Stockton, she was "the cheapest,

177

fastest, and most certain ship-of-war in the world."[11] Ericsson's biographer noted, "Her success was the final triumph of the principle of screw propulsion."[12]

On 17 October 1843 Stockton took her to New York to race what was regarded as the fastest steamer of the day, the trans-Atlantic sidewheeler *Great Western*. The *Princeton* was victorious on a twenty-one mile, using only steam while the *Great Western* used both sail and steam.[13]

The *Princeton*'s armament consisted of two 12-inch wrought iron guns and twelve 42-pounder carronades. The big guns fired a 212-pound shot and rested on pivot mounts on the forecastle and quarterdeck.[14] One of the 12-inchers was the "Orator," the other was the "Peacemaker," both purchased before undergoing proof, a violation of standard procedure owing to Stockton's influence.[15] Manufactured of Yorkshire iron at Liverpool's Mersey Iron Works, the "Orator" had a thirteen foot unchambered bore. Trunnions were installed in Philadelphia, and the gun was bored before it was proofed in 1842. During firing it had developed a small crack behind the trunnions.[16] Ericsson supervised a reinforcement. Beside the trunnion band, designed only to hold the trunnions and not provide reinforcement, four additional bands of iron totalling approximately nine inches in width and two and three-quarters inches in depth were shrunk on the breech, one above the other so as to appear as a single band. They had been precisely machined, heated to expand, and then positioned on the gun and allowed to cool down, in order to grip the gun with their tensile strength. Additional proof firings confirmed the gun as safe.[17]

During the test firing the crack in the "Orator" opened enough to allow water to drain through when the gun was swabbed out, but that was all. The subsequent Naval Court of Inquiry concluded that, "if a gun of this construction should yield to the force of the trial, it would be by a simple opening, and not, as in cast iron, a violent disruption and shattering of the fragments."[18]

The original plan had been for the *Princeton* to carry just one 12-incher mounted forward. The aft gun would be smaller, perhaps an 8-inch, 64-pounder. Stockton, who saw the advantage of having a battery of two 12-inch guns capable of firing in all directions, however, contrived to have another gun built on the same basic rule and installed aft. The owners of the Phoenix Foundry of New York City stated that Ericsson had "furnished and executed" the drawings of the gun and that boring and finishing were under his supervision. Ericsson also examined the gun after it was proofed, and there is no record that he ever doubted its strength. Certainly the new gun was hastily made, but concern was partially allayed by the belief that American iron was superior in strength and tenacity to that of English iron.[19]

The gun was made by the firm of Ward & Co., then bored and finished at the Phoenix Foundry under Ericsson's direction.[20] When completed it weighed 27,334 pounds and cost the government nearly $11,500. It was made, for the most part, of iron already on hand.[21] Described as "the better piece of worksmanship of the two," it was fifteen feet long and had the same size bore and a chamber similar to the "Orator" but about a foot greater diameter at the breech to compensate for the bands on the first gun.[22] Although the new gun was the same size as the "Orator," it had no shrunk-on bands for added strength, and thus suffered from the inadequacies of wrought iron guns despite its size. Ogden believed that the new gun, with its bands welded two inches greater than the first gun, "would be perfectly safe under any trial."[23]

Captain William Crane, head of the Bureau of Ordnance and Hydrography, and a tragic figure in this affair, was not happy with developments but was unable to influence Stockton. He did insist that Stockton proof the gun before it was paid for. It was fired only five times,[24] which in no way compared with the proof of the "Orator," or of other experimental guns. Ericsson always maintained that the "Peacemaker" had been poorly designed and proofed, but all present believed it "capable of sustaining any charge that could be put in her." Stockton noted: "The men who made it deserved their money. It is worth all the guns on board of any frigate."[25] On mounting the two guns--the one built in the United States, now named "Peacemaker," and the one built in England, now named "Oregon" as a result of the boundary dispute with England over that territory--on board the *Princeton*, Stockton mounted the "Peacemaker" on the forecastle, while Ericsson's gun was relegated to the quarterdeck.[26]

With the *Princeton* complete, Stockton sailed her in early 1844 to Washington for display, leaving Ericsson waiting with his suitcases at the foot of Wall Street when the sloop passed.[27] Stockton made no claim to be responsible for the innovations of both the sloop and her ordnance. But he did not deny the claims of others on his behalf, and in his widely circulated report of February 1844 on the warship's capabilities, Ericsson was nowhere mentioned.

When the *Princeton* arrived at Washington on 12 February 1844, interest in the sloop and her revolutionary ordnance was heightened by tensions with Britain over Oregon and with Mexico over talk of annexation of Texas. Stockton took the *Princeton* on a trial run three days later, followed by two excursions for publicity. During these three trips, the "Peacemaker" was fired a total of eight times.[28] Stockton was a staunch advocate of modernizing the navy, and the *Princeton*'s success would help overcome congressional opposition to President Tyler's request for similar ships, though larger size and more suited to carry heavy armament.

Interest in the *Princeton* and her guns was such that a grand outing was planned. On 28 February 1844 between 350 and 400 people, including President Tyler and cabinet officers and their families, boarded the sloop at Alexandria. On the way down the Potomac, the "Peacemaker" was fired twice, each time with a charge of twenty-five pounds, one round shot of 212 pounds and two wads. The *Princeton* was on its way back up the river when Stockton agreed, at the suggestion of Secretary of the Navy Thomas Gilmer, to fire the gun again with a charge of only twenty-five pounds of powder. This time the gun blew up.

The rupture occurred in the breech end just short of the trunnions, splitting the gun into three large, irregular fragments. Two of these blew out over the starboard bow, carrying away about twenty feet of the hammock rail. The other fragment, five feet long and more than half the circumference of the gun at the larger end, fell on the deck about thirty feet from the gun,[29] mowing down the front rank of onlookers, who had been standing to the left of the gun. Dead were Secretary of State (and former Secretary of the Navy) Abel Upshur, Secretary of the Navy Gilmer, and six others. Another nine, including Senator Thomas Hart Benton and Stockton (who had fired the gun), were injured. President Tyler, who had remained below in the company of Miss Julia Gardiner, was unharmed.[30] There was another belated casualty. In 1846, William Crane resigned his post of chief of the Bureau of Ordnance and Hydrography and committed suicide. His family blamed it on the "Peacemaker" episode.[31]

Stockton requested President Tyler to convene a court of inquiry that met on 7 March aboard the *Princeton*. Stockton did not attend, informing the court by letter that he had "not yet recovered from my wounds...."[32] Ericsson had been invited to present evidence but refused to be involved in any way. He was convinced that Stockton, who would not share triumph with him, now wanted him to share in the failure. His assumption was probably correct, but Ericsson's refusal was a great blunder. The inference was that this was proof of his responsibility.[33]

Experts concluded after examining the gun that "the fibrous quality of the iron appears to be wholly destroyed; large crystals form the mass; and the specific gravity is found to be nine per cent less than that of ordinary hammered iron." On 11 March the court completely exonerated all concerned and concluded that Stockton had been moved by patriotic motives.[34] It noted that he had solicited the advice of Colonel George Bomford of the army Ordnance Department on the proper proof; had "proceeded on well established practical facts"; had "resorted to men of science and practical skill for advice..."; and that the trials had justified "confidence in the durability and efficacy of the gun." The court concluded: "No shadow of censure...can be attached to any officer or any of the crew of the *Princeton*."[35]

Apparently at Stockton's instigation, a committee from the Franklin Institute also studied the explosion. Its report of 8 August 1844, limited to materials and workmanship of the gun, concluded that the iron used to forge the "Peacemaker" was of inferior quality, having only about three-quarters the strength of English iron. It could have been "rendered of a good quality by sufficient working," but this had not been done. Furthermore, the welding was also imperfect. The committee concluded that "in the present state of the arts, the use of wrought iron guns of large calibre, made upon the same plan as the gun now under examination ought to be abandoned...." This was based on the difficulty, "if not impossibility," of welding such a large mass and the weakening of the metal from its long exposure to the intense heat necessary in its manufacture with the trip hammers then available in the United States.[36] This negative judgment did not, however, rule on the issue of the practicality of all wrought iron guns.

Stockton continued to defend the wrought iron gun.[37] But many remained critical. The House Committee on Naval Affairs carried out its own investigation, the results of which were reported on 15 May 1844. It sustained the earlier board of inquiry by not blaming the officers and men of the *Princeton*, but by censuring the navy for allowing Stockton "to carry out his own peculiar views." It found that he had purchased the two large guns without "any express order from the Navy Department," and that the guns were ordered, not by the advice of the navy's Ordnance Department, "as would seem to be the proper course." It found that "it was irregular to permit an officer unconnected with the Construction or Ordnance department to proceed with so little restraint in the building and arming of a ship of war, as was the case with regard to the Princeton." It also cautioned against allowing individuals to order armament without concurrence by "the proper officers of the government." The Committee also questioned the wisdom of purchasing a replacement gun, suggesting that these "large guns," at least as far as the navy was concerned, were experimental and perhaps ought "to be specifically directed by Congress before they are procured."[38]

The bursting of the "Peacemaker" may well have given Congress an excuse to hold up construction of more steam warships and delay the modernization of the navy. It may also have impeded the introduction of heavy ordnance aboard ships,[39] but it does not seem to have retarded their development.

President Tyler completed Stockton's exoneration when, on 14 March 1844, he directed the secretary of the navy that another gun of the "size and dimensions of that lately destroyed [be] wrought, under the direct supervision of Captain Stockton."[40] It was forged by the Mersey Iron Works in England as a replacement piece. Secretary of the Navy John Mason sent Stockton on 28 February 1845 to Liverpool to collect the replacement gun. However, it was never mounted for service and only fired once.[41]

The explosion led to a policy giving the Bureau of Ordnance and Hydrography sole responsibility for the proof of naval weapons. There were new requirements gauging the standards whereby ordnance would be accepted into the service, and there was a series of government-ordered experiments over the next five years into metal casting techniques and quality control, resulting in better quality guns. The "Peacemaker" events motivated Lieutenant Thomas Rodman (later brigadier general and Chief of Ordnance of the U.S. Army) to patent a new process for casting guns to make them safer. Naval ordnance designer John Dahlgren also found inspiration for his work in the tragedy. Robert Parrott, inventor of the hooped gun of the American Civil War, acknowledged his debt to the banding technique employed in the "Oregon."[42]

Another result of the "Peacemaker" explosion was the reduction of powder charges for guns aboard ship. By the Civil War the maximum was fifteen pounds, and this was for the 11-inch Dahlgren gun.[43] This regulation, of which Ericsson disapproved, probably enabled the *Virginia* to escape destruction during her epochal engagement with the *Monitor*.

What of Ericsson and Stockton? The "Peacemaker" explosion led to a complete break between them, with the consequence that the inventer never did receive full compensation for his work on the *Princeton*.[44] Ericsson vowed never again to offer his services to the Navy Department. Fortunately for the Union he did not keep his vow, for he won lasting fame for his design of the *Monitor*. As for Stockton, he played a key role in the Mexican War as commander of the Pacific Squadron in securing the Pacific coast and earning the title, "Conqueror of California." He resigned from the navy in 1850 and served as a United States Senator from New Jersey from 1851 to 1853.

As for the *Princeton*, she lost her former luster and was evermore considered a jinxed ship. She was attached to the Home Squadron and served well during the Mexican War. From 1847 to 1849 she was in the Mediterranean, where she is said to have had some influence on both French and British naval design, both navies having powerful steamers with her characteristics by 1856.[45] Upon her return, her hull was too rotten for repair, and she was broken up at the Boston Navy Yard.[46]

Although accounts differ, President Tyler may have met Julia Gardiner for the first time the day of the explosion (some writers have them already engaged by that date). She was a striking twenty-four year old, and the president had tarried below in her company when the explosion occurred. Her father, Colonel David Gardiner, a state senator from New York, was killed in the explosion. When Julia Gardiner was informed of the news she promptly fainted, and when the *Princeton* docked, the president carried her off the ship. They were married in June.

Finally, the explosion may have altered foreign policy as well. Upshur's replacement as Secretary of State was John C. Calhoun, who favored accommodation with Britain over the Oregon boundary and also had considerable impact on the acquisition of Texas.

Notes

[1]Ericsson was a leader in the development of the steam locomotive and shared credit in 1836 with Francis P. Smith for the development of the screw propeller. Despite a successful demonstration by Ericsson's small (45' 8") screw steamer, the *Francis B. Ogden*, in the summer of 1837, the Lords of the Admiralty remained unconvinced (William C. Church, *The Life of John Ericsson*, 2 vols. [New York, 1906], I: 88-91).

[2]The *Robert F. Stockton* was the first direct-acting screw propeller engine vessel ever built. It was a 70-foot iron steamboat, of thirty tons, and powered by a thirty horsepower engine. For more than twenty-five years it was in service on the Delaware & Raritan Canal (Ibid., I: 87, 91-92, 94-95, 102).

[3]The gun was to have a bore twelve inches in diameter, be twenty-four inches in diameter behind the trunnions, and taper to eighteen inches at the muzzle.

Testimony of Francis B. Ogden before the Naval Court of Inquiry, in U.S. Congress, House Committee on Naval Affairs, *Accident on the Steam-ship "Princeton,"* 28th Cong., 1st sess., 15 May 1844, 45 [hereafter "House Report 479"]. Lee M. Pearson, "The *Princeton* and the Peacemaker," *Technology and Culture* VII (Spring 1966): 164, 166, 167.

[4]Ogden testified that Stockton formed his decisions about the construction of large wrought iron guns from Ericsson's calculations and his own experience. Ogden testimony in "House Report 479," 6.

[5]Lieutenant George F. Emmons, *The Navy of the United States, from the Commencement, 1775 to 1853* (Washington, 1853), 26, 34.

[6]Ericsson believed that he would design it. Church said that Stockton used an Ericsson-built model along with a set of plans with his presentation to the Navy Department (Church, *Ericsson*, I: 120). Both men hoped that the new 12-inch gun would be the prototype of the *Missouri*'s battery, but the navy decided that the *Missouri* was to be a duplicate of the *Mississippi*. In any case her command did not go to Stockton. Neither did the *Union*.

[7]Pearson, "*Princeton* and the Peacemaker," 168. Meanwhile, Ericsson enjoyed some success constructing commercial steamers using his propeller (Church, *Ericsson*, I: 107-111).

[8]She was 164 feet in length of deck and 673 tons burden. Extreme beam was thirty feet and six inches; total depth was twenty-one feet; displacement at deepest load, with two hundred tons of coal on board, was nineteen feet, four inches (George H. Preble, *A Chronological History of the Origin and Development of Steam Navigation*, 2d ed. [Philadelphia, 1895], 196).

[9]There is controversy over credit for her design. Stockton was responsible for her sail rig. Miles credits him with the hull design as well (Commander A. H. Miles, "The Princeton Explosion," *U.S. Naval Institute Proceedings*, LII [November 1926]: 2225). That, however, should probably go to Ericsson, who was responsible for the engines and the 6-bladed 14-foot diameter propeller (Ensign Henry C. Watts, "Ericsson, Stockton and the U.S.S. *Princeton*," Ibid., LXXXII [September 1956]: 963). Ericsson's biographer stressed that Ericsson, occupied with the project from September 1841 to September 1843, supervised all facets of the building (Church, *Ericsson*, I: 135, 155).

[10]Emmons, *Navy of the United States*, 32-33; Edgar Stanton Maclay, *A History of the United States from 1775 to 1901*, 3 vols. (New York, 1924), III: 18; James P. Baxter, *The Introduction of the Ironclad Warship* (Cambridge, 1933), 14; Horace Greeley, et. al., *The Great Industries of the United States* (Hartford, 1872), 598; Paolo E. Coletta, "Abel Parker Upshur," in *American Secretaries of the Navy*, ed. Paolo E. Coletta, 2 vols. (Annapolis, 1980), I: 184; Watts, "Ericsson, Stockton and the U.S.S. *Princeton*," 964.

[11]Stockton to Secretary of the Navy David Henshaw, 5 February 1844, quoted in Preble, *Chronological History of...Steam Navigation*, 197. In this long letter Ericsson is nowhere mentioned.

[12]Church, *Ericsson*, I: 136. In 1858 Senator Stephen R. Mallory of Florida, who had chaired the Naval Committee and later served as the Confederate secretary of the navy, called the *Princeton* "the foundation of the steam marine of the entire world...." Speech in the United States Senate, May 14, 1858. U.S. Congress, Senate, 35th Cong., 1st sess., 1858, XXVII, Pt. 3., 2131.

[13]Church, *Ericsson*, I: 135.

[14]All, according to Stockton, could be used at once on either side of the ship, giving her a greater weight of broadside than most frigates. Stockton to Secretary of the Navy David Henshaw, 5 February 1844, quoted in full in Preble, *Chronological History of... Steam Navigation*, 197-98.

[15]Person, "*Princeton* and the Peacemaker," 169.

[16]The gun had not been mounted, and Ericsson claimed, with considerable justification, that this was the result of burying the breech of the gun in sand where it could not recoil with powder charges of up to fifty-six pounds.

[17]Accounts differ on the number of times the gun was fired after original proof. Stockton subsequently put it at 180 with the gun "still in perfect condition" (Letter of 23 August 1844 to Stockton to secretary of the navy, 23 August 1844, Department of the Navy General Records, Record Group [hereafter RG] 74, entry 159, National Archives, Washington, D.C.). Lieutenant William Hunt, who took part in the proof of the "Orator," said it was fired between 120 and 150 times after being hooped ("House Report 479," 7).

[18]Ibid., 13. All involved believed that the gun had been successfully tested. There were those, however, who thought that it was too large for shipboard use. Ericsson later cited John Dahlgren as one of those who "opposed my 12-inch gun of 1841" (Church, *Ericsson*, II: 137).

[19]Pearson, "*Princeton* and the Peacemaker," 172; Church, *Ericsson*, I: 124; "House Report 479," 13.

[20]Manufacture of the gun is credit to either the Phoenix Foundry, to Peter Hogg and Cornelius Delameter who bought the Phoenix Foundry in 1842, or to the Hamersley Forge (Miles, "The Princeton Explosion," 2230; Watts, "Ericsson, Stockton and the U.S.S. *Princeton*," 964). Ward & Co.'s Hamersley Forge, also in New York City, worked as a subcontractor to the Phoenix Foundry (Pearson, "*Princeton* and the Peacemaker," 164).

[21]RG 45, entry 159, National Archives; Work on the gun began a few days after it was ordered in early July 1843 ("Report on the Explosion of the Gun on board the Steam Frigate 'Princeton,'" *Journal of the Franklin Institute*, Third Series, VIII [1844]: 209-210 [hereafter "Franklin Institute Report"]).

[22]*National Intelligencer*, 2, 16 March 1844 in *Niles' National Register* (Baltimore), 2 March 1844.

[23]Ogden's testimony in "House Report 479," 5.

[24]It was fired with various charges, beginning with fourteen pounds of powder and no ball and working up to forty-five pounds of powder, two wads, and a 212-pound shot. The powder was more powerful than normal and the last charge was equivalent to 49.6 pounds. Only the last firing was shot, however. Letter of Stockton to Crane, January 16, 1844 ("House Report 479," 41).

[25]A gunner and a lieutenant testified that Stockton, Ericsson, and one of the manufacturers (Mr. Hogg), examined the gun in and out after proof and found it "to all appearance, to be perfect" (Ibid., 7, 10; Stockton to Crane, letter of 16 January 1844, Ibid., 4).

[26]Ericsson designed other ordnance innovations, including a new wrought iron pivot carriage that dispensed with breeching, a first with heavy guns and a forerunner of the later monitor carriages of the Civil War (Church, *Ericsson*, II: 142-46). Elevated by tackle fixed to the breech, the gun had an automatic range finder and a self-actuating lock that caused it to fire at just the right elevation in the ship's motion. The range finder was awarded a prize at the 1851 London Exhibition. The self-acting gunlock had been invented as early as 1828 (Ibid., I:132). Although overstated, the press reported the gun to be so accurate "that it could hit on object 'the size of a hogshead' 9 out of 10 times half a mile away." *Niles' National Register*, 2 March 1844.

[27]Church, *Ericsson*, I:140.

[28]The "Oregon" was not fired at all. The first trip on 16 February was a trial run. That of 19 February included President Tyler, much of the Cabinet and Congress as well as newspaper reporters. Another such outing took place on the 20th.

[29]"Franklin Institute Report," 206-207.

[30]*The National Intelligencer* in *Niles' National Register*, 2 March 1844.

[31]The bursting of the "Peacemaker" led to the removal of the "Oregon" from the Philadelphia Navy Yard to Annapolis where it is today (Letter from Chief of the Bureau of Ordnance H. A. Wise to Superintendent of the Naval Academy David Dixon Porter, 5 July 1867, RG 45, entry 159, National Archives).

[32]Letter from Stockton to Judge Advocate Richard S. Coxe, 8 March 1844, in "House Report 479," 15. He was, however, represented by his attorney, John R. Thompson.

[33]Years later Ericsson said that the "Peacemaker" had "previously been destroyed by a hollow shot too large for the bore, and forced home with great effort. The hollow shot, which had stuck during the discharge, came out in small fragments. By this unfortunate occurence the gun was fatally ruptured" (Cited in Church, *Ericsson*, I: 134-35).

[34]"House Report 479," 5-6, 12.

[35]Bomford had not given a precise recommendation, but he shared the proof record for his gun (Letter from Bomford to Stockton of 25 November 1840, in ibid., 13-14, 16-17).

[36]"Franklin Institute Report," 215-16.

[37]He maintained that the "Peacemaker" would not have burst had it been made of sound materials (Letter to the Secretary of the Navy, RG 74, entry 159, National Archives).

[38]"House Report 479," 3-14.

[39]Samuel E. Morison, *"Old Bruin," Commodore Matthew Calbraith Perry* (Boston, 1967), 132; Edgar S. Maclay, *A History of the United States Navy from 1775-1901*, new and enl. ed., (New York, 1924), III: 19.

[40]"House Report 479," 43.

[41]Alexander L. Holley, *A Treatise on Ordnance and Armor* (New York, 1865), 86-87; Lieutenant General Sir Howard Douglas, *A Treatise on Naval Gunnery*, 3rd ed. (London, 1851), 214; K. Jack Bauer, "John Young Mason," *American Secretaries of the Navy*, I: 212. The gun came to be known as the "Brooklyn Navy Yard Gun," since for many years its location was the Sands Street entrance to the yard. Today, it stands next to the restored Commandant's House at the Washington Navy Yard, mounted on a 13-inch 1861 mortar carriage.

[42]Testimony of Major T. J. Rodman in U.S. Congress, Joint Committee on the Conduct of the War, "Heavy Ordnance," in *Report of the Joint Committee on the Conduct of the War at the Second Session, Thirty-Eight Congress* (Washington, 1865), 98, 136.

[43]U.S., Bureau of Ordnance, Navy Department, *Ordnance Instructions of the United States Navy*, 2d ed. (Washington, 1860), 141.

[44]Ericsson had received only $1,150 from Stockton for his part in designing the *Princeton*, but he claimed that an additional $13,930 was owed to him for his service and patents. When he presented a bill, the secretary of the navy referred the matter to Stockton who refused to approve it for payment with the claim that there never had been such an agreement (Letter from John Y. Mason to Ericsson, May 11, 1844, in Church, *Ericsson*, I: 143). Stockton also refused to acknowledge Ericsson's role in the *Princeton*'s design and construction, referring to him only as " a very ingenious mechanic." Stockton also asserted that he had no idea that Ericsson intended to come to the United States and that he had in fact "thrust himself upon me." He also maintained that he had never entered into an agreement with Ericsson for recompense by the government, and that Ericsson simply volunteered his services (Stockton to John Y. Mason, 20 May 1844, in Church, *Ericsson*, I: 143-45). The U.S. Court of Claims in 1857 authorized payment of $13,930, but no payment was ever made. See also Senate debate on bill (5 C.C. No. 90) for the relief of John Ericsson, 15 May 1858 in U.S. Congress, Senate, 35th Cong., 1st sess., 27, pt. 3: 2129-32.

The motivation was clear, judging from a remark by Stockton: "If Ericsson had not been a damned coward, there would have been no trouble about his getting his money for the vessel." This is quoted in a several sources. Church attributes it to Sargent (Church, *Ericsson*, I: 141).

[45]The French in 1843 and the British in 1844 each fitted a frigate with a propeller on Ericsson's plan (Ibid., 138).

[46]The *Princeton* was rebuilt in 1851-52 as a clipper ship, 177 feet long and 1,370 tons displacement, largely a result of Stockton's influence. The new ship used as much of the old machinery and timber as possible. Armed with a battery of four 8-inch guns, and six medium 32-pounders of 32 cwt, she was fitted out as one of the vessels in Perry's squadron to the East Indies, but trouble in her new boilers prevented her from taking part. She became a receiving ship and was sold in 1896 (Preble, *Chronological History... of Steam Navigation*, 199).

Secretary of the Navy Josephus Daniels and the Marine Corps, 1913-21

Merrill L. Bartlett

For the first century and more of its existence, the U.S. Marine Corps attracted little attention from successive civilian secretaries of the navy. Commandants and senior Marine Corps officers normally profited by this benign neglect as the secretaries focused their energies on the navy and not on its small sister service. Only after the turn of the century during the tenure of a weak commandant, did civilian involvement and the influence of partisan politics come to be felt in the Marine Corps. In this essay, Colonel Bartlett examines the role of Josephus Daniels in the development of the "smart and faithful force."

George F. Elliott came to the commandancy in 1903 ill-suited to head the Corps. For most of his thirty-three years in uniform, he had served at sea or abroad, and lacked the temperament and disposition for duty in Washington. The absence of bold administrative initiatives or worrisome problems at Headquarters Marine Corps (HQMC) provided a false sense of solace to civilian supervisors. Like his predecessors, Secretary of the Navy George von Lengerke Meyer paid scant notice to the administration of the Marine Corps except when trouble brewed. In 1910, an untoward situation involving Elliott and his staff threatened to taint the presidency of William H. Taft. Critics of the administration suggested that the disagreement between the commandant of the Marine Corps and his adjutant and inspector, the colorful Colonel Charles H. Lauchheimer, had anti-Semitic overtones. Meyer wisely separated the feuding members of the HQMC staff and put the matter to rest, but a panel of investigators recommended a single four-year term for future commandants of the Marine Corps, along

with other administrative changes which limited the tenure of officers on duty at HQMC. Changing the senior leadership of the Corps more frequently than had been the custom during the Age of Sail paved the way for partisan political involvement in both the selection of future commandants and the day-to-day management of the administration of the Marine Corps.[1]

President Woodrow Wilson's secretary of the navy, Josephus Daniels, came to his office convinced that the administration of the naval services demanded firm, steady civilian leadership. A North Carolina newspaper editor and party loyalist, Daniels satisfied Wilson's requirement for an articulate spokesman in his cabinet for the New South, prohibition, progressive reforms, and religious fundamentalism. As a Democratic national committeeman, Daniels supported Wilson's candidacy and received the secretary of the navy's portfolio in return.

The day before Wilson's inauguration in 1913, Daniels paid a courtesy call on the outgoing secretary. As he prepared to depart, the patrician Meyer offered a piece of advice that the new secretary of the navy followed for the next eight years: "'I do not wish to give you any advice, but merely to suggest that you keep the power to direct the navy [and Marine Corps] *here.*' For emphasis, he slapped his desk."[2]

The new secretary of the navy turned to his post with a passion and energy that few could remember in the history of the office. To begin with, Daniels sought to erase the difference in social class between officers and enlisted men, suggesting that sailors suffered "at the hands of an officer whose right to command is due to opportunities enjoyed at the outset of life rather than to superior natural capacity or character."[3]

Daniels turned the old-line navy on its ear quickly. On his first visit to a battleship, he waved away the official guard of honor and receiving party on the quarterdeck. Walking to the forecastle, he mounted a wooden box and asked the sailors to gather around him: "Boys, I've come to tell you that I am going to run the navy for you. There won't be anymore of this oppression by the officers.'"[4]

Daniels sought the allegiance and devotion of the enlisted force of the navy and Marine Corps for his stewardship of the Navy

Department. When he forbade the consumption of alcohol aboard ship, Daniels argued that sailors should not be denied a privilege enjoyed by the officers. Expanding his ukase ashore, the moralistic secretary found that his drive for temperance had waned. The sailors enjoyed the opportunity to purchase alcoholic beverages and tobacco in the commissary stores and canteens at prices considerably cheaper than in town. Daniels's critics failed to dissuade the determined prohibitionist.[5]

Navy officers observed Daniels's machinations with wry amusement and hoped that like most civilian interlopers, the new secretary's tenure would be mercifully brief. One disappointed observer waxed biblical: "The feelings of the Hebrew prophet as he descended into the menagerie of King Darius may now be shared by his namesake at the head of the Department of the Navy."[6]

Criticism of the new secretary ranged from flippancy to ferocity. When Daniels selected William S. Benson to be the first Chief of Naval Operations instead of the more senior and better qualified Bradley A. Fiske, most naval officers understood the secretary's determination to cast the naval services into a new mold. On the heels of the announcement of Benson's appointment, one of Daniels's most strident critics lashed out: "We could make shift to live under a debauchee or a tyrant, but to be ruled by a busybody is more than human nature can bear."[7]

During his first year in office, Daniels began to feel misgivings concerning the smaller of the naval services. Knowing all too well that the corpulent and lethargic Major General William P. Biddle had gained the Corps' highest post in 1911 because of his important Philadelphia connections and the powerful political support of Senator Boise Penrose, the new secretary began almost immediately to interject himself and his office into the affairs of the Marine Corps. Meyer had chosen to leave Biddle to his own devices, perhaps relieved because the troublesome Elliott had slipped into retirement. Daniels acted upon the recommendation of a board of inquiry which examined the heated acrimony of 1910. Apparently, the driving force behind the change in regulation precluding career-long tenure for the commandant and his principal staff officers was none other than the aid for inspections,

Captain William F. Fullam. The evidence Fullam presented to Daniels included a memorandum from HQMC indicating that Lauchheimer had served twenty of his thirty years of Marine Corps service in Washington. Fullam argued forcefully to limit the tenure of the commandant and his principal staff officers to single four-year terms, and to keep the size of the Marine Corps below ten thousand men lest it appear to be another "army."[8]

Under Daniels's close scrutiny, Biddle chafed. After less than a year under the new administration, he requested retirement. In the selection of the twelfth commandant, Daniels had the opportunity to influence the future of the Marine Corps for decades to follow. The secretary's office notified all Marine Corps commands that any colonel or lieutenant colonel could apply for the post of commandant. Daniels had eight colonels from which to chose, and all but one commanded barracks. Biddle had hoped to slide in his good friend, Colonel Lincoln Karmany, commanding the barracks in Norfolk, before any of the other contenders had sufficient time to marshal their political supporters. But when the moralistic secretary learned of Karmany's messy divorce in order to marry another woman, he dismissed his claim for the office immediately. The secretary's diary entry for 11 November 1913 leaves no doubt as to why the veteran, hard-drinking campaigner had lost out: "Karnody [Karmany]--divorced."[9]

Littleton W. T. Waller, the senior colonel in the Corps with a date of rank of 5 March 1905, appeared to have the most firm claim to the commandancy. Senator Claude A. Swanson of Virginia garnered the signatures of all thirty-one Democrats in the Senate in a forceful letter to Woodrow Wilson urging the appointment of the colorful bushwhacker. But it was not to be. Daniels reasoned that it made little sense to appoint an officer with a record of inhumane treatment of the Filipino people just when the Wilson administration promised a new and enlightened approach to the government of the Philippines.[10]

In his published memoirs, Daniels claims to have been more attracted to the candidacy of Lieutenant Colonel John A. Lejeune than to any of the Corps' colonels. But the secretary's self-serving recollection of the events of late 1913-early 1914 must be tempered with the knowledge of the maelstrom following the ouster of Major General George Barnett from the commandancy in 1920. Barnett had the strongest claim to the Corps' highest post by virtue of a superior and spotless record, a diploma from the Naval Academy, and--most important of all--the strong support of his Annapolis roommate, Senator John Weeks of Massachusetts.[11]

The selection of Barnett made good political sense, given his powerful Republican supporters. Senior navy officers expressed approval because, for the first time, an Annapolitan came to head the Corps. The senior officers of the Marine Corps chimed in to applaud Barnett's selection as well. His only noteworthy detractor was an obscure junior officer with a powerful political connection. Major Smedley D. Butler considered his future and that of the Corps to rest with bushwhackers and campaigners characterized by Waller. More than two decades later, the mercurial and colorful Butler still referred to Waller as "the greatest soldier I have ever known."[12]

Butler's father, Congressman Thomas S. Butler, sat on the powerful House Naval Affairs Committee. In a series of letters home, the younger Butler sought to persuade his father to join him at the barricades. When the announcement of Barnett's appointment had been made public, Butler's morale sank to new lows.

> I am so unhappy, I do not know what to do. All my hard work has been thrown away and I am broken. The only hope is Colonel Waller's appointment and I am losing faith in that. This cursed mail also brought news of Barnett's appointment. Oh, I don't know if I can stand anymore--if it were not for thee and the babies I would go on a terrible drunk--I just don't give a g--d d--m in [sic] what happens.[13]

Butler never would or could accept the appointment of someone like Barnett, who in his view, lacked the requisite powder burns and tropical sweat stains on his uniforms to head an elite body of fighting men. Through the years, Butler's smoldering anger and mounting frustration came to play an important part in Secretary

Daniels's machinations with regard to the future of the Marine Corps.

Despite Butler's histrionics and fears, Barnett measured up to the exacting demands of Secretary Daniels. Daniels added the commandant of the Marine Corps (CMC) to his advisory body. In a press release, Daniels claimed to hope for closer coordination between the two branches of the naval service. His confidence in Barnett had not yet ebbed. "He [Barnett] stands equal to the ablest men who have been at the head of this important branch of the service."[14]

In his professional relationship with Daniels, Barnett found a superior that paid close attention to administrative details. For example, when the CMC informed the secretary that enlistments for the Marine Corps appeared to be on the rise and would more than meet manpower requirements, Daniels responded by asking Barnett why he did not then take steps to close some of the recruiting stations in order to save money![15]

Like most administrators before them, both Daniels and Barnett spent their days preoccupied with personnel matters. During Barnett's tenure under the watchful gaze of Secretary Daniels, no issue came to dominate his commandancy--except for his untimely ouster in 1920--more than personnel increases. From an overly-committed small force numbering approximately ten thousand officers and men in 1914, the Marine Corps grew to more than seventy thousand by the end of the World War. For casual observers of the Corps' administrative scene, the spectacular increases appeared tied to the commitment on the Western Front; however, long before "over there" became a household phrase in the United States, Barnett and his staff had convinced first Secretary Daniels, and then both congressional naval affairs committees, to support legislation calling for increases in numbers of men wearing forest green.[16]

In October 1915, Barnett told Daniels of his concerns about personnel shortages. On the heels of a demand by the navy for an increase of seventy-five hundred men, Barnett argued for an increase in his ranks of fifteen hundred using the figure of 20 per cent of navy strength for the Corps. On 3 February 1916, a special personnel board headed by Assistant Secretary of the Navy Franklin D. Roosevelt issued a report supporting Barnett's argument. Daniels seemed to encourage Barnett in his aggrandizement, and the CMC shared his optimism with Colonel Joseph H. Pendleton. Just as Daniels suspected, the CMC hoped that the increases in personnel would result in the authority to promote several colonels to brigadier general.[17]

Daniels warmed to Barnett's argument that without the increases and authorization for more rapid and timely promotions of the officer corps, most officers would be too old to keep pace with their younger and more fit troops. In company with Daniels, Barnett informed the House Naval Affairs Committee that unless company grade officers received promotions at a more accelerated rate, the average captain would spend thirty-five years in uniform before becoming eligible for advancement to major. Then, in just five more years he would be forced to retire for age. Barnett's logic met with a ready reception from Daniels, already under siege from critics who argued that a bigger navy did not necessarily mean a better one. Then, the Butlers--father and son--fired a salvo that caused both Daniels and Roosevelt to waiver in their support for the CMC's proposed personnel increases.[18]

Congressman Butler argued forcefully against merging line and staff officers, and spoke out strongly against allowing staff officers to become eligible for promotion to brigadier general. Doubtless the elder Butler reflected the views of his ambitious son, then serving in Haiti. When news of the CMC's proposed legislation reached the Caribbean, Butler lost no time in venting his spleen in a letter home:

> tell him [father], the line officers... look upon this proposed Marine Corps Personnel bill with suspicion...it promotes practically no one but staff officers who went into a staff department because they preferred an easy life.[19]

The younger Butler's sharply-worded correspondence gained his father's attention sufficiently. After Congressman Butler discussed the matter with Daniels, the secretary ordered Barnett to bring Butler home to confer with Congressman Butler about the proposed personnel legislation. Despite the younger Butler's protests, the increases in manpower became law. And the principal staff officers at HQMC--adjutant and inspector, quartermaster, and paymaster--became brigadier generals.[20]

Daniels's support for Marine Corps expansion faltered only once--and then just slightly. On the heels of the U.S. declaration of war in 1917, Barnett argued for sufficient increases in manpower to allow a brigade of leathernecks to join the American Expeditionary Forces (AEF) in France. Admiral William S. Benson, the chief of naval operations (CNO), spoke out strongly against the plan because he feared it would detract from the Marines' primary mission. Barnett promised to meet the Corps' naval requirement, and then reminded his audience that the president had the authority to transfer naval forces such as marines to the army for the duration of the conflict. At first, Daniels appeared to agree with Benson, but in the end he accepted Barnett's argument that if the leathernecks failed to see action in the war in France, it would give a hollow ring to the Corps' colorful recruiting slogan, "First to Fight."[21]

Through Barnett's first four-year term of office, he and Daniels worked well together. The Corps met new commitments, including the manning of expeditionary brigades to Haiti and the Dominican Republic, while continuing to fulfill existing manpower needs abroad, at sea with the fleet, and at home. The fitness reports Daniels submitted on Barnett continued to be "excellent to outstanding."[22]

Leatherneck prowess on the battlefields in France calmed any fears that Daniels might have harbored over his decision to support Barnett's proposal to volunteer marines for duty with the AEF. Although senior army officers resisted all attempts to place an additional brigade of leathernecks--the Fifth Brigade--into the front lines, the Fourth Brigade won fresh laurels for the Marine Corps. Approximately thirty thousand marines served in France during the war out of the 72,963 leathernecks on active duty during that period. Of the number "over there," almost one-third suffered wounds; the brigade received more than thirteen hundred individual decorations for bravery, including six Medals of Honor.

Daniels shared Barnett's pride in marine elan and bravery, and was so moved after the epic battle of Belleau Wood that he composed a new stanza for the Marine Corps Hymn:

As we raised our flag at Tripoli
And again in Mexico;
So we took Chateau-Thierry and
The forest of Belleau.
When we hurled the Hun back from the Marne,
He said we fought like fiends,
And the French rechristened Belleau Wood
For United States Marines.[23]

Nevertheless, by 1918 the secretary of the navy and CMC had come to loggerheads. As Barnett's first four-year term of office neared its end in 1918, everyone expected him to be reappointed. Although the secretary had announced at the beginning of his administration that he planned to limit the CMC and bureau chiefs to single four-year terms in office (his "single-oak" policy), changing so many key officers in the middle of a war made no sense. Daniels summoned each of the incumbents and asked for an undated letter of resignation which he intended to use upon the cessation of hostilities. While each senior navy officer complied, Barnett hesitated.

According to Barnett's version of the incident, he refused to sign such a letter, claiming that as an officer he served at the pleasure of the president. When the commander-in-chief no longer required his services, he would leave office. Daniels then told the CMC to forget the matter. Understandably, Daniels's account differs. On 25 February 1918, when the secretary discussed the matter with Barnett, the CMC agreed. However, the following day he telephoned and asked to reconsider. Barnett then gave his word as an officer and a gentleman that a resignation would be forthcoming any time that Daniels wished it. Later, Daniels suggested that Mrs. Barnett probably goaded her husband into refusing his request. For the first time, Daniels used the expression "if Barnett was an Indian, his name would be 'the-man-who-is-afraid-of-his-wife'."[24]

198

While Mrs. Barnett might have enjoyed a reputation as one of the most sparkling hostesses among the smart set in the nation's capital, her charm failed to impress Daniels. Scorning inherited wealth, the secretary found Mrs. Barnett more irritating than amusing or clever. Shortly after Daniels announced that alcoholic beverages would no longer be served at official functions at naval installations ashore, Mrs. Barnett obtained his permission to continue to use liquor in cooking. She then served the secretary a dinner which he and the other guests would long remember. Every course except the roast beef came laced with alcohol!

Although out of his element in the vibrant social scene dominated by Mrs. Barnett, Daniels realized that far too often he came off as the butt of her clever witticisms. Moreover, Daniels's plain wife paled next to the beautiful and charming spouse of the CMC. On one occasion, Mrs. Barnett's name appeared on a list of the best dressed women in the nation. Neither Mrs. Daniels nor the second Mrs. Wilson received so much as a mention. Gossip columnists reminded their readers that Mrs. Barnett's prominence in social circles rubbed some sensibilities raw, especially those of Secretary of the Navy Josephus Daniels.

In the summer of 1919, Daniels learned that a young Marine Corps officer had filed suit for divorce after a brief and unwise marriage; furthermore, he seemed unwilling to pay the alimony dictated by the courts. Confusing the matter further was the fact that the officer was Mrs. Barnett's nephew and the son of an admiral. Daniels's request that Lejeune (now a major general) look into the matter "confidentially" underscores the increasing estrangement between the secretary and the CMC. Any semblance of cordiality and confidence between the two had already ended over the issue of the promotion of the CMC to the rank of lieutenant general the year before.[25]

In May 1918, Barnett's Republican supporters in the Senate placed a proviso in the annual naval appropriations bill calling for the promotion of the CMC to lieutenant general and each of the principal staff officers at HQMC to major general. News of the legislation reached the restless Butler in Haiti, and he lost no time in sharing his outrage with his father. When Congressman Butler learned that Daniels knew nothing of the proposed promotions before the Senate Naval Affairs Committee passed it, he rose in the House to denounce the legislation.

Arguing that such promotions should be saved for those fighting in France, he then referred to Barnett and the senior officers sitting in the visitors gallery as "rocking chair warriors." Warming to his audience, Congressman Butler exclaimed (to the obvious discomfort of Barnett, his wife, and the principal staff officers at HQMC): "When the rewards are handed out for service in the war, they will go to the men that have earned them, and not to those favored by certain beautiful social surroundings."[26] Barnett insisted that the proposed legislation had not been his doing, but sufficient evidence existed revealing that a third star had been on his mind for some time. Daniels knew that the CMC had used all of his influence on Capitol Hill to gain the promotion. Sadly, this incident, coupled with the difficulties over Barnett's reappointment months before, fueled Daniels's convictions that Barnett had become just the sort of entrenched bureaucrat that he sought to remove when taking office in 1913.

The relationship between the secretary of the navy and his CMC deteriorated rapidly. Daniels's scrutiny of Marine Corps administrative matters increased. When the Quartermaster of the Marine Corps ordered more blankets, the secretary complained in a memorandum to Barnett that sufficient quantities were in stock. Barnett then countered with the obvious: it gets colder in Quantico than at Parris Island. Unconvinced, Daniels revoked the CMC's authority to requisition supplies for the Corps. Petulant exchanges such as this came to dominate their working relationship following the strained events of early 1918, and foreshadowed the events that stunned Washington naval circles two years later.

On 20 June 1920, the wily Daniels sent the CMC a notice of dismissal to take effect at the end of the month. Lacking the courage to face the disgraced and humiliated Barnett, the secretary left town, claiming the press of official business. A family friend of the Barnetts and Woodrow Wilson's personal physician, Rear Admiral Cary Grayson, witnessed the meeting between the secretary of the navy and the president two days before. When the

Barnetts learned that Daniels told Wilson that the CMC had agreed to step down, they sought redress and support from Republican supporters in Congress. Meanwhile, Lejeune took office as ordered at noon on 30 June 1920. During the painful encounter when the two old leathernecks had to face one another, Barnett asked his successor an obvious question. "As an old friend, why didn't you let me know?"[27]

Lejeune earned any discomfort he felt during the confrontation. Beginning in September 1919, when Daniels first informed him of his plan--"in strictest confidence"--to oust the twelfth CMC, Lejeune had ample opportunity to inform Barnett of the duplicity. Clearly, he thought that he had no choice in the matter. But by 1919, Lejeune stood as Barnett's logical successor to the Corps' highest post. No other general officer could lay claim to the commandancy, given Lejeune's fame and superlative service during the world war. Leaving Barnett in office until the end of his second term in 1922 would have prevented the political scandal that threatened to tarnish the Corps' image.[28]

Daniels's motives for the untimely change in the commandancy stemmed from real or imagined political fears. An American electorate, weary of Wilsonian idealism and the haggling over the League of Nations and the Treaty of Versailles, yearned to put the world war era behind them. It seemed to most political observers that any candidate nominated by the Republicans would soon occupy the White House. As a life-long Democrat and not the least hesitant to display his political colors, Lejeune's candidacy could well become a casualty of the presidential race of 1920. Thus, Daniels feared for Lejeune's future and sought to place his good friend in the Corps' highest post when he had the opportunity to do so.

Butler turned his powerful father against Barnett after Waller's failure to gain the commandancy in 1914. Increasingly, the ambitious Butler saw the twelfth CMC and his coterie of "headquarters toadies" and Naval Academy graduates as a threat to his own ambitions. Inability to see action on the Western Front in 1918 turned his blind rage into hatred for Barnett and all he stood for.

I feel at the present time and have felt for the past five months that my days of soldiering are over. For over twenty years I have worked hard to fit myself to take part in this war which has just closed, and when the supreme test came my country did not want me.[29]

In the years following the turbulence surrounding the commandancy in 1920, Barnett's supporters--especially his indefatigable wife--argued that a cabal, consisting of Lejeune, Daniels, and the Butlers, had conspired to oust the twelfth CMC. But no evidence exists to support such a charge, although all parties to the duplicity had knowledge of Secretary Daniels's plan. More than a decade later and after Barnett's death, Mrs. Barnett came forward with new evidence of a Byzantine plot to oust her husband. In a painful letter to Lejeune, she accused him of complicity in the plot that helped kill her husband and threatened to turn her material over to the news media. Daniels calmed Lejeune's fears immediately by stating emphatically that "you never requested the appointment [to the commandancy], nobody ever requested it for you, and no influence was ever brought to bear upon me to appoint you."[30]

True enough, but Daniels's actions in 1920 reflect the worst sort of nepotism. Initially when called to task for his ouster of Barnett, Daniels explained his "single-oak policy." Even his most loyal supporters had difficulty stifling yawns. Then, Daniels claimed that Lejeune earned the Corps' highest post because of his outstanding performance during the World War. A new explanation took hold. "I always gave preference to men who won distinction at the cannon's mouth." Daniels's new *mot juste* gained quick acceptance even from Barnett's supporters.[31]

While the years of Secretary of the Navy Josephus Daniels have slipped mercifully into the dustbin of history, his tenure and the effect of his meddling in Marine Corps affairs have yet to be assessed accurately. Not since Smith Thompson (1819-23) has a secretary of the navy influenced the future of the Marine Corps in such a far-reaching fashion. For the most part, Daniels's biographers have chosen to devote themselves to navy and not naval matters.[32]

Even though the Republicans swept the Democrats from office in the fall of 1920, Daniels's influence continued to be felt. When the Senate set aside Lejeune's confirmation because it had originated from a lame-duck administration, Daniels urged Congressman Butler to bring the entire House Naval Affairs Committee to request that the new secretary of the navy, Edwin H. Denby, accept Lejeune as the CMC and not bring back the tarnished and wounded Barnett. The new secretary agreed and, with Lejeune's urging, restored Barnett to the rank of major general. Both supporters and antagonists of the twelfth CMC breathed a sigh of relief.[33]

Barnett strengthened the Marine Corps during his tenure and deserved better treatment from the nation he served so faithfully. The twelfth CMC brought the Corps back to efficiency and respectability after two successive commandants--one an alcoholic and the other a lethargic sinecure--weakened the Marine Corps by their administrative shortcomings. Barnett's untimely dismissal in 1920 was the result of personal animosities overriding judicious decision-making. Both the Butlers sought the secretary's favor, and the younger Butler even took Second Lieutenant Josephus Daniels, Jr., under his wing and made him an aide-de-camp. In 1918, Daniels congratulated Lejeune on his promotion to major general with a cordial note that foreshadowed the events of 1920:

> How gratifying it is for me to know that your appointment [to major general] was approved universally in and out of the Corps. I think of you often and have every confidence in your leadership of the Marine Corps.[34]

More than two decades later, apparently, the relationship had not lost its luster, as suggested in another warm note from Daniels: "Our deep friendship formed in the days when we were in the navy together is permanent and lasting on both sides. You know that nowhere outside your own kin have you friends who hold you in more affectionate esteem."[35]

Despite Daniels's bombastic rhetoric and carping moralizing for eight long years, observers of American naval affairs may be surprised to learn that the indefatigable secretary hoped to have Butler succeed Lejeune in the commandancy. Surely Neville, winner of the Medal of Honor at Vera Cruz and the commander of the Fourth Brigade (Marine Corps) in France during the World War, qualified as "having been at the cannon's mouth." Daniels's ambition to elevate a fawning subordinate to such an important position serves only to tarnish further his administration of the Department of the Navy.[36]

One can easily imagine Smedley Darlington Butler as the fourteenth CMC. The restless and indefatigable Butler's dislike for Naval Academy and War College graduates, and navy officers in general, had already become legend even before his memoirs appeared in print. A "headquarters toadie" and Annapolitan such as Ben H. Fuller would never have achieved the commandancy. More ominous and potentially disastrous for the future of the Corps would have been the absence of John H. Russell, an officer despised by Butler, but a man who succeeded in changing the Marine Corps' antiquated system of officer promotion--a legislative achievement that eluded Lejeune for nine long years. Indeed it was during Russell's administration that the Corps' amphibious doctrine was codified and published. Had Daniels succeeded in elevating Butler to the commandancy, most likely the Marine Corps would have entered World War II unprepared to accept its role for the spearhead in the amphibious assault across the Pacific. More likely as a result of Butler's legacy, the Corps would continue to cling to the role of the bushwhackers in fighting America's small wars in the Third World.

The U.S. Marine Corps suffered a perilously close call because of Secretary of the Navy Josephus Daniels. The forty-first public servant to hold the position of secretary of the navy left office with statements that matched the quality of his tenure. Senior naval officers exchanged wry smiles when they read Daniels's farewell message of 5 March 1921. "For eight years, I have been your commanding officer. All my life, I will be your shipmate."[37] The wry smiles, however, changed to guffaws when they heard the secretary's remarks at the ceremony honoring the service of the women marines during the World War. "We will not forget you. As we embrace you in uniform today, we will embrace you without uniform tomorrow."[38]

In a less jocular note, Assistant Secretary of the Navy Theodore Roosevelt, Jr., recorded his own opinion of Daniels in a candid and pungent diary entry.

> Secretary Daniels came in. He had nothing really on his mind, except to say How-do-you-do. He is a queer character, a combination of ignorance, kind-heartedness, and shifty opportunism.[39]

Notes

The author gratefully acknowledges the generous grants from the Marine Corps Historical Foundation and the Naval Academy Research Council supporting researches of the Corps' highest post from 1913 to 1929. The author's earlier thoughts on this subject may be found in the following materials: "The Road to 'Eighth and Eye': John Archer Lejeune, 1913-1920" (Paper presented at the Annual Meeting of the American Historical Association, Chicago, IL, 27 December 1984); "Ouster of a Commandant," *U.S. Naval Institute Proceedings* [hereafter *Proceedings*] 106 (November 1980): 60-65; and "Old Gimlet Eye," *Proceedings* 112 (November 1986): 73-79.

[1]Wayne A. Wiegand, "The Lauchheimer Controversy: A Case of Political Pressure During the Taft Administration," *Military Affairs* 40 (April 1976): 54-59; and "Maj. Gen. Elliott's 40 Years' Record," *New York Times*, 22 April 1928, pt. III, p. 1.

[2]Josephus Daniels, *The Wilson Years: Years of Peace, 1910-1917* (Chapel Hill, 1944), 119; Daniels's diary, 5 March 1913, container 2, Josephus Daniels [hereafter JD] Papers, Manuscripts Division, Library of Congress, Washington, D.C. [hereafter JD MSS]; and JD to Claude A. Swanson, 9 March 1934, container 101, reel 62, JD MSS.

[3]"Democratizing Daniels," *Nation*, 22 April 1915, p. 438.

[4]Archibald Douglas Turnbill, "Seven Years of Daniels," *North American Review* (November 1920): 607; For material in support of Daniels's initiatives, see "Secretary Daniels at Bay," *Literary Digest* 52 (8 April 1916): 955-56, and "Josephus Daniels—and the Navy," *Forum* 59 (January 1918): 18-20.

[5]JD to Henry L. Roosevelt, 17 February 1934, reel 97, and JD to Claude A. Swanson, 15 November 1933, reel 62, JD MSS; Hanson Baldwin, "The End of the Wine Mess," *Proceedings* 84 (August 1958): 82-91.

[6]"Daniels in the Lion's Den," *Literary Digest* 51 (24 April 1915): 941.

[7]George Harvey, "The R. Hon. N.C.B. [North Carolina Boy], Our First Lord of the Admiralty," *North American Review* (April 1915): 481.

[8]JD to Woodrow Wilson, 5 April 1913; Wilson to JD, 14 May 1913; and Fullam to JD, 5 December 1913, Marine Corps, general file 1899-1913, container 531, JD MSS.

[9]E. David Cronin, ed., *The Cabinet Diaries of Josephus Daniels, 1913-1921* (Lincoln, 1963), 83. See also, JD to Biddle, 14 November 1913, Marine Corps, general file, September-December 1913, container 531, JD MSS.

[10]Claude A. Swanson to Woodrow Wilson, 2 December 1913, Candidates for Commandant, 1913 file, container 531, JD MSS.

[11]John A. Lejeune [hereafter JAL], *Reminiscences of a Marine* (Philadelphia, 1930), 199; JAL to the commandant of the Marine Corps [1935], reel 6, JAL MSS, Manuscript Division, Library of Congress; Daniels, *The Wilson Era: Years of Peace, 1910-1917*, 322-23; Major Louis McGill to Colonel Joseph H. Pendleton, 27 December 1913, folder 10, Pendleton MSS, Marine Corps Historical Center [hereafter MCHC], Washington Navy Yard, Washington, D.C.; Rear Admiral Victor Blue to Pendleton, 30 January 1914, folder 11, Pendleton MSS; "Many Seek Post of Marines' Head," *New York Times*, 13 November 1913, p. 5; and "Marine Corps' New Head," *New York Times*, 3 February 1914, p. 4.

[12]Smedley D. Butler [hereafter SDB] as told to Lowell Thomas, *Old Gimlet Eye* (New York, 1933), 36.

[13]SDB to Mrs. Smedley D. Butler, 31 January and 16 February 1914, SDB MSS, Newtown Square, PA.

[14]JD to files, undated memorandum [1915], subject file--Navy Department, Bureau Chiefs, 1913-16, container 549, JD MSS. See also, JD to George Barnett [hereafter GB], 28 June 1915, Barnett 1914-1917 file, container 64, JD MSS; and Daniels's press release, 22 April 1914, Barnett's officer qualification record (OQR), HQMC, Washington, D.C.

[15]JD to GB, 16 March 1914, Barnett 1914-1917 file, container 64, JD MSS; "Annual Report by the CMC for 1913," in *Annual Report by the Secretary of the Navy* [hereafter *ARSN*], 1913 (Washington, 1914), 527-28; and "Annual Report by the CMC for 1915," in *ARSN*, 1915 (Washington, 1916), 755-58.

[16]Jack Shulimson, "First to Fight: Marine Corps Expansion, 1914-1918," *Prologue* 8 (Spring 1976): 5-16.

[17]GB to Joseph H. Pendleton, 30 September 1915, folder 12; and 25 January 1916, folder 13, Pendleton MSS, MCHC.

[18]GB's testimony before the House Naval Affairs Committee, 29 January 1916, U. S. Congress, House, Committee on Naval Affairs, *Hearings on Estimates Submitted by the Secretary of the Navy, 1916*, 64th Cong., 1st sess. (Washington, 1916) 2: 2119-2271.

[19]SDB to Mrs. Thomas S. Butler, 21 February 1916, SDB MSS, MCHC.

[20]GB to commander, U. S. Expeditionary Force, Haiti, 15 March 1916, 1916 file, SDB MSS, MCHC.

[21]U. S., Congress, House, Committee on Naval Affairs, 17 April 1917, *Hearings on Estimates Submitted by the Secretary of the Navy, 1917*, 65th Cong., 2d sess. (Washington: GPO, 1917), pp. 30-31.

[22]Barnett's fitness reports, signed by Daniels, are in his OQR.

[23]N.d. [1918], Curtis Wilbur file, container 558, JD MSS.

[24]JD to Franklin D. Roosevelt, 26 December 1934, container 95, reel 59, JD MSS (the original of this letter cannot be located in the Roosevelt MSS, Hyde Park, NY); GB's version is in his unpublished autobiography, "Soldier and Sailor Too," ch. 29, GB MSS, MCHC. See also, Daniels, *The Wilson Years--Years of War and After* (Chapel Hill, 1947), 155.

[25]GB to Arthur I. Caperton, 26 August 1919, Barnett June-December 1919 file, container 64, JD MSS; Mrs. Caperton to JAL, 29 May 1920, and JD to JAL, 29 May 1920. Lejeune 1920-1924 file, container 88, JD MSS.

[26]*Congressional Record*, 65th Cong., 2d sess., 27 June 1918: 8374; see also, Thomas S. Butler to Franklin D. Roosevelt, 27 April 1918, container 88, Roosevelt MSS, Hyde Park, NY; Congressman A. W. Gregg to GB, 23 May 1918, GB's OQR; GB to JD, 28 June 1918, Barnett January-June 1918 file, container 64, JD MSS; Leigh C. Palmer to William S. Sims, 29 May 1918, Sims MSS, MD, LC; and Daniels's diary entries, 23 May, 24 May, 3 June, and 26 June 1918, container 3, JD MSS.

[27]Tom Butler, interview with author, 17 July 1979; Oral Histories by Benis M. Frank, MCHC: Gen. Clifton B. Cates (28 March 1967); Maj. Gen. Ray A. Robinson (18-19 May 1968); and Maj. Gen. William A. Worton (31 January and 20 February 1967). See also, SDB to Alexander A. Vandegrift, 6 August 1920, SDB MSS, MCHC; William S. Benson to GB, 27 August 1920, "Barn-Barr" file, Benson MSS, Library of Congress; and Lelia Montague Barnett, "Command Performances" and "Washington Dinner Disasters" (unpublished memoirs, privately held).

[28]JAL to CMC [1935], reel 6, JAL MSS; Senator John Weeks to GB, 17 August 1920, and Senator Henry Cabot Lodge to GB, 29 June 1920, container 2, GB MSS.

[29]SDB to his father, 20 March 1919, and to his wife and children, 29 October 1918; see also, SDB to CMC, 18 May 1917; JAL to SDB, 1 June 1917, SDB to JAL, 22 June 1917; Thomas S. Butler to SDB, 19 June 1918, and GB to SDB, 8 December 1917.

[30]JD to JAL, 2 May 1932, container 88, reel 55, JD MSS; see also, JAL to JD, 28 April 1932, container 88, reel 55, JD MSS; Mrs. GB to JAL, n.d. [1932], and

Raymond J. Bartholomew to Mrs. GB, 11 January and 27 January 1932, GB MSS, MCHC. The Bartholomew letters are suspect in that they are typed and unsigned.

[31]JD to Claude A. Swanson, 27 July 1933, container 102, reel 62, JD MSS; Senator John Weeks to GB, 17 August 1920; and Weeks to Mrs. GB, 2 September 1920, container 2, GB MSS.

[32]See, for example, Joseph L. Morrison, *Josephus Daniels: the small-d Democrat* (Chapel Hill, 1966); Innis L. Jenkins, "Josephus Daniels and the Navy Department" (Ph.D. diss., University of Maryland, 1960); and Paolo E. Coletta, "Josephus Daniels," in Coletta, ed., *American Secretaries of the Navy*, 2 vol. (Annapolis, 1980), 2:525-81.

[33]Josephus Daniels, *The Wilson Years--Years of War and After*, 155-56; and Cronin, *The Cabinet Diaries of Josephus Daniels*, 2 March 1921, 604n.

[34]JD to JAL, 12 September 1918, JAL 1913-1919 file, container 88, JD MSS.

[35]JD to JAL, 5 March 1941, reel 9, JAL MSS.

[36]JD to Franklin D. Roosevelt, 26 December 1934, container 95, reel 59, JD MSS. Daniels even defended Butler over his inappropriate remarks concerning the Italian dictator, Benito Mussolini. See JD to Claude A. Swanson, 3 February 1931, reel 62, JD MSS.

[37]Navy Department press release, 5 March 1921, Edwin Denby MSS, Burton Collection, Detroit Public Library, Detroit, MI.

[38]Quoted in Linda L. Hewitt, *Women Marines in World War I* (Washington, 1974), 41.

[39]Diary entry, 6 December 1921, Theodore Roosevelt, Jr., MSS, MD, LC.

Forrestal and the Navy Plan of 1945: Mahanian Doctrine or Corporatist Blueprint?

Jeffery M. Dorwart

Immediately following World War II, the nation's victorious armed services engaged in lengthy and often bitter inter-service squabbling over the issue of unifying the military under a single Department of Defense. In this essay, Professor Dorwart examines the intellectual and organizational assumptions behind the navy's plan for unification, the backgrounds and attitudes of the architects of that plan, and the particular role of Secretary of the Navy James Forrestal in that process.

James Forrestal remains one of the most enigmatic and neglected figures in modern American naval history. Publication of diary excerpts in 1951 and two biographical works in the early 1960s are still the standard references.[1] Since then scholars have echoed the earlier emotion-charged interpretations that Forrestal was either an unstable Cold War ideologue driven by obsessive fears of Russia, or that he was the greatest spokesman for the U.S. Navy as the first line of national defense since Alfred Thayer Mahan. Writing about Forrestal's term as Secretary of the Navy, one historian observed: "It is no exaggeration to say that Forrestal at this time was beginning a period of leadership that was to have a more profound and lasting influence on the thinking and political behavior of the senior naval officer than any man since Captain Mahan."[2]

There were reasons why after the initial activitity scholars neglected Forrestal. His voluminous private papers contained boxes of trivial details but gaps on major issues. Those who worked closest with Forrestal seemed reluctant or unable to discuss him, while documentary collections that might add to an understanding remained closed. This has changed in recent years. New archival materials are available to Forrestal researchers at Princeton University, the Harry S. Truman Library, the Operational Archives of the Naval Historical Division, and the National Archives.[3]

In re-examining Forrestal, however, historians continue to confront the pervasive interpretations of the tragic Cold Warrior or brilliant modern-day Mahan. This paper suggests a possible methodological approach for conceptualizing Forrestal without the emotional, ideological implications of earlier works. The approach is by examining the strategy, structure, and bureaucratic politics of large-scale corporate organization and its relationship to public policy. Robert D. Cuff's important study of the War Industries Board provides a stimulating model of how to apply this method to "innovations in management structures for combining business, government, and defense."[4]

Simultaneously, historian Ellis Hawley finds that this search for innovation in management structures took on many characteristics of European corporatist theories and in his words became "an American variant of corporatism." In Hawley's construct, organizational managers such as James Forrestal were "corporatizers," or corporatists, because they favored corporative structures to coordinate, rationalize, and stabilize the many competing and conflicting social and economic groups that dominated the American liberal capitalist system. Corporatists sought to advise and guide president, Congress, and public toward a middle course between statism and socialism, centralization and decentralization, and tradition and innovation.[5]

Many historians remain unconvinced that corporatism helps explain the centrist forces that shaped recent American history. However, some have started to apply a "corporatist synthesis" to the study of economic, diplomatic, and military policy and organization between 1900 and 1950. Joan Hoff Wilson explains Herbert Hoover's associational state in corporatist terms. Robert Griffith argues that Eisenhower was driven by the vision of a "Corporatist Commonwealth," while Jordan Schwarz uses this construct as the basis for an analysis of Bernard Baruch. "He was not a democrat," Schwarz contends, "he was a corporatist" because Baruch wanted an enlightened organizational elite rather than elected representatives to run the country through coordinating agencies such as a national security council or a national economic parliament.[6]

Baruch's longtime Wall Street friend and associate, James Forrestal, shared this socio-economic, political, and organizational vision. But was he also a corporatist? Did Forrestal want to design a corporatist blueprint for America? Or was he, as earlier studies maintain, primarily a Mahanian ideologue? This brief paper cannot adequately answer these questions, but it can test them at a point in Forrestal's public service where private and public, civil and military, tradition and innovation, and business and government intersected most dramatically to create structural fault lines. That point occurred where Forrestal confronted the struggle to combine army, navy, and an autonomous air force in a single department of national defense, a movement that by mid-1945 was popularly called the "unification crisis." It was probably no exaggeration when Forrestal's assistant Marx Leva observed later that the Frankenstein monster of unification tore up and killed Forrestal.[7]

In 1945, though, Forrestal met the issue of military unification with all the substantial political and administrative savvy and bureaucratic power at his command. He approached the movement to consolidate the services into a single department of defense from a Mahanian perspective. Whether, as Secretary of War Henry Stimson suggested, Forrestal had become a pawn of the admirals and their Mahanian doctrine, or as was more likely, had absorbed Assistant Secretary of the Navy Franklin Roosevelt's fascination with Mahan's theory of sea power while serving in the Navy Department during World War I, Forrestal had become an enthusiastic and vocal proponent of the Mahanian concepts.[8]

In defending naval autonomy during the unification debates, Forrestal created his own *Mahanian hybrid* that combined naval aviation and amphibious doctrine into something that he called sea-air power. This sea-air power theory not only counteracted the army air force's crusade for air power as the post-war first line of defense but reflected Forrestal's recognition, as a former naval aviator, of the new role of carrier warfare then unfolding in the Pacific. As Forrestal wrote in June 1944 he hoped that one day some naval officer would write a book on the use of air in sea power comparable to what Mahan had done for the role of sea power in history.[9]

In early 1945 Forrestal tried to avoid altogether the issue of defense reorganization. His primary interest--reinforced by civilian, naval, and congressional allies--was to define post-war ship and naval manpower levels, overseas base requirements, and an organization that integrated naval aviation, the Marine Corps, and the fleet without having to compete directly with army and air force for post-war budgets, roles, missions, and force levels. At this point it was doubtful that Forrestal's growing concern for post-war rivalry with Russia influenced his views and actions so much as his conviction that traditionally the navy in peacetime provided the first line of defense and protected and extended American productive power overseas. Driven by his desire to keep a strong post-war navy as the dominant force in American defense, Forrestal wrote FDR in early April 1945 that he wanted to send a couple of his people down to Warm Springs with charts and tables to brief the president on the navy's post-war material, personnel, and base requirements. Forrestal knew that FDR would give them a sympathetic hearing.[10]

That meeting never occurred. Three days after Forrestal dispatched his message, Roosevelt died at his Georgia retreat. In Forrestal's mind, the president's death drastically changed the predicament for the post-war navy because instead of a disciple of Mahan in the White House, he now had to deal with an admirer of General John J. Pershing and a former army captain, Harry S. Truman. Forrestal believed that Truman had little understanding of sea power, was more sympathetic to the post-war desires of the army air force than those of the navy, and uncritically admired General George C. Marshall. Forrestal considered Marshall the prime force behind the movement for a single department of defense that sought to submerge the navy in a monolithic establishment under a single secretary and a single military chief of staff. It was Marshall, Forrestal wrote to Undersecretary of War Robert Patterson, who sought to rush through this single department scheme before the navy had an opportunity to secure legislation for naval organization. "I cannot accept this view," he told Patterson. "The Navy is by the very nature of its material forced to take definite action--ships either have to be laid up or kept in commission; they cannot be left hanging in mid-air."[11]

It had been Marshall's submission to the Joint Chiefs of Staff (JCS) in the fall of 1943 of his "Single Department of War for the Post-War Period" that had initiated this entire unification tangle for Forrestal. Marshall's single department memorandum set in motion a series of events that put Forrestal and the navy on the defensive, including the holding of hearings by the Woodrum Special House Committee on Post-War Military Policy and the formation of a JCS Special Committee on Reorganization under Admiral J.O. Richardson. Propelled to the center of the navy's post-war organizational struggle by Secretary Frank Knox's sudden death in April 1944, Forrestal had taken steps to postpone reorganization until after the war, and to mobilize the naval bureaucracy to protect itself in what he believed would be a difficult post-war organizational struggle.[12]

FDR's death accelerated the unification movement and caused increasing anxiety in an already war-weary Forrestal. In April 1945 the Joint Chiefs issued the long-awaited report on reorganization. They recommended, over Admiral Richardson's objections, a single defense department, a single chief of staff, and an autonomous air force. Forrestal's assistant secretary for air and personal friend Artemus Gates warned that this report was a dangerous proposal to subvert civilian authority over the military since the chief of staff could go to the president. Meanwhile Forrestal learned that the army and air force had put together sophisticated secret organizations to promote the single department idea among patriotic organizations, congressmen, and the press. Vigorous air force stories in the press seemed to confirm such reports in Forrestal's mind. Yet when he appealed to Stimson and Patterson to settle this unification mess quietly and privately before it got out of hand, he was rebuffed. It was a fundamental principle of the

War Department, Stimson replied, that post-war defense be based upon a single department.[13]

Worse still, Forrestal found the navy "lamentably unprepared to conduct any fight against consolidation." It had no coherent post-war plans, no consistent policies and was filled with what Congressman Christian Herter told Forrestal was so much loose thinking that navy friends in Congress had nothing concrete to support. The admirals provided little guidance. Acting General Board chairman Admiral Edward C. Kalbfus advised Forrestal simply to oppose anything the War Department proposed while Admiral Ernest J. King told Forrestal that when asked about the single department to "Just say I am 'agin' it." Finally, at a Top Policy Group meeting in May, Forrestal's civilian advisors, Ralph Bard, H. Struve Hensel, and Artemus Gates urged their boss to develop a navy alternative to the Marshall single department plan, to assemble a well-staffed navy organization of experts on post-war reorganization, and to sell a positive navy plan to the public.[14]

Simultaneously Senate Naval Affairs Committee chairman David Walsh, and House Naval Affairs Committee chairman Carl Vinson, both locked in a titanic executive-legislative struggle with the new president for leadership of post-war national security policies, urged Forrestal to come up with a plan to counter the Truman-Marshall program. Walsh, a waspish New England progressive Democrat and Wilsonian, favored an organization for post-war defense-similar to the British imperial defense cabinet, a federated system that left authority decentralized rather than merged under the executive through a tightly structured pyramidal organization.[15]

After much agonizing and indecision, Forrestal took the step in June 1945 to develop a navy plan for post-war national defense organization. As he had during the past forty years when confronted with crisis, he turned for help to his best friend, Ferdinand Eberstadt, a Wall Street investment banker. Forrestal asked Eberstadt to direct a comprehensive study of what the press now called the "unification controversy." Eberstadt agreed to return to Washington and help Forrestal, despite having been forced out of the war bureaucracy in 1943 in a bitter power struggle with FDR and his New Deal war administrator, Donald Nelson. The

Eberstadt-Forrestal relationship transcended such bureaucratic infighting. They had shared a lifetime personal, professional, and intellectual partnership. As Forrestal's newspaper editor at Princeton, personal lawyer, investment partner, and constant advisor between 1912 and 1939, Eberstadt had helped organize and stabilize Forrestal's career and life.

A profound student of European corporatist thought and political-economic theory, Eberstadt discussed often with Forrestal the need to find a middle way in America between too much governmental regulation and not enough control over the economy and society. Forrestal called this socio-economic value system "liberal capitalism," but it approximated that fundamental American variant of corporatism identified by Hawley and presented as the conceptual framework for recent studies of Hoover, Eisenhower, and Baruch. The interlinking mechanisms favored by Eberstadt and Forrestal to guide such a system rested with agencies such as Baruch's War Industries Board, the Federal Reserve Board, the Securities and Exchange Commission, and the Business Advisory Council of the Commerce Department. Ideally, such agencies coordinated government and business, stabilized economic cycles, and balanced national and private interests.[16]

During his service as vice-chairman of the War Production Board in 1942 and with active help from Forrestal and Baruch, Eberstadt had started to work on a coordinating mechanism to link and balance enlightened private business and labor interests with national policy through a Controlled Materials Plan.[17] Now, in June 1945, Forrestal offered him another opportunity to develop coordinating machinery and innovative structures. To provide an organizational blueprint Eberstadt assembled a brilliant team of research experts. He demanded and got the best Ivy League graduates who in 1945 served as naval reserve officers in Washington. Eberstadt's unification team included Harvard law professor Milton Katz; historians Elting E. Morison and Myron P. Gilmore; advertising executives Scott Harrod and Arthur E. Tatham; and corporate lawyers and investment bankers C. Douglas Dillon, Edward Hidalgo, Eugene Catron, and Maxwell Rabb. As advisors and assistants, Eberstadt consulted economists Bertrand

Fox and E. F. Willett, political scientist Robert Connery, Columbia engineering school dean J.W. Barker, operational research expert Philip M. Morse, intelligence expert Sidney Souers, and aviation expert Nicholas Ludington. To provide guidance Eberstadt recruited Harvard political scientist E. Pendleton Herring, whose 1941 book, *The Impact of War*, was the pioneering synthesis of national security affairs.[18]

The naval bureaucracy was not entirely happy with Eberstadt roaming about the department recruiting the best reserve officers for his personal use. He did not help matters by announcing that Mahanian doctrine no longer provided the answer for national defense. "In the past it is true that the Navy has been our first line of defense," Eberstadt observed, "but this may not be so in the future." His major concern, he announced, was to discover ways to integrate America's resources with its military and diplomatic commitments and policies. Suspicious naval officers remained uncooperative in assigning key personnel to Eberstadt, while Admiral King tried to get Eberstadt out of Washington to study Pacific bases. Unsuccessful in removing Eberstadt, King placed Captain George L. Russell on Eberstadt's organizing committee to keep an eye on this civilian intruder.[19]

Forrestal had given Eberstadt a blank check, ordering all naval officers to talk directly to him without going through the normal chain of command. Armed with this authority, Eberstadt and his experts brushed Russell aside, interviewing dozens of naval officers, war mobilizers, industrial and business leaders, corporate lawyers, academic experts, and nationally syndicated newspaper columnists. Absent from the interview schedule were vocal proponents of the single department scheme and anyone possibly called a New Dealer. Eberstadt wanted only those who saw national security as he did, as more than the uniting of army, navy, and air force into a single department, who understood national security as an extension of the productive capacities of the nation, and who believed that there were no longer distinct periods of peace and war, only periods of constant preparedness.[20]

Eberstadt submitted his final report to Forrestal in late October 1945. The report ranged over many elements of national security, including the interrelationship between economic resources and military strength, the importance of industrial and manpower mobilization planning, the linkage of foreign and military policies, the respective roles of sea and air power, the connection between scientific research and military technology, and the importance to national security of centralized intelligence. The Eberstadt report recommended structures and organizations to coordinate these elements of national security or, as he explained, to provide "strong ligaments of coordination expressed by formal interorganizational links." Specific recommendations included a National Security Council (NSC), a National Security Resources Board, a Central Intelligence Agency, a Munitions Board, a permanent Joint Chiefs of Staff, a Military Education and Training Board, and a National Military Establishment composed of three autonomous departments for air, land, and sea services. For Eberstadt the NSC was the most important interorganizational link. It was the "keystone of our organization structure," he wrote, the body by which to build a consensus for consistent and effective foreign and military policies and to balance military capacity with foreign objectives.[21]

Once again his friend had rescued Forrestal, providing an alternative to the army's single department program. Forrestal did not like Eberstadt's recommendation for a separate U.S. Air Force, but that feature gave the report added legitimacy as an impartial plan made by an outside expert with no axe to grind. Thus Forrestal could protect naval autonomy within a larger system of self-adjusting, interacting, and coordinating structures that comprised a corporate system like the decentralized operations of a General Motors or a DuPont corporation. Eberstadt urged Forrestal to get the navy "100% behind" the report. "I am convinced from the attitude and words of the air people, and perhaps to a lesser extent from the army, that if unification goes through, our sea power will be dealt a mortal blow." He urged Forrestal to assemble a research team on reorganization comprised of his study group experts, Admirals Forrest Sherman and Arthur W. Radford, and a "first class publicity man" to organize the navy's case.[22]

Assistant Secretary Gates was more direct. Forrestal had to take the Eberstadt plan and make it the navy plan if he hoped to combat the army plan. The secretary could no longer rest on the dead hand of tradition embodied in blind acceptance of Mahan's view of sea power still held by some naval officers. He had to introduce Eberstadt's innovative ideas of national security as the navy's position in the reorganization struggle. Several Eberstadt experts recommended that Forrestal whip key elements of the report into a slick advertising brochure with red, white, and blue organizational charts that promoted a navy plan. The pamphlet should be kept the size of *TIME* magazine for better distribution. By early December ten thousand copies of such a pamphlet entitled "The Navy Plan for National Security" were ready for circulation. "I understand the Secretary is talking about printing the pamphlet by the hundreds of thousands," one study group member wrote Eberstadt.[23]

Soon the "Navy Plan" circulated to every newspaperman, congressman, and bureaucrat in Washington. Budget Director Harold Smith found the president at his White House desk carefully going over the colorful charts. At the same time Forrestal observed Senator Warren Austin, a pivotal member of a committee to draft military reorganization legislation, using the pamphlet extensively during committee hearings.[24]

The Eberstadt Report and its offspring, the Navy Plan, sent shock waves through the bureaucracy. The army air force dissected it, looking for structural designs that might threaten its drive for autonomy. General J. L. Collins, who had just introduced his own version of the Marshall single department plan to the Senate Military Affairs Committee, charged that the navy had purchased the Eberstadt Plan, forcing Patterson to apologize publicly to Forrestal for the general's intemperate comment. The Navy Plan, Budget Director Smith told Truman, had driven the defense reorganization debate "completely out of bounds." More ominously, Smith's assistant Arnold Miles warned the White House that in the National Security Council and Central Intelligence Agency, Eberstadt and the navy report had created two powerful extralegal agencies outside the normal organizational channels that could bypass formal Cabinet deliberations and usurp executive authority.[25]

Presidential aides Clark Clifford and George Elsey, two naval reserve officers, were more supportive. They suggested that the president consider Eberstadt's report and the Navy Plan carefully when drawing up his defense reorganization message for Congress. Truman did. He showed interest in both the NSC and CIA, and in the end adopted certain aspects of the Navy Plan to win consensus from all parties to his national security reorganization. Thus while insisting on the single department and independent air force, Truman compromised on other issues to ensure navy support for the National Security Act of 1947.[26]

The question remains, was the Navy Plan of 1945 Mahanian doctrine or corporatist blueprint? It was both. The two concepts reinforced each other. Mahan had stressed the interlinkage of foreign and military policies, the need to control the seas for economic strength, and the importance of structural innovation to coordinate policy. He had testified for such reorganization before Congress in 1910. Of course, it is hindsight to attribute the complex national security machinery to Mahan's primitive steps. Moreover, the foundations for a national security state rested as much in the pioneering work of Elihu Root, Theodore Roosevelt, Wilson, and others. Nevertheless, the Navy Plan was consistent with much of Mahan's tradition. When adopted it assured a fighting chance for the navy in the post-war organizational scheme to politic with Congress, president, and public for an equal share of post-war budgets, roles, and missions. One can see in the work of Princeton scholars Harold and Margaret Sprout, asked by Forrestal to develop a text on national security, and whose work on sea power remains the strongest scholarly expression of Mahanian doctrine, the dovetailing of these two principles. The Navy Plan and its incorporation into the National Security Act of 1947 effectively institutionalized Mahanian tradition.[27]

Mahanian doctrine was designed to protect, expand, and promote American production, and as historian Thomas McCormick argued in a recent article, productionism was the cornerstone of corporatism.[28] Thus a system that preserved naval domination, control of the seas, and protection of foreign commerce had corporatist implications. More important, the architects of the Navy Plan subscribed to the associative state, the politics of adjustment, the middle course between state regulation and private enterprise, and between conflicting interests and groups that characterized Hawley's American variant of corporatism.

Corporatism and its application to American national security organization needs more research before any definitive conclusions can be made. Perhaps the value of examining the origins and politics of the Navy Plan lies more in what it reveals about Forrestal. He emerges as an administrator who was neither a tragic zealot nor a parochial defender of naval interests. He was a beleaguered bureaucrat in a modern national security power struggle, pursuing his job as he saw it to protect the Navy Department's integrity in a rapidly changing environment. He was able to identify threats to the navy's role as the first line of American defense, synthesize advice, balance factions both within his own bureaucracy and from outside, and in the end select the appropriate expert with the appropriate response--the Navy Plan of 1945--to further his objectives. Whether Forrestal would be as successful as the first Secretary of Defense in running the national security machinery outlined in that Navy Plan of 1945 was another question.

Notes

[1] James Forrestal, *The Forrestal Diaries*, ed. Walter Millis (New York, 1951); Robert Greenhalgh Albion and Robert Howe Connery, *Forrestal and the Navy* (New York, 1962); Arnold A. Rogow, *James Forrestal: A Study of Personality, Politics, and Policy* (New York, 1963).

[2] Vincent Davis, *Postwar Defense Policy and the U.S. Navy, 1943-1946* (Chapel Hill, 1966), 209. For the view of Forrestal as Cold War ideologue, see Richard F. Haynes, *The Awesome Power: Harry S. Truman as Commander in Chief* (Baton Rouge, 1973) and Lloyd C. Gardner, *Architects of Illusion: Men and Ideas in American Foreign Policy, 1941-1949* (Chicago, 1970). For the modern-day Mahan school, see Gordon W. Keiser, *The U.S Marine Corps and Defense Unification, 1944-47: The Politics of Survival* (Washington, 1982).

[3]Major new archival material on Forrestal includes the Eberstadt and Krock Papers, Seely Mudd Library, Princeton University; Marx Leva, John A. Kennedy, John Kenney, John L. Sullivan Oral History Transcripts, and the George Elsey Papers, Harry S. Truman Library, Independence, Missouri; Papers Relating to Secretary of the Navy James V. Forrestal, 1934-1951, Operational Archives, Naval Historical Division, Washington Navy Yard; Records of the Office of James V. Forrestal and Special Assistant Eugene S. Duffield, 1941-1947, Records of the Office of the Undersecretary Files and Secretary of the Navy (SecNav) files, Records of the Office of SecNav, Record Group (RG) 80, National Archives (NA), Washington, D.C.

[4]Robert D. Cuff, "An Organizational Perspective on the Military-Industrial Complex," *Business History Review*, 52 (Summer 1978): 261-62; Robert D. Cuff, *The War Industries Board, Business-Government Relations During World War I* (Baltimore, 1973). See Edwin J. Perkins, ed., *Men and Organizations: The American Economy in the Twentieth Century* (New York, 1977).

[5]Ellis W. Hawley, "The Discovery and Study of a 'Corporate Liberalism'," *Business History Review*, 52 (Autumn 1978): 315. See also Hawley, *The Great War and the Search for a Modern Order: A History of the American People and Their Institutions, 1917-1933* (New York, 1979).

[6]Jordan A. Schwarz, *The Speculator: Bernard M. Baruch in Washington, 1917-1965* (Chapel Hill, 1981), 544-46; see also Joan Hoff Wilson, *Herbert Hoover: Forgotten Progressive* (Boston, 1975); Robert Griffith, "Dwight Eisenhower and the Corporate Commonwealth," *American Historical Review*, 87 (February 1982): 87-122.

[7]Marx Leva, Oral History Transcript (January 1972), Harry S. Truman Library.

[8]Henry L. Stimson and McGeorge Bundy, *On Active Service in Peace and War* (New York, 1948), 506; Albion and Connery, *Forrestal*, 185-86; William E. Livezey, *Mahan on Sea Power* (Norman, 1981 rev.), 357 n. 45.

[9]Forrestal to Coudert, 30 June 1944, box 86, Forrestal Papers, Princeton University. (This and all other citations from the Forrestal Papers cannot be published without permission from Princeton University Library.)

[10]Forrestal Memorandum for the President, 9 April 1945, box 88, Forrestal Papers.

[11]Forrestal to Patterson, 7 November 1945, box 89, Forrestal Papers. See Truman, "Our Armed Forces Must be Unified," *Colliers* (26 August 1944): 16, 63-64.

[12]See James E. Hewes, Jr., *From Root to McNamara: Army Organization and Administration, 1900-1963* (Washington, 1975); Demetrios Caraley, *The Politics of Military Unification: A Study of Conflict and the Policy Process* (New York, 1966).

[13]Gates Memo for Forrestal, 3 January 1945, and "Exchange of Correspondence, May-Sept 1945 between Forrestal, Stimson and Patterson Re Study of Unification Problems," both in Forrestal Papers, Operational Archives, Naval Historical Division, Washington Navy Yard.

[14]Duffield to Forrestal, 14 April 1945, and Kalbfus to SecNav, 15 June 1945, box 28, Records of Forrestal and Duffield, 1941-1947, Records of the Office of Secretary of the Navy, box 27, RG 80, NA; telephone transcript of Herter to Forrestal, 9 April 1945, box 88, Forrestal Papers; Forrestal Diary, vol. 2, entry 10 May 1945, Princeton University; 20th Meeting of the Top Policy Group, box 2, RG 80, NA.

[15]Walsh to Forrestal, 15 May 1945, in Eberstadt Papers, Princeton University.

[16]See Calvin Lee Christman, "Ferdinand Eberstadt and Economic Mobilization for War, 1941-1943" (Ph.D. diss., Ohio State University, 1971). My forthcoming study, "Partners in National Defense: Eberstadt, Forrestal and the Building of a National Security State, 1912-1969," develops fully the Forrestal-Eberstadt relationship and education.

[17]Robert D. Cuff, "From the Controlled Material Plan to the Defense Materials System, 1942-1953," *Military Affairs* 51 (January 1987): 1-6.

[18]Gene M. Lyons and Louis Morton, *Schools for Strategy: Education and Research in National Security Affairs* (New York, 1965), 37, 59; list of Eberstadt's research group in Eberstadt Memo, 5 October 1945, Eberstadt Papers.

[19]Eberstadt Memorandum of Thoughts, 12 July 1945; Willett Memorandum, 13 June 1945; Eberstadt to King, 22 June 1945; Memo of Meeting Eberstadt, Fox, Willett, Russell, 8 and 15 June 1945, box 5, Eberstadt Papers.

[20]Secretary of the Navy to bureaus, officers, and shore establishments, 26 June 1945, and List of Interviews, Eberstadt Papers.

[21]*Report to Hon. James Forrestal, Secretary of the Navy on Unification of the War and Navy Departments and Postwar Organization for National Security, 22 October, 1945* (Washington, 1945), 5, 7.

[22]Forrestal to Krock, 17 October 1945, box 26, Krock Papers, Princeton University; Eberstadt to Forrestal, 15 and 18 November 1945, Eberstadt Papers.

[23]Gates to Forrestal, 20 October 1945, box 28, Forrestal Records, RG 80, NA; Harrod to Eberstadt, 5 November 1945, box 5, and Catron to Eberstadt, 8 December 1945, Eberstadt Papers.

[24]Conference with President, 13 December 1945, Harold Smith Papers, Franklin D. Roosevelt Library, Hyde Park, New York; Forrestal to Ogden Reid, 13 January 1946, box 123, Forrestal Papers.

[25]"Second Weekly Letter on Single Department," 16 November 1945, box 266, Spaatz Papers, Library of Congress; Patterson to Forrestal, 14 December 1945, Patterson Safe File No. 2, RG 165, NA; Smith Memo for the President, 30 November 1945, Smith Papers, FDR Library; Miles Memorandum for Judge Rosenman, 15 December 1945, Rosenman Papers, 5, Harry S. Truman Library.

[26]Elsey Memorandum for Judge Rosenman, 13 December 1945, Elsey notes, 14 December 1945, box 93; Elsey Papers, Clifford memorandum for Judge Rosenman, 13 December 1945, box 4, Samuel Rosenman Papers, Hensel to Rosenman, 11 December 1945, box 2, Rosenman Papers, all in Harry S. Truman Library.

[27]Livesey, *Mahan on Sea Power*, 239-40, 376-77.

[28]Thomas McCormick, "Drift or Mastery? A Corporatist Synthesis for American Diplomatic History," *Reviews in American History*, 10 (December 1982): 318-30.

"The Revolt of the Admirals"
Reconsidered

Jeffrey G. Barlow

The House Armed Services Committee's 1949 hearings on the B-36 program and on unification and strategy, and the events which led up to them, had a pivotal influence on the navy. At a time when naval aviation was dangerously close to enforced obsolescence, the hearings provided a forum which allowed the navy's grievances and concerns to be publicly expressed. Many of the records from 1949 have been declassified in the last decade, and in this essay, Mr. Barlow examines this important chapter in the history of the modern U.S. Navy in light of this new material.

INTRODUCTION

Four decades have passed since the navy fought for its life in hearings before the House Armed Services Committee. The events of the summer and fall of 1949 are remembered, if at all, as "The Revolt of the Admirals"--a pejorative phrase that is as inaccurate as it is sensational. It was never a revolt, and naval officers of almost every rank were actively involved in the effort. The phrase quickly stuck not only because of its eye-catching headline but also because of the assiduousness of anti-navy propagandists.

The events that are grouped as "The Revolt of the Admirals" occurred from May to November 1949. The new secretary of defense, Louis Johnson, directed on 23 April that construction of the navy's newly-laid flush-deck aircraft carrier, the *United States*, be discontinued.[1] Three days later, Secretary of the Navy John L. Sullivan tendered his resignation in protest of the way this action was taken. He was replaced by Francis P. Matthews, a man of no military or government experience, who saw himself as a servant of the defense secretary's policies.

In early May, several members of Congress received an "anonymous" document, subsequently revealed to have been written by Cedric Worth, special assistant to Undersecretary of the Navy Dan A. Kimball. Alleging that serious improprieties had taken place in the air force's procurement of the B-36 bomber, this document implied that Secretary of the Air Force Stuart Symington and Secretary Johnson had a financial stake in the program's outcome. The allegations contained in this document eventually led to the House Armed Services Committee's hearings on the B-36 bomber program and later hearings on unification and strategy. At those hearings the navy put forth the case that the secretary of defense was stripping away its naval aviation because of a dangerous overemphasis on the war-deterring and war-fighting properties of strategic bombing as propounded by the air force. In the aftermath of these hearings, the secretary of defense fired Chief of Naval Operations Admiral Louis E. Denfeld and punished other naval officers in an effort to bring the service into line behind his policies.

Since 1949 a sizeable number of books and articles of varying pretensions to significance have touched on the navy's fight. To date, however, the navy's actual role has been inadequately analyzed. In a paper of this length, events in all their historical complexity cannot be described. Nevertheless, an outline can put the events into better perspective.

The most significant work to deal with the incident remains Paul Hammond's 1963 study, "Super Carriers and B-36 Bombers."[2] It is a well-written study, being thorough and judicious in tone, and has become the standard account of the events. Several aspects, however, have diminished its final accuracy. For one thing, it is too dependent upon newspaper accounts for its facts. For another, its version of the incident is affected by a pro-air force perspective on the events--one no doubt influenced by air force briefing materials.[3] Other accounts which have followed in the wake of Hammond's study, even those by authors partial to the navy, have used many of his basic judgments uncritically.

225

Largely as a result of historians continuing to rely on press stories and dated or biased information, we have little more insight into the actual circumstances behind the so-called "Revolt of the Admirals" than did contemporary observers. This no longer needs to be the case. Most of the navy's classified files relating to the events are free of security restrictions, and the U.S. Naval Institute released a large oral history (the first of several projected volumes) in 1983, giving a detailed account of Op-23, the pivotal organization behind the preparation of the navy's case.[4] This oral history, which includes a substantial written text, was the product of a dedicated effort from 1979 to 1983 by Admiral Arleigh Burke, who had headed Op-23 during that organization's fateful ten-month existence.

"REVOLT OF THE ADMIRALS": IMPRESSIONS AND REALITY

A review of the writings on "The Revolt of the Admirals" shows that all suffer from certain misconceptions about the navy's involvement and, more specifically, the role that Op-23 played in organizing the navy's presentation before the House Armed Services Committee. One reason for this is that the authors lacked sufficient detailed background on the navy-air force fight to enable them to explain why certain things happened as they did. It is necessary to fill in a bit of that background before examining a few of the major misconceptions about the navy's role.

Background

The first point to understand is that, from 1946 to 1949, the air force was highly effective in putting its view of a proper defense posture before Congress and the press and in propagandizing against the navy's view. Much of the initial focus of this effort was on establishing its status as a separate service. Nonetheless, from the first, air force publicity was designed to accentuate the positive aspects of its doctrine of air power (even to the extent of distorting the record on occasion) and to minimize the positive aspects of the doctrines espoused by the other services.

From the beginning of its postwar drive for separate service status, the air force was aware that a strong public relations organization was a necessity. As retired Major General Follett Bradley wrote to General Carl Spaatz, then acting commander of the army air forces, in early 1946:

> In my view, the Army Air Forces will never be successful in your organizational objective until you can control your own publicity....
>
> If our objectives are to be attained, it will be necessary for one or more of the civilian organizations who back us to put on a publicity campaign employing all media, movies, newspapers, radio, etc., to convince the American public of the necessity for action now by Congress. Such a publicity campaign would be little different from marketing a new toothpaste or fountain pen.[5]

By 1948, the air force's Directorate of Public Relations had developed into a highly effective, centralized organ for controlling every aspect of air force public relations.[6] The message that the air force was selling was that only the strategic air power provided by the air force could attack effectively a continental land power such as the Soviet Union. However, since sufficient air power to accomplish the task would require a larger (70-group) air force, it was time for the Congress to decide that it could no longer allow competing and duplicative (air force/navy) air forces to squander available resources.

In contrast to the air force's information program, the navy's public relations effort was dismal. The navy seemed to view public relations as something of a necessary evil. The service's senior leadership had little understanding of the importance of getting their message across to the public until it was far too late to do much about it. One man who saw this deficiency all too well was Captain Walter Karig, who was serving as a special advisor for public relations on the staff of the chief of naval operations (CNO). He attempted to educate Admiral Louis Denfeld, the CNO, on the important nature of the navy's public relations effort throughout 1948 and 1949. Whatever success he had in educating Denfeld, it did not seem to have much of an effect on the state of navy public relations which, as an organizational entity, remained under the secretary of the navy's cognizance. In June 1948, Karig wrote to Denfeld:

> Vice Admiral Radford said at DCNO meeting Friday that the fate of the Navy will be determined in the next two years. I think the time is shorter than that, in a public relations sense. The effort must be to utilize every outlet of public expression to build up public appreciation for the Navy as a continuing component of the national defense, by abandoning our defensive and explanatory role and adopting a policy of vigorous, sustained coordinated propaganda (in the true, and best, meaning of the word).[7]

Karig campaigned unsuccessfully for an integrated navy public relations outfit headed by a professionally-qualified officer who would stay in the job long enough to make a difference. In November 1948, he wrote to Harold Brayman, a civilian who headed a committee making an inspection of public relations for the secretary, giving him a detailed look at his own thinking on the issue.

> The Navy prides itself on precision in gunnery, precision in bombing, precision in courts martial and real estate procurement, but in public relations it still uses the technique of the manure spreader (But it isn't spreading awfully good fertilizer). The output as a whole is dull, uninspired, tardy. The element of zeal, esprit de corps, all the devotion to a cause that the Air Force exhibits, is lacking. (I don't know how it can be acquired, either).[8]

In June and July 1949, even as the navy was finding itself becoming involved with the events that were to lead to the B-36 and the unification and strategy hearings, Captain Karig was pressing the CNO to obtain the transfer of the Office of Public Relations (OPR) from the secretary's shop to the CNO's. He also cautioned the CNO that the navy's attitude about the value of public relations would have to change if the organization was going to work as it should. He explained:

228

One of the handicaps OPR has always suffered from is the attitude within the Navy itself that Public Relations is somehow on a par with garbage collecting. Too many senior officers hold the "feather merchant" concept of Public Relations, and then wonder why in hell naval aviation is on the way out, the fleet is shrinking to a ferry service, and Admirals are called "brass hats" and cartooned as pompous nitwits--all products of anti-Navy press agentry, unopposed.[9]

However, by July 1949, nothing the navy could have done about its public relations organization would have had a significant impact on the struggle that summer and fall.

Another important point concerns the navy's view of the strategic air offensive as set forth by the air force. Because the overwhelming number of studies on "The Revolt of the Admirals" fail to delve into the nature of navy thinking on strategic air warfare before the events of 1949, they imply that the navy's opposition to the B-36 and to the air force's idea of strategic bombing in mid-1949 was in direct response to Secretary Johnson's cancellation of the navy's flush-deck aircraft carrier. Since this was the gist of contemporary anti-navy news stories (many inspired by the air force and its supporters), there is the overall impression that the navy's opposition was unprincipled--largely designed to strike back at the air force for what had been done to the navy. This was not the case.

The navy's concern about the likely success of the air force's proposed strategic air offensive in case of war with the Soviet Union can be traced to the early postwar period. Naval aviators, in particular, remained unconvinced that the results of strategic bombing in World War II (as analyzed in the many reports of the United States Strategic Bombing Survey and those of its British counterpart) had validated the inherent decisiveness of strategic bombing in warfare.[10] And as navy strategic planners working on the preparation of the Joint War Plans began to compare the air force's projected strategic air offensive with its assumptions about available overseas bases, the ability to penetrate Soviet air defenses, and many other issues, they began to express serious concerns about the viability of the air offensive.[11] The navy shared these concerns with appropriate outside agencies. It made some of its reservations clear in October 1948 in its presentation before the Eberstadt Committee, which was looking into national security organization and planning.[12] The CNO made a blunt presentation of his concerns about the success of the strategic air offensive to Secretary of Defense James Forrestal and the Joint Chiefs of Staff (JCS) during meetings on the 1950 budget in early October 1948.[13] Thus, by 1949, the navy's questions about the air force's capability of carrying out the strategic air offensive were well known within the national military establishment and in other appropriate quarters.

With the above information supplied to provide a bit of background to the events of mid-1949, one can now analyze several of the major misconceptions about Op-23 and the navy's actual role in the hearings that are present in writings about "The Revolt of the Admirals." Two have to do with Op-23 itself, while the last concerns the longer term effects of the unification and strategy hearings.

Op-23: A Dirty Business?

Paul Hammond asserted that the navy treated Op-23 like a "dirty business." He wrote:

Set up for a normal and wholly legitimate purpose--to study Navy organization, and formulate Navy policy towards the organizational problems incident to unification--Op. 23 was treated by the Navy from the beginning like a dirty business; and the press had soon drawn the same conclusion. Upon its establishment it was located next to the Office of Naval Intelligence, and its activities from the beginning were subject to an unusual degree of secrecy. The press was soon aware of its existence, but could obtain no satisfactory explanations from the Navy.[14]

230

This same negative appraisal of Op-23 (though without it being directly named) comes through in other accounts of the navy's fight, such as that by Paolo Coletta.[15]

This is a point that needs clarification. From the first, Op-23 was designed to be a regular division in the office of the CNO. It was neither devised to do "dirty business" (however Hammond might define it), nor was it an *ad hoc* organization,[16] as its predecessor organizations, SCOROR and UNICOM, had been.[17] It was created because the secretary of the navy and the CNO believed the navy was in need of a permanent organization that could provide advice on the complex issues involving unification of the services. Brigadier General Samuel Shaw recalled what was said by Marine Corps Commandant General Clifton B. Cates:

> He said he'd spent several conferences with the Secretary of the Navy and [Admiral] Denfeld, his Chief of Naval Operations. And they were determined that something had to be done to get the Navy back into believing in itself. That was the...principal thread of the problem--[to] get the Navy to believe in itself.[18]

At first, it was thought that the new organization could be just a re-established SCOROR--a committee under the cognizance of the secretary. Eventually, however, Secretary Sullivan, Admiral Denfeld, and General Cates decided that it would have to be set up under the CNO. General Shaw remarked:

> First,...[SCOROR] was the Secretary's organ and that wouldn't necessarily get all the uniformed Navy to think they ought to get up and follow whoever happened to be the Secretary of the Navy. And furthermore, SCOROR had not endeared itself to lots of Navy people. So,...if I remember what Cates was saying correctly, they'd decided it [the head of the new organization] had to be a guy--a uniformed Navy guy--who when he was announced, everybody [would believe]..."let's go with that guy." So apparently...[in] one of the last conversations they had they decided it was going to be Arleigh Burke....[19]

231

When Captain Arleigh Burke reported to his new boss, Rear Admiral Charles Wellborn, Jr., the Deputy Chief of Naval Operations for Administration (Op-02), he found that his new organization had been assigned a tough and demanding job and one that was still in the process of being defined by the navy's senior leadership. When Admiral Denfeld briefed Burke the following day, he asked the CNO for concrete ideas on what Op-23 could do to help. As Admiral Burke recounted:

> He [Denfeld] replied to my query by saying the charter included the best guidance he could give me: OP-23 was to familiarize itself on all matters pertaining to unif ication; advise him and keep him and other senior officers involved and informed on all unification matters; keep other navy commands informed of the situations; and be the clearing house within the navy for unification matters.... He said it was our job to do what was necessary and proper to be able to advise navy groups on unification matters. The navy was being castigated for the stands it had taken, and we had not been very successful in persuading either the other services or the administration and the Congress of the correctness of our stands.[20]

Within the first few hours of his taking over, Arleigh Burke realized that he had been put on a spot.

> I realized that what I was to do was to do a job that nobody else would do or could do...which is [to] fight what we thought was [going] to be an effort to consolidate [the navy and the other services] into a single Service....
>
> People were very fearful. They were very much afraid...of their own personal careers. And...everybody...felt that if you opposed...what the powers-that-be wanted--what we thought the powers-that-be wanted--you were very likely to be in a bad way in the future, because you probably wouldn't be able to win it [the fight to avoid consolidation] and if you didn't win it, why you would be labeled, correctly so, as antagonistic to the ideas of the people who were in

charge.... Nobody wanted the job. I don't blame them. I didn't want it either.[21]

Burke also realized that in order to retain its success in the face of opposition, whether from within or without, Op-23 would have to be entirely above board in its activities. He noted:

> The biggest thing--the biggest trouble--is people want you to do things quietly, confidentially,...without a lot of other people knowing about it. It can't be done.... That's one thing I had learned... before the Op-23 thing that...not only did God know everything you did but so did everybody else--eventually.[22]

To ensure that Op-23 would be effective and yet be permitted to continue to operate, Captain Burke established a set of rules for the staff to follow. These included: avoiding involvement in secret activities or anything that the rest of the navy could not know about; remaining scrupulously ethical in everything Op-23 did (even if people in other services were not operating that way); distributing Op-23's products through regular navy channels to all sections that could use them so that they all were aware of what the organization was doing; and making sure that facts stated by Op-23 were indeed facts and not opinions.[23] In regard to this last rule, General Shaw recalled:

> [I]n the B-36 query,...we did a lot of research. We were made available to anybody who wanted the stuff written for 'em. Burke had one requirement there--that if we put our hand to the thing and we said this is not true or this is not accurate or this is illogical, they had to accept it or quit using us at all, you see.[24]

Probably the one aspect that most links Op-23 to "dirty business" in the eyes of authors such as Hammond is the unlikely coincidence of the actions by Cedric Worth and Captain John Crommelin which began the B-36 investigation and then helped to keep the House Armed Services Committee hearings going long enough for the navy to present its case. They remain convinced that these actions were part of an organized navy plan, and since Op-23 was the focal point of the navy's fight, they assume that Op-23 was involved in Worth's and Crommelin's activities.

This was not the case. Cedric Worth's plans to release the "anonymous document" on the B-36 were known to no one in Op-23 (and likely no one else in the Navy Department) until the day he released it. Op-23 staff member Commander Thomas Davies, who acknowledged during the navy court of inquiry that he had supplied technical information on the B-36 bomber to Worth at his request, was not informed of Worth's planned use of the material until just before the "anonymous document" was turned over to members of Congress. As Davies later recalled:

> I had no idea what Cedric was going to do with the information, and, as a matter of fact, I was completely taken aback when he showed me the document that he had written, which had all kinds of stuff in it which I hadn't told him.... [H]e showed it to me just--oh--a few hours before he handed it to [Congressman James] Van Zandt.... So I didn't really see it until it was essentially in Van Zandt's hands....
>
> I knew that Cedric Worth was doing something, but on the other hand, he had done about fifteen other things.... And I didn't really know what the hell he was gonna do with it, because it never occurred to me in a million years that he would give it to a Congressman to make a speech on the Hill....[25]

Similarly, General Shaw recalled that the first time that he and Arleigh Burke learned that Cedric Worth was suspected of writing the "anonymous document" was in mid-July 1949, some two months after it had first been given to several members of Congress.[26]

As with Cedric Worth, Captain John Crommelin's surreptitious activities were neither sponsored nor condoned by Op-23 or the senior naval officers involved in the navy's presentation. Admiral Burke remembered:

> [W]hen the situation became more critical and when it appeared that the hearings might be called off before the

Navy could be heard on [Committee Agenda] items 3 to 8,...[Crommelin] had grown very tense. He deplored the inaction of the SecNav and CNO. He thought that OP-23 should take more positive action and insist that the Navy take a very strong stand.... My arguments [against this] did not convince John who wanted to take the controversy public and who felt OP-23 was not doing its duty properly because we insisted that our cause was just and that if we presented our case clearly, logically and forcefully we would eventuall [sic] win.[27]

This account is enriched by additional comments by Rear Admiral J.L. Howard, another former Op-23 staff member, who noted:

I...was the only other person present at one of the conversations between Captain Burke and Captain Crommelin (in Burke's office) and in capsule form, Crommelin's view was that we should (as he had been doing) leak anything we deemed appropriate to the press to make the Navy's points, make a big public "splash," call curbstone interviews, go on the stump nationwide, and "martyr" ourselves if necessary to get our message to the world. This was apparently Crommelin's opinion of the "courageous" way to go.

Burke, on the other hand, argued that we should operate completely within the system, using proper channels and forums, and conduct ourselves in a wholly correct manner... [ellipsis in text] and let the full force of our effective arguments influence the decisionmakers in both the Executive and Legislative branches.[28]

Several senior naval officers also did their best to convince Crommelin not to speak out and thereby jeopardize the navy's case. In early September 1949, several days before Crommelin first spoke out, Admiral Radford sent Burke a message asking him "to convey the following message...to John Crommelin.... In particular the Admiral would appreciate it if John will hold his horses and not jeapordize [sic] the Navy's presentation and the selection of witnesses now being arranged by the Task Force."[29] Vice Admiral Felix Stump, Commander Air Force, Atlantic Fleet, was similarly moved to caution Crommelin about taking unilateral action which might endanger "results you are patriotically endeavoring to accomplish."[30] However, these appeals, too, failed to sway John Crommelin from his course of public protest.

Op-23 Poorly Prepared for the Hearings?

Another charge that is commonly made about Op-23 is that it was inadequately prepared for the unification and strategy hearings in October. For example, Paul Hammond stated:

> The major avoidable handicap for the Navy was its lack of thorough preparation.... The results of their preparation indicated their inadequacies. What the witnesses said showed that their preparatory work had not been carefully coordinated, for the statements were sometimes unfounded, often exaggerated, and not always consistent;.... In short, irrespective of its inherent merits, the Navy's case was inadequately prepared and poorly coordinated.[31]

Interestingly, Hammond contrasted what he thought to be the navy's poor presentation with the air force's highly effective one. Despite the strength of the assertion, however, it lacks merit.

Where Hammond apparently went wrong in his assessment of navy preparation was in attempting to judge the navy and air force presentations according to the same set of criteria. The air force's testimony during the B-36 hearings, masterminded by Harvard Law School Professor W. Barton Leach, was designed to follow the lines of a legal presentation before a court. In their prepared remarks, the air force witnesses, for the most part, denied out-of-hand the allegations contained in the "anonymous document," presumably because to admit that aspects of the document might have some validity could have undermined the air force case. And when air force witnesses such as Stuart Symington and General Hoyt Vandenberg returned to answer the navy's charges during the unification and strategy hearings, they stuck to the air force testimony previously given in order to avoid lending credence to the navy's positions.

The navy's case, on the other hand, was fashioned like a military-style briefing--one presented to acquaint the members of the committee with the navy's differing conception of strategic air warfare and the role which it desired to play in the country's national security. The case's preparation stressed interlocking presentations, a certain amount of repetition for effect, and the use of expert testimony delivered by relatively junior officers. While the navy's case may have proven difficult for the members to follow at times, it showed that there existed important divergences in navy and air force thinking. While in some senses it may have seemed less polished than the air force presentation, in most regards it was just as professionally handled.

The Results of the Hearings

Most of the works that touch on "The Revolt of the Admirals" appear to conclude that the navy either lost its case before the committee or that its testimony had only a very modest influence on congressional thinking. For example, Hammond noted that "the Navy appeal was not so successful as to make the House Armed Services Committee an ally of the Navy. At best, it secured a slight shift in committee sympathies."[32] And Paolo Coletta claimed that the navy presentation had little positive influence.[33]

Did the navy's hard-fought campaign really have only a minor impact on the House Armed Services Committee's view of the navy? The answer to that question is in an understanding of how far the navy had to go in attempting to change the view which the committee, and particularly its chairman, Carl Vinson, then held about the navy's role in the atomic age.

To fully grasp the magnitude of the navy's task, one must turn back to mid-January 1949 when newspaper columnist Stewart Alsop had a riveting interview with Vinson. He recounted the important aspects of this conversation a few days later, in a letter to an editor at *The Saturday Evening Post*.

I talked with Carl Vinson the other day. His long love affair with the Navy is now definitely at an end---if he talks to the Admirals the way he talked to me they must be muttering about the sharpness of serpents' teeth. His line is---and it seems to me a sensible line---that our only potential enemy is Russia, that we can't touch Russia with a navy, that we can't hope to equal Russia in ground forces, and that the only way we can really and immediately bring our superiority to bear is by air.[34]

Thus, it can be seen that at least six months before Cedric Worth's "anonymous document" helped to trigger the B-36 hearings, Carl Vinson, the powerful chairman of the House Armed Services Committee and a longtime friend of the navy, had accepted, apparently without reservation, the air force's assertion that against a continental power such as the Soviet Union, the U.S. Navy was useless. This shows the difficulty of the task which the navy had to face in convincing the committee that it had a significant role to play in the country's defense.

That it had achieved its goal of changing the committee's thinking regarding the navy's usefulness was demonstrated finally in March 1950, when the Armed Services Committee released its report on the unification and strategy hearings. On most of the significant issues raised by the navy witnesses, the committee sided with the navy. Among the most gratifying conclusions for the proponents of naval aviation were its statements that:

6. Intercontinental strategic bombing is not synonymous with air power. The Air Force is not synonymous with the Nation's military air power. Military air power consists of Air Force, Navy and Marine Corps air power, and of this, strategic bombing is but one phase.

and

9. Difficulties between the Air Force and the naval air arm will continue because of fundamental professional disagreements on the art of warfare. Service prejudices,

jealousies and thirst for power and recognition have had only a bare minimum of influence on this controversy.[35]

Some historians, viewing these events from a vantage point of perfect hindsight, have argued that even if the navy fight had not taken place, the eruption of the Korean conflict in June 1950 would have pulled naval aviation out of its doldrums. Yet, it can be argued with even more plausibility that if the navy had not made known its case for modern carrier aviation during the unification and strategy hearings, the Korean War-generated Congressional funding for naval aviation would have gone merely for keeping the existing types of naval aircraft and carriers in commission. Under the circumstances then likely to be obtaining, the U.S. Navy would not have gotten congressional approval for the *Forrestal*-class super carriers and the long-range attack aircraft that provided the navy with its primary offensive striking power during the bulk of the 1950s and 1960s.

Whatever the second guessing on the outcome of the hearings, the senior officers who put their careers on the line to fight the navy's fight evidently believed that it had been a successful effort. For example, Rear Admiral Ralph Ofstie wrote to Captain Fitzhugh Lee: "Personally, Fitz, I feel that we are now well over the hump, or rather the low point, in the fortunes of the post-war Navy.... I think things are looking up very definitely and in good measure this is a result of the fracas of last fall."[36] Similarly, Admiral Radford wrote to Captain Roy L. Johnson, then on staff of Second Task Fleet:

> I am very optimistic about the long range effects of the recent Hearings in Washington, and see no reason why any intelligent naval officer should feel otherwise. Naturally, I have no illusions as to the difficulties we face in the immediate future, but what is particularly gratifying to me is to feel that for the first time we are on the offensive. You can quote me to any individual in the Navy as saying that it behooves all naval officers to thoroughly acquaint themselves with what went on in Washington, and to make an effort to understand what was behind it all. Also tell

them, before they arrive at any conclusions, to estimate what the situation would have been if the Hearings had not taken place. The Navy is not in a horrible mess, but just coming up out of a deep pit, and we have good times ahead.[37]

And in a letter of Christmas greetings to Admiral Richard Conolly, commanding naval forces in the Eastern Atlantic and Mediterranean, Radford expressed his optimism about the future. "I look back on the last twelve months with mixed feelings, but arrive at the conclusion that, if I had to do it all over again, I would not change one thing I did or said. I sincerely hope that you feel the same way in spite of the developments of the last two months."[38]

CONCLUSION

The events of the summer and fall of 1949 were pivotal for naval aviation and, in a larger sense, for the navy's future as a component of the country's armed forces. But for far too long, this navy fight for survival has been seen only in a highly distorted fashion.

Now that the documentation is available to analyze the true dimensions of the fight over the B-36 and over unification and strategy, the task of historians must now be to re-examine the standard interpretations of the navy's role. The naval and marine officers who took an active part in preparing and presenting the case for naval aviation when it appeared to many that all had been lost deserve to be known for what they accomplished on the navy's behalf.

Notes

The author would like to thank Admiral Arleigh Burke, Admiral Charles Griffin, Vice Admiral Fitzhugh Lee, Rear Admiral Thomas Davies, Rear Admiral A.B. Metsger, Brigadier General Samuel Shaw, and colleagues Bernard Cavalcante and Wes Pryce of the Naval Historical Center's Operational Archives, for help with this article. The views expressed are those of the author alone and do not necessarily represent those of the Department of the Navy or the Department of Defense.

[1] For a brief background review of the *United States*, see Arleigh Burke to the Judge Advocate General, 11 May 1949, "History of the 6A Carrier Project," "A21/1-1/1 Carrier" folder, Section II, Op-23 Records, Operational Archives, Naval Historical Center (hereafter OA), Washington Navy Yard, Washington, D.C.

[2] Paul Y. Hammond, "Super Carriers and B-36 Bombers: Appropriations, Strategy and Politics," in *American Civil-Military Decisions: A Book of Case Studies*, ed. Harold Stein (Birmingham, 1963), 465-564.

[3] See Hammond's acknowledgement that W. Barton Leach, the Harvard Law School professor (and air force reservist) who headed the air force team preparing for the B-36 hearings, "made available...a portion of his personal file covering the B-36 investigation." Ibid., 555.

[4] Admiral Arleigh Burke, USN (Ret.), "A Study of Op-23 and its role in the Unification debates of 1949, Special Series: Volume IV," Naval Institute Oral History Project, 1983.

[5] Follett Bradley to Carl Spaatz, 21 February 1946, "Diary, 1946 - Feb" folder, Box 25, Papers of General Carl A. Spaatz, Manuscript Division, Library of Congress (hereafter MD-LC), Washington, D.C. In his reply, Spaatz noted that "I am doing everything possible to put into my organizational objectives a set-up along just the lines you suggested." Spaatz to Bradley, 28 February 1946, ibid.

[6] On the organization of the air force's Directorate of Public Relations as of mid-1949, see Vice Admiral J.W. Reeves, Jr., to Admiral Arthur W. Radford, 16 September 1949, and the enclosed excerpt from *Air Force Public Relations Letter*, 29 July 1949, "J.W. Reeves" folder, Box 36, Papers of Admiral Arthur W. Radford, OA.

[7] Memorandum from Captain Walter Karig (Op-004) to the CNO, 21 June 1948, "Public Relations" folder, Box 4, Double Zero Files 1948, OA. This and several later memos by Karig on the state of navy public relations were copied and sent to Secretary of the Navy Sullivan by Denfeld in July 1948. See "Personal and Confidential" memorandum from Denfeld to Sullivan, 10 July 1948; "ADM DENFELD FILE CONF-SEC Jan-Dec 48" folder, Box 3, Double Zero Files 1947-1950, Admiral Louis E. Denfeld Papers (hereafter Denfeld Papers), OA.

[8] Karig to Brayman, 8 November 1948, "ADM DENFELD PERS FILE Nov & Dec '48" folder, Box 3, Denfeld Papers, OA. At the end of this letter, Karig commented: "Admiral Denfeld, his Vice Chief of Naval Operations, Admiral Radford, and Under Secretary Kenney are all very much worried over the Navy's public relations operation.... The concern of these men would be useful, if public relations were under their jurisdiction, which it is not. But it's good to know that the top men in the Navy are aware that there is a problem that is damn near a crisis.

Ten years ago there wasn't a man in the Navy who knew or cared what the public thought." Ibid.

[9] Karig to CNO, 25 July 1949, "ADM DENFELD PERS FILE Jul-Aug '49" folder, Box 4, Denfeld Papers, OA.

[10] For just one example, see Radford to SecNav on "Strategic Bombing of Germany," n.d. [early February 1948], "SecNav" folder, Box 2, Double Zero Files 1948, OA.

[11] See, for example, the memorandum from Op-30V (Captain Herbert D. Riley) to Op-30 (Director, Strategic Plans) on "World War III - Strategic Concept," 7 February 1947, "A 16-3(5) War Plans" folder, Box 111, Subject Files, 1947, Strategic Plans Division Records, OA.

[12] The documentation and drafts for the navy's presentation are available in the John L. Sullivan SecNav Papers. See particularly memorandum for distribution list from Captain Paul E. Pihl on "Presentation before the Eberstad Committee on 18 October 1948 Justifying the Navy's Position Regarding Air Power and the Organization of the Air Forces," 4 October 1948, "A18, A21 LEGISLATION, CONFERENCES, AVIATION 1948-1949" folder, Box 3, Classified Correspondence of Sec. John L. Sullivan, Record Group (hereafter RG) 428, National Archives (hereafter NA).

[13] See "MEMORANDUM BY THE CHIEF OF NAVAL OPERATIONS" marked "Presented orally by CNO to JCS and BAC [Budget Advisory Committee] about 4 Oct 1948"; unlabeled folder, Box 21, Radford Papers, OA. The complete transcript of this meeting is in the Records of the Joint Chiefs of Staff-- CCS 370 (8-19-45), B.P. [Bulky Package] Part I, RG 218, NA.

[14] Hammond, "Super Carriers and B-36 Bombers," 505.

[15] Paolo E. Coletta, "The Defense Unification Battle, 1947-50: The Navy," *Prologue: The Journal of the National Archives* 7 (Spring 1975): 25.

[16] Vincent Davis called Op-23 an *ad hoc* agency in his discussion of naval officers' "covert and rejected" political techniques. Vincent Davis, *The Admirals Lobby* (Chapel Hill, 1967), 286-87.

[17] For a brief but informative discussion of the roles of these previous organizations, see Burke, "A Study of OP-23," 98-123. The section on UNICOM was written by Captain Robert A. Rowe, a former UNICOM staff member.

[18] Brigadier General Samuel R. Shaw, USMC (Ret.), interview with author, Alexandria, VA, 29 July 1987 (hereafter, Shaw interview).

[19] Ibid.

[20] Burke, "A Study of Op-23," 75.

[21] Admiral Arleigh A. Burke, USN (Ret.), interview with author, Fairfax, VA, 25 September 1986.

[22] Ibid., 27 April 1987.

[23] Burke, "A Study of Op-23," 141-42.

[24]Shaw interview.

[25]Rear Admiral Thomas D. Davies, USN (Ret.), interview with author, Washington, D.C., 11 August 1987.

[26]Shaw interview. For Admiral Burke's comments on Cedric Worth's activities, see Arleigh Burke, "Notes in regard to Op-23," (renumbered) 242-43, photocopy of a typescript manuscript with inked corrections in green binder marked "ADM Burke Oral History Docu. OP-23 I," Box 23, Subject Files, Papers of Admiral Arleigh A. Burke, OA. Admiral Burke prepared this manuscript for his oral history on Op-23.

[27]Burke, ibid., 291.

[28]"Comments on Admiral Burke's OP-23 Draft (Beginning p. A188) by J.L. Howard," 4/5-5/5, "OP 23 Oral History Project Comment & Documents by RADM J. Howard" folder, Box 19, Subject Files, Burke Papers, OA.

[29]Photocopy of letter from Captain Fitzhugh Lee to Burke, 8 September 1949, "Burke Papers: Subj; OP-23" folder, "OP-23 News Clippings" Box, ibid.

[30]Photocopy of letter from Stump to Crommelin, 16 September 1949, enclosed with a note from Stump to Burke of the same date; ibid.

[31]Hammond, "Super Carriers and B-36 Bombers," 541, 543.

[32]Ibid., 554.

[33]See Paolo Coletta, *The United States Navy and Defense Unification, 1947-1953* (Newark, 1981), 201-202.

[34]Stewart Alsop to Martin Sommers of *The Saturday Evening Post*, 12 January 1949, in "SPECIAL CORRESPONDENCE 'Sat. Evening Post' Jan-May 1949" folder, Box 26, Papers of Joseph & Stewart Alsop, MD-LC.

[35]House Committee on Armed Services, *Unification and Strategy: A Report of Investigation*, 81st Cong., 2d sess., 1 March 1950, H. Doc. 600, 54.

[36]Ofstie to Fitzhugh Lee, 17 March 1950, "*1950* Letter File Outgoing" folder, Box 5, Papers of Vice Admiral Ralph A. Ofstie, OA.

[37]Radford to Johnson, 19 December 1949, "J" correspondence folder, Box 33, Radford Papers, OA.

[38]Radford to Conolly, 20 December 1949, "Admiral Conolly" folder, Box 31, ibid.

Part IV

Culprits or Scapegoats?
Some Views on the Japanese
Attack on Pearl Harbor

Secretary of the Navy Frank Knox and Chief of Naval Operations Admiral Harold R. Stark

George H. Lobdell

Two of the most important figures connected with the Pearl Harbor attack, and around whom much controversy has centered, are those men who occupied the navy's top civilian and military offices below that of president. In this essay, Professor Lobdell looks at the careers, qualifications, and responsibilities of Frank Knox and Harold Stark and offers some conclusions about the degree of responsibility or blame they have had for the debacle of 7 December 1941.

In Chicago, the day after Hitler's May 1940 assault on the Low Countries, an alarmed Frank Knox, publisher of the *Chicago Daily News*, started his front page editorial with the dire warning, "In a world where might makes right, there is neither pity nor mercy for a nation unprepared." A few lines later, using bold capital letters, he declared, "WE MUST HAVE THE MOST POWERFUL FLEET IN THE WORLD AS SOON AS IS HUMANLY POSSIBLE."[1]

The same day, in Washington, D.C., Chief of Naval Operations (CNO) Admiral Harold R. Stark wrote a colleague that his earlier pessimism about the passage of the proposed 11 per cent naval expansion bill had changed to optimism.[2] The fears aroused by Hitler's successes made possible the realization of Knox's call for and Stark's plans for the most powerful fleet in the world.

On 11 July 1940, Frank Knox and Admiral Stark became colleagues, for on that day Knox was sworn in as secretary of the navy. Knox's appointment marked the beginning of a warm personal friendship between the two men, a friendship which reached its most important climax on 7 December 1941 with the Japanese attack on Pearl Harbor.[3] Who were these two men whom fate seemed to bring together at a critical time in their navy's history?

Admiral Stark was nearly sixty years old when he became CNO on 1 August 1939. His selection for the navy's top billet came after thirty-six years of outstanding service as an officer. An able captain with seven successful ship commands, he was also a skillful, competent administrator. As chief of the Bureau of Ordnance from 1934 to 1937, he showed ability not only in directing the bureau but also in dealing tactfully and effectively with Congress. His appointment as CNO meant that fifty flag officers senior to him were passed over, yet his selection was apparently accepted by these seniors with little serious discontent because he was liked and respected throughout the naval service.[4]

If Stark was well known to his service colleagues, Frank Knox was almost a total stranger to the navy, for when he became secretary he did not have a single close friend among its captains or admirals. Soon, however, Navy Department officials found they had an aggressive, able, and experienced administrator in their midst who was completely dedicated to the best interests of both the navy and the nation.

Knox was an unusually successful journalist. During the depression he reached the pinnacle of this career by reviving the sagging fortunes of the *Chicago Daily News*. He was, by contrast, a failure in his main avocation, politics. His lack of political success reached its climax in 1936 when he failed to win the Republican presidential nomination and then, as Alf Landon's vice presidential running mate, he experienced the most colossal defeat of his political career. It was fortunate that he was a near genius as the manager of newspaper properties for it does not appear he would have made much of a living as a politician.

Knox was also a part-time soldier. In 1898 he enlisted in the Rough Riders and fought in Cuba. In 1917 he left his thriving Manchester, New Hampshire, newspaper, enlisted, earned a commission, and fought in France as an artillery officer. After the war he remained in the army reserves becoming a colonel before he retired.

As an old fashioned patriot, Knox believed the platitude that politics ends at the water's edge. As soon as World War II broke out in Europe, he abandoned his strident anti-New Deal attacks and supported vigorously the president's internationalist foreign policy. When Roosevelt, for the second time, asked him in June 1940 to be secretary of the navy, he accepted. "We are in danger because we are inadequately prepared," the old Rough Rider told reporters upon his appointment. "If I can help [the president] ...prepare for any emergency, I must do so."[5] Soon his new colleagues in the Navy Department knew he meant what he said.

From the very beginning the new secretary resolved not to meddle in strategy or operations except when it was his responsibility to carry out presidential orders or suggestions, or to endorse or give force to a policy recommended to him by Stark. His strength was in business management, and here he applied himself with characteristic vigor. He concentrated on improving the Navy Department's internal office efficiency, coordinating teamwork between the professional navy officers and the civilian secretariat, and promoting the navy's public image.

As a newspaper publisher Knox knew how to delegate authority and then trust his subordinates to carry out their duties with a minimum of interference from him. He also had learned how to weigh advice and act on it promptly. Often, after presented with some persuasive statement with which he agreed, he would show his approval by declaring, "That represents my views exactly." If action was then called for, it followed without delay. Stark was not as impetuous as Knox, but he and the secretary were much alike in the ways they directed subordinates. Stark was more deliberate and cautious in judging evidence than was Knox, but like Knox, he moved quickly if a decision required orders.[6]

Though Knox stuck to his resolve of not interfering with technical naval matters, he knew he had to learn as much about the navy as he could as rapidly as possible. By the end of his first month as secretary, he ranged from the base at Pensacola to the navy yard at Portsmouth, New Hampshire. In early September he inspected west coast installations before flying on to Pearl Harbor.

Knox knew he was flying into a situation which was more than just an inspection trip. In the spring of 1940 the fleet was in Hawaiian waters finishing an exercise just as Hitler was conquering Europe. Roosevelt ordered the fleet to remain at Pearl Harbor fearing the Japanese would consider its return to the west coast as a retreat in a time of crisis. When Admiral James O. Richardson, in command of the fleet, insisted on knowing why he was being retained in Hawaii and how long he might be there, Stark, without any explicit guidance from the White House, answered, "You are there because of the deterrent effect which it is thought your presence may have on the Japs going into the East Indies." Stark could give Richardson no information on how long he would remain there.[7]

Richardson immediately campaigned to have the fleet returned to its home bases since holding it in Hawaii presented him with severe problems of supply, planning, maintenance, and morale. Stark fully sympathized with him and pressed the president for clarification with no results. When Knox arrived at Pearl Harbor, Richardson continued his efforts to remove the fleet to San Diego and San Pedro.

Knox and Richardson did not get along well. On the surface the admiral was correct and proper. He did everything which was expected of him to make the secretary's visit useful to both men. However, he did not care for journalists and considered Knox very limited in his knowledge of naval matters.[8] He complained that Knox complicated the visit by unexpectedly changing his travel schedule and did not send an appropriate signal of thanks to the fleet at the end of his trip. Knox appreciated Richardson's efforts, but came away from Hawaii with reservations about the admiral.[9]

Still, the trip to Pearl Harbor was a valuable journey for the secretary. Impressed by what he saw, he sailed on several ships and met all the flag officers in Hawaii including Admiral Husband E. Kimmel. He felt Richardson "was obsessed" with the personnel problem and that he was "too social minded." Though Knox told the press he believed Pearl Harbor was "tremendously well defended," he knew its defenses were inadequate and he thought there was a lack of "war mindedness" in the fleet, which Richardson took as a negative reflection on himself. At the end of the visit, Richardson gave Knox a long memorandum why the fleet should not stay at Pearl Harbor; a document with which Knox did not agree.[10]

Secretary of War Henry Stimson was among those interested in what Knox had seen in Hawaii and invited the navy secretary to his office. Stimson, a lifelong Republican, had joined the cabinet when Knox took office, and the two men became good friends. Knox admired Stimson's service as secretary of state under Hoover and as secretary of war under Taft. When Stimson spoke of matters involving department administration or foreign affairs, Knox listened with respect.

Their talk that October afternoon ended with Stimson giving Knox "a little memorandum" which was Stimson's historical summary on Japanese-American relations. Stimson confided to his diary, "Knox was delighted with it and said that it represented his views exactly." The final paragraph was a summary of what both Stimson and Knox used as a guide for dealing with the Japanese. "Japan has historically shown that she can misinterpret a pacifistic policy of the United States for weakness," Stimson declared, and then concluded, "For the United States now to indicate either by soft words or inconsistent actions that she has no...clear and definite policy toward the Far East will only encourage Japan to bolder actions."[11]

It was useful for Knox to have Stimson as a civilian mentor and Stark as his navy teacher for there seemed to be an unending multitude of matters competing for his attention besides affairs in the Pacific. His weeks were filled with such tasks as testifying before Congressional committees, attending cabinet meetings, holding press conferences, presiding at ceremonial occasions, helping solve labor disputes, making inspection trips, sitting on committees, and keeping up with the tremendous task of materiel procurement for the rapidly growing navy. As the months passed, developments in the European war and the increasing intensity of the Battle of the Atlantic claimed a large share of his time. Stark's hours were equally crowded.

Yet, often, in spite of all else which demanded their attention, the problems in the Pacific claimed a share of both men's time. Stark had already established a fine working relationship with army chief of staff General George C. Marshall and had contacts with officials in the State Department as well. Starting in October 1940 Knox and Stimson met weekly at the State Department with Secretary of State Cordell Hull to discuss developments in foreign affairs and at each of these conferences they reviewed the situation in the Far East.

In January 1941 Knox and Stark were included on the very limited distribution list of ten men to receive daily, selected English translations of important secret Japanese diplomatic dispatches intercepted and decoded by the army-navy process known as "MAGIC." Knox rarely spoke of the MAGIC material to anyone; he realized the great importance of keeping secret that the Japanese diplomatic code was being read. Since he saw each message briefly and made no notes, he apparently did not develop a sense of any pattern in the Japanese communications. He knew the same messages were being read by Stark, the chief of the war plans division, Rear Admiral Richmond Kelly Turner, and the director of naval intelligence. There is no evidence that Knox felt these dispatches required any action on his part. In keeping with his resolve to stay out of technical matters he was willing to let Stark and Turner judge what was important in MAGIC.[12] Apparently he assumed if the admirals needed his support for action based on intercepted Japanese messages, he would understand their request since he had already seen what they had reviewed.

Stark probably discussed MAGIC messages almost exclusively with Turner, for Turner insisted that he and his war plans division be the only division to interpret such intelligence. Thus, the director of naval intelligence was cast in the role of collecting information and disseminating it to those who needed to know, principally Turner and his associates, for evaluation.[13]

One decision, reinforced by the Stimson principle of displaying strength in the face of Japanese aggression, and later by MAGIC intelligence, was the one to base the main fleet at Pearl Harbor. Admiral Richardson was ordered to Washington in October 1940 and took advantage of the opportunity to campaign, once more, for the return of the fleet to the west coast. Richardson lost his argument and eventually his assignment after he confronted Roosevelt in a blunt and undiplomatic way.[14]

When Richardson returned to Pearl Harbor he surveyed all army and navy security measures at Stark's request. The resulting report described vividly the deficiencies present, especially the army's inadequate defensive capabilities.[15] Since the army had responsibility for land and air protection of the islands, Turner and Stark composed a carefully worded, formal letter for Knox to send to Secretary of War Stimson.

"If war eventuates with Japan," the letter declared in its first paragraph, "it is believed easily possible that hostilities would be initiated by a surprise attack upon the Fleet or the Naval Base at Pearl Harbor." The dangers the navy anticipated in order of importance and probability were: first, air bombing, second, air torpedo attack, followed by sabotage, submarine attack, mining, and bombardment by gunfire. The letter concluded by urging the army to increase the number of pursuit aircraft and anti-aircraft guns and to establish an effective air warning net in the islands.[16]

Stimson replied two weeks later expressing "complete concurrence as to the importance of this matter." He then promised to send to Hawaii within six weeks thirty-one obsolescent P-36 pursuit planes, fifty new P-40 fighters, and to increase the number of anti-aircraft guns. He promised that aircraft warning equipment would be delivered in June and installed immediately.[17]

A few weeks later, Knox was no longer nervous about Pearl Harbor's defenses. On 22 April Knox, Stark, Stimson, Marshall, and Admiral Ernest King, commander of the Atlantic Fleet, conferred with Roosevelt. King needed more ships for his command, and Stimson urged sending the whole fleet into the Atlantic. Marshall, supporting his chief, stated that Hawaii was invincible whether any ships were there or not. Stimson's diary recorded, "Knox...chipped in that he agreed perfectly that Hawaii was impregnable." Stark and Roosevelt focused on Stimson's suggestion that the fleet be sent to the Atlantic, instead, and the security of Pearl Harbor was not examined.[18]

Late spring and summer 1941 were crowded with events filled with serious implications for Knox, Stark, and the navy. American troops occupied Greenland and Iceland, Germany invaded Russia and gave an entirely new dimension to the war in Europe, and Roosevelt and Churchill met at the Atlantic Charter conference. Shortly after, the navy engaged in an undeclared war against German submarines on the Atlantic. Soon, American merchant ships were sunk, and in rapid succession one U.S. destroyer was attacked, another torpedoed, and a third sunk.

Through August and September, Knox gave very little attention to the Pacific, though Stark was in constant touch with Admiral Husband E. Kimmel, now the fleet commander in Hawaii. After mid-October, Far Eastern affairs demanded more and more of their daily attention. On 16 October Roosevelt called Knox, Stark, Stimson, Marshall, Hull, and presidential assistant Harry Hopkins into special conference when the news announced the fall of the Konoye government in Japan. These men reviewed the Far East situation and speculated that Japan might now attack Soviet Siberia. Stimson's diary tells that the conferees considered "the delicate question of diplomatic fencing...to be sure that Japan was put in the wrong and made the first bad move."[19]

Apparently these men felt war would come soon in the Far East, but whether Japan would strike U.S. interests directly was unclear. Stark wrote Kimmel the next day, "Personally, I don't think the Japs are going to sail into us...but we should be on guard, at least until something indicates a trend."[20] Knox, on the other hand, told a group of manufacturers a week later that if Japan persisted in its expansionist program, a collision with the United States "was almost certain, and on very short notice."[21]

Knox was excited by developments and not at all discouraged by the crisis. "Japan has evidently reached the point where she must either fish or cut bait," he wrote a friend in a revealing letter on 10 November.

I have seen the crisis approaching and I am delighted with the firmness with which it is being met by the President and the cabinet. So far as the Navy is concerned, we have anticipated this event and are as thoroughly well prepared for it as it is possible for us to be. Frankly, deep down in my heart, I doubt that the Japs will have the guts to go through with their program of aggression when they find out they are confronted with war with both the United States and Great Britain. It would be tantamount to committing suicide.[22]

By the time Knox wrote these lines, Stark had changed his mind. In a letter to Kimmel of 7 November, Stark observed, "It continually gets 'worser and worser.' A month may see, literally, most anything."[23] A few days later Stark cautioned the President, saying, "War between the United States and Japan should be avoided while building up defensive forces in the Far East... [recommending] No ultimatum be delivered to Japan."[24]

Soon both Knox and Stark knew the Japanese were not going to back down. On 24 November Stark warned all fleet commanders that "chances of a favorable outcome of negotiations with Japan very doubtful..." and concluded that recent Japanese movements "indicate in our opinion that a surprise aggressive movement in any direction including an attack on the Philippines or Guam is a possibility."[25]

On the next day, the navy received reports that the Japanese were embarking a large force--from thirty to fifty ships--from Shanghai, and the first elements were proceeding south along the China coast. That same day Roosevelt told Knox, Stimson, and Hull, "We are likely to be attacked without warning."[26] For the next few days all eyes in Washington were fixed anxiously on the inadequately defended Philippines.

Two days later both the army and the navy sent their Pacific area commanders "War Warning" messages. The navy's dispatch was carefully drafted by Admiral Turner, edited by Stark, and based on the best information and intelligence available to them at the time.

This dispatch is to be considered a war warning. Negotiations with Japan looking toward stabilization of conditions in the Pacific have ceased and an aggressive move by Japan is expected within the next few days. The number and equipment of Japanese troops and the organization of naval task forces indicates an amphibious expedition against either the Philippines, Thai or Kra Peninsula or possibly Borneo. Execute an appropriate defensive deployment preparatory to carrying out the tasks assigned in WPL-46. Inform district and Army authorities. A similar warning is being sent by War Department....[27]

Reading this message, Admiral Kimmel in Hawaii did not sense any unusual threat to his command, since there was no specific mention of Pearl Harbor in the dispatch.[28]

Any lingering doubts Knox and Stark may have had about the imminence of a Japanese aggressive move vanished during the first days of December. Knox and Stark read MAGIC messages which told Japanese embassies all over the world to destroy code machines, and Stark relayed this information to his fleet commanders. Guam was ordered to destroy all secret and confidential publications on 4 December, and two days later other outlying Pacific islands were included in the order.[29]

Thursday, 4 December, was an unusually grim day for Knox and Stark. The McCormick-Paterson newspapers, which included Knox's old isolationist competitor, *The Chicago Tribune*, published accurate extracts of the army and navy's top secret Rainbow 5 war plan. This plan outlined the strategy the armed forces would follow if the United States went to war against Germany, Italy, and Japan. Knox and Stark were angry and frustrated for they feared that the security of the navy's documents had been compromised. Any panic over security of top secret material inevitably caused concern for the reliability of measures protecting the secrecy of MAGIC.[30]

The Secretary and Stark had their worries about Admiral Kimmel's safety in recent weeks. Some of the MAGIC messages were menacing, such as the one in which the Japanese divided Pearl Harbor into specific areas to make the reporting of ship locations easy. So they asked questions. In November, Knox sent his naval aide to find out if Admiral Kimmel had a machine for deciphering the MAGIC intercepts and was reading the same messages he, Stark, and Turner were reading. "Of course he is," Admiral Turner told the aide. "He has the same 'magic' setup we have."[31] Stark also asked the same question two or three times and each time Turner gave the CNO the same answer he had given to Knox's aide.[32]

When Admiral Turner was questioned during the post war Congressional Pearl Harbor hearings, he claimed he was misinformed on this point by the chief of the communications division, Admiral Leigh Noyes. Noyes maintained he knew that Pearl Harbor did not have a "Purple machine" and could not understand why Turner did not know. At best, this episode was a colossal failure of communication between two key officers; a failure of great consequence as things turned out.[33]

On 5 and 6 December the office of naval intelligence briefing for Knox, Stark, Turner, and others included a chart study which showed the large Japanese fleet of transports and escorts nearing the Malay Peninsula. It also showed a possible carrier group in the Marshalls. There was nothing hostile located on the map anywhere close to Pearl Harbor.[34]

At the Saturday, 6 December, session, Knox asked the group, "Gentlemen, are they going to hit us?" Admiral Turner answered, "No, Mr. Secretary, they are not ready for us yet; they are going to hit the British." No one in the room disagreed.[35]

That evening the officer courier handling MAGIC found Knox at his residence and waited while the secretary read without comment the thirteen parts of a message to the Japanese ambassador which showed that negotiations between Japan and the United States were at an end. Apparently Knox did not regard this intercept as especially alarming for he later made arrangements with his personal secretary, John O'Keefe, to fly to Chicago the next day to take care of important newspaper business.[36]

The next morning, Sunday, 7 December, O'Keefe found that Knox had postponed their flight and had gone to the State Department to meet with Hull and Stimson. During their conference a MAGIC message was read in the Navy Department which revealed that the Japanese ambassador was directed to deliver the message ending negotiations at 1:00 P.M. that day. Told of this intercept, Marshall and Stark realized that 1:00 P.M. in Washington was just past dawn at Pearl Harbor. Marshall wanted to send another warning to Hawaii but Stark hesitated. He felt that enough alarming messages had been sent to his commanders already. Within minutes he changed his mind, however, and called Marshall asking him to inform Kimmel of this latest message. Marshall's transmission reached Pearl Harbor hours after the Japanese had attacked.[37]

If the three conferees at the State Department ever heard of the 1:00 P.M. delivery message, they missed its significance. They were certain the Japanese were "planning some deviltry" but assumed the United States was not going to be attacked. Instead, they discussed what convincing arguments could be presented supporting a declaration of war on Japan should that nation attack either Malaya or the Netherlands East Indies but not the American possessions.[38]

Knox returned to his office about noon, and Stark and Turner joined him. It seems probable that Stark told the secretary that another warning message had been sent. Later Knox indicated that he knew a dispatch had been transmitted, but for some unknown reason he came to believe it had been sent the night before.[39]

At the end of this conference, Knox started to leave his office. He got as far as the desk of his confidential assistant when a communication watch officer handed him a brief message which had just been received. It read simply, "AIRRAID ON PEARL HARBOR X THIS IS NOT DRILL." "My God, this can't be true," he exclaimed in astonishment. "It must mean the Philippines." He passed the paper to Stark, who noted its origin was CINCPAC, and replied, "No sir, this is Pearl."

Knox's unintentional eloquence when he cried out in amazement, "My God, this can't be true. It must mean the Philippines," makes emphatic his total surprise at the news. Stark was equally astounded. The Pearl Harbor attack so shocked him psychologically that when he testified about the event years later he could not remember where he was either the night before or when he heard the news.[40]

Was either Knox or Stark a scapegoat or a culprit? These two terms are not an exact assessment of either man's role in the Pearl Harbor tragedy. Yet each of these words can be useful in a summation of the part each man played in the drama.

Stark's actions have been recorded in detail in his extensive testimony before the Navy Court of Inquiry in August 1944, and before the Congressional Pearl Harbor Investigating Committee in 1945 and 1946. His prepared statements and his responses to the many questions fired at him have been weighed and summarized in several studies of the Pearl Harbor attack such as those by Wohlstetter or Prange.[41] His testimony and the many documents available in the Navy Historical Center are the foundation stones of a forthcoming biography of Stark by B. Mitchell Simpson. The evidence from both the sources and the secondary works points to a verdict that the admiral was neither a scapegoat, a person taking blame for others, nor a culprit, a person guilty of a fault or a crime.

Knox's role in the Pearl Harbor drama has never been the object of careful study. He died unexpectedly in April 1944, and therefore, was not available for questioning after the war. The Pearl Harbor Congressional Investigating counsels could find very little in his files which was of use and so his part is, to this date, a missing piece in the Pearl Harbor puzzle.

Scapegoats? After the war there was both a partisan and scholarly effort to place the blame for the Pearl Harbor defeat on Roosevelt. If proven, the charge against the president--of deliberately placing the fleet at the Hawaiian base as bait which the Japanese could not resist so he could bring the nation into war--would not only discredit him, but his party as well. The president's closest advisors in the Navy Department would have had to be an essential part of any such conspiracy and the conspiracy would have had to include deliberate withholding of vital information from Admiral Kimmel's command so the fleet would continue to be an irresistible target for the Japanese to the last moment. Knox and Stark were totally incapable of participating in such a scheme.

Stark had known Roosevelt since World War I and the two men admired and respected each other. But Stark was a man of such unquestioned integrity that he would never have participated in any sort of conspiracy which would have jeopardized the fleet. If he disagreed with something Roosevelt wanted to do which he thought was wrong or illegal, he would have resigned rather than be a party to such an act. In fact, he almost did step down as CNO during the 1940 destroyers-for-bases deal, and he would have had he not been convinced that his role was not only legal but in the best interests of the nation's security. Stark, a man of honor, simply could not have a part of any shady scheme or the cover-up of any such deal. Roosevelt knew this. There is no evidence in any of the source materials that Stark was Roosevelt's scapegoat, nor anyone else's scapegoat.

Knox was an old, conservative Republican who had blasted Roosevelt's New Deal every chance he had. Yet, when he felt the nation was in peril and he perceived that Dr. New Deal was being supplanted by Dr. Win-the-War, he served willingly as secretary of the navy. If ever, in that capacity, his newspaperman's nose for concealed fact detected the possibility of being used as a part of the scheme which smacked of conspiracy, he not only would have refused to be a part of it, he would have resigned and then turned on Roosevelt. He was nobody's scapegoat.

Culprits? A culprit, by definition, is a person guilty of a fault or a crime. Neither Knox nor Stark could be accused of any crime in the Pearl Harbor matter, nor was there ever any serious attempt to do so. The major fault flung at Stark, and it would have included Knox had he lived, was stated by Kimmel at the beginning of his testimony before the Pearl Harbor investigating committee. He declared, "I shall describe how the Pacific Fleet was deprived of a fighting chance to avert the disaster of December 7, 1941, because the Navy Department withheld information which indicated the probability of an attack at Pearl Harbor at the time it came."[42]

The genuine astonishment of both Stark and Knox when they received the news of the attack is evidence that no information they had seen "indicated the probability of an attack on Pearl Harbor at the time it came." They simply could not have conspired to withhold information of an impending attack which they themselves did not know was going to happen.

There is one final matter which acquits Knox and Stark of the charge of being either culprits or scapegoats. Both men believed that Kimmel was reading the same MAGIC messages they were seeing in Washington. Both believed, erroneously, to be sure, but believed, nevertheless, that Kimmel knew of such key messages as the so-called bomb plot intercept, the 6 December, 14-part Japanese message ending negotiations, and even the 7 December, 1:00 P.M. delivery instructions to the Japanese ambassadors. No conspiracy charge of withholding information from Kimmel can be made against the secretary of the navy and the chief of naval operations when each of these men thought the commander-in-chief in the Pacific was receiving the very messages he later accused them of denying him.

There may very well have been failures in communications and even failures in superior judgement, but there is no evidence which sustains any accusation of a conspiracy or a cover-up by Knox and Stark. They were neither culprits nor scapegoats.

Notes

[1]*Chicago Daily News*, 11 May 1940.

[2]Harold R. Stark to Admiral Claude Bloch, 11 May 1940, Stark Papers, Naval Historical Center, as cited in B. Mitchell Simpson, "A Biography of Admiral Harold R. Stark" (MSS, Newport, RI, 1985), 102.

[3]Knox to Stark, 21 March 1942, in Congress, Joint Committee on the Investigation of the Pearl Harbor Attack, 79th Cong., 1st and 2nd sess., 1945-1946, Pt. 5, 2402-3 [hereafter PHH (Pearl Harbor Hearings)].

[4]Simpson, "Stark," 55.

[5]*Chicago Daily News*, 22 June 1940.

[6]George H. Lobdell, "Frank Knox," in Paolo E. Coletta, ed., *American Secretaries of the Navy* (Annapolis, 1980), II: 682, 688; Simpson, "Stark," 56-7.

[7]Stark to Richardson, 27 May 1940, PHH, pt. 14, 943.

[8]James O. Richardson with George C. Dyer, *On the Treadmill to Pearl Harbor: The*

Memoirs of Admiral James O. Richardson (Washington, c.1972), 171, 401.

[9]Ibid., 376; Richardson to Stark, 18 September 1940, PHH, pt. 13, 953.

[10]Richardson, *Memoirs*, 378-80; *Honolulu Star Bulletin*, 14 September 1940; PHH, pt. 14, 955-57.

[11]Henry L. Stimson, Diary, 2 October 1940, Stimson Papers, Yale University Library, New Haven, CT.

[12]Roberta Wohlstetter, *Pearl Harbor: Warning and Decision* (Stanford, 1962), 180.

[13]PHH, pt. 4, 1914.

[14]Richardson, *Memoirs*, 435.

[15]Ibid., 363-64.

[16]Knox to Stimson, 24 Jan 1941, PHH, pt. 1, 279-80.

[17]Stimson to Knox, 6 February 1941, ibid., 280-81.

[18]Stimson, Diary, 22 April 1941.

[19]Ibid., 16 October 1941.

[20]Stark to Kimmel, 17 Oct 1941, PHH, pt. 5, 2134.

[21]*New York Times*, 25 October 1941.

[22]Knox to John Winant, 10 November 1941, Frank Knox Papers, Library of Congress, Washington, D.C.

[23]Stark to Kimmel, 7 November 1941, PHH, pt. 5, 2134.

[24]Stark to Roosevelt, 14 November 1941, ibid.

[25]Secret Dispatch to fleet commanders, 24 November 1941, ibid., 2135.

[26]Stimson, Diary, 25 November 1941.

[27]PHH, pt. 14, 1406.

[28]Ibid., pt. 6, 2518.

[29]Ibid., pt. 5, 2135.

[30]Ladislas Farago, *The Game of Foxes* (New York, 1971), 561-62.

[31]Frank E. Beatty, "Another Version of What Started War With Japan," *U.S. News and World Report*, 28 May 1954, p. 50.

[32]PHH, pt. 5, 2175.

[33]Ibid., 1975-6.

[34]Beatty, "Another Version," 49.

[35]Ibid.

[36]PHH, pt. 4, 1763; Interview by author with John O'Keefe, 12 February 1954.

[37]PHH, pt. 32, 160, and pt. 5, 2132-33.

[38]Stimson, Diary, 7 December 1941.

[39]Beatty, "Another Version," 50; PHH, pt. 8, 3815-16.

[40]Ibid., pt. 5, 2149, and pt. 10, 4664, 5154; Interview by author with John H. Dillon, 15 July 1959.

[41]Wohlstetter, *Pearl Harbor*; Gordon W. Prange, *At Dawn We Slept: The Untold Story of Pearl Harbor* (New York, 1981).

[42]PHH, pt. 6, 2498.

Rear Admiral Patrick N.L. Bellinger, Commander Patrol Wing Two, and General Frederick L. Martin, Air Commander, Hawaii

Paolo E. Coletta

Nearly fifty years after the fact, the Japanese attack upon the U.S. Pacific Fleet at Pearl Harbor continues to attract attention, debate, passion, and controversy. In this essay, Professor Coletta addresses two important questions. First, why were neither U.S. Army nor Navy long range patrol planes able to detect the approach of the Japanese carrier fleet to Pearl Harbor on 7 December 1941? Second, if the local army and navy air commander was held not responsible for this failure, who was?

Patrick N. L. Bellinger assumed command in November 1940 of the Hawaiian-based Patrol Wings and Patrol Wing Two at Ford Island, Pearl Harbor. He reported via commander, Aircraft Scouting Force, based in San Diego, to the commander-in-chief of the Pacific Fleet, Admiral James O. Richardson. But he also wore four other hats. To Richardson he reported as commander, Task Force 9, which included Patrol Wings One and Two and aircraft tenders assigned to him by Richardson. Second, he reported to Richardson as commander, Fleet Air Detachment, Pearl Harbor. Under that hat he administered all the aircraft at Ford Island Naval Air Station and furnished planes requested by task force commanders. Under hat number three he reported to Admiral Claude C. Bloch, commandant, Fourteenth Naval District, for aviation developments in the district including Hawaii, Midway, Wake, Palmyra, and Johnston islands and so to Australia. Under hat number four he reported to Bloch as commander Task Force 4, Naval Base Defense Air Force.

Upon his arrival at Pearl Harbor Bellinger questioned why the Navy Department overlooked the lessons of history as they concerned the defense of a vitally important Pacific outpost.[1] In January 1928 Rear Admiral William A. Moffett, Chief of the Bureau of Aeronautics, had predicted that an aerial attack would be made on Pearl Harbor and that local defense forces could not stop it. The only effective means to ward off such an attack, he said, was "to maintain a continuous patrol offshore at such a distance that no enemy carrier or raider equipped with aircraft, can approach within striking distance, and in sufficient strength to destroy such a carrier before it comes within effective striking range." Second, on 7 February 1932, a Sunday, Admiral Harry E. Yarnell, with the *Saratoga*, *Lexington*, and Bellinger's *Langley*, approached Oahu from the northeast, launched aircraft when sixty miles out, and successfully attacked the installations, hangars, and fuel storage tanks there. A similar attack under the same conditions was made in February 1933. Finally, on another Sunday in April 1938, Admiral Joseph M. Reeves launched an air strike from the *Lexington* against Pearl Harbor and caught army and navy pilots still in their beds.[2]

Moreover, Lieutenant Commander Logan C. Ramsey had postulated in 1937 that the only way to prevent an attack upon a fleet in port was to destroy enemy carriers before they launched their planes. Because a carrier at thirty knots could cover 360 miles during a night, this meant the maintenance of constant aerial reconnaissance out to a radius of four hundred miles.[3] As Bellinger's chief of staff in 1941, one could expect that Ramsey briefed Bellinger about the dangers of leaving a fleet in port.

In addition, in studying the problem of how many aircraft it would take to prevent a surprise attack on a fleet at Pearl Harbor, Rear Admiral Frederick J. Horne predicted that enemy carriers would steam at night to a point about 250 miles off Oahu and launch at dawn. Because air patrols were ineffective at night, daytime patrols must be extended to cover all areas where enemy carriers might be during the day preceding an attack. For a continuous inner and outer 360 degree search, 159 planes were needed at Pearl Harbor.

If the Orange War Plan was carried out, Horne continued, during the first six months of a war 715 patrol aircraft were required, with 159 of them to cover the area between Hawaii and Samoa. For fiscal year 1939 the chief of naval operations, Admiral Harold R. Stark, allotted Bellinger 110 planes rather than the 159 Horne recommended.[4]

The army was responsible for defending the Hawaiian Islands. Although pleased with its military and naval defenses when he visited Oahu in September 1940, Secretary of the Navy Frank Knox soon questioned Admiral Bloch about them and early in January 1941 told Secretary of War Henry L. Stimson that "If war eventuated with Japan, it is believed easily possible that hostilities would be initiated by a surprise attack upon the Fleet or the Naval Base at Pearl Harbor"[5]--the same conclusion Bellinger voiced to Admiral Richardson. On 1 May 1941 Block appointed committees to study the defense problem, called for additional army-navy cooperation, and initiated various passive defense measures on Oahu's naval airfields, but he knew that there were not enough patrol aircraft on Oahu to prevent a surprise air attack. On 17 October he noted that the situation was "still bad" and asked Stark to take "extraordinary measures." Although Stark's office replied on 15 November that "We are doing the best we can," it failed to supply Bellinger with the planes he vitally needed. The Roosevelt administration's decision on 19 June 1940 of a "Europe first" strategy also meant that military commanders in Hawaii could expect little support.[6]

In December 1940 Stark sent an officer to tell Admiral Richardson and also Admiral Thomas C. Hart, commanding the Asiatic Fleet, that the new policy was to adopt an offensive stance in the Atlantic and a defensive one in the Pacific. Kimmel, Richardson's prospective relief, thereupon voiced great concern over the defense of Pearl Harbor. He suggested the use of barrage balloons, torpedo nets, and greater army-navy cooperation. However, Stark provided no balloons or torpedo nets. Kimmel also raised the point that personnel and material not be worn out by alert watches. He and Richardson then jointly wrote to Stark on 15 January 1941 that "Surprise raids on Pearl Harbor, or attempts to block the channel, are possible." Stark replied in February that "The Japanese did not plan an attack in the foreseeable future."[7]

On 9 May 1940 President Roosevelt had ordered Richardson to keep the Battle Force at Pearl Harbor. Richardson objected strongly, saying that Pearl Harbor was a "God-damned mousetrap." However, Roosevelt considered three options: withdrawing the fleet to home ports in California, a move that might cause the Japanese to think that he was leaving the Pacific to them; sending it to the Philippines, which might provoke the Japanese to war; and leaving it in Pearl Harbor to deter the Japanese. He chose the last, thereby leaving the fleet two thousand miles closer to Japan and increasing the chances of an attack by the Imperial Navy. When Richardson questioned his leadership, Roosevelt had him relieved by Kimmel on 1 February 1941.[8]

Lacking sufficient numbers of them, Richardson had patrol planes scout to about three hundred miles only to the northwest and south of Oahu and around fleet operating areas. After Kimmel relieved Richardson, Bellinger informed Kimmel that he had only fifty-seven old PBY-3s, eight of which were awaiting spare parts in order to be repaired, and that his planes had flown an inordinate number of hours since October 1940. Spurred by Stark telling him that his patrol wings would be among the last to be equipped with modern planes, on 16 January 1941 he had written to Stark a very strong letter.

In his letter Bellinger noted that he was operating on a "shoestring." He listed the planes, munitions, facilities, and personnel he needed to prepare his wings for war. His letter showed that he was much surer than Washington that the Japanese would attack Pearl Harbor. He also made it part of the record that if the deficiencies he pointed out were not rectified, then someone else, not he, would be responsible for whatever happened. The letter was endorsed first by Richardson, then by Kimmel.[9]

Stark told Kimmel on 1 February 1941, the day he assumed command, that Ambassador Joseph Grew, in Tokyo, had reported that the Peruvian Minister had heard that the Japanese planned a surprise attack on Pearl Harbor. Kimmel thereupon drafted a paper on "Security of the Fleet at Base and in Operating Areas."

While ships patrolled the channel entrance, boom, and harbor, Patrol Wing Two would search the assigned fleet exercise areas and in addition search to a radius of thirty miles from the entrance channel buoys. Army anti-aircraft guns and marines would defend against air attack, and all embarked and shore based aircraft would augment local air defenses during an attack. Lastly, he set levels of readiness in descending order from general quarters in all ships in condition I to the anti-aircraft battery of at least one ship in each sector manned and ready in condition III.[10]

Kimmel rather than Bellinger controlled the aircraft of the Pacific Fleet. Even when at war, Kimmel would not only provide security against attack by Japan but "continue training operations as practicable." He agreed that when construction was completed at the outlying islands seventy-two of Bellinger's patrol and observation planes would be based there, with the rest remaining on Oahu. But toward the end of November 1941 no more than 65 percent of the construction work at the Hawaiian islands was completed. Moreover, Bellinger thought that the Japanese would attack Pearl Harbor, Kimmel that they would attack Wake first, then Midway, with equal chances for Palmyra and Johnston. In any event, Kimmel fully supported Bellinger in requesting that "materials for outlying Pacific bases [be] given the highest priority in order to insure early completion." By endorsement of 17 October 1941, Bloch agreed with Kimmel and forwarded his request to Stark. On 18 November Stark called for representatives of the bureaus and offices involved to confer on 27 November. Seen from the vantage of hindsight, this was too little and too late.[11]

Per his confidential letter 14-41, Kimmel directed Bellinger to plan for training in an expansion program first and patrolling second. Given his number of planes and personnel, Bellinger found that training and search were mutually exclusive. After flying searches for eighteen-hour days, seven days a week, his crews had no time to train new aviators coming into their squadrons. With the planes they had, about noon they could search for 360 degrees to between six and seven hundred miles yet just miss an enemy carrier making for a launching point the next morning, and only some half a dozen ships in the Pacific Fleet had radar. Further, after three days every plane engine needed a check. Because there were no spare mechanics, exhausted crews had to check their own planes. New orders then called for less search and more training, but there were no spare personnel to train spare crews. In addition Bellinger had to use pilots to help army air forces (AAF) B-17s get from Hawaii to the Philippines.[12]

When Bellinger called upon Kimmel, still the commander of the Cruiser Force, Pacific, in January 1941, he understood him to say that he should get army air to cooperate in augmenting Hawaii's defenses. Bellinger asked, "Are you telling me to give such orders to Army air?" Kimmel replied, "I have no authority to tell you to do anything now, but if I become commander in chief, I hope to arrange some unified effort."[13] About a month after he became the commander in chief he directed Bellinger to report to Bloch and work out a joint air defense plan for Pearl Harbor. Bloch told Bellinger to see Major General Frederick L. Martin, the Hawaiian AAF commander, and go into the problem in detail.

Martin, who had been in the army air service since 1920, was a command pilot, combat observer, and technical observer and had attended the Command and General Staff School. He had direct access to the chief of the AAF, Major General H. H. Arnold, but served under the army's commanding general on Hawaii, Major General Walter C. Short, a foot soldier to the soles of his boots. Short, who assumed command of the Hawaiian Department on 7 February 1941, fully cooperated with Kimmel, and the army chief of staff, General George C. Marshall, assured him that Hawaii was receiving more equipment and troops than any other overseas installation.

What Marshall said was true, but demands for the vast expansion program and the need to strengthen bases in the North Atlantic and Caribbean delayed the sending of some modern planes and additional anti-aircraft artillery to Hawaii until early 1941. On 7 December 1941, Martin had a bombardment wing at Hickam Field and a pursuit wing at Wheeler Field, a total of 231 aircraft, of which about half were modern. The latter included only twelve B-17Ds and a few smaller bombers, the rest being fighters. Were he called upon to provide his own reconnaissance, he would need seventy-two B-17s--more than were in the entire AAF. Moreover, his strength was sapped by his having to train personnel to deliver reinforcements to the Philippines, which by early 1942 were to receive most of the heavy bombers produced.[14]

Martin told Bellinger that the army was responsible for inshore patrol and the installation of radar nets. He also said that his planes would search for suspicious objects a bit offshore and hold the periodic joint air exercises Bellinger suggested whenever his planes were not otherwise employed. He and Bellinger then prepared a joint estimate of the situation upon which to base operation plans and orders. This done, on 31 March the estimate was forwarded to Kimmel. Thus came about the Joint Coastal Frontier Defense Plan, signed by Short and Bloch on 11 April.

The Martin-Bellinger estimate noted that a Japanese attack most likely would come from the Japanese mandated islands to the south. Because carriers could strike from any direction, however, it called for 360 degree reconnaissance sweeps as far as possible to sea. All hands recognized that such sweeps could be maintained by current personnel and planes for only a very short period and that they should not be undertaken "unless other intelligence indicates that a surface raid is probable within rather narrow limits of time."

Both sides also agreed that Japan had never preceded hostile action with a declaration of war and that "the most likely and dangerous form of attack on Oahu would be an air attack." At dawn of the day of the attack several carriers would launch planes 233 nautical miles from Oahu and achieve "a complete surprise" to which Hawaii's defenders would be slow to respond. It was agreed that the army would use its planes to intercept enemy planes over the islands while Bellinger's Naval Base Air Defense Force, with whatever planes the army could spare, would try to track down and discover the hostile carriers.[15]

Bloch was responsible to Kimmel for the development of the forward island bases and provision of services to the fleet. With the army he would exercise joint control over the defenses against attack, and under the Joint Coastal Frontier Defense Plan he would provide distant aerial reconnaissance. He recognized that the navy could hardly conduct continuous distant reconnaissance, had no fighters to lend the army, and that the army in turn had no aircraft warning system and no bombers worth anything to lend the navy. Further, engaging in joint operations vitiated expansion of training activities. Lastly, the Naval Base Defense Air Force Operation could be carried out only after Kimmel recognized an emergency. As for Bellinger, he was responsible to Kimmel for training and operating his patrol wings when they were part of the fleet but was responsible to Bloch when the planes were acting as part of the Naval Base Defense Force.[16]

The Martin-Bellinger estimate was highly praised by Stark's office and by all later investigations into the Pearl Harbor disaster. The report of the congressional investigation, for example, stated: "The outline of possible enemy action as set forth in the Martin-Bellinger estimate is a startling harbinger of what actually occurred."[17] However, again, it had a major flaw. Because of his lack of planes, pilots, and crews and because they must patrol the fleet when it exercised at sea, Kimmel could not transfer fleet planes to Bloch as Naval Base Defense Officer unless he had advance knowledge that an attack was to be expected within narrow limits of time.

When told by Stark on 7 February 1941 about shortcomings in the army's defense of Pearl Harbor, General Marshall replied that Hawaii was in better shape than all other army commands. In May 1941 Marshall told President Roosevelt that the thirty-five thousand troops, modern pursuit planes, coast defense guns, and anti-aircraft artillery made Pearl Harbor secure. In June, however, Kimmel told Stark, Admiral Ernest J. King, the Atlantic Fleet Commander, and Roosevelt himself of the problems he faced, including the possibility of an air attack on Pearl Harbor. But rather than support Bellinger's and Bloch's demand for more patrol planes, he listened to his war plans officer, Charles H. McMorris, who held that the Japanese would never attack Pearl Harbor. Forced to compromise, he emphasized training more than reconnaissance.[18]

Between 4 February and 4 December 1941 Bloch asked Stark twenty-four times to strengthen the defenses of Oahu and of the outlying islands. Stark warned his fleet commanders that the Germans and Japanese favored weekends for attacking and that the Japanese could strike in any direction, but he did nothing beyond furnishing Bellinger some new aircraft in late October and November.

When he visited Bellinger, Under Secretary of the Navy James V. Forrestal congratulated him for his close teamwork with army air. Bellinger replied that interservice cooperation would not work in time of war and that what was needed was unity of command. Another visitor, Representative Melvin Maas, an aviator and a colonel in the marine corps reserve, also suggested a unified command for the islands. Bellinger agreed but in turn recommended that Maas tell Congress of such and that he would succeed only if Congress "lights a bomb."[19]

Bellinger received eighteen PBY-5s and PBY-5As (amphibians) on 28 October 1941, twelve on 8 November, and twenty-four on 23 November--the last just two weeks before the Japanese attack. They not only lacked spare parts and replacement crews, but his men at Ford Island had to fit them with leakproof gasoline tanks and armor and so make them war-ready.

On 17 October Kimmel directed the outlying islands to go on alert and had Bellinger send twelve planes to operate from Midway and to prepare six planes to be sent to Wake. But he failed either to order long-range reconnaissance from Oahu, reduce the training activities of his fleet or Bellinger's wings, or change the training routine of the ships in his task forces. The last, he ordered, would spend eight days at sea and thirteen including weekends in port.[20]

On 16 November Kimmel again asked Stark to give more consideration to his shortages. Furthermore, uninformed except from what he read in newspapers about what was going on in Washington and its international relations, he directed Commander Joseph J. Rochefort, head of Communications Intelligence, to submit an estimate of the disposition and intentions of the Japanese fleet to him and to communications intelligence units in Washington and Corregidor for comment. On 26 November Rochefort reported that the Japanese had strong naval and air components at Hainan Island and Formosa and others in the Palau and Marshall Islands. It thus appeared that an attack would be made on Southeast Asia and the Netherlands East Indies. Based in part on this report, Stark on 27 November sent a "war warning" message to Kimmel, Hart, and the naval commander at Panama. The message noted that negotiations with Japan had ceased and that Japanese action could be expected within the next few days particularly against "the Philippines or the Thai or Kra Peninsula or possibly Borneo." The message then ordered its addressees to "Execute an appropriate defensive deployment preparatory to carrying out the tasks assigned in WPL 46. Inform district and Army authorities. A similar warning is being sent by War Department." There was no mention of Pearl Harbor in the message because the best information available showed that an attack would be made on the places mentioned in it. Moreover, the message applied to Admiral Hart more than to Kimmel, yet Kimmel was expected to take appropriate defensive measures.[21]

Kimmel told most of his staff officers and task force commanders about the war warning message, but not Bellinger. Meanwhile Washington did not inform him about the fourteen-part message in which Japan stated that diplomatic sparring with the United States would end at 1400 on 7 December, Washington time--0700 Hawaii time. Kimmel ordered depth charges dropped on all submarine contacts in the fleet operating areas near Pearl Harbor and the destruction of classified material in the outlying islands. However, he kept his ships and aircraft following their training schedules and maintaining the lowest condition of readiness he had prescribed. He discussed long-range air reconnaissance with his staff but decided not to initiate it. Without an emergency or directive from him, Bloch, as the Naval Base Defense Officer, could not alter Bellinger's patrol plane schedules or direct him to stop training and engage in reconnaissance.[22]

On Kimmel's order, however, Bellinger sent an island commander, servicing crews, and radio personnel to Wake Island so that patrol planes could be based there as required. Moreover, on 28 November Kimmel ordered Bellinger to have his twelve patrol planes at Midway search from there to Wake and to a distance of 325 miles therefrom and also have a relief squadron sent to Midway to cover Halsey's *Enterprise* force, which on 3 December would fly marine planes off to Midway.

On 1 December, his Fleet Intelligence Officer, Edwin T. Layton, told Kimmel that an unusual change of Japanese radio call signs signified "an additional progressive step in preparing for operations on a large scale." For the next six days Layton noted a great increase in Japanese radio traffic but had no indication that a Japanese carrier fleet was heading for Pearl Harbor.[23]

Between 1 and 4 December Bellinger conducted daily scouting flights covering ninety degrees for three hundred miles to the southwest of Oahu as part of patrol wing exercises. The planes he had sent to Midway returned to Pearl on 7 December. The southwestern approaches to Oahu had thus been well covered, but not the northwestern sectors where, he unavailingly pointed out, a northeasterly wind facilitated the recovery of carrier aircraft. On his own recognizance he instructed his aviators to arm their planes and be ready during a peaceful mission to shift to a war mission without returning to base.[24]

On 6 December Bellinger had sixty-one planes on Oahu, but the planes returned from Midway and Wake needed overhaul. Had he used the forty-nine planes available to him, they could have flown a 360-degree search at best for four or five days. Had Kimmel ordered him to search in this manner, the northwestern sectors about Oahu would have been covered and the Japanese carrier fleet might have been discovered.

General Short reacted to his war warning message by placing in effect only an anti-sabotage alert because stronger ones would have stopped all air training. Kimmel did not ask him for long-range reconnaissance planes, and Short did not report that fact to Washington because he had few such planes and the mission belonged to the navy. Subsequently, the order to send about fifty percent of Hawaii's modern fighters to Wake and Midway caused Kimmel and Short to conclude that the War and Navy Departments did not anticipate an attack on Pearl Harbor. For some unknown reason, joint defense exercises previously held for two months on Sunday mornings did not occur on 7 December. As a result, it took up to six hours to draw and distribute ammunition to Short's guns and four hours for Bellinger to arm his planes.[25]

If Kimmel ordered planes on reconnaissance, he would deny protection to the operating fleet and dilute his training program. Bellinger often told him that his few patrol planes could not search 360 degrees about Oahu for an extended time and that both he and Martin had to help army B-17s get to the Philippines. Moreover, Short was not getting any B-17s, which in emergencies could be used for long-range reconnaissance, or enough fighters to intercept enemy fighters, and his staff disregarded the report by a mobile radar station at 0700 on 7 December that planes were approaching Oahu from 132 miles to the north because of an expected flight of B-17s from the mainland.[26]

Not furnished intelligence by Washington about Japanese activities subsequent to 27 November, Kimmel still thought that the Japanese would attack Wake or Midway before Pearl and that any attack on the last would come from the south. Although he had Bellinger beef up the defenses of Wake and Midway, he let the battleship fleet remain in Pearl Harbor during weekends and ordered only the lowest condition of readiness. Bellinger instead believed that an attack would be made on Pearl from the northwest. However, no superior asked him to search the sector northwest of Oahu on 7 December. Uninformed by Kimmel of the war warning message and therefore seeing no need for a continuous search, and knowing that he could expect no B-17s from the army, at least he had the good sense to direct his aviators to be ready to shoot at any time.

Were Bellinger and Martin culpable? Could they had done more within the limits of their equipment and authority? Secretary Knox arrived in Pearl Harbor on 11 December and spent thirty-two hours on "fact finding." Secretary of War Stimson sent his own investigators on 12 December and a general to relieve Short. In his report, approved by Roosevelt, Knox stated that both Kimmel and Short had admitted that their services had not been prepared to defend against a surprise air attack. Similar admissions were later made by Generals Marshall and Martin, and by Layton. While Knox noted deficiencies in fighter aircraft and anti-aircraft guns, matters for which Washington was responsible, he did not reveal that the Hawaiian commanders had been denied vital intelligence by Washington. He held Kimmel to be blameworthy and removed him from his post.[27]

On 17 December Roosevelt asked Justice Owen Roberts "to ascertain the facts relating to the attack...[which could] provide bases for sound decisions whether any dereliction of duty or errors of judgment on the part of the United States Army and Navy personnel contributed to such successes."[28] The board report, made public on 23 January 1942, failed to mention Magic intelligence and found no fault with Knox, Secretary of State Cordell Hull, General Marshall, or Admiral Stark about their having kept Kimmel and Short informed. While such subordinate commanders as Bellinger and Martin were not held responsible for the state of readiness of Pearl Harbor, Kimmel and Short had been "in dereliction of duty"--for not having cooperated better--and had committed "errors in judgment."[29] Kimmel and Short thereupon asked for court martials so that they could clear their names. These were never provided.

Protests against the Roberts Board report in the press, Congress, and military services led to three army and three navy investigations and to a congressional investigation between 1944 and 1946. The army inquiries and the inquiry by Admiral H. Kent Hewitt reversed the Roberts Board's conclusion that Kimmel and Short had been culpable. A navy board comprised of three admirals agreed that Kimmel and Short should not have sent out reconnaissance planes until an attack appeared imminent. When Kimmel noted that Stark had not sent him all the Magic messages, Washington had to be investigated. President Harry S. Truman refused to let the congressional investigators see the Magic messages on the grounds of national security. The investigators reported on 20 July 1946 and centered more upon Bloch than Bellinger, but in the end the buck rested with Kimmel. On the other hand, Washington had been derelict in keeping the commanders on Oahu fully informed.

Without revealing how he reached his conclusion, Admiral George C. Dyer has assigned twenty percent of the responsibility for the Pearl Harbor disaster to President Roosevelt--presumably for leaving the fleet at Pearl Harbor and waiting for the Japanese to commit the first act--forty percent to Stark, and forty percent to Kimmel.[30] In sum, officials in Washington were more culpable than Kimmel. Bellinger and Martin stand fully cleared while Bloch's reputation is tainted. The Roberts Board's conclusion that Kimmel and Short had been derelict in duty and had committed errors of judgment has been reversed. Although about as many military people and historians have upheld Roosevelt as others have charged that Kimmel and Short were made scapegoats for his administration, evidence supports the conclusion that they were not culprits.

Notes

[1]Vice Admiral Patrick N. L. Bellinger, "The Gooney Bird." MSS autobiography, 1960, p. 36 (Naval Historical Center, Operational Archives Branch, Washington, DC) [hereafter NHC:OAB].

[2]Edward Arpee, *From Frigates to Flat-tops: The Life of William A. Moffett* (Lake Forest, IL, 1935, 49-50; John D. Hayes, "Admiral John Mason Reeves, USN," *Naval War College Review* 23 (November 1970): 54-55; Eugene E. Wilson, *Wings of the Dawn* (Palm Beach, 1950), xxii-xxx.

[3]Logan C. Ramsey, "Aerial Attacks on Fleets at Anchor," *U.S. Naval Institute Proceedings* 63 (August 1937): 112-40.

[4]A copy of Horne's paper is in General Board Records, File 449, NHC:OAB; Stark to Horne, 10 June 1940, copy in Admiral Claude C. Bloch Papers, Manuscript Division, Library of Congress.

[5]Knox to Bloch, 9 September 1940, copy in Bloch Papers; Knox to Stimson, 24 January 1941, in U.S. Congress, *Hearings before the Joint Committee of the Pearl Harbor Attack: Congress of the United States*, 39 vols. (Washington, 1946), pt. 1, p. 279 (hereafter *Pearl Harbor Attack*).

[6]*Army Pearl Harbor Board Report* (Washington, 1945), 99-101; Bloch to Stark, 1, 5 May, 17 August 1941, Bloch Papers; Stark to Bloch, 12 November 1941, copy in Special Collections, Nimitz Library, U.S. Naval Academy.

[7]*Army Pearl Harbor Board Report*, 101-103.

[8]*On the Treadmill to Pearl Harbor: The Memoirs of Admiral James O. Richardson, USN (Ret.), as told to Vice Admiral George C. Dyer, USN (Ret.)* (Washington, 1973), 223-26.

[9]Bellinger, "Gooney Bird," Addendum B; Gordon W. Prange, in collaboration with Donald M. Goldstein and Katherine V. Dillon, *At Dawn We Slept: The Untold Story of Pearl Harbor* (New York, 1981), 362.

[10]B. Mitchell Simpson, *Admiral Harold R. Stark: A Biography* (s.l., s.n., 1985), 126-33; *Narrative Statement of Evidence at Pearl Harbor Investigations before Admiral T.C. Hart, USN, the Naval Court of Inquiry, and Admiral H. Kent Hewitt, USN*, 3 vols. (Washington, 1945 [?]), I: 80-84, 149, 157-61.

[11]Chief of Naval Operations to Chief of Bureau of Ordnance, 5 February, 10 March 1941, Strategic Plans Division (Series V), Box 90; "Pacific Bases. Study of Defense Installations at Outlying Bases," ibid., Series III, Box 64; (NHC:OAB).

[12]Commander Fleet Air Wing Two [Bellinger], "History of Fleet Air Wing Two, 1 November 1942-12 April 1945" (NHC: OAB); Homer N. Wallin, *Pearl Harbor: Why, How, Fleet Salvage and Final Appraisal* (Washington, 1968), 41-44, 52; Lloyd J. Graybar, "Pearl Harbor Scapegoat," *Louisville Courier Journal*, 3 December 1978, 11-18.

[13]Bellinger, "Gooney Bird," 306; John Toland, *Infamy: Pearl Harbor and Its Aftermath* (Garden City, NJ, 1982), 7-8.

[14]*Army Pearl Harbor Board Report*, 99, 183, 184-87.

[15]The entire Martin-Bellinger report appears in *Pearl Harbor Attack*, pt. 22, pp. 349-54; See also *Army Pearl Harbor Board Report*, 104.

[16]*Narrative Statement of Evidence*, I:63, 430-35; *Pearl Harbor Attack*, pt. 4, p. 1941; Barbara Wohlstetter, *Pearl Harbor: Warning and Decision* (Stanford, 1962), 22-23, 25; Prange, *At Dawn We Slept*, 93-95.

[17]*Pearl Harbor Attack*, pt. 38, p. 304, and *Report*, 84, 97-98.

[18]*Army Pearl Harbor Board Report*, 65-66, 95-96; Narrative *Statement of Evidence*, I:235-36, 249-53; Forrest Pogue, *George C. Marshall: Ordeal and Hope, 1939-1942* (New York, 1966), 173.

[19]Bellinger, "Gooney Bird," 313-14; Maas, "Random Notes on My Observations on Pacific Island Bases, 20 Oct. 1941." Copy in William F. Halsey Papers, Manuscript Division, Library of Congress.

[20]*Narrative Statement of Evidence*, I:197-98, 403-405.

[21]Ibid., 23:419-20; *Pearl Harbor Attack*, pt. 14, p. 1406; Prange, *At Dawn We Slept*, 354.

[22]*Narrative Statement of Evidence*, II:430, 431, 575.

[23]Ibid., 465-59, 518-22, 563-64.

[24]Bellinger, "Gooney Bird," 318.

[25]*Army Pearl Harbor Board Report*, 114-14, 1245-27; Prange, *At Dawn We Slept*, 414.

[26]*Army Pearl Harbor Board Report*, 60-5, 157-62.

[27]*Pearl Harbor Attack*, pt. 5, p. 2338; Husband E. Kimmel, *Admiral Kimmel's Story* (Chicago, 1955), 136; Edwin T. Layton with Roger Pineau and John Costello, *"And*

I Was There": *Pearl Harbor and Midway--Breaking the Secrets* (New York, 1986), 307, 309-10.

[28]*Pearl Harbor Attack Report*, 269.

[29]Bellinger, "Gooney Bird," 333; Layton, *"And I Was There"*, 336-37, 341, 343-44.

[30]George C. Dyer, "My God, They Can't Do That To Me," Paul Stillwell, ed., *Air Raid Pearl Harbor! Recollections of a Day of Infamy* (Annapolis, 1980), 48.

Part V

The Tonkin Gulf Incident, 1964

Tonkin Gulf: Fact and Fiction

America's involvement in Vietnam continues to attract much scholarly attention as well as passionate opinions and intense controversy. In this essay on one of the most significant and controversial events in the war, Mr. Marolda examines the historical and journalistic coverage of the naval incidents known as the Tonkin Gulf Affair and the American public's changing view of it.

Reminiscent of another Sunday, twenty-three years before, on 2 August 1964 the morning-watch calm of the navy's Pentagon command center was suddenly shattered. A "flash," or top priority, message arrived from the destroyer *Maddox*, then in the Gulf of Tonkin: "Being approached by high speed craft with apparent intention of torpedo attack. Intend to open fire if necessary [in] self defense."[1] Then, around 1600 local time, the *Maddox* reported an actual attack on her by hostile PT boats. Two days later, on the evening of 4 August, another attack occurred, this time involving the *Maddox* and the destroyer *Turner Joy*.

This naval confrontation, collectively the Tonkin Gulf Incident of 1964, was of seminal importance to the Vietnam War. It is essential to establish, as nearly as possible, an accurate picture of the causes, circumstances, and results of this major event in U.S. and Vietnamese history. The immediate importance of the Tonkin Gulf Incident was obvious. For the first time in the long Southeast Asian conflict, U.S. and North Vietnamese forces engaged in open combat. The effect on the administration of President Lyndon Johnson, the Congress, and the American people was electric. Some writers have likened the incident to the Japanese attack on Pearl Harbor for its effect on American public opinion. There was widespread support for the Seventh Fleet's retaliatory carrier strikes against the North Vietnamese navy on 5 August.[2]

Further, the naval actions off the Indochinese coast inspired passage by Congress on 7 August of the Southeast Asia Resolution, better known as the Tonkin Gulf Resolution. As often in times of crisis, the Congress, and indirectly the American people, rallied around the flag. The House of Representatives passed the Tonkin Gulf Resolution unanimously. In the Senate, the vote was eighty-eight to two.

Only Senators Ernest Gruening of Alaska and Wayne Morse of Oregon voted against the measure.[3] These were not popular acts. As some indication of public sentiment, Senator Morse revealed that he received telegrams from some of his constituents that "questioned my human paternity."[4] Conversely, in August 1964, most Americans echoed the expression of Georgia's Senator Richard Russell regarding the perceived North Vietnamese aggression. He believed that "our national honor is at stake." The United States could not just "turn tail and run" from the North Vietnamese.[5] Senator J. William Fulbright, powerful Chairman of the Senate Foreign Relations Committee, acted as the floor manager for the Tonkin Gulf Resolution and vigorously pushed its adoption in the senior legislative body. After all, the Tonkin Gulf measure was only the latest in a long line of similar postwar resolutions. The Formosa Resolution of 1955 over the defense of Taiwan, the Middle East Resolution of 1957 in regard to the Suez Crisis, and the Cuba Resolution of 1962 during the Missile Crisis all expressed congressional confidence in the president's plans for managing serious international confrontations.[6]

The Tonkin Gulf Resolution, which stated that the United States was prepared, "as the President determines, to take all necessary steps, including the use of armed force, to assist any member or protocol state of the Southeast Asia Collective Defense Treaty [better known as the SEATO Pact] requesting assistance in defense of its freedom,"[7] gave Lyndon Johnson great latitude in the conduct of U.S. policy in Southeast Asia. Without a formal declaration of war, the Tonkin Gulf Resolution was seen by many as the legal basis for American participation in the Vietnam conflict. At one point, Assistant Secretary of State Nicholas Katzenbach testified before Congress that the Tonkin Gulf Resolution was the "functional equivalent"[8] of a declaration of war.

When Senator Fulbright's Foreign Relations Committee convened hearings on the Tonkin Gulf Incident in February 1968, a dramatic change in the American perception of the Vietnam War had occurred. By then more than half a million U.S. troops had been committed to the struggle, with little prospect of victory. The enemy's bloody Tet Offensive was in full swing then, and President Johnson would shortly call off the failed Rolling Thunder bombing campaign against North Vietnam. Opposition to the war had mounted steadily in the United States since the heady, muscle-flexing days of August 1964. Secretary of Defense Robert McNamara, who represented the Johnson administration at the hearings, was seen by many in Congress as an "adversary--the symbol of an unsuccessful war, the author of unfulfilled optimism."[9]

Senator Fulbright and many other Americans felt they had been consistently deceived and misled by the Johnson administration over the conduct of the war in Southeast Asia; the contemporary term "credibility gap" was much in use. Critics of the government then and in later years of the war were especially exorcised over the Tonkin Gulf Resolution. Convinced that LBJ had used it to circumvent the constitutional requirement for Congress to declare war, opponents of the war vowed that this not happen again. Fulbright in particular felt that he had been "hornswoggled" by Johnson, his former close friend and Senate colleague; that the president had used the resolution as a *carte blanche* in Southeast Asia. Fulbright and others hoped to make further escalation of the war difficult. To do this they had, in the words of one writer, "to impugne [*sic*] the legitimacy of the Tonkin [Gulf] Resolution."[10] Importantly, opponents of the war took aim at the administration's account of the Tonkin Gulf Incident of August 1964, which motivated and substantiated the Tonkin Gulf Resolution. Some

283

critics leveled serious charges; that the administration and the navy deliberately provoked the North Vietnamese into attacking U.S. destroyers on patrol off North Vietnam in order to get public support for an expanded war; we needed another "Remember the Maine!" rallying cry. Several writers have even suggested that the administration hoped for the "death of Americans, the sinking of a U.S. ship on the high seas [because it would be] dramatic, shocking, and unique. It was the stuff of headlines."[11]

Other commentators, including the North Vietnamese, assert that the U.S. ships intruded repeatedly into North Vietnamese territorial waters during their August surveillance mission, code-named the Desoto patrol. Another charge is that the U.S. ships were working directly with South Vietnamese coastal raiders conducting a sabotage and bombardment operation, code-named 34 Alpha, in North Vietnam.[12] Although U.S. naval forces had been active ashore and afloat in Southeast Asia since 1950, one writer avers that this operation "offered the U.S. navy its first chance to get involved in Vietnam."[13] The most common allegation is that the engagement on 4 August was a "phantom" battle, with jumpy sailors afraid of the dark shooting at shadows and ghostly contacts, and that U.S. civilian and military leaders, before determining the validity of this night action, rashly ordered retaliatory carrier strikes against North Vietnam the next day.[14]

Perhaps the most damning charge of all was that the government and the navy staged a "sham battle" on the night of 4 August as a justification for widening the war. The North Vietnamese, of course, were the first to label the action a fabrication and a pretext for bombing the North.[15] Many Americans, however, also believe the incident was "rigged" or "staged" by the United States. Journalist I.F. Stone, writing in 1968, saw it as "one of the great military frauds of world history, the curtain raiser for our disastrous Vietnamese adventure, which may easily and soon turn into a wider and nuclear war. There are no limits to what such leadership may cook up."[16]

For their part, Johnson administration leaders advanced explanations for the Tonkin Gulf Incident that soon strained their credibility. Immediately after the naval actions of 2 and 4 August, and during the Senate hearings in 1968, Secretary of Defense Robert McNamara assured Congress that the *Maddox* was "carrying out a *routine* [italics added] patrol of the type we carry out all over the world at all times," when subjected to an unprovoked attack by North Vietnamese warships. Admiral Ulysses S. Grant Sharp, commanding all U.S. forces in the Pacific during this period, also emphasized the "routine" character of the *Maddox* and *Turner Joy* intelligence collection patrol off North Vietnam.[17] McNamara contended that there was no connection between the patrol and the South Vietnamese 34 Alpha operation and that the navy knew nothing about it. Finally, administration leaders stated that the primary purpose of 34 Alpha was to prevent infiltration into South Vietnam.[18] Information on the Tonkin Gulf Incident surfacing after 1964, however, called into question each of these assertions.

Much of what happened in August of that watershed year related to the Johnson administration's new strategy for Southeast Asia. At the beginning of 1964, the United States began applying military pressure on North Vietnam to induce that country to stop directing and supplying the communist guerrillas in South Vietnam and Laos; the object of this pressure campaign was to influence the North Vietnamese to "leave [their] neighbors alone."[19] Ironically, when Senator Fulbright published his book, *Old Myths and New Realities*, in May 1964, he concurred with this strategy and suggested carrying the war to the enemy by "equipping the South Vietnamese armed forces to attack North Vietnamese territory, possibly by means of commando type operations from sea or air."[20]

By early 1964, South Vietnam especially needed that help. President Ngo Dinh Diem had been assassinated and his government overthrown the previous November; political turmoil followed in their wake. Hoping to capitalize on the disarray in the South Vietnamese body politic, the Hanoi leadership stepped up combat activity. Viet Cong guerrillas attacked and destroyed a growing number of regular units of the South Vietnamese forces. The enemy also crippled the government's pacification program.

A key feature of the U.S. effort to help the South Vietnamese was Operation 34 Alpha. It entailed covert sabotage and raiding actions along the North Vietnamese coast. Its primary purpose was not to monitor or impede infiltration into South Vietnam. Although South Vietnamese commandos landed by South Vietnamese-crewed *Nasty*-class fast patrol boats carried out these missions, U.S. leaders with the Military Assistance Command, Vietnam (MACV), in Saigon, and others in Washington, controlled the operation. Further, the U. S. Navy supplied the *Nasty*-class fast patrol boats, or PTFs, and trained the South Vietnamese raiders at Da Nang, one hundred miles south of the Demilitarized Zone. Most details of the 34 Alpha operation were known at the Seventh Fleet level. Indeed, fleet representatives coordinated with their MACV counterparts to avoid interference between the 34 Alpha and Desoto Patrol operations.

The U.S.-Vietnamese maritime venture, begun 1 February 1964, initially was a flop. South Vietnamese casualties were high and the boat force failed to accomplish more than a few successful missions. The lack of good intelligence on North Vietnamese targets, coastal naval forces, and shore defenses was a major cause of failure. To get better intelligence for the 34 Alpha program, Admiral Harry D. Felt, Commander in Chief, Pacific, ordered patrols along the North Vietnamese coastline by U.S. destroyers.

These surveillance missions, part of the Desoto Patrol program, had been conducted along the Chinese, North Korean, and North Vietnamese coastlines since 1962. For the first time, however, U.S. ships were authorized in early 1964 to steam as close as four nautical miles to only one communist country--North Vietnam. The destroyer *John R. Craig* carried out the first patrol from 25 February to 9 March. As naval leaders later observed, however, persistent coastal fog and other factors limited the intelligence return.

Commander Seventh Fleet assigned the July-August mission to the *Sumner*-class destroyer *Maddox*, a venerable veteran of World War II and Korea. Captain John J. Herrick, commanding Destroyer Division 192, was designated the on-scene commander. The ship was to steam along a pre-set track off North Vietnam, no closer than eight miles to the mainland or four miles to offshore islands. Under international law, North Vietnamese territorial waters extended to three miles offshore. As it happened, no

American ship came closer than five miles to any part of the Democratic Republic of Vietnam during the August Desoto Patrol.

In the meantime, the 34 Alpha operation began to register success. South Vietnamese commandos destroyed several bridges, storage buildings, and other military structures ashore. On the night of 30-31 July, for the first time, the PTF force stood offshore and bombarded targets on the islands of Hon Me and Hon Nieu. Although North Vietnamese naval forces tried throughout the spring and summer of 1964 to intercept these raiders, they were unable to catch the fast craft.[21]

Into this situation steamed the *Maddox* on the morning of 31 July. For that day and through 1 August, the destroyer proceeded without incident generally northward along her coastal patrol track. Intelligence revealed, however, that the North Vietnamese monitored the ship's progress visually and on radar throughout her patrol. Thus, the North Vietnamese did not mistake the destroyer for the South Vietnamese boats that raided the coast the previous night, as has been alleged.

This air of normality changed suddenly. In the early morning hours of 2 August, U.S. intelligence learned that North Vietnamese naval headquarters had ordered its coastal fleet to get ready for battle and deployed naval vessels to a small cove on the island of Hon Me, southeast of Thanh Hoa. The assembled force consisted of the three Soviet-built P-4 motor torpedo boats of Division 3, PT Squadron 135, and two Swatow motor gunboats. Around 1400 this force was ordered to attack the "enemy" with torpedoes.[22]

Between 1500 and 1600, the three PTs were picked up on an intercepting course, at fifty knots, first by the *Maddox* radars and then visually by topside personnel. Commander Herbert L. Ogier, commanding the *Maddox*, sounded general quarters, increased the ship's speed to twenty-seven knots, changed course to the southeast away from the threat, and called for air support from the aircraft carrier *Ticonderoga*, then 280 miles to the southeast. In addition, Herrick sent the "flash" priority message that so jolted Washington awake that day.

By 1600 the fast approaching P-4s, now in column formation, closed to 9,800 yards off the *Maddox*'s starboard quarter. It is important to note that the North Vietnamese made no attempt, by radio, lights, flares, or signal flags, to clarify their menacing approach.[23]

At 1605 the *Maddox* fired three warning shots from her 5-inch guns in an unsuccessful attempt to deter further approach by the PT boats. Three years after this engagement, Lieutenant Raymond P. Connell, the *Maddox* weapons officer, stated that these first shots were aimed to hit, not warn away, the enemy craft. He explained, however, that "the chances of long-range naval guns hitting a target at that range with the first shot, before corrections are applied, is very slight." Other witnesses, including Captain Herrick, contend that the shots were to warn. Samuel Halpern, the ship's doctor, distinctly heard a call for warning shots over the PA system.[24] At 1608 the *Maddox*, by then twenty-five miles off the coast of North Vietnam, opened fire in earnest. Some writers have faulted the navy for firing the first shot. The issue is bogus. Captain Herrick had intelligence of a planned torpedo attack on an "enemy"; torpedo boats, for the first time that year called south from their far northern base at Van Hoa, were closing his ship on an intercept course; and his warnings went unheeded. The captain later stated: "This is like pointing a gun [at you] as far as I'm concerned. The torpedo is sitting there and he's pointing it where it will hit you if he lets it go. That's an attack."[25] Herrick would have been derelict in his duty if he allowed the PTs to get within torpedo range.

Between five and nine thousand yards from the destroyer, the lead PT launched one torpedo and turned away to the south. The second vessel, with the third right behind, closed to three thousand yards and launched two torpedoes. Simultaneously, 5-inch gunfire hit the lead PT and she retired from the battle with difficulty. As the *Maddox* changed course to avoid them, two North Vietnamese torpedoes passed by her two hundred yards to starboard. The third PT then crossed the destroyer's wake without firing torpedoes and moved out of the action. At that point, the first boat returned to the attack. Closing to two thousand yards, the P-4 dropped one torpedo in the water and fired her dual 14.5-millimeter guns at the

Maddox. One round hit the pedestal of the destroyer's M56 fire control director.[26]

This battle at close quarters was more costly to the North Vietnamese, however. The boat commander was killed at his station near the wheel by *Maddox* gunfire. Paying tribute to the enemy's daring, Captain Herrick stated later that the "attacking boats were aggressive and showed no tendency to abort their torpedo run even though they were confronted with a heavy barrage of fire."[27]

By 1630, the surface action was over. The PTs put about and headed for shore. The *Maddox* continued to the southeast. At that point, four F-8 Crusaders from the *Ticonderoga* arrived on the scene. Led by squadron commander James B. Stockdale, later Vice Admiral, Medal of Honor recipient, and impassioned writer, the navy fighters made for the enemy PTs. They shot up the three craft with their Zuni rockets and 20-millimeter cannon fire and left one boat dead in the water and burning. Intelligence verified that this vessel later sank.[28]

Enemy losses might have been much higher if the American side had not taken steps to avoid further combat. Fleet commanders recalled a second group of *Ticonderoga* aircraft dispatched to attack surviving North Vietnamese PTs and prohibited their pursuit into the enemy's air space.

Furthermore, President Johnson ruled out retaliation for North Vietnam's naval assault on 2 August, the cause of which baffled his chief advisors. Aside from publicly warning the North Vietnamese not to make the same mistake twice, he took no escalatory action. Even Senator Fulbright, a later opponent of the war effort, was impressed with the administration's measured response. In August 1964 he stated: "I...think the restraint with which you used overwhelming power in the area is a new attitude on the part of a great power that is extremely beneficial and I think will be effective."[29]

In view of this clear attempt to limit the consequences of the naval confrontation, it is hard to understand why some of Johnson's critics contend that he used the later incident on 4 August as a pretext for striking North Vietnam. Certainly, he had justification enough after the 2 August action, and on the next day he authorized resumption of the Desoto Patrol. Some critics have concluded that this act was unduly provocative, given the events of the previous day. Johnson and his naval commanders, however, were determined to reaffirm the traditional American support for the principle of freedom of navigation. They would not allow the North Vietnamese to designate the Gulf of Tonkin a *mare nostrum* even as current leaders refuse to recognize Libya's claim to all the Gulf of Sidra or Colonel Gaddafi's "Line of Death."

During daylight on 3 August, the *Maddox*, now joined by the *Forrest Sherman*-class destroyer *Turner Joy*, continued the interrupted coastal surveillance off North Vietnam. Their passage was not contested. At dusk the ships retired to the open sea. Farther south in the gulf, around midnight on the 3rd, the South Vietnamese 34 Alpha maritime force carried out another harassment action. Three *Nasty*-class PTFs shelled a radar facility and a security station on the coast near Vinh Son.

The *Maddox* and *Turner Joy*, which patrolled the coast unhindered throughout 4 August, steered to the east with the sunset. Captain Herrick wanted his ships to steam in relative safety near the center of the gulf during the night, as they had the previous night. The men of the *Maddox* and *Turner Joy* would not enjoy a peaceful open sea orbit, however, for that afternoon North Vietnamese naval headquarters had ordered some of its P-4s and Swatows to prepare for military operations that night. Between 2041 and 2145, surface search radars in the *Maddox* picked up three contacts forty-two miles to the northeast, in the area where the Americans had intended to pass the hours of darkness. The contacts moved at greater than thirty-knot speeds, suggesting fast, PT-type vessels, and they shaped their course to intercept with that of the destroyers.[30]

Fearing a trap, Captain Herrick steered his units more to the southeast away from the approaching contacts. James Stankevitz, a radar operator in the *Maddox* Combat Information Center (CIC), later stated that "they were definitely contacts and moving fast."[31] For a time the three contacts hung back at a distance, and radar contact was lost as the destroyers opened the range and made for the mouth of the gulf at thirty knots. The fast craft, however, resumed the chase and soon fell in behind the *Turner Joy*, deployed in column formation one thousand yards astern of the *Maddox*. When the contacts closed to thirteen miles, the sophisticated fire control radars of both destroyers locked on these targets.[32]

Much has been made of the supposed unreliability of each ship's radars and of their operators' reports. As one journalist opined, they were "victimized to some extent by peculiar weather conditions and other problems" which included "scattered thundershowers, fishing junks, schools of fish, and American aircraft." This same writer concedes, however, that "all of the scope-watchers interviewed by me [years after the incident] insisted that 'something was out there.'"[33]

A wealth of information supports the conclusion that the ship's radars picked up "something out there." The official reports prepared by each ship shortly after the battle state emphatically that weather, sea, and other anomalies were quickly identified as such and dismissed. No fishing junks operated after darkness that far out to sea.[34] Further, most of the radarmen in these ships had long experience with their equipment.

The statements made by both ships' operators right after the engagement and years later affirm the validity of the night's radar contacts. One of the *Turner Joy*'s surface search operators, Seaman Dennis Plzak, stated on 7 August: "I have spent many hours on the surface search and I evaluate them as definite contacts. It appeared to me that there was a definite plan used by the craft. At one time I held clearly three contacts."[35] Ensign John M. Leeman, positioned on the *Maddox*'s bridge, recalled in 1967 seeing "with my own eyes, five or more high-speed contacts approaching on the surface-search radar."[36] Of related importance, surface warfare officers attest that when the intensified, pencil-like beam of a fire control radar locks onto a contact, that contact is a hard target. The *Maddox* and *Turner Joy* fire control radars locked onto and held targets throughout the night. Commander Robert C. Barnhart, the *Turner Joy*'s commanding officer (CO), recently affirmed that his ship's fire control and surface search radars held strong and constant contacts.[37]

Returning to the action, at 2234 the *Maddox* and *Turner Joy* radars picked up another contact, alone, approaching from the east at thirty-five to forty knots. When it closed to seven thousand yards, at 2239, the *Turner Joy* opened fire in earnest. The *Maddox* soon joined in. Soon afterward, this lone contact turned hard to port and moved off; this is a classic torpedo launch maneuver and the watch officer in the *Maddox* CIC, Lieutenant (jg) Frederick M. Frick, evaluated it as such. Shortly, the *Maddox*, steaming on a steady course at thirty knots, picked up the distinct sound of a torpedo running. Captain Herrick heard it over the bridge speaker system when his sonarman reported the sounding.

As the *Turner Joy* veered to starboard, to avoid the torpedo reported by the *Maddox* shortly before, Lieutenant (jg) John J. Barry, high atop the ship at Fire Control Director 51, spotted "a distinct wake...on the port side about five hundred feet from the ship...moving from aft forward on a parallel course to this ship," adding "the wake itself appeared light in color and more just below the surface than anything cutting the water on the surface."[38] Several times in later years Barry, retired from the navy, reaffirmed the accuracy of his sighting. On one occasion, he stated: "I was an anti-submarine officer at the time and I had seen many torpedoes fired from submarines during practice exercises. It was right under the surface of the water.... As we turned it just ran up on our side." This sighting was corroborated by Barry's subordinate in the gun director, Seaman Larry O. Litton, and two other topside personnel. When interviewed by *Esquire Magazine* in 1968, Litton stated that "there definitely was [a torpedo]. I never want to see one that close again."[39]

On the other hand, there were many other reports of torpedoes in the water that night. Except for the first report, most can be attributed to the noise generated by the *Maddox*'s own screws as she zigzagged violently at better than thirty knots. The destroyer's inexperienced sonarman was unable to differentiate between these sounds and the real thing. Thus, while both Captain Herrick and Commander Ogier have long considered at least the first torpedo report valid, they dismissed the rest to "overeager sonarmen."[40]

Even before the *Turner Joy* opened fire, air support arrived overhead. An F-8 Crusader, piloted by Commander Stockdale, an A-4 flown by Commander Wesley McDonald, and another Skyhawk made repeated passes over and around the destroyers in search of hostile vessels. They could find none. This also was the experience of eleven other naval aviators from the *Ticonderoga* who overflew the ships that night.[41]

There is no puzzle here. The night was pitch black. The ship's doctor, Samuel Halpern, related that it was the "blackest night I've ever seen, no moon, no stars... nothing. Total absence of light."[42] Moreover, the cloud ceiling hung low at between fifteen hundred and two thousand feet, and the star shells, flares, and other pyrotechnics used by the American ships and aircraft provided little illumination. They were simply enveloped in clouds. Commander McDonald, later a vice admiral and Deputy Chief of Naval Operations (Air), has observed that "he was only able to see the wakes of the destroyers when he was fairly close to them, and they were not highly conspicuous even then."[43] Captain Andy Kerr, a retired surface warfare officer and avid small-boat sailor, adds that "every sailor knows that searching aviators often do not see what is surely there, even in broad daylight."[44] Additionally, the *Turner Joy*'s malfunctioning radio equipment would not allow the air controller to communicate effectively with aircraft. The *Maddox* air controller was excitable and inexperienced, which led to a "confused" air control situation.[45] Despite the extreme difficulty of making any visual observation from the air on the night of 4 August and because the action continued for an hour after he departed the area, Admiral Stockdale has often and vehemently asserted that there were no hostile boats present that night. He has written that he was "the prime observer of the Tonkin Gulf affair" and the only person in the world who had a good firsthand look "at the August 4th and the August 2nd episodes."[46]

There were, of course, many in the *Turner Joy* positioned to make visual observations as were two naval aviators. Commander George Edmondson, the CO of Attack Squadron 52, and his wingman, Lieutenant Jere Barton, orbited the *Maddox* and *Turner Joy* for almost three hours. In contrast to the jet aircraft flown by

Stockdale and others, the prop-driven A-1 Skyraiders piloted by Edmondson and Barton cruised at a relatively slow one hundred fifty-knot speed. Both men were experienced at night search. At one point during the night action both men sighted gun flashes on the surface of the sea followed by bursts of light at their altitude that they identified as antiaircraft fire.[47] Edmondson has more precisely defined this fire as "patterned tracer fire that swept up past him from astern of his aircraft."[48]

During the latter part of the action, when Commander Stockdale was gone from the scene, Barton reported seeing a dark object half-way between the two destroyers that shortly moved off into the darkness. Even later, Edmondson observed a snake-like wake a mile and a half ahead of the lead destroyer, the *Maddox*. He saw it from a perilously low four hundred feet and added that he "couldn't have seen that wake from a thousand feet."[49] Edmondson and Barton, the latter of whom was killed flying combat missions in South Vietnam later in the war, stuck by their eyewitness accounts. Edmondson has been interviewed several times since the incident and still supports the accuracy of his earlier observations.[50]

Throughout the night, the destroyers fired on contacts. At 2310 the *Turner Joy* fired on and damaged or sank a contact that approached from the west. A third contact followed in the ship's wake and closed to twenty-five hundred yards at forty-eight knots before being saturated by shell bursts on radar. Commander Barnhart, the *Turner Joy*'s CO, and others saw explosions and smoke emanate from this target. Besides visual sightings of explosions on target by topside personnel, radar operators witnessed contacts hit by gunfire that soon disappeared. This also impressed Commodore Herrick.[51]

A fourth contact, following the *Turner Joy*, overshot the destroyer's wake when the ship veered to starboard. In the light of star shells and flares, three sailors in Gun Mount 32 sighted what they identified as a PT boat. One of the men, Boatswain's Mate 3rd Class Donald V. Sharkey, stated that the "outline of this contact was clearly seen by me and was definitely a PT boat." The next day, looking through intelligence materials, they further identified the vessel they had seen as a Soviet-made P-4 motor torpedo boat.[52] To get at this closely trailing craft, the *Turner Joy* dropped depth charges astern and at one point tried to ram it. Within minutes, however, this contact was stopped dead in the water by gunfire and evaluated on radar as sunk.

During the latter part of the action, the *Turner Joy*'s bridge personnel, including Commander Barnhart and several experienced signalmen, saw a bright light, aft of the ship in the area from which the hostile boats were operating. The light was extinguished when American aircraft were vectored toward the source. Signalman 2nd Class Richard M. Bacino stated that "as a Signalman, I feel I can tell a searchlight from any other light that could possibly be mistaken for such." Senior Chief Quartermaster Walter L. Shishim observed the light "by eye and its beam...by binoculars" and related that it "remained at constant brightness and the beam was an elongated fan shape pointing up."[53] This is close to Commander Barnhart's later description of the light as a "Hollywood type of light" that shined its beam "up into the sky."[54] Other witnesses described the light as being played on or around the *Turner Joy*. Critics often focus on this variation in observations. Regardless of its use, one thing is clear; all observers identified it as a light and it did not belong to either the *Maddox* or *Turner Joy*. It revealed the presence near the ships of another vessel, which under the circumstances could only be considered hostile.

Shortly after this episode, the *Maddox* and *Turner Joy* dropped depth charges astern to ward off contacts that trailed the ships. Captain Herrick and Commanders Barnhart and Ogier believed that the enemy PTs used this tactic of following the destroyers' wakes throughout the night because the small craft did not want to use their radar to locate the American ships.[55]

For the next hour, both ships fired on contacts and dropped depth charges as they headed for the mouth of the gulf. By 0010 on 5 August, neither ship held contacts. The momentous engagement was finally over.

The men of the *Maddox* and *Turner Joy* were not to rest, however, for everyone in the chain of command all the way to Washington wanted information. Scores of messages flowed from and to the ships. Dr. Halpern relates that "through the night, through the next day and the next, [his ship's officers] rarely slept, they just prepared data." He added, "I have no idea how the information was presented to Congress and the president, but I knew the officers who wrote the facts and they were honest men."[56]

This last consideration is important, because since the event in August 1964 some commentators and even serious scholars have stated or implied that the Johnson administration needed to exert "pressure [on] Herrick and other Pacific commanders for confirmatory evidence"[57] and that U.S. surface sailors and aviators relayed false information under this pressure.

What motivated the call for confirmatory evidence were two messages sent by Captain Herrick at the end of the engagement that expressed doubt about some of the information he had dispatched earlier. In particular, he believed some of the radar contacts and sonar soundings from the *Maddox*, from which he commanded, were false readings, and no one in the *Maddox* had made credible visual sightings of the enemy. As shown previously, this was an accurate assessment about the *Maddox*, which was not the focus of enemy action that night and steamed an average of six miles ahead and to the west of the *Turner Joy* during the engagement.

Thus, the officer in charge of the destroyer task unit acted wisely when he suggested a complete evaluation of the evidence before additional action was taken. Soon, however, information flowed to him from the *Turner Joy* that laid many of his doubts to rest. Thereafter, the torrent of messages sent through the Pacific command to Washington reflected his fuller understanding of the night's events. In addition, he communicated that he was "certain that original ambush was bonafide."[58] Six years later, in retirement, Captain Herrick was asked if he would still be sure there had been an attack on his ships without the existence of supporting intelligence (discussed below). He responded: "I'd still be sure. The intercepts to me were [only] the clincher, the frosting on the cake."[59]

That same intelligence also helped convince Pacific commanders and their civilian and military superiors in Washington, then and later, that the North Vietnamese navy had indeed attacked the U.S. destroyers on 4 August. The North Vietnamese reported after the battle that they had shot down enemy aircraft and damaged an enemy vessel. While no American aircraft were lost that night, this report can be ascribed to misinterpretation of the many falling flares and star shells or to the usual battlefield exaggeration. Finally, the enemy reported losing two vessels. This coincides with the number of craft determined sunk by the *Maddox* and *Turner Joy* and with the report of a North Vietnamese naval officer captured in 1967. Thus, the contention that U.S. intelligence agencies confused reports of the 4 August action with those of 2 August, does not square with the fact that only one P-4 was sunk on 2 August.[60]

Shortly after the engagement of 4 August, Admiral Roy Johnson, commanding the Seventh Fleet, dispatched Commander Andy Kerr to the scene to evaluate all available information. The experienced surface warfare officer gathered material from both ships and compiled a composite chart that incorporated radar, sonar, and visual data and identified relevant times, ranges, and bearings. When completed, the chart revealed "great consistency between all of the contacts made by both ships" and the "tracks of the attacking vessels, as plotted independently by both the *Maddox* and *Turner Joy*, coincided and were precisely what one would expect from attacking torpedo boats." Kerr concluded, and in this he was joined by Admiral Johnson and others of his staff, that the "composite track chart left no doubt whatsoever. An attack had taken place."[61]

Besides Kerr, other officials investigated the evidence on the Tonkin Gulf actions. Lieutenant General David A. Burchinal, USAF, and his joint chiefs of staff secretariat reviewed information held in Washington while a Defense Department team composed of high level civilians and several naval officers sent to the Far East pored over the messages, track charts, action reports, witness statements, and other relevant materials. These officials concurred that the *Maddox* and *Turner Joy* had been subjected to a torpedo attack by the North Vietnamese navy.[62]

Several conclusions can be drawn from the voluminous information on the Tonkin Gulf Incident. Of prime importance, the

Johnson administration and the navy did not deliberately provoke the North Vietnamese to attack American destroyers in August 1964. The overriding object of U.S. strategy in Southeast Asia was to contain the conflict by deterring the North Vietnamese from inflaming the insurgencies in South Vietnam and Laos. The instrument of this strategy was the military pressure campaign applied on North Vietnam by the 34 Alpha operation and similar activities. The underlying assumption of this strategy was that at some point the North Vietnamese would back down in the face of the overwhelming military power of the United States, but before undesired open warfare ensued.

Thus, the Johnson administration was genuinely surprised by the North Vietnamese naval attack of 2 August on the *Maddox*. American civilian and military leaders obviously misread Hanoi's intentions and underestimated North Vietnamese resolve to resist U.S. pressure. Specifically, U.S. leaders believed the North Vietnamese unwilling, unable, because of their small navy, and unlikely to challenge the mighty U.S. Navy at sea.

In a formal sense, the 34 Alpha operation and the Desoto Patrol were not connected. The Military Assistance Command, Vietnam, ran the former while the U.S. Navy directed the latter. The destroyers and PTFs did not operate together, or even near each other while in the gulf. Captain Herrick knew almost nothing about the maritime raiding actions.

On the other hand, both operations were coordinated at the MACV and Seventh Fleet levels. Further, the navy ran the PTF facility at Da Nang and trained there the South Vietnamese commandos and boat crews. Finally, gathering intelligence for the 34 Alpha program was an important responsibility of the Desoto Patrol which, in July-August 1964, cannot be described as a "routine" coastal surveillance mission.

Although the fleet was not looking for a fight in August 1964, the presence of the Desoto Patrol ships off the coast of North Vietnam did inflame the predicament. The ships did not enter North Vietnamese territorial waters, but the North Vietnamese certainly saw the destroyers and the 34 Alpha PTFs as involved in a combined campaign mounted against them.

While U.S. naval activities in the Gulf of Tonkin were not routine, there is no credible evidence that the Johnson administration or the navy "staged" or "rigged" a "sham battle" on the night of 4 August. Not one of the hundreds, perhaps thousands, of civilian officials, military officers, sailors, and aviators connected in some way with the night action has surfaced with supporting information in the twenty-three years since the incident.

Conversely, there is a wealth of solid evidence that the action on the night of 4 August was no "phantom battle" but a concerted attack by the North Vietnamese navy on U.S. naval forces. The intelligence information gathered from several sources is persuasive. More important, however, are the visual sightings by the *Turner Joy* personnel of a torpedo running parallel to the ship, of a PT boat passing close aboard, of smoke and fire emanating from other targets, and of a bright light in the area aft of the destroyer; sightings by an aviator of a snakey wake ahead of the two ships and antiaircraft fire at his altitude and of a boat-like object by another pilot; radar plots by surface search and fire control systems, operated by cool, experienced men, of hard, fast contacts, gunfire hits on target, and target sinkings; and bonafide reports from sonar of at least one torpedo in the water.

Sufficient positive information was available to national leaders when they ordered the retaliatory strike against North Vietnam on 5 August. Investigation of all the evidence available shortly after the action by naval officers on the scene, by Seventh Fleet representatives, by other military personnel in the Far East and Washington, and by Defense Department officials confirmed the earlier analysis. Years after the battle, and in retirement, almost all the principals reaffirmed their earlier observations.

What, one might ask, possessed the minuscule North Vietnamese navy to attack the mighty U.S. Pacific Fleet, destroyer of the Imperial Japanese Navy in World War II, and queen of all she surveyed? Was this the impulsive act of a local PT boat commander or even the North Vietnamese leadership? It did not seem logical that a relatively weak, developing "Third World" country, barely born, could hope to prevail against U.S. power.

From all we now know, however, North Vietnam was conducting its own pressure campaign in late 1964 and early 1965. The Tonkin Gulf actions were followed within a few months by attacks on U.S. forces at Bien Hoa, Saigon, Pleiku, and Qui Nhon in South Vietnam. The object was to convince the United States that additional aid to South Vietnam would be costly and ultimately futile. With good reason, Hanoi saw South Vietnam on its last leg and wanted to deter major U.S. intervention in support of its Southeast Asian ally. As CIA director John McCone told President Johnson at the time, the Tonkin Gulf attacks were a "signal to us that the North Vietnamese have the will and determination to continue the war. They are raising the ante."[63]

In essence, the Tonkin Gulf affair was the first real indication of what would become crystal clear in the following years; neither side was prepared to forego its policy goals in Southeast Asia without a fight.

Notes

[1]Msg. CTG77.5 021008Z August 1964, Naval Historical Center [hereafter NHC], Washington, D.C.

[2]David Wise, "Remember the Maddox!", *Esquire Magazine* (April 1968), 123; Ralph Stavins, Richard J. Barnet, and Marcus G. Raskin, *Washington Plans an Aggressive War* (New York, 1971), 98.

[3]Senator Gruening felt that "all Vietnam is not worth the life of a single American boy." Quoted in Stanley Karnow, *Vietnam: A History* (New York, 1983), 375.

[4]Quoted in John Galloway, *The Gulf of Tonkin Resolution* (Rutherford, NJ, 1970), 81. This was not the first time Morse had dissented from congressional pronouncements in support of a president. He opposed similar resolutions backing presidential action during the major international crises of the 1950s and early 1960s. By 1964, however, Morse had little influence in the Senate, regarded by many of his colleagues as a "sanctimonious bore." According to Karnow, he was the "Typhoid Mary of Capitol Hill." Karnow, *Vietnam*, 374, 375.

[5]Quoted in Anthony Austin, *The President's War* (Philadelphia, 1971), 92-93.

[6]Galloway, *Gulf of Tonkin Resolution*, 86-87; U.S. Congress, Senate, Committee on Foreign Relations and Committee on Armed Services, *Joint Hearings on Joint Resolution to Promote the Maintenance of International Peace and Security in*

Southeast Asia (88th Cong., 2nd sess.) (Washington, 1966) [hereafter *Southeast Asia Resolution*], 3; Austin, *President's War*, 10-11.

[7]Public Law 88-408 (78 Stat. 384).

[8]Quoted in Austin, *President's War*, 7.

[9]Joseph C. Goulden, *Truth Is the First Casualty: The Gulf of Tonkin Affair--Illusion and Reality* (Chicago, 1969), 210.

[10]Galloway, *Gulf of Tonkin Resolution*, 137. See also Wise, "Remember the Maddox!," 123; Goulden. *Truth Is the First Casualty*, 210, 239; Andy Kerr, *A Journey Amongst the Good and the Great* (Annapolis, 1987), 201.

[11]Stavins, et. al., *Washington Plans an Aggressive War*, 98. See also Gabriel Kolko in *The Washington Post Potomac Magazine* (17 March 1968); Wise, "Remember the Maddox!," 123; I.F. Stone in *I.F. Stone's Weekly* (4 March 1968).

[12]Galloway, *Tonkin Gulf Resolution*, 499; Stone in *I.F. Stone's Weekly*, 3-4; Morse in ibid., 6-7.

[13]Karnow, *Vietnam*, 365.

[14]Eugene G. Windchy, *Tonkin Gulf* (Garden City, 1971), 283; "The 'Phantom Battle' That Led To War," *U.S. News and World Report* (23 July 1984); Karnow, *Vietnam*, 372; Wise, "Remember the Maddox!," 127, 129; Goulden, *Truth Is the First Casualty*, 239.

[15]Austin, *President's War*, 333; Wise, "Remember the Maddox!," 129; Galloway, *Tonkin Gulf Resolution*, 501.

[16]Kolko in *Potomac Magazine*; Stone in *I.F. Stone's Weekly*, 1-4.

[17]*Southeast Asia Resolution*, 14. See U.S. Congress, Senate, Committee on Foreign Relations, *Hearings on the Gulf of Tonkin, the 1964 Incidents* (90th Cong., 2nd sess.) (Washington, 1968) [hereafter *Hearings on the Gulf of Tonkin*], 10; U.S.G. Sharp, *Strategy For Defeat* (San Rafael, CA, 1978), 39; U.S.G. Sharp and W.C. Westmoreland, *Report on the War in Vietnam* (Washington, 1969), 11.

[18]Goulden, *Truth Is the First Casualty*, 59, 61.

[19]"Phantom Battle," 56. See also Edward J. Marolda and Oscar P. Fitzgerald, *From Military Assistance to Combat, 1959-1965*, Vol. II in series, *The United States Navy and the Vietnam Conflict* (Washington, 1986). 334-43, 366-73, 392.

[20]J.W. Fulbright, *Old Myths and New Realities* (New York, 1964), 42.

[21]Marolda and Fitzgerald, *From Military Assistance to Combat*, 334-43, 393-410.

[22]Ibid., 414. Key primary sources treating the Tonkin Gulf naval engagements are the following: *Maddox*, Patrol Report, ser 002 of 24 August 1964, NHC; *Maddox*, Action Report, ser 003 of 24 August 1964, NHC; *Maddox*, Action Report, ser 004 of 25 August 1964, NHC; *Turner Joy*, Action Report, ser 004 of 11 September 1964, NHC; Destroyer Division 192, Action Report, ser 002 of 13 August 1964, NHC; Deck, CIC, Sonar, and Quartermaster Logs of *Maddox* and *Turner Joy*, August 1964, NHC. See also High-Level Military Institute, Socialist Republic of Vietnam,

Vietnam: The Anti-U.S. Resistance War for National Salvation, 1954-1975: Military Events (Hanoi, 1980), 60.

[23]Marolda and Fitzgerald, *From Military Assistance to Combat*, 415.

[24]Wise, "Remember the Maddox!," 124; Samuel E. Halpern, *WEST PAC 64* (Boston, 1975), 183.

[25]Goulden, *Truth Is the First Casualty*, 132-33, 240; Associated Press, "Events of 3 Years ago in the Gulf of Tonkin Reconstructed," *Denver Post* (16 July 1967).

[26]That round is now on display at the Washington, D.C. Navy Museum. Senator Gore later complained that every time administration spokesmen came up to the hill to testify, "they waved that bullet around," adding, "one bullet and you went to war--Helen's [of Troy] face is insignificant in comparison." Quoted in Goulden, *Truth Is the First Casualty*, 202.

[27]*Maddox*, Action Report, ser 003 of 24 August 1964, NHC, 10.

[28]Jim and Sybil Stockdale, *In Love and War: The Story of a Family's Ordeal and Sacrifice During the Vietnam Years* (New York, 1984), 4-10; Marolda and Fitzgerald, *From Military Assistance to Combat*, 417-19; Conversation with Everett Southwick, of 8 November 1986.

[29]Lyndon B. Johnson, *The Vantage Point: Perspectives of the Presidency, 1963-1969* (New York, 1971), 113; *Southeast Asia Resolution*, 10.

[30]Marolda and Fitzgerald, *From Military Assistance to Combat*, 419-29.

[31]Wise, "Remember the Maddox!," 125.

[32]Marolda and Fitzgerald, *From Military Assistance to Combat*, 429.

[33]Windchy, *Tonkin Gulf*, 282. See also Karnow, *Vietnam*, 370, 371; Stockdale, *In Love and War*, 13.

[34]*Maddox*, Action Report, ser 004 of 25 August 1964, NHC; *Turner Joy*, Action Report, ser 004 of 11 September 1964, NHC. See also Halpern, *WEST PAC 64*, 202, 204, 205.

[35]Dennis P. Plzak, Statement of 7 August 1964, NHC. See also Robert E. Johnson and Marshall L. Hakala, Statements of 7 August 1964, NHC.

[36]"Events of 3 Years Ago in the Gulf of Tonkin Reconstructed," *Denver Post* (16 July 1967).

[37]Conversation with Robert C. Barnhart, 12 June 1987. See also *Maddox*, Action Report, ser 004 of 25 August 1964, NHC; *Turner Joy*, Action Report, ser 004 of 11 September 1964, NHC.

[38]Statements of Frederick M. Frick, John J. Herrick, and John J. Barry of 7 August 1964, NHC.

[39]Quoted in Wise, "Remember the Maddox!," 126. See also Windchy, *Tonkin Gulf*, 271-73; and Statements of Larry O. Litton, Roger N. Bergland, and Edwin R. Sentel of 7 August 1964, NHC.

[40]Msg, CTG72.1 041727Z August 1964, NHC. See also Wise, "Remember the Maddox!," 126; "Events of 3 Years Ago", Halpern, *WEST PAC 64*, 219.

[41]Stockdale. *In Love and War*, 17-24: Conversation with James B. Stockdale, of 26 February 1986; Conversation with Everett Southwick, of 8 November 1964, NHC: Marolda and Fitzgerald, *From Military Assistance to Combat*, 431-32.

[42]Halpern, *WEST PAC 64*, 200.

[43]From Moise conversation with McDonald of 3 February 1987, in Edwin B. Moise, draft chapter, "The Tonkin Gulf Incident, 1964," 42.

[44]Kerr, *Amongst the Good and the Great*, 206.

[45]Windchy, *Tonkin Gulf*, 201.

[46]Stockdale, *In Love and War*, 106, 454.

[47]Msg, CTF77 070252Z August 1964, NHC; See also Windchy, *Tonkin Gulf*, 204, 279.

[48]Conversation with G. Edmondson, of 15 June 1987.

[49]Quoted in Windchy, *Tonkin Gulf*, 209. See also 279.

[50]Conversation with G. Edmondson, of 15 June 1987. See also Msg. CTF77 070252Z August 1964, NHC; Windchy, *Tonkin Gulf*, 209.

[51]"Events of 3 Years Ago", Statements of Barnhart, McWeeney, Bergland, Abney, Reed, Johnson, Plzak, and Hakala of 7, 8 August 1964, NHC.

[52]Statements of Donald V. Sharkey, K.E. Garrison, and J.B. Spanka of 7, 9 August 1964, NHC.

[53]Statements of Richard M. Bacino and Walter Shishim of 7 August 1964, NHC.

[54]Quoted in Wise, "Remember the Maddox!," 127.

[55]*Maddox*, Action Report, ser 004 of 25 August 1964, NHC, 4, 11; Destroyer Division 192, Action Report, ser 002 of 13 August 1964, NHC, 3, 7, 8; *Turner Joy*, Action Report, ser 004 of 11 September 1964, NHC, VI-2.

[56]Halpern, *WEST PAC 64*, 221.

[57]Goulden, *Truth Is the First Casualty*, 242. See also Karnow, *Vietnam*, 371; Moise, draft chapter, "The Tonkin Gulf Incidents," 49-55.

[58]Msg. CTG72.1 041848Z August 1964, NHC. See also Kerr, *Amongst the Good and the Great*, 177; Marolda and Fitzgerald, *From Military Assistance to Combat*, 440-41.

[59]Quoted in Austin, *President's War*, 292.

[60]Marolda and Fitzgerald, *From Military Assistance to Combat*, 441-42; Kerr, *Amongst the Good and the Great*, 202-06; Sharp, *Strategy for Defeat*, 43-44; Johnson, *Vantage Point*, 114; Stockdale, *In Love and War*, 453-55; "Phantom Battle," 56-67; *Hearings on the Gulf of Tonkin*, 92.

[61]Kerr, *Amongst the Good and the Great*, 178.

[62]Marolda and Fitzgerald, *From Military Assistance to Combat*, 443.

[63]Quoted in "Phantom Battle," 64.

Tonkin Gulf: Reconsidered

Edwin E. Moise

Taking advantage of new materials recently made available and most specifically interviews with participants in the 1964 incidents, Professor Moise attempts a new and long overdue synthesis of the incidents, real or alleged, of the Tonkin Gulf Affair in order to shed more light on this important chapter in the Vietnam War and on recent American history.

The Tonkin Gulf Incidents of August 1964 constituted a major turning point in the Vietnam War. They led directly to the first U.S. bombing of North Vietnam, and they paved the way for the campaign of systematic bombing that began early the following year. Exactly what happened, however, is still a matter of considerable controversy.

The background to the incidents included a program of covert operations against North Vietnam, which the United States and South Vietnam had been conducting for some years. This program was too limited to cause any real weakening of the North. It may have been intended as a threat that if Hanoi persisted in supporting the guerrillas in South Vietnam, the U.S. might escalate attacks on the North to a level that did real damage. But the main logic behind the campaign seems simply to have been that the U.S. and South Vietnam should retaliate in some way for the trouble that North Vietnam was causing them.

In January 1964, the U.S. placed the various programs for raids against the North within a single framework, called OPLAN

(Operations Plan) 34-A. This involved drops of propaganda leaflets, an expanded version of the existing program for airdropping commandos and agents into the North, and maritime operations by small vessels along the coast of North Vietnam. These raids were to be "non-attributable" (the U.S. had to be able to pretend it was not responsible for them).[1] Indeed, every effort was made to prevent the public from learning that any such raids were occurring at all. The aspect of OPLAN 34-A most directly relevant here is the program of maritime operations conducted by eight fast vessels about the size of PT boats, based at the port of Da Nang. Two were old PT boats, with the torpedo tubes removed. The other six were new *Nasty*-class vessels built in Norway.

On 31 July 1964, in an operation separate from but not totally unrelated to OPLAN 34-A, the destroyer *Maddox* began what was known as a "DeSoto Patrol" in the Gulf of Tonkin. The ship had a special "communications van," containing electronic equipment and a team of specialists, capable of monitoring and translating North Vietnamese radio communications. Commander Herbert Ogier was commander of the *Maddox*, but for this voyage Captain John Herrick, commander of the Seventh Fleet's Destroyer Division 192, was on board in charge of the mission.

The primary purpose was to gather intelligence about the coastal defense system for the benefit of the vessels conducting OPLAN 34-A raids from Da Nang. The frequency and intensity of raids against North Vietnamese installations was increased at the time the *Maddox* was making this cruise, and it seems very likely that this was deliberate: U.S. planners believed that the *Maddox* would learn more about the coastal defenses if raids kept those defenses at a high state of activity.[2]

The Incident of 2 August

On the night of 1 August the *Maddox* was near Hon Me island, which had been shelled by the OPLAN 34-A vessels from Da Nang two nights earlier. Radio traffic among units of the coastal defense forces began to include some very ominous messages.[3] One of these ordered boats to strap explosives to their bows and attack by ramming.[4] The message apparently called for an attack on "imperialist interlopers" or some such phrase, rather than explicitly specifying a destroyer, but there seems no real possibility this referred to anything other than the *Maddox*. The tactic of ramming would have been preposterous against the small, fast, elusive vessels used in the OPLAN 34-A raids against the North Vietnamese coast. It made sense only against a larger target such as a destroyer, and the *Maddox* was the only such target in the area.

Captain Herrick decided the risks close to shore had become unacceptable, and at 0340H[5] on 2 August, he turned eastward away from the coast. Even when he returned to the coast a few hours later, he did not approach it as closely as he had on 1 August.

Early in the afternoon of 2 August, a radio message was intercepted ordering a force of three PT boats to carry out an attack using torpedoes.[6] It apparently did not specify an attack against a destroyer, but no other possible target for a torpedo attack was in the area.

At this point, the record of events becomes confused. The torpedo boats were at Hon Me; the *Maddox* was to the northeast of the island, and steaming farther northeast on the next leg of her reconnaissance cruise. Most accounts state that the radar of the *Maddox* acquired three torpedo boats, coming toward the destroyer at thirty knots from Hon Me, at 1500H.[7] The ship's logs, however, show that the torpedo boats were acquired on radar about half an hour after this time. The entries for acquisition of the three PT boats on radar show times of 1535H in the Surface Search Radar Contact Sheets,[8] 1535H in the Combat Information Center (CIC) Log, and 1538H in the Deck Log. It is likely that these entries were made only after a few minutes had been taken to compute the course and speed of the PT boats, and that their first acquisition on radar was at about 1530H. The ship went to general quarters at 1530H, which would not have been likely to occur without something having been acquired on the radar.

The *Maddox* had increased speed and turned away from the coast before 1530H. It seems likely that the misleading report of radar acquisition at 1500H arose from the need to present an explanation of this that would not reveal U.S. communications intercept capabilities. Interception of the message ordering the PT boats to attack had given the destroyer a considerable advantage, helping to ensure that the PT boats would end up pursuing her southeast instead of pinning her against the coast. As Commander Ogier commented long afterward, "The PT boats were behind us because we had already started moving away from them as a result of the messages we received. They approached from astern because that was the only option that we gave them."[9]

The *Maddox* fired warning shots at ninety-eight hundred yards, and began continuous fire at nine thousand yards. This was well beyond the effective range of the PT boats' torpedoes, and because they were overtaking from the rear, they were not able to get within effective range until the *Maddox* had been shooting at them for a considerable time. They suffered substantial damage, and scored no hits when they finally did fire torpedoes. They then retreated. The *Maddox* briefly pursued, but then turned southward, out of the Gulf, while four jets from a U.S. aircraft carrier attacked the fleeing torpedo boats. Captain Herrick also got orders to retire from the area rather than to pursue, but these appear to have been sent to him only after he had already turned southward for reasons purely involving the local situation.[10] By the time the jets had exhausted their ammunition, one torpedo boat was dead in the water, and it is believed later to have sunk.

It is crucial to note that in the hours before the 2 August incident, the U.S. had intercepted orders for North Vietnamese military action that did not specify a destroyer as the target, but were interpreted as referring to an attack on a destroyer. The interpretation was correct, and the attack did take place. This experience may have predisposed U.S. personnel to interpret ambiguous messages they intercepted on 4 August as referring to a second attack on the destroyer. That time the interpretation would be wrong.

The Incident of 4 August

Captain Herrick believed that the North Vietnamese considered themselves at war with the United States. He predicted that they would "attack U.S. forces on sight with no regard for cost."[11] He suggested that his mission be ended, but his superiors rejected the idea. A second destroyer, the *Turner Joy*, joined the *Maddox*, and the DeSoto patrol resumed.

On the night of 3 August the OPLAN 34-A vessels from Da Nang made another raid, this time shelling targets near the Cape of Vinh Son, to which the *Maddox* had paid prolonged and obvious attention two days before.

On 4 August Herrick did a reconnaissance cruise from north to south along the coast; his closest approach to the shore was sixteen miles. He then headed out to sea for the night. It was very dark and most of those involved say that the weather was poor, from drizzle to thunderstorms.[12] Weather of this sort had the capacity to generate spurious radar images. The Tonkin Gulf was later to acquire a reputation in the U.S. Navy as an area where spurious radar images, arising sometimes from weather and sometimes from other causes, were frequent.[13] The U.S. had not, however, operated much in the Tonkin Gulf in the early 1960s, so the men involved in the August 1964 incidents were not aware they were in an area characterized by radar ghosts that were both more numerous and more convincing than those to be encountered in most regions; so sharp and clear, indeed, that fire-control radars could lock onto them, which cannot happen with the rather diffuse ghosts created by weather in more normal regions.

Different radar operators were to reach different conclusions about what appeared on their screens during the night of 4 August; some appear to have been convinced they were spotting real enemy vessels, but Ensign Richard Corsette, who directed fire from the two forward gun mounts on the *Maddox* that night, later commented, "I know the way our radar was acting, my firm belief was that everything I locked onto was weather."[14]

Early in the evening, another ominous radio message was intercepted, ordering two Swatow boats, and perhaps also one PT boat, to make ready for military operations. As with the messages intercepted on 2 August, the target of the operation was not specified, and as on 2 August, American officers interpreted it as directed against their ships. This time, however, it seems almost certain they were wrong. Swatow boats were patrol vessels carrying no torpedoes, totally unsuited to attacks on a destroyer. Swatows would have been, however, the best thing North Vietnam had for defense against OPLAN 34-A raids.

Starting at about 2045H, the radar of the destroyers began to acquire what were assumed at the time to be hostile vessels. Those who believe that there was an attack on the destroyers that night have often presented descriptions suggesting a coherent pattern, with hostile vessels first acquired at long range, gradually getting closer, and finally attacking. What shows in the logs of the destroyers, however, is a series of completely separate incidents. Images would appear on the radar screens, remain on the screens for a few minutes, and then disappear, often without ever having come significantly closer than they had been when first acquired. Then other images would appear in completely different locations.

The first three images, designated skunks "N," "O," and "P," were acquired between 2045H and 2050H. The account in the recently published U.S. Navy history by Marolda and Fitzgerald gives the impression that these apparent enemy vessels headed southward, attempting to close the destroyers.[15] The actual positions recorded for these skunks aboard the destroyers that night, however, show them moving generally west on a course taking them nowhere near the destroyers. By 2145H, these skunks had been left behind, and had faded from the radar screens as the U.S. vessels retreated southward.

The next crucial acquisition, three or four high-speed images close together, collectively known as skunk "U," was made at 2208H. They were not behind the destroyers as is stated in Marolda and Fitzgerald,[16] giving the impression that the newly acquired vessels were or at least could have been the three that had been lost from the radar behind the destroyers half an hour before. They were to the east, abeam of the destroyers or even a little ahead of them, and far enough from the location of the previous skunks to leave no possibility that a PT boat could have covered the distance in the available time.

By this time, Herrick had air support overhead. The planes were vectored (guided by radio) to the location of skunk "U", but found nothing there, despite water conditions that should have made the wakes of high-speed vessels very conspicuous (see below). The skunk roughly paralleled the course of the destroyers, and then vanished at 2233H,[17] a fact that most later accounts neglect to mention.

To sum up the radar evidence for this period: the first six (or seven) supposedly threatening radar contacts--"N," "O," "P," and the three (or four) collectively known as "U"--all vanished from the radar screens without ever having come significantly closer to the destroyers than they had been when first acquired, although their speed was such that they easily could have closed the destroyers. There are three possible interpretations: that they were surface vessels unaware of the location of the destroyers, that they were surface vessels that did not wish to close the destroyers, or that the radar was playing tricks and they were not surface vessels at all. If one takes the time to consider "U" at least, the negative reports of the pilots and the abrupt disappearance of the skunk from radar make the third interpretation overwhelmingly probable. The men on the destroyers, however, had their attention diverted before they could reconsider their initial evaluation of "U" as a group of hostile vessels.

Immediately after "U" vanished, the *Maddox* acquired skunk "V" on the radar, coming from the direction of the last known location of "U," but again too far from that location for there to be any possibility that it could have moved from one place to the other in the available time. The *Turner Joy* almost immediately acquired "V-1" in the same area, and opened fire on it. Radar contact with "V" was lost at 2242H, range 9,000 yards and opening; contact with "V-1" was lost at 2244H, range under 5,000 yards. Despite the differences between the movements of "V" as recorded on the *Maddox* and of "V-1" as recorded on the *Turner Joy*, these skunks are often assumed to have represented the same PT boat, the first one believed to have launched a torpedo that night.[18]

For the next two hours, the images appearing on the radar screens (mainly those of the *Turner Joy*) were similarly ephemeral; they would appear and then disappear. Some observers interpreted this as meaning that they had been sunk by the destroyers' gunfire.

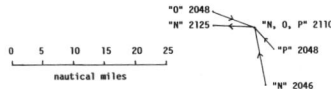

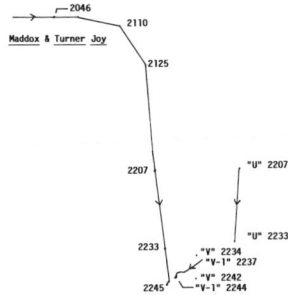

MAP 1: Destroyers and radar contacts, 2046H to 2254H, 4 August 1964. Tracks of radar contacts based on ranges and bearings from destroyers. Tracks of destroyers based on positions recorded by the *Maddox*.

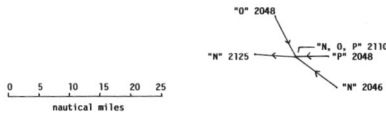

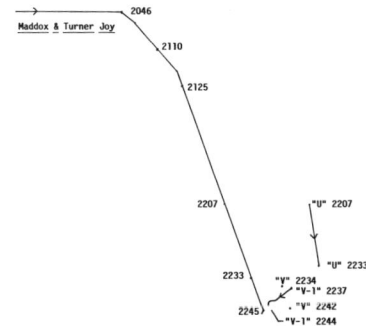

MAP 2: Destroyers and radar contacts, 2046H to 2245H, 4 August 1964. Tracks of radar contacts based on ranges and bearings from destroyers. Tracks of destroyers based on courses and speeds recorded in after-action reports of the *Maddox*.

Skunk "V-3," for example, was acquired by the *Turner Joy* at 2321H. The destroyer opened fire at 2324H, and the contact disappeared from the radar four minutes later. It was believed that this meant the target was a PT boat, and that it had disappeared from the radar because it had been sunk.[19]

Skunk "V-4" was acquired by the *Turner Joy* as an intermittent contact about 2328H, and a firm one at 2342H. The destroyer fired at it from 2347H to 2348H, and lost it on radar at 2354H. It was reacquired at 2359H, and the destroyer resumed fire at 2400H. When it disappeared three minutes later, this was interpreted as meaning it had been sunk.[20]

Comparison with the events of 2 August, however, contradicts this interpretation. Real North Vietnamese PT boats, on 2 August, showed no tendency to disappear even when subjected to prolonged pounding with 5-inch guns. It is not plausible that real PT boats would have vanished within three or four minutes after the *Turner Joy* opened fire on them on the night of 4 August, even if the conditions for gunnery then had been ideal, and the ship's commander considered the conditions very far from ideal. Captain Barnhart later wrote a remarkable report on the handicaps under which his gunners had operated, including under-manning of the loading crews, much difficulty with premature detonation of shells, and heavy reliance on a gun director that had never been used to control fire against surface targets in gunnery drills because it was less accurate than the main gun director, which was not functioning that night.[21]

For much of this period, radar on the *Maddox* could not detect the vessels appearing on the radar of the *Turner Joy*. Commander Ogier later commented on this portion of the incident:

> The *Maddox* did not have any unidentified blips on its radars.... We were relying on reports from the *Turner Joy*. I was very concerned about our inability to pick up the *Turner Joy*'s radar targets. I have since concluded that false targets may be picked up by some radars and not by others because of the difference in their frequencies or other differences.[22]

Evaluation

There can be no serious doubt that North Vietnamese torpedo boats attacked the *Maddox* on the afternoon of 2 August. Two torpedo tubes are now on display in a Hanoi museum, with a label stating that they were used against the *Maddox* on that date.

The U.S. government believes that the incident on the night of 4 August was another such attack, a running battle involving several North Vietnamese PT boats and lasting about two hours. The evidence that has been cited includes not only the skunks appearing on radar, but also communications intercepts, torpedo noises reported by the sonar operator of the *Maddox*, visual sightings by pilots overhead, and visual sightings by personnel aboard both destroyers.

Hanoi, however, has always denied any attack against the *Maddox* and the *Turner Joy* on the night of 4 August.[23] Democratic Republic of Vietnam (DRV) naval personnel captured by the U.S. in later years all said the same,[24] and it is very likely that they were correct; no Vietnamese vessels attacked the destroyers on the night of 4 August. The evidence that there was an attack could all easily exist even if there was not any attack. The evidence that there was no attack cannot be explained away; it could not exist if there had been an attack.

In considering the evidence, one must pay attention to timing. On the first day after the incident, messages from Washington to the destroyers asked what had happened on the night of 4 August. On 6 August, however, the Joint Chiefs of Staff (JCS) sent out a message saying that "An urgent requirement exists for proof and evidence" that the North Vietnamese had attacked the U.S. destroyers on the night of 4 August. "Material must be of type which will convince United Nations Organization that the attack did in fact occur...."[25]

In response to this demand, the commanders in the Pacific provided more support for the idea of a real attack than they had provided before. It should not be assumed that this was simply a matter of telling the Joint Chiefs whatever lies they wanted to hear. Captain Herrick and Commander Ogier both state that at the time they wrote their replies to the JCS on 7 August, the review they had made of the sighting reports had left them convinced that the attack had been real.[26] Both men have established records of honesty that entitle them to belief, though it seems permissible to note that the message from the JCS would have given them an incentive to convince themselves that the attack had been real.

In general, however, evidence of an attack that appears in the record for the first time on 7 August, in messages specifically labelled replies to the demand from the JCS, should be approached with a certain caution.

Reports by the Pilots Overhead

Of all the Americans present on the night of 4 August, Commander (later Admiral) James Stockdale eventually became the most vocal in saying that there had been no PT boat attack on the two destroyers on 4 August. His conviction was based on the fact that he and other pilots had not seen any PT boats, but it would be difficult to argue that he was not entitled to treat his lack of sightings as proof that there had been nothing to see. Two days before, on 2 August, he had had the opportunity to compare the wakes of North Vietnamese torpedo boats with that of the *Maddox*. When PT boats were moving at high speed on 2 August, they had left "long, foamy wakes, much more pronounced than the wake of a destroyer at full speed."[27] On the dark night of 4 August, water conditions made wakes luminous. The wake of a destroyer was terribly conspicuous, "just a spotlight in a dark pit."[28] When Stockdale was guided to places where the destroyers' radar showed high-speed torpedo boats, and he saw no wakes, he had all the justification he needed to be certain that there had been no high-speed torpedo boats there. He is "sure" he would have seen anything within five miles of the two destroyers.[29]

Up to the time of the message of 6 August from the JCS, no pilot appears to have reported any evidence that there had been PT boats near the destroyers. The carrier *Ticonderoga* told Washington, "Returning pilots report no visual sightings of any vessels or wakes other than Turner Joy and Maddox. Wakes from Turner Joy and Maddox visible for 2-3000 yards."[30]

314

On 7 August, however, the *Ticonderoga* reported sightings by two pilots, Commander George Edmondson and Lieutenant Jere Barton. Edmondson had supposedly seen the wake of an enemy vessel. Aside from this,

> ...flying at 700-1500 feet, they reported seeing gun flashes on the surface of the water and bursting light at the approximate flight altitude. Cdr Edmondson and his wingman were at this time flying on opposite sides of a large circle, orbiting to the northwest of the *Maddox* attempting to visually sight the contact reported there. Firing would commence when one or the other of the aircraft had passed abeam or over the firing vessel, and would cease when the aircraft turned in toward it. Firing would only commence when aircraft lights were turned on. The two aircraft attempted unsuccessfully to get in a firing run on the vessel for about 10-15 minutes, after which they broke off and returned to their original position circling the *Maddox*.[31]

Quite aside from the question of why this would not have been reported before 7 August, this account is very implausible. Among other things, North Vietnamese torpedo boats did not have guns large enough to fire the sort of shells that burst at the altitude of the plane at which they are shooting.

Lieutenant Barton is now dead, but Admiral James Stockdale recently contacted senior pilots who were with Barton in the squadron in 1964 to get an idea about Barton's motivation in these affairs. Their answers showed that Barton had been a very conscientious officer and had not liked being taken before the captain and asked to change his prior report of no sightings. Afterward, "He just wouldn't talk about it."[32]

In communications with this author, Edmondson has denied that he saw bursting lights at his approximate altitude, and he says that he denied seeing them when questioned by his superiors in August 1964. He says he did see moving lights, appearing to be tracer bullets, come past him from the rear. He denies that there was anything to suggest that he was passing over or abeam of a vessel that was firing these tracers; he had no idea where they were coming from. He now believes these tracers were fired by one of the other American aircraft in the area. He also did see what appeared to be a wake, at a somewhat later hour. He now believes it probably to have been generated by wave action. He recalls saying, when questioned about this in August 1964, that it could not have been the wake of a PT boat; it was too narrow.[33] Indeed, it was so narrow that he says he could not have seen it had he been at an altitude of one thousand feet or higher;[34] the wake of a PT boat would have been visible from a much higher altitude.

Commander Edmondson had also been "in the very near vicinity" of both "V-3" and "V-4" (see above) during the times that the *Turner Joy* was firing at those radar targets and reporting PT boats damaged or sunk. "There were no PT boats, therefore none could have been damaged or sunk."[35]

In fact, of the three pilots known to have been at a low altitude over the destroyers that night, Stockdale, Edmondson, and Barton, none saw at any time what they regarded as convincing evidence of PT boats, and the two still alive both feel that they had a good enough view that they would have seen convincing evidence if there had in fact been PT boats present.

The following morning, there was an exhaustive aerial reconnaissance of the area where the incident had supposedly occurred. No signs of battle were found. Lieutenant (later Captain) James Bartholomew, the Targeting and Reconnaissance Officer on the staff of the Seventh Fleet, believes this reconnaissance would "definitely" have found wreckage or oil slicks if the destroyers had sunk any PT boats there during the previous night.[36]

The Sonar Evidence

The sonar evidence was the first thing to come under suspicion aboard the destroyers themselves. The operator on the *Maddox* was inexperienced, and the more than twenty torpedoes he had reported seemed preposterous, given the total number of torpedo boats North Vietnam had. Experimentation revealed that during high-speed maneuvers, the destroyer's own propeller and/or rudder produced what the sonarman interpreted as torpedo noises. The most anyone now claims is that some of his torpedo reports were valid, and there is no solid evidence for this.

Visual Sightings on the Destroyers

The issue of the visual sightings by personnel on the destroyers is too complex to be dealt with adequately here. It should be noted, however, that some of the most important of them appear in the record only on 7 August, and that where there are records dating from before 7 August, these often differ in odd ways from the later versions. It should also be noted that extreme darkness punctuated by gunfire, rocket fire from the planes, and so forth, must have constituted an environment in which men who believed they were under attack might have seen almost anything.

To give a particular example: the after-action report of the *Turner Joy* states that just after radar had shown that skunk "V-3" had been sunk by gunfire (see above), personnel on the *Turner Joy* "observed a thick column of smoke rising from the vicinity of the contact. No flames were seen. Believe contact did not burn on surface but sank immediately."[37] This report loses plausibility, however, if one asks how a PT boat that sank immediately upon being hit, instead of burning on the surface, could have produced enough smoke for this to be visible as "a thick column" on a dark night. It loses more plausibility if one notes that the only records for the sighting of smoke in the ship's logs show times about five minutes before the destroyer even commenced fire at skunk "V-3."[38]

Electric Intelligence

What has often seemed the strongest evidence that an attack had occurred was in another radio intercept. This was picked up by a listening post at Phu Bai shortly after Herrick first reported himself under attack. NSA believed, but could not prove, that it was from North Vietnamese Naval Headquarters in Haiphong to an operating unit in the field. Paraphrased, it read: "Have engaged enemy and shot down two planes. Starting out on hunt and waiting to receive assignment. Morale is high as men have seen damaged ships."[39]

This has often been interpreted as referring to the incident taking place at the time, despite a striking lack of resemblance between the battle described in the message and anything believed to have occurred on the night of 4 August. The two highest-ranking intelligence analysts known to have considered the problem, CIA Deputy Director Ray Cline and NSA Deputy Director Louis Tordella, both concluded that this message did not refer to the events of 4 August at all, but to the events of 2 August. The headquarters believed to have sent the message could not have learned about the events of 4 August fast enough to have sent this message as a description of those events, at the time the message was intercepted.[40]

Another similar message was picked up soon after. These two messages simply do not make sense as reports of the combat supposedly taking place at the time they were intercepted. Neither said that the combat was still going on; neither said anything about the location of the combat.[41] These omissions are particularly conspicuous in the first, intercepted before the supposed attack on the U.S. destroyers was even half over.

The claim that two planes had been shot down is odd, on a totally black night that would have given the light, optically aimed guns of torpedo boats essentially no chance of hitting aircraft. On the other hand, the muzzle flashes of a futile attempt to do so should have stood out like beacons. Even the sightings sometimes attributed to Edmondson are for a considerably later hour; for the period covered by this report, no pilot saw the slightest indication that any Vietnamese vessels were anywhere in the area, much less that they were firing enough anti-aircraft rounds to convince themselves they had shot down two planes.

Even if the boats had thought they had shot down aircraft, how would the shore station that originated this message have known about it? The listening gear on the *Maddox* detected no sign of reports from any vessels in the area to their superiors on shore.

How would North Vietnamese vessels have "seen damaged ships" on such a night?

The comment about starting out on hunt and waiting to receive assignment seems the most bizarre of all, if the main part of the

318

message is interpreted as a description of a battle in progress. It makes excellent sense, however, if we interpret the message as describing the battle two days before. James Stockdale has analyzed the very close resemblance between what the North Vietnamese believed had happened on 2 August and what this message describes (notably the shooting down of the two planes).[42]

This interpretation is strengthened by the fact that the second message specifies the unit number and the name of the commanding officer of the naval unit involved in whatever action it described. Interrogation of a prisoner captured in 1967 revealed that this unit, under this officer, had conducted the attack on the *Maddox* on 2 August.[43]

The *Maddox* had been specially equipped to monitor enemy radio communications and enemy radar. It simply is not credible that a coordinated attack by several North Vietnamese vessels[44] could have been mounted against the *Maddox* and *Turner Joy*, sixty miles from the North Vietnamese coast, on a moonless night in poor weather, without the *Maddox*'s electronic devices having picked up so many radio messages between the attacking vessels, and so much radar use by the attacking vessels, as to leave no doubt of what had happened. In particular, the idea that torpedo boats could have attempted to aim torpedoes without radar help at relatively maneuverable targets such as destroyers, on a dark night with poor visibility, strains credibility. No such radio or radar use was detected.

Summing Up

The traditional story of the incident of 4 August is that several North Vietnamese vessels stretched their attack out for two hours, when their armament was such that they could have fired in the first twenty minutes everything they had that was capable of harming a destroyer. They somehow remained invisible to the planes overhead the whole time. They kept track of the wildly weaving destroyers and maintained their attack, in bad weather and extreme darkness, without either using radar or communicating with one another by radio, in spite of the shells falling on them from the *Turner Joy*, which could have left them in no doubt that the American radar had them spotted and that trying to hide by maintaining radar and radio silence was futile. They suffered heavy losses, but somehow the rest of the very small DRV navy never heard (to judge by later interrogations of prisoners) that the incident had ever happened at all.

This scenario is preposterous. The reports of various men who claim that under conditions of great emotional tension they glimpsed mysterious moving lights, or a silhouette in the distance, cannot counterbalance the impossibility of this version of events.

Captain Herrick, faced with evidence both contradictory and incomplete, decided on the morning of 5 August 1964 that he could not be certain what had or had not happened the previous night. He has remained uncertain for most of the following twenty-three years. He now believes, however, that it is *unlikely* that any torpedoes were fired at any time on the night of 4 August, unlikely that the radar image making the supposed first torpedo run was genuine, unlikely that any enemy vessel came within ten thousand yards of the *Maddox* on that night.[45] Commander Ogier similarly feels it is improbable that any attack was made against the U.S. destroyers that night.[46] The available evidence provides ample justification for their doubts.

Notes

[1]U.S. Congress, House, Committee on Armed Services, *United States-Vietnam Relations, 1945-1967: A Study Prepared by the Department of Defense* (Washington, 1971), Book 3, IV-C-2-a, 2.

[2]Dr. Ray S. Cline, letter to the author, August 1987. See also transcript, "Vietnam: A Television History" (Boston: WGBH TV, 1983), 4:6.

[3]For the actual content of the Democratic Republic of Vietnam (DRV) message traffic intercepted by the U.S., there is a published record going back to 1964, recently supplemented in a very useful way in Edward J. Marolda and Oscar P. Fitzgerald, *The United States Navy and the Vietnam Conflict*, vol. II, *From Military Assistance to Combat, 1959-1965* (Washington, 1986). This author has also gotten

information, the most important part of which constituted confirmation that certain items in the published record were accurate, from personal communications.

In regard to which U.S. units intercepted DRV messages and how they did so, the published record is less complete, and this author has not been able to supplement or confirm it through personal communications.

[4]Commander Herbert Ogier, letter to the author, September 1986.

[5]This paper will use Hotel Time (-8) throughout, in order to achieve compatibility with other published accounts. The *Maddox* was in fact using India Time (-9) on 2 August, and Golf Time (-7) on 4 August. WARNING: some of the records of the *Maddox* for the period when the ship was on Golf time are mistakenly labeled India time.

[6]Marolda and Fitzgerald, *Military Assistance to Combat*, 414; Ogier, letter to the author, September 1986.

[7]For example, see Marolda and Fitzgerald, *Military Assistance to Combat*, 415.

[8]These can be found as Enclosure 5 of Ogier to Chief of Naval Operations (CNO), "July-August DeSoto Patrol," Ser: 002 of 24 August 1964.

[9]Ogier, letter to the author, September 1986.

[10]COMSEVENTHFLT to CTG72.1, 020859Z (1659H) August 1964.

[11]Msg., CTG72.1, 021443Z August 1964, quoted in Marolda and Fitzgerald, *Military Assistance to Combat*, 420.

[12]Commander Ogier is an exception; he does not recall the weather having been as bad as some others have suggested. Personal communications.

[13]Captain John Herrick, telephone interview, 19 April 1986; Ogier, personal communications.

[14]*Arkansas Gazette*, 16 July 1967, reprinted in *Congressional Record*, 28 February 1968, 4582.

[15]Marolda and Fitzgerald, *From Assistance to Combat*, 427-29.

[16]Ibid., 429.

[17]*Turner Joy* Action Report, Barnhart to CNO, 11 September 1964, II-A-1; personal communications, Lieutenant Commander Richard B. Corsette.

[18]*Turner Joy* Action Report, II-A-l, II-C-3, II-C-4; Report of Tonkin Gulf, Action of 4 August 1964, Ogier to CNO, 25 August 1964, 5; personal communications, Richard B. Corsette.

[19]*Turner Joy* Action Report, II-A-2.

[20]Ibid., and IV-1.

[21]Ibid., esp. III-1, III-2, VI-1, VII-1, VII-2.

[22]Ogier, personal communications, September 1986.

[23]There is a totally unfounded claim in Douglas Pike, *PAVN* (Novato, 1986), 108, 118-19, repeated in Lt.Gen. Phillip B. Davidson, *Vietnam at War* (Novato, 1988), 320 that Hanoi has admitted attacking U.S. destroyers on the night of 4/5 August.

[24]There is a very convincing excerpt from a U.S. Navy report on the interrogations in U.S. Congress, Senate, Committee on Foreign Relations, *The Gulf of Tonkin, the 1964 Incidents*, hearing of 20 February 1968, 90th Cong., 2d sess. (Washington, 1968), 75.

[25]JCS to CINCPAC (copies to *Ticonderoga, Maddox, Turner Joy*, etc.), 061642Z August 1964.

[26]Personal communications.

[27]Jim and Sybil Stockdale, *In Love and War* (New York, 1984), 7.

[28]Admiral James Stockdale, in NBC White Paper on Vietnam, 27 April 1985.

[29]Kim Willenson, et. al., *The Bad War: An Oral History of the Vietnam War* (New York, 1987), 31.

[30]CTG77.5 to COMSEVENTHFLT, 041928Z August 1964.

[31]"Desoto Ops--Afternoon 5 Aug 1964--Verification Proof of Attack," CTF77 to CINCPACFLT, 070252Z August 1964.

[32]Admiral James B. Stockdale, letter to the author, April 1987.

[33]Commander George Edmondson, personal communications.

[34]Edward Marolda, "Tonkin Gulf in Fact and Fiction" (Paper presented at Naval History Symposium, Annapolis. MD, 25 September 1987), 10-11.

[35]Edmondson, letter to the author, 15 September 1987.

[36]Captain James Bartholomew, telephone interview, 15 October 1987.

[37]*Turner Joy* Action Report, II-A-2.

[38]*Turner Joy* CIC Log, entries for 2218G and 2220G (2318H and 2320H).

[39]"The 'Phantom Battle' that Led to War," *U.S. News and World Report*, 23 July 1984, 63.

[40]Ibid., 63-64; see also "Vietnam: A Television History," 4:7.

[41]Cline, letter to the author, March 1986.

[42]Stockdale and Stockdale, *In Love and War*, 453-55.

[43]Anthony Austin, *The President's War* (New York, 1971), 339-40.

[44]Secretary of Defense McNamara estimated three to six boats. *Southeast Asia Resolution*: Joint Hearing before the Committee on Foreign Relations and the Committee on Armed Services, United States Senate, 6 August 1964 (Washington, 1966), 7.

[45]Captain John J. Herrick, letter to the author, April 1986.

[46]Ogier, letter to the author, September 1986.

Tonkin Gulf: Comments

James A. Barber, Jr.

I would like to preface my remarks by sketching briefly the personal experience I bring to the task on commenting on these two papers. I was not in the Tonkin Gulf in August 1964. Rather, I was in the more pleasant surroundings of Palo Alto, California, completing work on my dissertation. Beginning in the summer of 1965, however, I spent many nights in the Gulf, on three different ships, continuing until 1972. While I was executive officer on the *Henry W. Tucker*, we conducted anti-torpedo boat exercises on several occasions with the same fast *Nasty*-class boats out of Da Nang used in the OPLAN 34-A covert operations. Though I lack personal familiarity with the events of August 1964, I nevertheless have a good feel for the field on which those actions occurred.

Both papers are well researched, well documented, responsible, and judicious. Yet in certain key respects they reach diametrically opposed conclusions. Let me first show a few minor points on which I take issue with one or the other of our two authors, then go on to an attempt to assess what one may reasonably conclude.

Ed Marolda reports testimony from surface warfare officers that "when the intensified, pencil-like beam of a fire control radar locks onto a contact, that contact is a hard target." He continues that the fire control radars of both destroyers "locked onto and held targets throughout the night." Based on extensive personal experience with the false radar target phenomenon, known as the "Tonkin Gulf ghost," I do not agree that anything a fire control radar will lock onto is necessarily a hard target. It is true that a fire control radar is *less* likely to be fooled by a Tonkin Gulf ghost than is a search radar. It overstates the case, however, to say that a fire control radar lock equates to a hard target. I have observed them tracking ghosts for several minutes at a time. More persuasive is evidence that a target is being tracked by multiple sensors of differing frequencies and different locations. It appears that on the night of 4 August only a single sensor tracked some targets, while several sensors tracked others simultaneously. I am much more likely to be persuaded by evidence of the latter sort.

Both authors devote attention to the reports from participating aviators, particularly Admiral James Stockdale, that they did not see any torpedo boats. There is no reason to question that assertion. What *is* worth examination is the assertion "they were certain that they would have seen them had they been there." My own experience leads me to doubt this certainty. When we ran night exercises with the *Nasty* boats from Da Nang, we had much difficulty talking our assigned Combat Air Patrol [CAP] onto the targets, despite positive knowledge of the identification and location of the boats. The pilots were unable to locate the targets in the dark a high percentage of the time even when vectored directly on top. I remember vividly an incident in which, after twenty minutes or so of unsuccessful attempts to talk our CAP onto the *Nasty* targets, we heard a triumphant "I've got him! Rolling in to attack," followed ten seconds later by the roar of a jet engine one hundred feet overhead as our CAP made a simulated attack on us. Thus I do not put great weight on the absence of firm visual sightings by the participating aircraft.

Ed Moise emphasizes the lack of electronic intercepts, by either of the two destroyers, of radar or radio from any attackers on the night of 4 August. I do not think this is a strong point. Under circumstances such as those that existed, the attackers would be likely to exercise stringent emissions control. More important, the existing intercept capabilities on the two destroyers were not the sort that would provide high probability intercepts on short transmissions on unknown frequencies. It is easy to believe that attackers could have used radar and radio intermittently without being detected.

Some additional testimony on the events of 4 August worth examining is that provided by Commander Andy Kerr in his book, *A Journey Amongst the Good and the Great*. In August 1964 Kerr, a former line officer with both surface and submarine experience, was a legal officer on the staff of the commander of the Seventh Fleet, Vice Admiral Roy Johnson. They embarked on the *Oklahoma City*, which after the 2 August attack on *Maddox* was steaming at high speed for the South China Sea.

Kerr recalls that intelligence reports on the *Oklahoma City* before 4 August showed that a second attack might take place. When the reports of the 4 August attack were received, however, Kerr, who had previous experience with the phenomenon of the Tonkin Gulf ghost, expressed doubts to Admiral Johnson about the reported attack. Johnson, based on Kerr's qualifications as a line officer and as a lawyer skilled in examining evidence, told Kerr: "When we get to the Gulf, I want you to go aboard those two ships and compare all of their logs and plots. Since you're a skeptic, you'd be a good one to do that."[1]

Transferring to the *Maddox* by helicopter, Commander Kerr was joined by the *Turner Joy*'s operations officer, along with all that ship's data. Kerr summarizes his investigation as follows:

> We carefully constructed a composite chart. It reflected all of the information available on both ships during the incident. The tracks of both ships were plotted. All radar, sonar, and visual data, with times, ranges, and bearings were entered. The chart showed remarkable correlation. False contacts are usually random and do not persist for long periods. The same false contact would seldom be

sensed by two ships that were in different positions. There was great consistency between all of the contacts made by both ships. Furthermore, the tracks of the attacking vessels, as plotted independently by both the *Maddox* and *Turner Joy*, coincided and were precisely what one would expect from attacking torpedo boats. Lastly, the plotted speed of the contacts was comparable to the speed of the North Vietnamese torpedo boats that had attacked the *Maddox* in daylight two days before....

On Admiral Johnson's staff, the chart was analyzed by the chief of staff, Captain Lloyd ("Joe") Vasey and the staff operations section. They then reviewed it with the admiral. All reached the same conclusion: The composite track chart left no doubt whatsoever. An attack had taken place. Admiral Johnson dispatched that information to the commander of the Pacific Fleet at Pearl Harbor, Admiral Tom Moorer. The chart was then flown back to Moorer's headquarters.[2]

Four years later, Kerr served under Assistant Secretary Robert McNamara preparing his testimony before the Fulbright Committee investigating the Tonkin Gulf incidents. As such he received special intelligence clearance and reviewed the intercepted and translated texts of the North Vietnamese messages before, during, and after the incident. About this review he wrote:

My recollection of the intercepted messages is as follows: On the afternoon before the attack, the Vietnamese torpedo boat division commander reported that he was tracking our two destroyers. The latitude, longitude, course, and speed coincided with the known data. During the evening, the North Vietnamese commander ordered his ships to take an attack position. One of the torpedo boat captains reported that he was making a torpedo run. He later reported that he had completed his attack and was withdrawing. He said that he had sunk one of the U.S. ships. All of these messages were seen by McNamara and reported to President Johnson during the evening of the incident. Those officials, of course, were also aware of the messages from the *Maddox* and *Turner Joy* reporting that they were under torpedo attack.[3]

The events on the evening of 4 August 1964 were a classical demonstration of the fog of war, and even with the benefit of nearly twenty-five years of hindsight, it is still difficult to sort out reliably exactly what did take place.

There are several points on which reasonable men may agree:

1. The *Maddox* was attacked by North Vietnamese PT boats on 2 August.

2. All those officers in command positions on both the *Maddox* and *Turner Joy* believed sincerely that they were under attack on 4 August.

3. The message reports to higher authority were sufficiently definite to support a good faith belief by senior officials that such an attack had taken place.

4. An experienced and skeptical observer, in the person of Commander Kerr, became convinced after reviewing the track data that both ships were tracking the same contacts.

5. There is no evidence that any of the naval commanders involved has offered anything other than honest reporting.

6. There is no evidence of an orchestration of events by higher authority.

On the other hand:

7. There is a lack of hard evidence: no photos, no shrapnel on deck, no bullet holes in aircraft, no recordings of electronic intercepts on attacking PT boats.

8. The prevailing atmosphere, which includes the 2 August attack, threatening intelligence reports, and a pitch black night, were all conducive to tension and perhaps imagination.

9. In the ensuing years none of the confirming evidence that one might expect has appeared from Vietnamese sources, although the North Vietnamese navy would likely withhold such evidence.

Am I going to say whether there was or was not an attack on 4 August? No, I am not. One must read the evidence and reach one's own conclusions. Whether there was an attack upon the *Maddox* and the *Turner Joy* on the night of 4 August 1964 remains a subject upon which reasonable men and women may disagree.

Notes

[1]Andy Kerr, *A Journey Amongst the Good and the Great* (Annapolis, 1987), 178.
[2]Ibid.
[3]Ibid., 202.